CW01187954

Peter Bunde & Markus Gaertner

Co-Author Thomas Hemmann

Translator: Richard L. Sanders

THE WESTPHALIAN ARMY IN THE NAPOLEONIC WARS 1807–1813

Authors	Peter Bunde Markus Gaertner
Co-Author	Thomas Hemmann
Translator	Richard L. Sanders
Layout	Stefan Müller
Maps	Bernhard Glaenzer & Erik Bauer
Publisher	Zeughaus Verlag GmbH Knesebeckstr. 88 10623 Berlin, Germany
Telephone	0049 (30) 315 700 30
Fax	0049 (30) 315 700 77
Email	info@zeughausverlag.de
Internet	www.zeughausverlag.de

Originally published in German as
"Die Westphälische Armee der Napoleonzeit 1807–1813."

Printed in der European Union, 2019

Bibliographic information from the Deutschen Bibliothek: The Deutsche Bibliothek lists this publication in the German National Bibliography; detailed bibliographic information is available at http://dnb.ddb.de.

ISBN: 978-3-96360-022-7

National Coat of Arms of the Kingdom of Westphalia 1810
Watercolor by Wilhelm Hewig in the Wehrgeschichtliches Museum (WGM) Rastatt

We dedicate this book to
Paul Meganck
(1945 - 2018)
Paul was our close friend for many years.
He shared our passion for the uniforms and military history of the Napoeonic era.
His extensive archives were always open to us.

ACKNOWLEDGEMENTS

During our many years of work on this book, we received support and encouragement from many sides. We owe special thanks to our co-author Thomas Hemmann who wrote a major portion of the introductory chapter, the history of the Westphalian Army's campaigns and the overview of the order of battle.

In addition we thank the following individuals and institutions:

Markus Stein, Paul Meganck, Pierre-Yves Chauvin, Dr. Frank Bauer, Bernhard Glänzer, Jean-Yves Forthoffer, Yves Martin, Digby Smith, Alfred Umhey, Peter Harrington (Anne S.K. Brown Military Collection, Brown University Library, Providence, R.I., USA), Ingrid Knauf (Museumslandschaft Hessen Kassel), Jérôme Croyet (Musee l'Emperi (Collection Brunon), Salon de Provence), Pierre Lierneux (Musée Royal de l'Armée et d'Histoire Militaire, Brussels), Dr. Thomas Weissbrich (Deutsches Historisches Museum, Berlin), Anne Dorte Krause (Stiftung Deutsches Historisches Museum) and Dr. Joachim Niemeyer (Wehrgeschichtliches Museum, Rastatt).

Our friend Richard L. Sanders, Colonel U.S. Army Res. Ret., who took on the laborious task of preparing an English translation of the work for us.

We had extensive discussion with Lutz Amsel concerning the army ranks and their designations and Oliver Schmidt helped eliminate ambiguities through his critical review.

In conclusion we expressly thank Stefan Müller, who undertook publishing our book in his publishing house Zeughaus Verlag and who always supported us exceptionally energetically and far beyond the norm. He is also responsible for the final and in our opinion very successful layout. We also thank Katja Leipnitz for her expert and unrelenting editing.

CONTENTS

Part I

Introduction

The Organization of the Westphalian Army

Part II

Organization, Structure and Uniforms of the Individual Military Positions and Units

The Army's First Formations

The Guard

Part III

The Army in Action – The 1808–1813 Campaigns

Appendices

TRANSLATOR'S NOTES

The Westphalian Army was essentially Napoleon's creation, so the French language was used extensively, e.g., officially for its ranks and duty titles. But the army's German speaking personnel were more comfortable in their own language, so both tongues were in use. Because many of the terms were officially in French, a number have been retained in that language. For example, the French "*chef de bataillon*" is often both the rank and duty title of a battalion commander. In some cases, there are even hybrid French-German terms, e.g., *"Premier-Leutnant"* and *"Seconde-Leutnant."* Place names are given in their Anglicized form when there is a common equivalent, e.g., "*Westfalen*" is translated as "Westphalia," the state "*Braunschweig*" as Brunswick," but the cities Kassel and Braunschweig are in the original German. Otherwise, personal and place names are shown in their native spelling. The term *"Kurhessian"* is used for the adjective form of Eletorate of Hesse, the earlier core area of the Kingdom of Westphalia. For place names, many of the locations are no longer in German-speaking countries and are not always easily recognizable by their current names, so whenever possible, the old German name is given along with the current name the first time it is used, and if the place is not well-known, then the country is noted as well. For example, the German name *"Küstrin"* is used, but the current Polish name *"Kostrzyn"* is given initially as well. Major rivers, such as the Vistula, are given in English, minor rivers and lakes are given in the native language or German. Generally the German designation will be followed by the French designation.

Richard Sanders

Part I

"The young king with his sallow, pale, but interesting face ... is a small, dainty man, thin, with dark hair and black eyes. His face has somewhat strong, prominent cheekbones, and already shows some light wrinkles around the eyes despite his youth. His chin and strong neck remind one of pictures of the Emperor, his brother, who he does not look like otherwise. He is more handsome."

From: *König Jérôme Napoleon, Ein Zeit- und Lebensbild* by Moritz von Kaisenberg, Leipzig 1899

King Jérôme in his Coronation Regalia
Painting around 1809 by Francois-Joseph Kinson, Museum Versailles Palace.

INTRODUCTION

THOMAS HEMMANN

THE FOUNDING OF THE KINGDOM OF WESTPHALIA AND ITS ARMY

After the outbreak of French-Prussian War in October 1806, Napoleon occupied the Electorate (*Kurfürstentum*) of Hesse-Kassel at the turn of October to November. Elector Wilhelm I then fled to safety in Denmark. Napoleon likewise declared the Duke of Brunswick, who had commanded the Prussian forces, as well as his descendants, as deposed. Hessen-Kassel, the country of Brunswick as well as the former Hanoverian Electoral territories were placed under temporary administration of the French military.

In the Treaty of Tilsit (7 July 1807), Napoleon had the Russian Tsar Alexander[1] recognize his youngest brother, Jérôme, as King of Westphalia. Additionally, Napoleon got a free hand to cobble together the Kingdom Westphalia from former Prussian and other territories. After Jérôme learned about his appointment, he immediately sent two Adjutants (Colonels Morio and Rewbell) to his new kingdom to get a first impression.[2] Then a provisional government for Westphalia was formed in Paris, which consisted of the imperial French State Counsels Simeon, Beugnot and Jollivet. This new government, also designated a regency, took over affairs of state in Kassel on 28 August 1807. Furthermore a constitution for Westphalia was drafted in France, signed by Napoleon, on 5 November[3] and imposed on the new country. All of this lets one imagine that the Kingdom of Westphalia was created as a satellite state dependent on France. According to the constitution, Jérôme's sovereign reign began on 1 December 1807 and on 10 December the newly baked King ceremoniously arrived in Kassel, his newly created Kingdom's capital.

1 Compare Hessen, p. 357ff.

2 For further details, see Kleinschmidt, pp. 7-38.

3 Officially dated 15 November 1807 because Napoeon transmittted it to Jérôme on that day.

Oath to the Westphalian Flag, 1810

"Serment au drapeau Westphalien" Detail, unfinished painting by Louis Dupre, Chateau Fontainebleau.

THE POLITICAL AND SOCIAL DEVELOPMENT

The Westphalian Constitution[4] (in Article 7) initially established that Jérôme, although the King, was still subject to the imperial family's pact. Also, according to the constitution's Article 2, half of the royal domains were under Napoleon's authority.

Along with these provisions that were contrary to Westphalia's and its population's interests, precepts in the Constitution were introduced that were progressive and granted advantages to broad sectors of the citizens. Article 10 established equality before the law and freedom of religious practice for all subjects. Article 13 abolished serfdom. Per Article 14, the nobility continued to exist but limited its prerogative for certain official positions and honors. Unitary taxes, coins, weights and measures were established (Articles 16 - 18). A State Council *(Staatsrat)* and the Imperial Estates *(Reichsstände)* were created as representative bodies *(Volksvertretung)* (Articles 26 - 28, 29 – 31 respectively). Other articles provided a modern organization of the Executive, e.g., Ministers responsible for Justice, Internal Affairs *(Inneres)*, War, Finance; creation of Departments *(Departements)* etc. Article 45 ultimately prescribed the Code Napoleon as the civil legal authority, effective on 1 January 1808.

With that, modern, common legal principles were created for the entire Kingdom. The subjects were to benefit from far reaching legal and social equality. Previous limitations (lack of rights, e.g., for Jews, limitations on guilds, etc.) were dropped without replacement. On the other side, the state's Finance Administration and the extensive police and informer system lay like blight over the entire country.

With respect to the military, in Westphalia's Constitution it was specified that the country would be part of the Confederation of the Rhine *(Rheinbund)* and that an army of 20,000 infantry, 3,500 cavalry and 1,500 artillerymen had to be raised. Additionally, conscription was introduced through the Constitution (Article 53) with a simultaneous prohibition against hiring for money. By the decree of 9 January 1808, all Westphalian-born persons were forbidden to serve in foreign armies and the country's sons were forced – under penalty of confiscation of property – to leave the service of foreign countries and to enter the newly created Westphalian Army. Additionally the first decree regarding desertion was issued on the 24th of the month. A further decree, of 25 April 1809, regulated the way conscription would be carried out. The former Military Governor of conquered Hessen-Kassel, the French Major General Lagrange, became Westpha-

4 For the constitution, see Kleinschmidt, p. 13ff.

Nro. 80. PLACE d'ELBING.

Messieurs les Magistrats de la ville d'Elbing sont invités a ~~faire~~ ...

Pour

a Elbing, le 7 ... 1813

Le Commandant de la Place.

Receipt for quartering for an officer in Elbing in 1813
Document collection of Markus Gaertner.

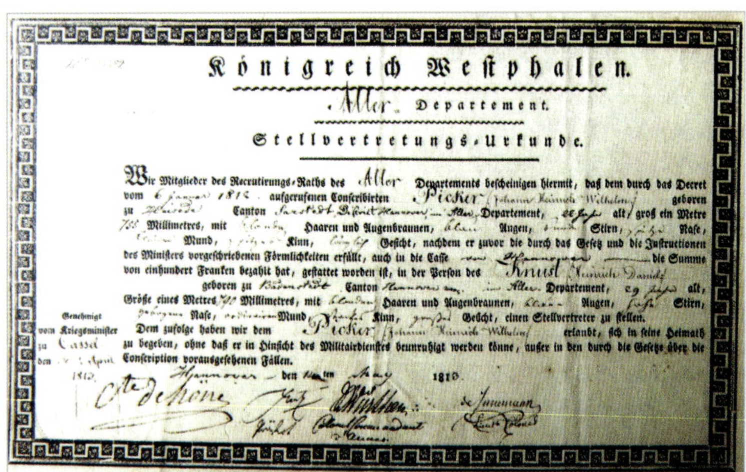

Königreich Westphalen.

Aller Departement.

Stellvertretungs-Urkunde.

Wir Mitglieder des Recrutirungs-Raths des Aller Departements bescheinigen hiermit, daß dem durch das Decret vom ... aufgerufenen Conscribirten Picker ... geboren zu ... Canton ... Departement, ... alt, groß ein Metre ... Millimetres, mit ... Haaren und Augenbraunen, ... Augen, ... Stirn, ... Nase, ... Mund, ... Kinn, ... Gesicht, nachdem er zuvor die durch das Gesetz und die Instructionen des Ministers vorgeschriebenen Förmlichkeiten erfüllt, auch in die Casse ... die Summe von einhundert Franken bezahlt hat, gestattet worden ist, in der Person des Knust ... geboren zu ... Canton ... Departement, ... alt, Größe eines Metres ... Millimetres, mit ... Haaren und Augenbraunen, ... Augen, ... Stirn, ... Nase, ... Mund, ... Kinn, ... Gesicht, einen Stellvertreter zu stellen.

Dem zufolge haben wir dem Picker ... erlaubt, sich in seine Heimath zu begeben, ohne daß er in Hinsicht des Militairdienstes beunruhigt werden könne, außer in den durch die Gesetze über die Conscription vorausgesehenen Fällen.

Genehmigt vom Kriegsminister zu Cassel den ... April 1813.

Hannover den ... 1813.

Heinrich Wilhelm Picker's Deputizing Certificate (*Stellvertreterurkunde*) from 14 May 1813, Hanover
Photo: Markus Gaertner, at Landesausstellung König Lustik, Kassel 2008.

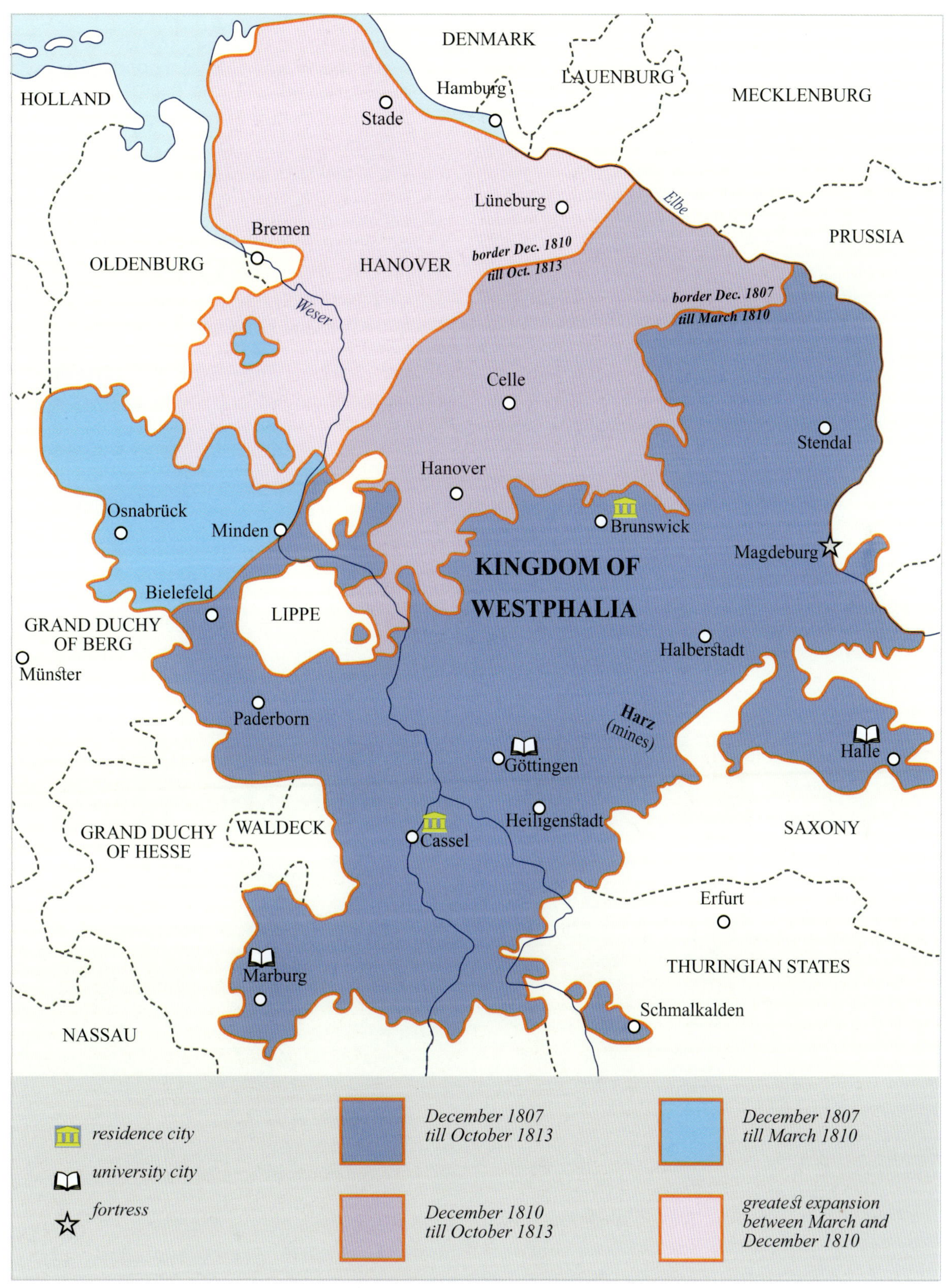

The Kingdom of Westphalia in its Development and its major Expansion up until 1810
Map by Bernhard Glaenzer.

lia's first Minister of war. He was followed quickly – provisionally – by Morio mentioned above, now a brigadier general. Starting in December 1807, the administration worked feverously on the army's organization.

The first measures were to set up the command structures for the Departments and consolidate additional departments – similar to those in France – into so-called Military Divisions *(Militärdivisionen)* (as administrative technical units).[5] So the following organization was introduced:[6]

1st Military Division:

- Department of the Fulda, Major General and Department Commandant Rewbell (Governor of Kassel)
- Department of the Weser, General Diemar (Osnabrück)
- Department of the Werra, General Börner (Marburg)

2nd Military Division:

- Department of the Oker, Major General and Department Commandant Rivaud[7] (Brunswick/ *Braunschweig*)
- Department of the Harz, General Webern (Heiligenstadt)
- Department of the Leine, General Lehsten (Göttingen)

3rd Military Division:

- Department of the Elbe, French Major General *(Général de division)* and Department Commandant Eblé (Magdeburg)
- Department of the Saale, General Motz (Halberstadt)

The Military Divisions formed the administrative framework for the Army's actual military organization, which will be discussed later.

5 A purely military administrative technical term. The "Military Divison" (*"Militärdivision"*) had nothing to do with the tactical unit "division" (that consisted of two to three brigades) used in the field

6 See Hellrung, p. 391f..

7 Alternative spelling: Rivaud de la Raffinière, compare Six, Georges, Vol. 2, p. 373f and Lünsmann, p. 50.

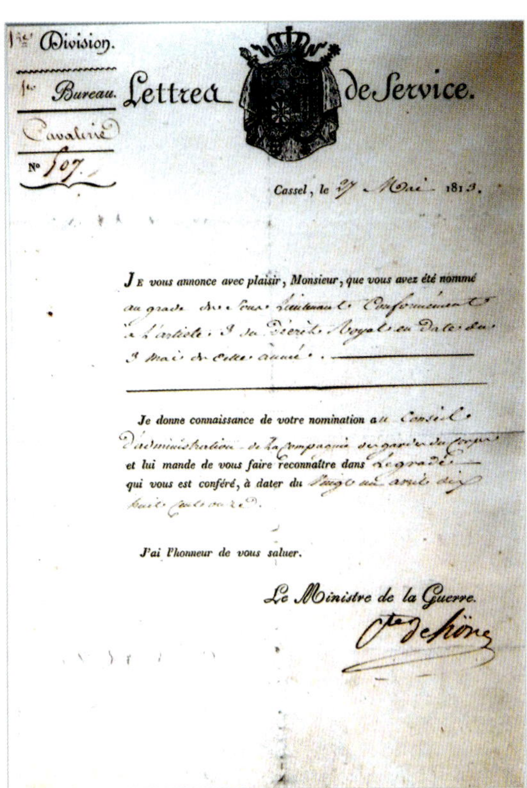

1re Division.
1er Bureau.
Cavalerie
No 507.

Lettres de Service.

Cassel, le 27 Mai 1813.

Je vous annonce avec plaisir, Monsieur, que vous avez été nommé au grade de ...

Je donne connaissance de votre nomination au Conseil d'administration de la compagnie des gardes du corps et lui mande de vous faire reconnaître dans le grade qui vous est conféré, à dater du ...

J'ai l'honneur de vous saluer.

Le Ministre de la Guerre.

Promotion Certificate for Promotion to Lieutenant 1813
Photo: Markus Gaertner, from Bomann Museum, Celle.

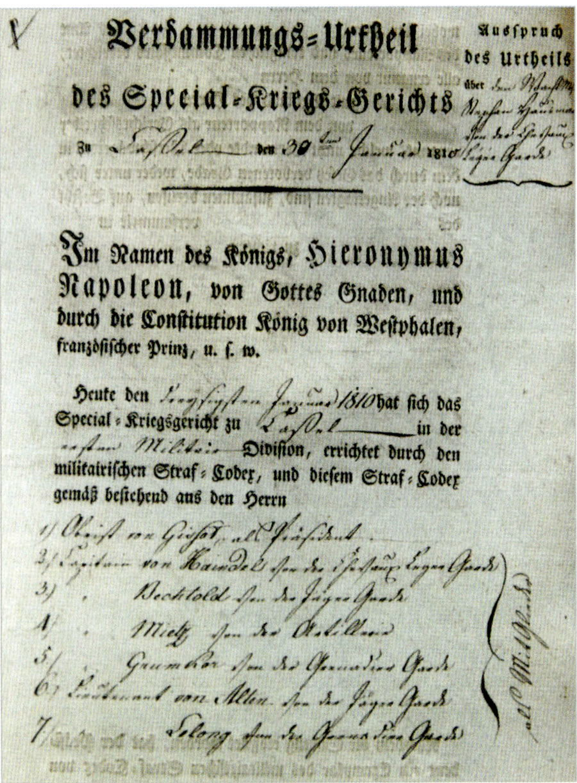

Verdammungs-Urtheil des Special-Kriegs-Gerichts

Ausspruch des Urtheils über ...

zu Cassel den 30 Januar 1810

Im Namen des Königs, Hieronymus Napoleon, von Gottes Gnaden, und durch die Constitution König von Westphalen, französischer Prinz, u. s. w.

Heute den ... 1810 hat sich das Special-Kriegsgericht zu Cassel in der ... Division, errichtet durch den militairischen Straf-Codex, und diesem Straf-Codex gemäß bestehend aus den Herrn

1) ...
2) ...
3) ...
4) ...
5) ...
6) ...
7) ...

Death Penalty Document from the Kassel Court Martial, of 30 January 1810
Photo: Markus Gaertner, from Landesausstellung König Lustik, Kassel 2008.

Bemerkung.
Die Ausfertigung der Anwerbungs-Urkunde muß spätestens vier und zwanzig Stunden nach der Anwerbung in triplo an den Unterpräfecten des Districts geschickt werden.

Linien Infanterie
5ten Regiment.

Departement Harz
Arrondissement Heiligenstadt
Canton Heiligenstadt
Gemeinde Heiligenstadt
den 25ten Junii 1812
No. 9

Freiwillige
Anwerbungs-Urkunde.

Heutigen Tages, den 25ten Junii 1812 ist erschienen vor uns Canton Maire der Gemeinde Heiligenstadt Canton Heiligenstadt Arrondissement Heiligenstadt Departement Harz benannter Joseph [illegible] alt 18 Jahr geboren den 3ten Februar 1794 wohnhaft zu Günterode Canton Heiligenstadt Arrondissement Heiligenstadt Departement Harz Sohn von Joseph [illegible] und von Anna Catharina geb. Feldmann dessen Signalement hier folgt:

Größe 1 Meter 500 Millimeter, Haare braun, Augenbraunen braun, Augen grau, Stirne [illegible], Nase spitz, Mund klein, Kinn spitz, Gesicht länglich, Gesichtsfarbe gesund besondere Auszeichnungen keine Profession keine welcher erklärte, daß er gesonnen sey, in Folge der Anordnungen des königlichen Decrets vom 16. November 1809, eine freiwillige Dienstanwerbung bei dem 5ten [illegible] Regiments [illegible] welchen Dienst er am meisten vorzieht, zu contrahiren.

Nachdem obbenannter durch den Herrn Med. [illegible] Chirurgus [illegible] untersucht, zum Kriegsdienst tauglich befunden worden, derselbe auch die Versicherung ertheilt hat, daß er alle nöthige Eigenschaften, um bei dem 5ten [illegible] Regt. angestellt zu werden, besitze; desgleichen das Attestat seiner guten Aufführung von dem Herrn Maire Armbrecht seiner Gemeinde vom Günterode vorgezeigt, habe ich ihm das officielle Protocoll, welches aus dem Decrete vom 16ten November 1809 und dem Militair-Strafcodex gezogen worden, und die Pflichten der Militairpersonen, so wie auch die Strafen gegen die Deserteurs enthält, vorgelesen; und nachdem benannter Joseph [illegible] erklärt, mich vollkommen verstanden und begriffen zu haben, sich auch allem diesen unterwerfe, habe ich ihn als Angeworbenen erklärt, und hat mit mir zugleich unterzeichnet.

Der Canton Maire
[illegible]

Comparent erklärt, daß er nicht schreiben könne.
[illegible]
Mairie Secretaire

Voluntary Enlistment Certificate of the 5th Line Regiment 1812
Photo: Markus Gaertner, from the Landesausstellung König Lustik, Kassel 2008.

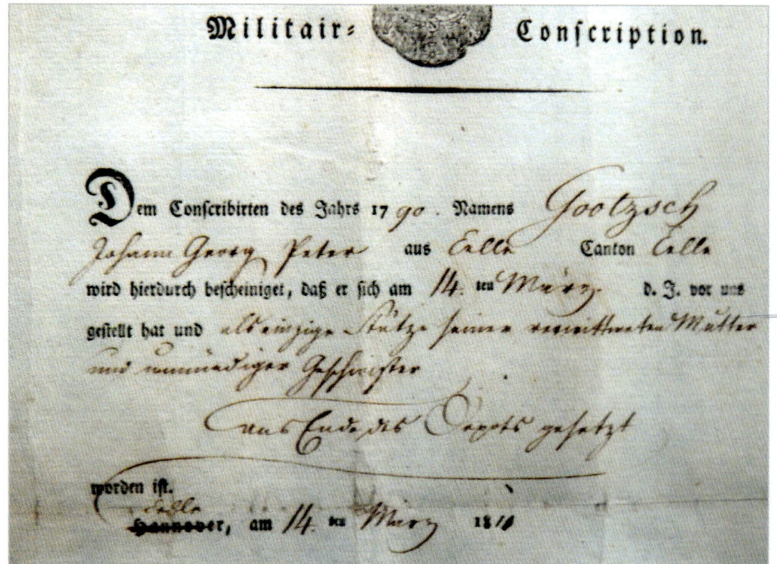

Militair-Conscription.

Dem Conscribirten des Jahrs 1790. Namens Gootzsch Johann Georg Peter aus Celle Canton Celle wird hierdurch bescheiniget, daß er sich am 14ten März d. J. vor uns gestellt hat und als einzige Stütze seiner verwittweten Mutter und unmündigen Geschwister ans Ende des Depots gesetzt worden ist.

Celle ~~Hannover~~, am 14ten März 1811

Certification for Conscription/ Call-Up from Celle; March 1811
Photo: Markus Gaertner, from Bomann Museum, Celle.

THE ORGANIZATION OF THE WESTPHALIAN ARMY

MARKUS GAERTNER

OVERVIEW OF THE DEVELOPMENT OF THE ARMY AND THE INDIVIDUAL BRANCHES

The new kingdom faced a difficult situation in creating a military force.

A large portion of the units from the former principality had already been disbanded or furloughed. Since 1803, the overwhelming portion of the Hanoverian officers and troops had gone abroad, especially to Great Britain. There, in many cases, they had enlisted in the newly established King's German Legion (KGL - German: *Königliche Deutsche Legion*) to fight against France. In August 1803, Napoleon attempted to create a counter-pole for winning recruits with the *"Legion hanovrienne."* But it saw no success and the unit never reached its planned total strength.

Also there was a similar situation in the Brunswick, Prussian and Hessian parts of the country. From the former military personnel, only a few experienced and willing soldiers were available.

In November 1806, the General-Governor of the French Administration in Hessen, General Lagrange, had already issued a proclamation with the goal of obligating the soldiers of the former Electorate of Hesse *(Kurhesse)* to service (in the *Legion franco-hessoise*). However, the resonance was slight. Only two weak infantry regiments were formed after many recruitment attempts; they later formed the core of the 1st and 2nd Westphalian Infantry Regiments.

In December 1806, the administration tried to use the formation of the *"Regiment de Westphalie"* also in the old Prussian territories to win soldiers for service. But the desired success eluded them here as well. Only one weak regiment, later battalion fought as an individual unit in Spain.

Immediately after Jérôme's accession to the throne, the raising of the army was begun with great energy. The King took the military seriously and involved himself with many technical matters and concerning the evolving forces. As an incentive, the pay was set higher than in other German states.

Article 5 of the Kingdom's Constitution established: "The Kingdom of Westphalia is a part of the Confederation of the Rhine. The contingent shall consist of 25,000 men. Of that, 20,000 infantry ..."[8]

The entire military administration was built on the French model.

The technical administrative foundations were created with the establishment of the Ministry of War and by dividing the Kingdom into Military Divisions.

At first, a 12,500 man French force was to guarantee the military security in the country. This transitional solution proved to be a lasting condition in the following years. During the establishment of the Kingdom, numerous garrisons, especially the Magdeburg Fortress had to be salaried and maintained.

The formation and organization of individual regiments started off with difficulty. Recruitment of officers did not attain the expected flow. It was only with the laws that penalized native officers for service abroad and with the introduction of conscription on the French model (at the end of May 1808), that there were enough soldiers available to effectively make progress in forming individual units.

In the course of the first months former soldiers also gathered at the military posts mostly due to economic need.

The Army was divided into four areas, i.e., the Royal Guards *(Königliche Garde)* with its own staff, the General Staff of the Line *(Generalstab der Linie)*, the line units as the nucleus of the armed forces and the Formations for Domestic Service and Security *(Formationen für den Dienst im Landesinneren and für die Sicherheit im Land)*.

In January 1808, the two regiments of the Franco-Hessian Legion were taken into Westphalian service. In February, a light Infantry battalion was raised from non-Prussian prisoners of war. Additionally in February, the National Guard *(Nationalgarde)*, the Department Companies *(Departement-Kompanien)* as well as a Gendar-

8 *"Das Königreich Westphalen ist Bestandteil des Rheinbundes. Das Kontingent soll 25,000 Mann betragen. Hiervon 20,000 Mann Infanterie ..."*

merie corps were formed. A Veterans Company *(Veteranen-Kompagnie)* was created in each Department to take care of wounded veterans *(Invaliden)*.

In April, the organization of the Guard was begun in Kassel. The King, contrary to his brother Napoleons' idea, saw the Guard more as a representational unit than as an elite fighting force.

So Jérôme formed a Garde du Corps as a personal bodyguard *(Leibgarde)*.

The Grenadier and the Jaeger Battalions were formed with volunteers, suitable recruits and 300 French veterans. For the Cavalry of the Guard, they began initially by forming of a Chevaulegers Regiment whose nucleus was filled with Polish lancers *(Vistula-Legion)*.

In the Line, starting in March 1808, a Jaeger Carabinier Company, using foresters, the 3rd and 4th Line Infantry Regiments, the 1st Cuirassier, as well as the Line Chevauleger Regiment could be formed. Until the end of 1808, an Artillery Corps also came into being with a strength of four foot companies and one mounted company. Although the creation of individual regiments was always a priority, most of the units still lacked their necessary complement of soldiers.

So by the end of the year, the Army reached a strength of ca. 14,000 men, of which 2,100 men were in the Guard. The Army's expansion spurred with newly conscripted personnel. Starting in February 1809, four additional infantry regiments, i.e., the 5th, 6th and starting in July the 7th and 8th Regiments, as well as a new light infantry battalion, were formed with 9,000 new recruits, among other personnel. The cavalry was increasing in strength, initially only with cadre for the 2nd Cuirassier Regiment starting in July.

For the campaign against Austria, which took the Westphalian forces to Saxony, a division had to be placed under the command of the King. In the spring, a second division with three infantry regiments, a light infantry battalion and attached artillery had already marched off to Spain. The Chevauleger Regiment had already been directed to this theater of war.

After the annexation of the remaining former Hanoverian territories in March 1810, one could also form the two hussar regiments with volunteers from the new departments. Personnel drafted in 1810 were used as replacement troops for the badly decimated regiments in Spain and to reinforce the existing units. Additionally, the 5th Infantry Regiment, which had been destroyed in Halberstadt by the Duke of Brunswick's *Freikorps*, had to be raised anew.

Organizing of a third light Infantry battalion with soldiers returning from Spain was begun in 1811. Regiments Nos. 2 and 7 were each expanded with a third battalion. The Technical Troops *(technischen Truppen)* along with the artillery were also beefed up with a sapper and artisan unit.

Until the end of the year, the Army had a strength of ca. 32,400 men.

In 1812, Jérôme provided the Grande Armée's 8th Corps with his army for the upcoming Russian campaign. During the catastrophic process, all the participating regiments were almost completely destroyed. Only 18 officers and ca. 600 men assembled at the mustering location in Thorn (now Torun, Poland) at the beginning of 1813. A "March Battalion" (*"Marschbataillon"*) was formed from the able-bodied men that by the end of January 1813 had melted to 120 men. Infantry Regiments Nos.1, 4 and 5, which were still mostly combat capable, were tied down as garrisons in Prussian fortresses.

In the course of the year 1812, the expansion of the army continued without letup and in August a new Queen's Guard Regiment *(Garderegiment Königin)*, later the *"Füsilier-Garde,"* was formed. At the end of September, raising a 4th Light Infantry Battalion began. Then in October, a second chevauleger regiment as well as a 9th Infantry Regiment followed.

The heavy losses during the Russian campaign demanded reestablishment of the entire Army. So the administration tried to at least bring the still existing regiments up to acceptable strengths. The just newly formed 2nd Chevaulegers Regiment was taken over into the new Guard Chevauleger Regiment.

The Foot Guards *(Garde zu Fuß)* was filled out with the line infantry's elite companies. The *Garde du Corps* was reinforced by a squadron with a company.

In the infantry, there were still a small number of reserves in the depot companies, so that only eight battalions of four companies each, of various strengths, were available for all regiments

With great effort, using new call-ups until March 1813, it was possible to bring most of the Guard as well as the 1st, 4th, 5th and 9th Line Infantry Regiments up to appreciable strengths. The 6th Infantry Regiment was not formed further. The light Infantry was restructures and brought up to strength with a third battalion

For the cavalry, forming the cuirassiers and hussars was more difficult. While it was possible to "quantitatively" fill a few units, the old "quality" could no longer be achieved due to the shortage of horses and the inexperience of the freshly called-up recruits.

Until June 1813, the Army again had a strength of ca. 20,000 infantry, 2,800 cavalry and 26 cannon. A division went to the *Grand Armée* in mid- August, where it was divided among various Army corps, used as garrisons, or took part in the autumn campaign in Saxony.

In August, Napoleon handed over a half-formed hussar regiment (of Frenchmen and Italians) for support and as a reliable bodyguard, which the King took into has forces as the Guard Hussars *(Garde-Husaren)*.

Until the autumn, the Army stood ready with 27,000 men on paper, although the loyalty and fighting ability were already viewed as questionable. Desertions increased by leaps, for example, at the end of August both hussar regiments had already decided by defect to the Allies.

Also the attempt in October to protect the Kingdom against the advancing Allies showed no more success. The remaining remnants of the Army put up little or no resistance in the fighting around Kassel. The individual units were wiped out, taken prisoner or simply dissolved. After his flight from Kassel, Jérôme disbanded the remaining parts of his Garde du Corps in Cologne on 1 November 1813. The last fighting forces, the Chevauleger Regiment located in Spain, were disarmed by the French in December 1813.

Only the 1st Westphalian Infantry Regiment, located in Danzig (Gdansk), remained in existence as a unit. After the capitulation of the Danzig Fortress, the Prussians took the remainder of the regiment into their own units until the unit was merged into the 27th Infantry Regiment in March 1815.

THOMAS HEMMANN

RECRUTING

The principles for recruiting,[9] named after France's conscription model, were already expressed in Article 12 of the Constitution:

"Military conscription is the basic law of the Kingdom of Westphalia; no recruitment for money will take place."[10]

Up until the French Revolution the predominant system in Europe was the mercenary army, an army of professional soldiers, which due to the expensive recruitment and difficult actions in wartime, was also only used with care. In contrast, in France the massive call-up was already in use since the beginning of 1793, the so-called *levée en masse*. It had become necessary in order to oppose the at least numerically strong armies of the coalitions of Great Britain, Austria, Prussia, Russia etc. With the Law of 23 September 1798, this form of recruiting, under the term *"conscription"*[11] was lastingly established in France.

In Westphalia, based on the Constitution's article mentioned above, the King issued his own conscription law by a royal decree of 25 April 1808. Numerous more detailed provisions followed in the next years, so that in 1810 the printed edition of the law was already in two volumes, each 500 pages long. Every male citizen of the kingdom was – from age 20 to 25 years – subject to conscription. The service obligation was five years in peacetime, and an extension was possible.

The Conscription Process

Initially by the authorities prepared lists of all the men obligated for conscription in the cited age group. Then a lottery was held, in which a recruiting officer as well as a gendarmerie unit – to maintain public peace – participated. The conscript had to pull a lottery chit depending on the lottery number was assigned to one of three classes:

1. Conscripted to march *(zum Marschieren konskribiert)*, i.e., for immediate call-up;
2. To the Reserve, i.e., slated for possible later call-up;
3. Free from conscription.

The lowest lottery numbers went to the 1st Class *(1. Klasse)*, the next higher numbers to the 2nd Class *(2. Klasse)*, etc. After the lottery a physical examination was carried out. If the recruits were less than 5 foot (1.54 meters) tall or very overweight, they were mustered out and the next lottery number was called in for call-up. There were also exceptions for the sole sons of parents older than sixty and the sons from families without parents but with minor children, so long as the men subject to conscription were responsible for the support of their family members.

Like in France, using a replacement was legally permitted, conditional upon an approval by the authorities. In this case, the conscripted man had to pay 100 Francs to the treasury and to pay his replacement – depending on the circumstances – about 5,000 to 7,000 Francs in compensation. Naturally the economically better situation members of the wealthy citizenry or the nobility profited from this rule.

Along with conscription, voluntary enlistment for military service was possible. But of course there was no cash bonus for doing so, however, the volunteer did get the privilege of being able to select his branch.

9 We base this again on the description in Lünsmann, pp. 27-40, as well as the special investigation *(Spezialuntersuchung)* by Pavkovic.

10 *"Die Militairkonskription ist Grundgesetz des Königreiches Westphalen; es sollen keine Werbungen für Geld stattfinden."*

11 Conscription here means as much signing into the mustering rolls on whose basis then a particular number of those signed up *(Konskribierten)* were actually drawn from the lottery for military service. Paying for a substitute was allowed.

THE CALL-UPS FROM 1808 TO 1813

The first conscription was carried out in 1808 and affected those born in 1788. The call-up took place in the shadow of providing contingents for Napoleonic France's war against Spain, to which the Westphalian Army had to supply a division. Nine thousand draft-eligible mean were chosen by the lottery for the 1st Class, and another 3,000 for the 2nd Class. Out of the 1st Class, 4,500 men were called up immediately and the remainder later. Organizational reasons were supposedly decisive for this staggered process.
In 1809, the year of the Austrian-French war, a total of 7,000 recruits were selected for the 1st and 2nd Classes. From 1810 to 1811 there were only small-scale call-ups in order to replace troops[12] who had been released.
The next major call-up took occurred in July 1812, i.e., at a time when almost the entire active Westphalian Army was already on the Russian campaign. Four thousand men born in 1792 were immediately called up. Another 4,000 men born in 1792 and 1793 were enlisted the beginning of 1813. In addition in 1813, when the entire army had been destroyed in Russia and had to be reestablished, one had to go back and call up those who had been spared during the years 1809-1812.

Handling of Noncompliant Men and Deserters
Special depots were set up for those conscripted, who tried to elude the lottery, refused the call-up, or feigned infirmity (the so-called *"Refraktäre"* or *"Widerspenstige"* – recalcitrants). The depots were similar to the punishment companies *(Strafkompanien)* of later times. Deserters could be sentenced to heavy monetary fines, public (forced) labor, ball-and-chain gangs (*Kugelschleppen* i.e., strict confinement) or the death penalty. In the spring of 1813, a special "Public Workers' Corps" (*"Korps öffentlicher Arbeiter"*) was created copying the French model for those apprehended for multiple desertions, self-mutilators and those sentenced to public labor.
Lünsmann estimates the portion of losses/separations from "noncompliants" and deserters came to 7-9% of the total strength of the Westphalian Army. The closer to the Kingdom's fall at the end of 1813 came, the more the various forms of misconduct and desertion increased. Accordingly increasingly stricter provisions were issued against them.

12 These two years were relatively peaceful, because only a few contingents from the Westphalian Army were fighting (in Spain). Otherwise the existing statistical information for the years 1810-1813 is very scanty.

THE MILITARY ADMINISTRATION

The Ministry of War *(Kriegsministerium)*
The Ministry of War was responsible for all of the administration of the Army. In peacetime, it was the authority over all the units,[13] which corresponded directly with it. Again, the French Army was the model for the Ministry of War's organization. In the beginning, the Ministry was divided into four Divisions, which in turn were divided into so-call bureaus *(Büros)*.[14]

The 1st Division *(Division Personnel)* was concerned with new formations, personnel matters and troop inspections. It had five Büros: for Infantry, Cavalry, two for the Artillery, Engineer System *(Geniewesen)*/Gendarmerie. The 2nd Division *(Division matériel)* was responsible for army materiel, caserns and hospitals; it was not divided into bureaus *("Büros")*. The 3rd Division, also without subordinate Büros, administered the Provision System *(Proviantwesen)* and carried out oversight of all war commissary officers.[15] The 4th Division *(Division de la Conscription)* with four Büros was responsible for all conscription matters. Additionally it had a *Büro* for financial accounting, pay, pensions etc.

13 The activities of the Ministry of War are based on the information in Lünsmann, p. 47ff, who in turn got his information from the *Almanach Royal de Westphalie*.

14 The term "Division" used here is also purely an administrative technical one. The "Divisions" correspond to Germany's present day Ministerial Departments *(Ministerialabteilungen)*, the Bureaus *(Büros)* to more or less the Branches *(Unterabteilungen)* and Offices *(Referaten)*. A restructuring took place in 1812.

15 These Commissary Officers *(Kommissare)* were responsible for the delivery of provisions to the units during march movements.

The Ministers of War, in chronological order, were:

- Major General Lagrange[16] (December 1807)
- Colonel Morio[17] (December 1807 - August 1808)
- Finance Minister v. Bülow[18] (August - October 1808)
- Major General Eblé[19] (October 1808 - January 1810)
- Großstallmeister (Grand Equerry) General D´Albignac[20] (February - September 1810)
- Justice Minister Simeon[21] (September 1810)
- General Salha[22] (September 1810 - October 1813)

16 Previous Military Governor in conquered Electorate of Hesse *(Kurhessen)*.

17 A favorite of Jérôme, but not well liked by Napoleon. In 1809 he was the commander of the Westphalian Division in Spain. Murdered in 1811. See "Short Biographies" in the Appendices.

18 Von Bülow as simultaneously the Minister of War and Minister of Finance.

19 He became well-known in 1812 for having constructed the two bridges over the Berezina River. Although Eblé was exceptionally capable, he had to give up the office of the Westphalian Minister of War because he refused to resign from the French Army.

20 He was a favorite of the King, and in May 1810 he received the title of Count of Ried (Graf von Ried). An equerry, from French *écurie 'stable'*, and related to *écuyer 'squire'*) is an officer of honour. Historically, it was a senior attendant with responsibilities for the horses of a person of rank, such as a king, prince or noble.

21 For a feew days he was both the Minister of War and of Justice.

22 He was a prior French naval Commander and old companion of King Jérôme.

THE INDIVIDUAL POSITIONS IN THE MILITARY ADMINISTRATION

The Mustering Inspectors and the Army Commissary Officers (*Musterungsinspektoren* and *Kriegskommissare)*

The War Commissariat *(Kriegskommissariat)* was also set up on the French model.[23] The highest authority was a commission that consisted of the General Mustering Inspector *(Generalmusterungsinspektor)*, four Mustering Inspectors *(Musterungsinspektoren)* and six adjutants that belonged to them. These Mustering Officers were responsible for the oversight of all administrative matters, accounting and discipline. In addition, they held troop reviews *(inspections)* and checked on the service's details.

Borcke, Then a Lieutenant in the 1st Light Infantry Battalion, commented about the inspections: *"The musterings were held with great minute exactness, especially with regard to the weapons and uniforms. The King himself and often the generals on such occasions took the musket out of the hands of the best soldier of a company, inspected it for its serviceability and were very serious with the unit's company commander or officer in which they found the slightest negligence. They viewed the pieces of clothing with the same exactness, had the backpacks unpacked, satisfied themselves with the presence of all the prescribed items and in this manner intruded in all the minutia. Naturally this stimulus descended on the deputy commander; as a result the administrative officials came under the closest scrutiny and provided those responsible for the soldiers with everything of the best quality. The army was as it could not be otherwise, soon clothed and equipped with the best and most effective items. Admittedly there was also no end of the reviews, inspections, and the officers were busy from early to late every day after day."*[24] Along with the normal reviews/inspections, there were also mustering before departing garrison, on marches, on days of rest and after returning.

In the larger towns there were so-called "weapon commandants" *(Waffenkommandanten)* who were responsible for all local military administrative affairs like personnel on leave, the sick, transportation, etc. They were the supervisors of the War Commissary Officers *(Kriegskommissare)*, some of who also occupied the office of the "Review Inspector" *(Revueinspektor)* or "Junior Review Inspector" *(Unterrevueinspektor)*. Finally during wartime a Field War Commissariat *(Feldkriegskommissariat)* was mobilized that was responsible for the provisioning of the forces in the field.

23 Again we base this on the investigations in Lünsmann, p. 53ff.

24 Quoted from Borcke, p. 119f. *"Die Musterungen wurden with großer Peinlichkeit und Genauigkeit, vorzüglich hinsichtlich der Waffen und der Bekleidung, abgehalten. Der König selbst und nicht selten die Generale nahmen bei solchen Gelegenheiten dem ersten besten Soldaten einer Kompanie das Gewehr aus der Hand, untersuchten es auf seine Brauchbarkeit und hielten sich sehr ernstlich an den Kompagniechef oder Offizier, in dessen Abtheilung sie die geringste Nachlässigkeit fanden. Ebenso genau besichtigten sie die Kleidungsstücke, ließen die Tornister auspacken, überzeugten sich von dem Vorhandensein aller vorgeschriebenen Dinge und drangen auf diese Weise in alle Kleinigkeiten ein. Dieser Antrieb ging natürlich auf die Unterbefehlshaber über; die Verwaltungsbehörden standen infolge dessen unter der schärfsten Aufsicht und lieferten alles dem Soldaten Zuständige von bester Beschaffenheit. Die Armee war so, wie es gar nicht anders sein konnte, bald auf das Beste und Zweckmäßigste bekleidet und ausgerüstet. Freilich nahmen auch die Paraden, Revuen and Inspektionen kein Ende, und die Offiziere waren Tag für Tag von früh bis spät beschäftigt."*

The Medical System (*Sanitätswesen*)

In the hospital system there were also authorities established that were long-term and temporary – just for wartime. The permanent facilities were subordinate to a Health Council *(Gesundheitsrat)* that reported to the Ministry of War. It led the hospitals in Kassel, Magdeburg, Brunswick, Hanover, Hameln, Halberstadt, Halle and Celle. Additionally, applicants for military doctors' posts had to take a test in front of this council.

In case of war, field hospitals *(Feldlazarette)* were set up consisting of field hospital depots *(Feldlazarettdepots)*, field hospital detachments *(Feldlazaretteabteilungen)*, field hospital sections *(Feldlazarettesektionen)* and mobile hospitals *(fliegenden Lazaretten)*. In addition, the regiments and battalions had their own small medical treatment elements for which their respective military doctors were responsible.

But one cannot conclude that there was a well-organized hospital system in the field based on this extensive administrative organization. Both the care for the soldiers on the battlefield and the subsequent treatment in the military hospital were extremely lacking under the poor conditions, especially in Spain and Russia, where the hospitals also were constantly threatened by the enemy units swirling around them. Furthermore, the surgeons' training was inadequate. In the best case the practice was by surgeons who had at least been toughened up, having gained a certain skill in operations and amputations.

Exemplary would be the story of Lieutenant Colonel Boedicker, who was badly wounded at the Battle of Borodino (with a bullet lodged in his throat) and despite his high rank could not get a Westphalian doctor on the battlefield. He wrote:"

"After I had been taken over a great portion of the battlefield in my sad condition, we can upon the French Old Guard. My people asked to let me through, but this was refused and disregarding that one could clearly recognize me as a staff officer from my uniform and that blood was streaming from my mouth, nothing helped – I was not allowed to pass those intervening, but my people were forced to go to one of the flanks with me."[25]

After being dragged around for a long time, I was finally brought to a large aid station where such a crowd of wounded officers from all countries was arriving, that all my hopes for quick help were taken from me. My pleas to be freed of my bullet remained fruitless for a long time, until finally a doctor (whom my boys offered 10 Louisdor [gold coins]) took pity on me. He had to go to work very carefully in order to not injure the artery, which would have resulted in inevitable death. He succeeded in dislodging the bullet after four incisions, which was enough for me; in doing so my face was so swollen that I was unrecognizable to my men. That night I had to remain lying on the battlefield where then next morning my men arrived, and then dressed me, lay me in a small wagon, and gave me some coffee poured through a quill, which refreshed me indescribably. Because the bandage on my wound had come undone, I was taken to a monastery in the hopes of finding the same medical attention. I went into a room in which more than one hundred wounded officers were lying, without counting those who were situated in the hallways and the courtyard. Because I could not speak, I expressed my need via signs and asked to at least be bandaged; all of my pleas and the efforts of my men to talk to a doctor were in vain. I wanted to tried to accomplish it with money and my servant offered 6 to 8 Louisdor, that that did not help at all, the doctors were so overburdened with work and wanted to first help the wounded who had arrived earlier. In the meanwhile, my condition had become worse and worse and I was having so much difficulty breathing that I almost suffocated.

In anticipation of my death, I decided to leave the monastery and wrote a note to the sergeants who were with me to bring me forward to the battalion, no matter how long it took. On the way, we passed a small woods in which thousands of wounded lay; I demanded to speak to the commander, who to my greatest joy came to my little carriage in the person of Lieutenant Colonel Byrs[26] *of the 5th Westphalian Infantry Regiment. This good man found me a doctor immediately who bandaged my wound very carefully and well, who also had me brought some bouillon, which refreshed me very much.*

On the following morning my man took me further and brought me, after much going back and forth, to the battalion, at Moschaisk to the rear of the battlefield. I remained with it, went with it to Moscow and can only thank my survival to the help of the battalion doctor and the good care of the battalion itself."

25 Quoted from Boedicker, p. 274, in modernized German.

26 Lieutenant Colonel Byrs is not included in the roster *(Rangliste)* from Lünsmann, p. 207f; in it the battalion commander's position is left unfilled and according to that would have been completed with Lieutenant Colonel Byrs.

THE MILITARY JUSTICE SYSTEM

The Westphalian Army's military justice system was again copied from the French example, a modern establishment by contemporary standards. Corporal punishments were essentially prohibited.[27] They tried wherever possible to appeal to the soldiers' morals and to avoid degrading punishments. This appeal to the soldiers' feelings of honor naturally had its limits in an army, which used forced recruitment and went to the field in the interest of foreigners.

For the military courts there were against standing and temporary institutions. The standing military courts included the courts of original jurisdiction *(Gerichtshöfe 1. Instanz)*: i.e., two military courts *(Kriegsgerichte)* at each of the Military Divisions and at each army division. In addition, there was a third permanent court that functioned as a court of appeals *(2. [Revisions-]Instanz)*. Furthermore, exceptional courts were formed under certain circumstances (e.g., military crimes by staff officers, *Revueinspektoren* and *Kriegskommissaren*) that were adjourned after a judgment was made.

Typical punishments were, depending on the severity and frequency of the infraction: fines, reduction in rank, public work, the already mentioned "ball-and-chain" and finally the death sentence. In addition, for minor offenses the company commanders could impose a few days of arrest or (for NCOs and officers) restriction to quarters.

27 Nonetheless, there was, for example, the punishment of *"Kugelschleppen"* for deserters. It was the convict was put in irons and had to, sometimes for years, drag attached heavy balls after him, in English "ball-and-chain."

THE FIELD POSTAL SERVICE

The Field Postal Service *(Feldpost)* was a temporary organization that took over the delivery of letters and packages for the Westphalian Army.[28] It was subordinate to the General Direction of the Westphalian Royal Postal Department. In 1812, the Feldpost consisted of one Senior Inspector *(Oberinspektor)*, two Postal Directors *(Postdirektoren)*, a Controller *(Kontrolleur)*, cashier *(Kassierer)*, accountant *(Rechnungsführer)*, six post masters *(Feldpostmeistern)*, eight couriers and 16 postmen *(Postillionen)*, for a total of 36 men with 52 horses.

During the 1812 Russian Campaign, the Feldpost supported the troops until they reached Russia's interior. For example, the Hussar Master of Music *(Musikmeister)* Klinkhardt[29] reported how during the retreat from Russia he encountered an acquaintance, who was serving as a courier with the Westphalian *Feldpost*, and in relatively short time got from Dorogobuzh to Warsaw.

28 We base this on the description in Lünsmann, p. 55, and in Klietmann, *"Post und Feldpost des Königreichs Westphalen 1808 – 13."*

29 Klinkhardt, p. 59ff.

THE MILITARY SCHOOLS

The Corps of Pages *(Das Pagenkorps)*

The Corps of Pages functioned as a nursery for the army's Officers.[30] The Pages were thoroughly schooled in mathematics, fortification science, drawing, history, geography, French, religion, riding, fencing, dancing swimming, drilling, artillery service and surveying. They were housed in barracks under the supervision of a governor and several assistant officials. Along with the – primarily military – education, the pages had to perform service at court, i.e., to escort and serve the King and Queen at many events. Lünsmann says that over the years 56 pages visited the Page School *(Pagenschule)*, of whom about 30% were French. A portion of the pages went into the army as junior lieutenants when they were about 17 years old; the remainder went to other careers.

The War and the Artillery Academies

Copying the military education system in France, Westphalia also had a Military Academy *(Kriegsschule)* and an Artillery Academy *(Artillerieschule)*.[31] Both schools had the mission to train the offspring of capable officers.

30 Our description is based on Lünsmann, p. 73f, and the information in Lehsten, p. 3ff, who was a royal page. There were page corps at the French court as well as at the German courts.

31 According to Lünsmann, pp. 69-72, and Poten, Vol. 5, pp. 301-312.

Ninety years later, Poten assessed the Westphalian Military education institutions during King Jérôme's reign to be among the "various good institutions" and termed them as *"vortrefflich"* – "excellent."
The seat of Kriegsschule, founded in 1808, was Brunswick. The head of the school was initially General Heldring, who was later replaced by Major v. Sommer because of being overworked. The number of students varied over the years between 50 and 70. A part of the spaces was designated as so-called "full pension positions" *(Vollpensionärsstellen)* or "partial pension positions" *(Teilpensionärsstellen)*, i.e., the *Kriegsschule* students were supported with stipends from the state. The demand for the positions was corresponding great. Aspiring students had to be in good physical condition, be able to read and write German, have mastered the beginning level of Latin and be able to perform the basic mathematical calculations. The entrance age was between 14 and 17 years. The subject taught were – similar to that for the Corps of Pages – writing, arithmetic *(Rechnen)*, mathematics, drawing, surveying of fortifications, geography, history, German and French languages, training in drill, in the battalion and on cannon. The graduates were transferred to the army as junior lieutenants *(Unterleutnants)* after two to three years of instruction. Students who were examined and found to not be suitable for military service were to be employed in civilian careers.
The establishment of the Artillery Academy in 1810 was part of a package of measures to reorganize the Westphalian Artillery. The school was subordinate to the General Director of the Westphalian Artillery and Engineer Corps *(Artillerie- und Geniekorps)*, General Allix. Pupils were taken on in the ages 16-20 years (exception military personnel up to 22 years), if they could present a birth certificate, a certificate of good conduct *(Führungszeugnis)* and a cowpox vaccination. The acceptance examination required a basic understanding of arithmetic, geometry, trigonometry and algebra. Correspondingly and in appropriate recognition of the demands of the technical branches (Artillery and Engineer), the instruction was also strongly oriented on the natural sciences. Mathematics, chemistry, physics, mineralogy, astronomy, fortification studies, artillery science, drawing, general military science, horsemanship, gymnastics, fencing, religion, history, German, French, geography and handwriting. The exam was given after a two-year course of instruction. The successful graduates were assigned to the artillery as junior lieutenants.

DUTY IN GARRISON AND IN THE FIELD

The Garrison and Billeting

Little is known about garrison duty in the Westphalian Army.[32] Only the Guard had an established garrison – the capital Kassel. It was housed there in casernes. For the Line units, which were intermittently garrisoned in Kassel, a permanent barracks camp was erected on the so-called *"Forst"* (training area near Kassel).
The garrison locations of the other units changed frequently. When they were available, they made use caserne buildings from the old times of the Electorate of Hesse. If there were insufficient numbers of barracks buildings, the troops were quartered in their respective cantonments with the citizens. Along with Kassel, the Westphalian units were above all housed in Brunswick (the Kingdom Westphalia's second capital), Magdeburg (formerly the Prussian primary fortress), Hanover and Ziegenhain (small, former Kurhessian fortress).

The Guard Duty and Guard Duty (Wachdienste)

Garrison duty in the Westphalian Army was codified by the Regulation *(Regelement)* of 1808.[33] There were external guards (*Außenwachen* – outside the cities, towns, villages and camps), security guards (*Sicherheitswachen* – on gates, magazines etc.), honor guards (*Ehrenwachen* - for the King, more senior commanders, etc.) and police guards (*Polizeiwachen* - in garrisons, to maintain public order and safety). The latter also performed police duty, i.e., they apprehended troublemakers or persons they encountered who were out at night without a lantern. The heed of the guard (usually an officer in accompanied by a sergeant) also had the task to go on a *"Ronde"* (patrol or rounds) and to visit the individual guards. When doing that the password (*"Parole"* - response) had to be called out. And *"wie bitte?"* – "What, please?"
A watch normally lasted twenty-four hours. The guard duty began in each case at 12:00 noon with an inspection and issuing of the password. The guards were provided by all the branches of a garrison whereby the elite personnel (e.g., grenadiers and voltigeurs) were usually taken for the honor guard. A watch command most frequently consisted of a captain, a lieutenant, two ser-

32 We used Lünsmann again who for his part essentially bases his work on Borcke and the *Ordrebuch des Artillerieregiments für 1813* by Gerland.

33 This German language instruction was a literal translation of the corresponding French instruction of 1792.

geants, four corporals, four senior privates *(Gefreiten)* and 24 privates *(Gemeinen)*. After guard duty normally a soldier was excused from the next six to twelve watches).

Inspections and Parades

Corresponding to the French Army's practices, many inspections *(Musterungen)* were held, as noted in the descriptions by Borcke. There were regular inspections (by the *Revueinspektoren*) and exceptional inspections by higher officers and generals all the way up to the King. In those, they checked on the presence for duty, condition and completeness of equipment, the meals, but possibly the complaints about shortcomings among other things. This meant a constant burden especially for the officers and NCOs of the inspected units, particularly because comprehensive lists had to be maintained. In the autumn major reviews and maneuvers were conducted. In those maneuvers usually certain evolutions of large troop units were carried out in response to a previously established arrangements. In 1810 and 1811, large-scale maneuvers were held in the forest near Kassel under King Jérôme's direct leadership. In the latter exercise, 21 battalions and 20 squadrons were employed, which portrayed historic battles among other activities.

Discipline

The available information about maintaining discipline in the Westphalian Army is not consistent. Like was generally common in the French Army, the discipline while on duty was very strict, but when not on duty it was more lax. Borcke already eloquently describes the disciplinary difficulties in the 1st Light Battalion (that was however formed with former Prussian prisoners of war and therefore not generally typical) that led to the battalion having to be transferred from Kassel into the province.

A tendency to neglect discipline can be seen in general in connection with the end of the 1812 Russian campaign. The newly called up privates could receive the same basic training as had been provided in previous years, which naturally was disadvantageous in its effects on the cohesion of the units. Along with that there was the influence on morale from the 1813 Prussian uprising as well as the fact that large parts of the Westphalian population were opposed to the conscription and the use of the young soldiers in theaters that had nothing to do with the Westphalian citizens' interests (like Spain and Russia). This was recognizable in the general hatred of the Gendarmerie, which was considered a tool of repression.[34]

The low point of lack of discipline in the Westphalian Army was reached with the mass desertion of both Westphalian hussar regiments under Hammerstein in August 1813. Alongside that, the endless complaints about disciplinary problems in the Westphalian Artillery Regiment (still in its garrison in Kassel) in 1813 shed light on the symptomatic disciplinary situation at the end of the Kingdom (see Gerland). So it is no surprise that the units that accompanied King Jérôme on his flight from Kassel practically dissolved due to desertions.[35]

Field Duty

Also here – besides the known memoirs – there is little reliable information. The regulations for duty in the field, similar to in the French Army, were not used all that strictly. What was important was only that the soldier fought well. How he spent his time in camp, how he obtained and prepared his food as was commonly practiced in the countryside, all that was mostly left up to the individual's efficiency and imagination in the field.

Before deploying a thorough inspection usually was conducted in which, along with accounting for personnel, put emphasis on whether the equipment and munitions were complete. When they were available, a gendarmerie detachment accompanied the march column in order to assist the officers in ensuring marching discipline. A rearguard detached from the march column made sure that no one remained behind while the unit was underway. In the infantry only the higher ranking officers and their adjutants could ride, while all the other officers had to march on foot. Some of the marches were very long, up to 25 miles (40 km) per day. A five-minute break was included for each hour's march, in addition one for two hours at mid-day in order to allow the troops to cook their meals.

As much as possible the troops were quartered when on the march. If a bivouac had to be established, then a more senior officer or adjutant chose the site. Because there were no tents for the soldiers, each time improvised hut or tent-like shelters were built using whatever materials were at hand (e.g., trees, tree limbs, haystacks, straw, and parts of houses like doors or windows). Detachments were sent out to "organize" foodstuffs from the close-by settlements. When they brought back something, it was cooked and then the overnight camp was occupied. Of course, depending on how close the enemy was – a watch (i.e., sentries and so-called pickets - *Piketts*) was posted. When needed, the troops were called to be under arms *("unter das Gewehr")* even before daybreak, that is they had to form ranks by battalions or squadrons with their weapons in hand and could only put down the weapons when the patrols that had been sent out indicated no enemies had been discovered.

When possible the units looks for herds of sheep or cows to requisition and take along on the march in order to be able to prepare a meat meal or soup underway. In addition, provisions were obtained from sutlers and sutleresses who sold food and alcoholic beverages to the soldiers. Of course, above all officers and more senior NCOs with respectively better pay, could improve their menu.

34 See Ruthe.

35 Compare Gebauer and Kaisenberg.

In battle the combination of column and linear tactics was practiced exactly like by the French forces. The fighting was usually opened with artillery fire and a swarm of riflemen. Then, as a rule decisively – the column advanced. The infantry defended itself from cavalry attacks by forming a square. Along with that there was the tiring laying siege to fortresses (Gerona, 1809) or their defense (Küstrin, 1813) as well as fighting in built-up areas (e.g., the 1809 defense of Halberstadt). Further details about fighting techniques are handled in the section on the Training Regulations. (See below).
Toward the end of the Kingdom, i.e., in 1813, the tactical art had considerably suffered due to the short training during the Army's rapid new stand-up. Along with that was the fact that in 1813 the Westphalian Army was no longer employed in consolidated large units (divisions, corps), but was dispersed by regiments and brigades to many French Army corps (supposedly because Napoleon no longer trusted the Westphalian Army's reliability).

The Drill Regulations *(Exerzier-Reglements)*

The recruits were initially given the basics of military training. Then they simple formations and movements with and without muskets were drilled into them. Following that, they had training on firing their weapon. That was followed by training in increasingly large units, from platoon *(Peleton)* (six chapters) about the company / squadron / battery up to the battalion and regiment level. The recruit training for the cavalry was similar to that for the infantry, but mounted training was only begun after about six weeks of dismounted service. The prescribed sequence was the ideal case. Depending on the pressure of the circumstances, in 1813 at the latest, the training was significantly shortened and simplified.
The outdated French regulation of 1791 (based on the French regulation of 1775) was the model for the infantry.[36] This regulation was also established for the Westphalian Army– in the German language – in 1810. In addition there was a handbook for the infantry *(Manuel d´ Infanterie)* from 1811 that took up the further development of the tactical practices from the wars during the French Revolution and since the Empire's creation. It gave rules for the deployment of regiments for battle *(Ordre de Bataille)*, the structure of two to three battalions, their division into fusilier and elite companies, the positioning of the officers and NCOs as well as the kinds of fire (by ranks, platoons, two ranks and battalion fire). Along with the line formation, additional formations (e.g., columns, hollow and filled squared) were specified.
The cavalry trained on the basis of the French "Provisional Instruction on the Training and Maneuvers of Cavalry " *("Ordonnance provisoire sur l'exercice et les manoeuvres de la cavalerie")* (Strasbourg, 1809).[37] Also like for the infantry, the tactical structure (here in squadrons), the positioning of the officers and NCOs (differing for the heavy and light cavalry regiments), as well as the formations in line and in column were specified. The most important cavalry missions were reconnaissance and massed attacks. The latter occurred in line or in squadrons *(Staffeln)* formations.
There was no fixed instruction for the artillery. The valid French regulations appeared in 1792. They were supplemented by a collection of instructions that appeared in 1808 plus a handbook, *"Petit Manuel de Canonier"* from the year 1812. A battery consisted of a maximum of six cannon and two howitzers, i.e., eight cannon, but there were also batteries of six cannon. Tactically the battery could be divided into two half-batteries and these further into sections with two. A battery had its own train with an ammunition wagon and special vehicles like spare carriages, lifts, field forges, etc. Besides when in the march column, the placement of the battery was expected to be primarily like the other vehicles in a line further to the rear. The normal "battalion fire" *("Bataillenfeuer")* with cannonballs and grenades took place sequentially from one cannon to the next. Canister shot was fired as pairs each time by two cannon of a section.

36 See *Planches Relatives au Règlement concertant l´Exercice et les Manoeuvres de l´Infanterie.*

37 Compare also *Reglement für die französische Cavallerie ihr Exercieren und Manoeuvriren* which refers.

THE OFFICER CORPS

Composition and Evolution

The Westphalian officer corps was assembled from the most diverse elements.[38] At the establishment of the Westphalian Army, former Kurhessian officers formed the lion share of the officer corps - 323 from the Electorate of Hesse of the total 661 transferred into Westphalian service. To that were added about sixty Brunswick officers, and a few Hanoverians[39] and many former Prussian officers.[40] Another important part was that Frenchmen streamed into the country after its creation and occupied important positions. There were also officers from other armies (especially the Dutch), who were forced by Jérôme to take up service in the Westphalian Army under threat of expropriation of property if they or their families came from Westphalian territories.[41]

Lünsmann gives the following composition of the officer corps in 1810:

Officer's Origin from:	Percentage of the Officer Corps
Hessian Service	ca. 50 %
French Service	ca. 15 %
Prussian Service	ca. 10 %
Brunswick Service	ca. 7 %
Hanoverian Service	ca. 7 %
Other countries' Service	ca. 5 %
NCO, Military Academy graduates, etc. from the Westphalia. Army	ca. 6 %

In the later years the ratio changed more in favor of native elements because the military schools and the corps of Pages increasingly provided more officers for the Army. The officers' duty was already very arduous in peacetime. Borcke remarks: *"After my appointment I was sufficiently busy with very strict service, frequent training and constant supervision of the soldiers who lay in the caserne and were not allowed to be let out from under one's eyes for an instant."* And further, *"Because, despite all strictness and supervision, the discipline of the battalion in which I was assigned did not improve, frequent arguments and fistfights occurred among the men, so the battalion was officially banned from Kassel and suddenly in April 1801 received the order to march to Paterborn. On 14 April, I began, not being used to it at all, my first march on foot, which due to my unhealthiness made me very mad because I had never before in my life walked for eight to ten hours. Necessity and the example of others made the apparently impossible, if with great exertion, possible; I arrived in Paderborn with sore feet but completely safe and well."*[42] Naturally even greater demands were made of the officers during their wartime assignments especially in Spain and Russia.

The material conditions (pay, etc.) were adequate in so far as one did not ask for any luxury. For the lower officer's grades the level of pay corresponded to that of the Prussians; in the higher grades it was lower than in Prussia.

The opportunities for promotion were good, not least from vacancies caused by the many deaths in the constant wars. There are many examples of officers who climbed from Lieutenant to Lieutenant Colonel or even higher in Westphalian service in a few years. Efficiency and bravery in the lower grades were primarily the deciding factors; promotions in the more senior grades mostly went to those with better relations with the royal court.

Relations within the officer corps, after initial frictions (due to the heterogeneous regional composition), were mostly good due to military spirit and comradeship. However, disbanding of units and desertions in the officer corps became apparent toward the end of the Kingdom. Borcke and Morgenstern reported growing mistrust between the French and German generals and officers the closer it got to the downfall of the kingdom in 1813.

38 Our description is based on the analysis in Lünsmann, pp. 125–127.

39 However, most of the former Hanoverian officers took up service starting in 1803 in the King's German Legion *(KGL, Königlich Deutschen Legion)*, created in England i.e., on the side of Napoleon's opponents. Compare the rosters *(Ranglisten)* in Schwertfeger, Bd./Vol. 2. There were even case where Westphalian officers faced close relatives who served in the KGL in Spain. See for example, Bussche, p. 81ff.

40 As a reminder, the Kingdom of Westphalia was put together by Napoleon essentially by using former Electorate of Hesse, Brunswick, Hanoverian and Prussian territories.

41 For example, Meibom, who with his brother, formerly was in the Dutch service in a Waldeck regiment Meibom.

42 Borcke, p. 115, and p. 121. For understanding, it should be added that Borcke had had a horse during his earlier service (as a Subaltern) in the Prussian army. *"Nach meiner Anstellung war ich hinlänglich with sehr strengem Dienst, häufigem exerzieren und beständiger Aufsicht über die Soldaten beschäftigt, die in einer Kaserne lagen and keinen Augenblick aus den Augen gelassen werden durften."* ... *"Da trotz aller Strenge und Aufsicht die Disziplin des Battalion, bei welchem ich stand, sich nicht verbesserte, häufige Streitigkeiten and Schlägereien zwischen Leuten stattfanden, so wurde das Bataillon förmlich aus Kassel verbannt und erhielt plötzlich in April 1808 den Befehl, nach Paderborn zu marschieren. Am 14. April trat ich, dessen ganz ungewohnt, meinen ersten Marsch zu Fuße an, der mir wegen meiner Kränklichkeit recht sauer wurde, denn ich war in meinem Leben noch nie acht bis zehn Stunden weit gegangen. Notwendigkeit und das Beispiel Anderer machten mir das unmöglich Erscheinende, wenn auch with Anstrengung, möglich; ich kam zwar with wunden Füßen aber ganz wohlbehalten in Paderborn an."*

Part II

MARKUS GAERTNER & PETER BUNDE

ORGANIZATION, STRUCTURE AND UNIFORMS OF THE INDIVIDUAL MILITARY POSITIONS AND UNITS

"The wagon was escorted by a platoon of the Garde du Corps in their white coats and in my mind's eye I saw Thee riding among. The uniform did look beautiful indeed, the white dress coats have blue collars, cuffs and lapels, plus aiguillettes, the steel breastplates with a yellow sun.... Only the trumpeters have red coats."

"Der Wagen wurde von einem Zuge der Garde du Corps in ihren weissen Kollets eskotiert, und ich sah im Geiste schon Dich dazwischen reiten. Die Uniform sieht doch sehr schön aus, die weissen Galaröcke haben blaue Kragen, Aufschläge und Rabatten, dazu Fangschnüre, die Brustharnische von Stahl mit gelber Sonne ... Nur die Trompeter haben rote Röcke."

From: *König Jérôme Napoleon* by Moritz von Kaisenberg (Leipzig 1899).

Officer of the Jaeger Carabiniers in field uniform, 1812
Watercolor by Herbert Knötel, Anne S.K. Brown Military Collection, Brown University Library.

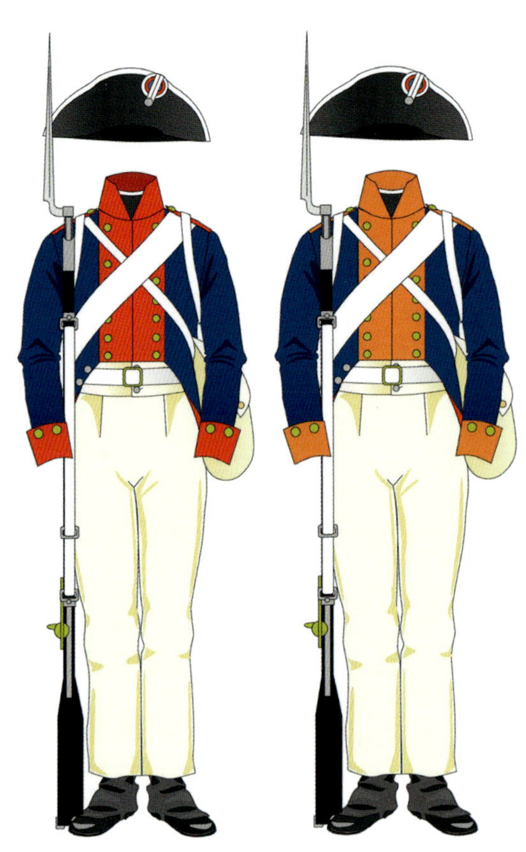

THE ARMY'S FIRST FORMATIONS

Guard Grenadier Regiment coat, 1803–1807
Schloss Friedrichstein (Bad Wildungen), Museumslandschaft Hessen-Kassel.

THE FRANCO-HESSION LEGION 1806–1807 *(LÉGION FRANCO-HESSOISE)*

ESTABLISHMENT

The Landgraves of Hesse-Kassel had always maintained close political and personal ties with Prussia. That also did not change with the elevation in rank from a landgrave to a prince in 1803. Napoleon tried repeatedly – also within the framework of the establishment of the Confederation of the Rhine in July 1806 – to pull Hesse-Kassel onto his side. The Elector always refused. In the conflict between France and Prussia in the autumn of 1806, he declared himself neutral in the hope of protecting his sovereignty. But this was unsuccessful. After the Prussian defeat, the French occupied the electoral principality in October 1806, and the Elector had to go into exile in Prague.

The Kurhessian Army was disarmed without any fighting and was declared to be disbanded. As a whole, the disbanding took place without any large incidents, also the overwhelming part of the officer corps initially went along with the suddenly occurring changes.

Napoleon quickly came up with the plan to secure the military potential, which was considered excellent and was now freely available.

He ordered the Governor General (*Generalgouverneur*) assigned in Kassel, Major General Lagrange, to conduct an appeal to the Hessian military and to advertise for joining a Hessian Legion (*Légion Franco-Hessoise*). The Legion was to consist of several regiments and be formed exclusively with former Hessian soldiers.

Recruitment attempts were begun in November and they initially focused on voluntary entry. Despite the promise of higher pay and promotions and to continue serving in the Hessian uniforms, it was only possible to establish two weak regiments of one battalion each by April 1807. Starting the end of July, the Legion's two regiments were designated as the 1st and 2nd Hesse-Kassel Regiments (*1. et 2. Régiment de Hesse-Kassel*).

The 1st Regiment was formed from the former members from the two Hessian Guard regiments (*Regiment-Garde* and *Garde-Grenadier Regiment*) and the *Füsilier-Bataillon von Todenwarth*; the 2nd Regiment was constituted from soldiers from the four disbanded infantry regiments (Kurfürst, Kurprinz, Landgraf Carl and Biesenroth). In December 1807, both units were combined and formed the 1st Line Infantry Regiment of the new Westphalian Army.

Fusilier of the former Guard Grenadier Regiment
Watercolor by Herbert Knötel, WGM, Rastatt.

STAFF

Each regiment was supposed to consist of three battalions, which again were formed on the French norm of four fusilier, one grenadier and one voltigeur (*Schützen*) company. Each regiment received an eight-man band (*Musikkorps*) with "Turkish Music" *("türkischer Musik")*.

Authorized Strengths

Regimental Staff (3 men)	**Battalion Staff** (5 men)	**Per Company** (139 men)
1 Colonel *(Oberst)* 1 Major 1 Regimental Surgeon	1 Battalion Commander 1 Adjutant-Major 1 Quartermaster 1 Battalion Surgeon 1 Company Surgeon	1 Captain *(Kapitain)* 1 Senior Lieutenant *(Premier-Lieutenant)* 1 Second Lieutenant *(Seconde-Lieutenant)* 1 Sergeant Major *(Feldwebel)* 4 Sergeants *(Sergeanten)* 1 Quartermaster Corporal *(Fourrier)* 8 Corporals *(Korporale)* 2 drummers/buglers 120 privates

The total strength of a battalion with the staff consisted of 850 men (including musicians) according to this guideline.
These authorized strengths were mostly not achieved. At the review of the 1st Battalion of the 2nd Regiment on 30 March 1807, the strength was only 265 men of all ranks. The second fusilier company, with 35 soldiers, was registered as the strongest company. The voltigeur company could report a strength of 27 jaegers (voltigeurs). The battalions of the 1st Regiment reported a strength of 366 men, organized in 6 companies on 27 April 1807.
The two regiments never reached the full strength of a battalion.

Along with the infantry, a gendarmerie detachment was assigned. However, this is not stated in the Legion's official roster, but Hahlo's contemporary illustrated manuscript (*Bilderhandschrift*) shows such a Hessian gendarme.
It can be concluded that a separate unit with reliable men from the French Military Administration was assigned as the Gendarmerie. The aversion to service, the danger of flight/desertion and the inflamed mood within the former Kurhessian units were highlighted repeatedly in the sources. The Legion's soldiers had enlisted for service more or less due to financial necessity, not from political conviction.
Nothing is known about the strength of the Gendarmerie.

COMMANDERS

1807–1808

1st Regiment: Major von Müller as *Großmajor* (Lieutenant Colonel); Chef de Bataillon Montier de Benneville
2nd Regiment: Colonel Schraidt; *Chef de Bataillon Gissot*

When the regiments were transferred to Alsace, the regiment commanders, von Müller and de Benneville, remained in Kassel in Major General Lagrange's staff, so that the regiment were actually led by the two battalion commanders *(Chefs de Bataillon)*.

ACTIONS

Until the middle of June individual detachments of the 1st Regiment marched initially to Weissenburg in Alsace, where on 21 June 1807 the establishment of the unit was declared as complete. A part of the regiment then went on further to Hagenau.
The 2nd Regiment was in Eschwege starting the middle of January, then in Kassel in garrison. On 6 July 1807 it also received marching orders to Weissenburg and arrived there on 22 July. Finally it occupied its new post in Pfalzburg (Phalsbourg) on the 25th. There the officers and privates were sworn in to the emperor.
The regiments only performed garrison duty during their short existence.

Franco-Hessian Legion *(Légion Franco-Hessoise – Legion Hessen-Kassel)*,1806–1807

1: Guard Regiment; **2:** 2nd Regiment's flag, front and rear; **3:** Guard Grenadier Regiment; **4:** Kurfürst Regiment; **5:** Kurprinz Regiment; **6:** Landgraf Carl Regiment; **7:** Biesenrodt Regiment.

Sources: 1, 3, 4, 5, 6 and 7 – according to the *Decree* of 1806 and H. Boisselier's pattern;
2 – after an original artifact in Museum Schloss Friedrichstein, Bad Wildungen.

INFANTRY UNIFORMS

In the Decree of 17 December 1806 Napoleon established:
Art IX. These regiments shall continue to wear the uniform that they have worn as Hesse-Kassel units; the headgear, clothing and equipment should remain completely after the mode of the Hessian infantry. And to this end one will, therefore, make all use of whatever is on hand in the Hessian stores.

PRIVATES AND NCOs

Headgear: Prussian style bicorn with white braid around the edge and French tricolor cockade.
Coat: The soldiers initially received the old Kurhessian uniforms. With that, the two regiments were not dressed very uniformly. Over time all of them were to be clothed in the uniforms of the old Kurhessian Guard Regiment: Blue coat with red facings and white braiding, white pants.
The officers wore silver epaulets in the French pattern as rank insignia. The NCOs also received French rank braid on their sleeves.

DRUMMERS AND MUSICIANS

There is no information available about them.

FLAGS

On 20 June 1807, Napoleon promised the Legion flags for the battalions. They corresponded to the French model of 1804 without the eagle. The flag of the 2nd Battalion of the 2nd Regiment is still preserved today because it was never issued to the unit. It is noteworthy that it was considerably larger than the corresponding French flags.

Front side of the flag of the 2nd Battalion of the 2nd Regiment
Original cloth displayed in the Schloss Friedrichstein (Bad Wildungen) Museumslandschaft Hessen Kassel.

THE GENDARMERIE UNIFORM

Uniform: Tall bicorn hat (German: *Zweispitz*) with a white plume with a red base. Like the infantry this unit wore the blue coat with red facings and edging. Red under-vest *(Unterweste)*. As a mounted detachment they wore light leather pants with heavy cuffed boots. Broad white, red-bordered cavalry bandoliers of the former *Kurhessian Garderegiment Gens d'armes*. As armament the Hessian cuirassier straight saber *(Pallasche)*.

Gendarme of the Hessian Legion
Watercolor by Herbert Knötel based on the *Manuscrit du Canonier Hahlo*, 1807–1808, in WGM, Rastatt.

Elite and Center Company of the Lancer Regiment, 1807.

Left: **Polish Grenadier with shako, 1807.**

Right: **Polish Grenadier, 1807.**

Copies by W. Hewig after Samuel Hahlo's: *Manuscrit du Canonier Hahlo*, 1807–1808. Collection: Edmund Wagner.

POLISH-ITALIAN LEGION 1807-1808 *(LÉGION POLACCO-ITALIENNE)*

ESTABLISHMENT

At the beginning of 1807, Napoleon had all the available Polish Legion units – especially from Italy – transferred to Silesia and assemble in Breslau (Wrocław, Poland). The various units, which had previously been French, Italian as well as Neapolitan service, were newly formed into two infantry regiments and a cavalry (*lancier-*) regiment with 600 men. This received the new designation as the Polish-Italian Legion on 5 April of that year.

However, the new Legion itself did not take part in any further important fighting in East Prussia. In May 1807 Jérôme Bonaparte (IX Army Corps) also commanded two squadrons of *Lanciers* from the Legion that successfully participated in a withdrawal in contact against the Prussian Army at Struga (Adelsbach) on 15 May.

After the Treaty of Tilsit, Legion was supposed to be incorporated into the Army of the Duchy of Warsaw, which Napoleon rejected for financial reasons. Instead the Polish units were transferred to Westphalian service in October 1807 in order to give Jérôme, as the new king, an experienced body of troops to serve as the nucleus of the new army. It was reorganized and brought up to a strength of three infantry regiments with ca. 5,000 men. Furthermore the *Lanciers*/Chevauleger Regiment was reorganized with two squadrons.

The *Lanciers* served as Jérôme's escort when the new king entered in Kassel on 11 November 1807. They were garrisoned in the new capital temporarily.

On 28 March 1808, the entire body of troops was pulled into French service again and shortly thereafter ordered to the Spanish theater of war as the "Vistula Legion." A part of the officers requested to be taken into the Westphalian Army. They were transferred into the new *Garde-Chevauleger* Regiment and the Garde du Corps Company.

UNIFORMS

According to a contemporary description by Samuel Hahlo, the Lanciers were seen in and around Kassel. Another artist - Mathias Bayer – also had recorded the cavalry in his drawings. The infantry also had been observed moving from the north via Magdeburg and Brunswick and briefly also in Kassel. However, by the end of March the infantry moved by way of Fulda on to Frankfurt and then in the direction of Metz, so that its stay in the kingdom was only of short duration.

Both branches still wore the typical dark blue uniforms of the Legion's units, then with yellow distinctions. The czapka was the characteristic headgear, which had become the fashion in Italy, and the Kurtka cut for the coats.

S. Hahlo also shows the light infantry shako as the replacement for the missing czapkas during duty in Westphalia.

The Infantry coat had short, closed yellow lapels and yellow turnbacks. Close-fitting dark blue pants that were cut very narrow toward the bottom. In the field more often they wore blue or white linen pants. The armament was from Prussian stocks and the equipment of French origin.

The cavalry wore an open coat like the mounted jaegers with its lapels turned back and short coattails. Close fitting pants with low boots. As armament a light cavalry saber and new for the Westphalian army – the lance with a pennant in the Polish blue, white and red colors. The saddlecloth was of white fleece with yellow wolves teeth trim.

The officers also wore the busby with a yellow bag and a white plume. A yellow vest with silver cording was visible under the open coat.

THE GUARD
(DIE GARDETRUPPEN)

The King's Uniforms

The Royal Household

Garde du Corps

Grenadier Guards

Jaeger Guards

Guard Light Horse

Guard Fusiliers (Queen's Regiment)

Guard Hussar Regiment (Jérôme-Husaren)

Jaeger Carabiniers

Guard Artillery

King Jérôme in uniform of a Westphalian General, 1808
Watercolor from the Carl Collection of paper soldiers, Musée l'Armée Paris, photo: Paul Meganck.

THE KING'S UNIFORMS

As a member of the imperial household, King Jérôme was already being shown in paintings and other depictions in uniform as early as 1804–1805, for example in a painting by Francois J. Kinson,[43] the later court painter, which shows the Emperor's brother in the uniform of a French Navy officer. It emphasized his military service in the navy. This painting was used as a model for Jérôme's portraits until 1810 when he was already a king. Various artists copied this form or prepared engravings based on it.

In the 1807 campaign in Silesia Jérôme then appears as a major general in a pose as a victor, for example at the surrender of Breslau (Wrocław). Then he was presented as a successful and meritorious member of the imperial family.

Though he was already a king in 1808, Jérôme had himself depicted as an imperial prince posed as a field commander, and in 1809 in coronation regalia as a legitimation of his kingship. Later variations were produced on these themes.

Jérôme loved to appear in uniform following his brother's example, whereby he preferred the Guard uniform. In his daily appearance, Jérôme stressed the "simple" ("*einfache*") and "casual" ("*legere*") uniform coat. For example, he was depicted in the Napoleonshöhe (now Wilhelmshöhe) Park at the Kassel Schloss [palace]) or in garden scenes.

Around 1809-1810 Jérôme had a portrait done (by Kinson) of himself as a colonel of the Garde du Corps, in the unit's white dress uniform, with his wife Catharina. An interesting detail on the margin is the depiction of the saber from the Battle of Marengo (1800) that Jérôme had received as a gift from his brother Napoleon and that is conspicuous due to its open form of hilt. The same model appears again in later depictions.

Many variations of portraits and etchings with the Guard white uniform exist, so these depictions of Jérôme in this attire are widespread.

Then around 1810 a depiction in the new blue Garde du Corps uniform. He wears the daily outfit without lace trim. Only the rank insignia with aiguillettes, as a sign of belonging to the Guard, enhance the appearance.

The King also wears a comparable outfit, here with trim on the collar and cuffs, in a painting by Louis Dupré[44] around 1812.

An original coat belonging to the King as the Colonel of the Garde du Corps still exists today (in the Musée Napoleon in the Fontainebleau Palace, France) and is nearly identical to those in the various pictures. On the extravagant lace trim on the collars and also on the cuffs show the coat as being more richly worked.

Around 1812 Jérôme is depicted in more illustrations as a colonel in the dress uniform of his Guard Chevauleger Regiment.

The King is also documented (by Gros in 1809 and Kinson in 1810) as the army's commander-in-chief and also as a major general of the Westphalian Army. In both representations he wears the regular uniform and appears with a sash and white plumage on the hat with appropriate rank distinctions.

Around 1808 the King is pictured several times in an outfit of his own creation here a white uniform with medium blue distinctions and rich lace decoration on the collar, lapels, cuffs as well as turnbacks. This uniform is compared with that of a Westphalian general, but there is only a color reference to the Westphalian national colors of white and medium blue.

43 Francois Josephe Kinson, 1771-1839, a sought after painter in Ghent, Brugges and around 1805 in Paris, worked initially at the French emperor's court and after 1808 was the cout painter in Kassel and did numerous paintings and portraits of the Westphalian court. After 1813 he was back in Paris.

44 Louis Dupré, 1789-1837, French court painter, active for Jérôme in Kassel starting in 1811, 1813 emigrated to Rome where he remained for many years.

King Jérôme with his wife Catharina in the dress uniform of the Garde du Corps ca. 1809
Painting around 1810 by Francois-Joseph Kinson, Museum Schloss Versailles.
Copyright akg-images.

King Jérôme in der Uniform der Guard Chevaulegers, 1811
Painting by Francois-Joseph Kinson, Bowes Museum, Durham, UK.

Jérôme in the uniform of a naval captain
Engraving by L. Buchhorn after the painting by Francois-Joseph Kinson, ca. 1805.

Jérôme in the uniform of the Garde du Corps 1811
Watercolor by F. Neumann, collection of Paul Meganck, Brussels.

Portrait of Jérôme Bonaparte (1784–1860)
ca 1804, private collection.
Heritage Images/Fine Art Images/akg-images.

"JÉROME BONAPARTE"
Colored etching ca. 1845,
24 × 135 cm.
From a series on costumes and uniforms at the time of Napoleon I's reign.
Plate No. 76.
akg-images.

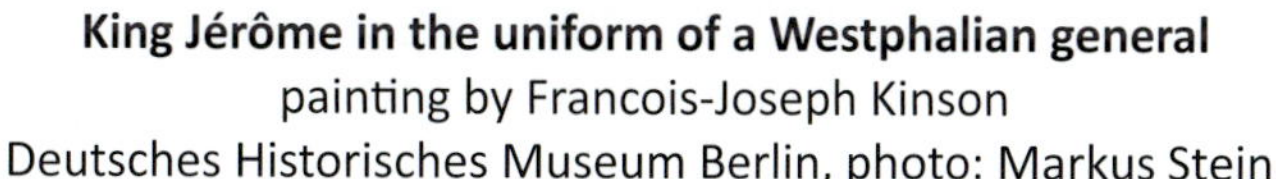

King Jérôme in the uniform of a Westphalian general
painting by Francois-Joseph Kinson
Deutsches Historisches Museum Berlin, photo: Markus Stein.

Adjutant in Undress Uniform 1811
Detail from the painting *"Jérôme sauve un garde du corps de la noyade dans la Mulde"* (Jérôme rescues a Garde du Corps member from the Mulde River) by Louis Dupre, 1811, privately owned, photo: Markus Gaertner.

THE ROYAL HOUSEHOLD *(MAISON DU ROI)*

King Jérôme established an extensive state court, copying that of his brother Napoleon. The state court – *Maison du roi* – was divided into a civil and a military sector.

Civil Sector *(Ziviler Bereich)*

The civil sector included:

- Grand Marshal of the Palace (*Grand maréchal du palais*) with various adjutants *(Adjutants Supérieurs)*. He carried out oversight of all the parts of the royal court.
- Grand Chamberlain with chamberlains *(Junkern)*. Had the important function in the protocol area surrounding the King (serving at the royal table, protecting the royal seal, constant access to the King).
- Grand Equerry (the Master of the [Royal] Stables/*Ecuyer d´honneur*) with equerries (stable masters) and instructors *(Bereitern)*. Oversight of the royal stables *(Marstall)*.
- Grand Master of the Hunt *(Grand maître chasseur)*.
  He oversaw the kingdom's forests and wildlife.
- Marshal of the Palace *(maréchal du palais)* with valets, among them the King's personal servants – Mameluks.

Corps of Pages *(Pagenkorps)*

The Corps of Pages was part of the civil functions and was subordinate to the Office of the Court Marshal (*Hofmarschallamt*). But the Corps also had a military aspect. The selected sons of wealthy, respected as well as noble families were supposed to enter carriers in the officer corps after serving at the royal court. The corps was under the leadership of a Governor (Gouverneur), who with an educational staff was responsible for the pages' schooling at the court. Furthermore the pages had various duties to perform at court. When they were 17 years old, they were taken into the army as junior lieutenants. In 1810 the corps initially consisted of twenty-one pages. In 1813 twenty-six pages from various countries were assigned.

Military Sector *(Militärischer Bereich)*

The military sector consisted of the King's adjutants (*aides de camp du roi*), who numbered five or six officers from 1808 to 1813 and who served the King directly. They each held the rank of a general or colonel. Among them were Colonel Prince zu Salm-Salm and Colonel Hans von Hammerstein. Furthermore up to five officers carried out the function of the King's orderly officers (*Ordonnanz-Offiziere/officiers d'ordonnance*). They were not staff officers.

How many officers served the King's in person cannot be definitively established based on the rosters in the almanacs based on ranks because the separation of adjutants and orderlies' functions and tasks were flexible and resulted from the situation and the assigned duties. In the graphic depictions both types of officers, whose uniforms differed, are shown next to one another. The Guard regiments also belonged to the military sector of the court (*Maison du Roi*).

Maison du Roi – Royal court
Mameluk of the King, Grand Equerry and Senior Chamberlain to the King, Watercolor by Henri Boisselier after notes by Colonel Darbou, collection of Markus Gaertner.

UNIFORMS

THE KING'S ADJUTANTS

Dress *(Grosse)* Uniform

Headgear: Bicorn with white plumage for generals and black for colonels. Broad embroidered edging on the hat, loop and tassel were all silvered.

Coat: Dark green coat with pointed, cut out lapels that were piped in red. The collar, the cuffs and the turnbacks were red and decorated with rich silver oak leaf embroidery. The lapels and the flaps on the coattail pockets were also embroidered in that manner. Silver epaulets and aiguillettes. A red vest with silver cording or a white vest was worn under the coat.

Gala Coat of the Prince zu Salm-Salm

Coat cut like that for a general, made of green cloth with silver oak leaf embroidery. Collar, cuffs and turnbacks red; all trimmed silver.

Trousers: White pants with tall cavalry boots or breeches with buckled shoes.

Armament: Sword with silvered sword-knot (French: *Portepée*) on the waist belt.

Undress *(Kleine)* Uniform

Headgear: Hat without braid but with plumage.

Off duty a green forage cap (*Lagermütze,* French: *bonnet de police*) with red piping and silver trimming was worn.

Coat: Coat in the same cut but without embroidery. The waist pockets are á *la soubise* with red piping. The sources also show the collar in green or the collar and the cuffs with simple embroidery as variations.

Trousers: Pants made of dark green cloth or made of light deerskin worn in hussar boots.

Armament: Sword or saber on a black leather belt. Also a Mameluk style saber was used.

Greatcoat: A dark green, double-breasted coat (*Überrock/*redingote) was worn during inclement weather. The collar and the cuffs were red with silver braid.

The green greatcoat only had the collar in red. He folded down collar was decorated with a silver braid along the edge.

Saddlecloth: The green cloth shabraque with pointed ends had a silver trim on the edges with a red piping. In the rear corner was the royal cypher with a crown both in silver.

King's Adjutants – *Aides du Roi*, 1808–1812

1: Coat, Prince zu Salm-Salm's 1811 dress uniform; **2:** coat, dress uniform; **3:** undress uniform coat, 1811; **4:** adjutant (colonel) in undress uniform when mounted, 1811; **5:** adjutant (general) Prince zu Salm-Salm in dress uniform, gala, 1813; **6:** adjutant (general) in dress uniform, daily duty; **7:** adjutant (colonel) in undress uniform; **8:** adjutant (general) in redingote; **9:** adjutant (colonel) in the greatcoat with forage cap.

Sources: 1, 5 – from Prince zu Salm-Salm's original coat; 2, 6 – A. Sauerweid, S. Pinhas, H. Boisselier; 3, 4, 7 – from paintings by L. Dupre, H. Boisselier, 8, 9 – H. Boisselier, H. Knötel.

1
2
3
4
5
6
7
8
9

King's Adjutant in gala dress uniform
Sauerweid, Alexander Iwanowitsch: *Uniformen der Königlich westphälischen Armee*, 1810, Dresden.

King's Adjutant in dress uniform
Pinhas, Salomon: *Recueil de planches représentant les troupes des différentes armes et grades de l´armée Westphalienne*, 1811–1813.

Prince zu Salm-Salm's full dress coat, Adjutant to the King ca. 1811
Original piece from the Prince zu Salm-Salm collection.
The coat's original color was green and has faded.
Wasserburg Anholt, photo: Historisches Preußen-Museum Wesel.

ORDERLIES *(Ordonnanz-Offiziere)*

The orderly's uniform was very similar to that of the King's adjutants. The main difference was the blue basic color in place of the green. The dress uniform coat had straight cut lapels and cuffs. The undress coat and the *Überrock* were completely blue without color distinctions. The blue pants for the undress uniform were decorated with the rank chevrons in the style of light cavalry officers.

Saddlecloth: Like for the adjutants but in royal blue. Another version was a dark blue rectangular blanket edged in silver. In the corners were the silver initials JN with a like-colored crown above them. In the front were holsters rounded at the bottom in the color of the lower blanket, without initials. The leather saddlery was black.

Orderly officer in dress uniform 1812
Suhr, Christoph: Album du Bourgeois de Hambourg, 1806 - 1815, Lipperheide Kostümbibliothek, Berlin. Westphälische Truppen: 7 sheets, 1809–1812.

Adjutant and Orderly - officer in undress uniform 1810
Detail from the painting "Serment au drapeau Westphalien" (Oath to the Westphalian Flag) by Louis Dupre, 1810 – 1812, Chateau Fontainebleau, photo: Markus Gaertner.

King's Orderly Officers, 1808–1812

1: Coat, dress uniform; **2:** undress uniform coat; **3:** captain in dress uniform when mounted; **4:** officer in dress uniform; **5:** officer in undress uniform; **6:** officer in redingote.

Sources: 1, 3, 4 – C. Suhr, *Album du Bourgeois de Hambourg*, 1806–1815; 2, 5 – Louis Dupre; 6 – reconstruction H. Boisselier.

CORPS OF PAGES *(Pagenkorps)*

The Pages had a wide variety of uniforms corresponding the numerous duties they had at court.

Dress Uniform
For duty at the court and for escort duty.
Headgear: A black velvet beret with three light blue and three white ostrich feathers attached on the front. For escort duty a black bicorn with gold edging and white plumage.
Coat: Dark blue, knee-length coat without turnbacks, with semicircular gilt edging on the collar; chest and seams. A white sash with golden fringes was tied around the waist. On the left shoulder a wide shoulder knot of light blue silk decorated with golden fringes. The cloth was embroidered with golden bee and lion emblems.
Trousers: The breeches and the vest were red. For gala events and duty on foot, white stockings and shoes with buckles were worn. For escort duty, high cavalry boots with blue pants were worn.
Armament: Sword with gilt *Portepée* on the waist belt.

Undress Uniform
According to the memoirs of von Lehsten, a former page under King Jérôme:
Headgear: Bicorn without a border.
Coat: Dark blue with long coattails. Collar and cuffs were light blue. All parts, the tails as well as seam on the chest were decorated with a silver edging worked through with gold. The coat was single-breasted and closed with seven buttons. These were decorated with silver and golden braids in the form of laces or loops. The light blue shoulder knot was also attached at the shoulder.
Trousers: White breeches with silk stockings and shoes with buckles.

Pages in dress uniform, 1810
Detail from the painting *"Serment au drapeau Westphalien"* (Oath to the Westphalian Flag) by Louis Dupre, 1810–1812, Chateau Fontainebleau, photo: Markus Gaertner.

Hunting Uniform
Short dark blue stable jacket, closed in front with one row of silver colored buttons.
Silver piping on the collar and pointed cuffs.
Close fitting pants in the same color with two wide silver stripes on the sides. Boots with cuffs.

Uniform for the 1812 Campaign
For the campaign in Russia the King took three pages with him to the field. For this campaign, he had them outfitted in hussar uniforms.
Headgear: Shako with silver cording, chin-scales and edging. The silver plate had the form of a shield with the coat of arms, as the monogram the gilt "JN". Medium blue and white plume.
Dolman and Pelisse: All dark blue with silver cording and buttons. The pelisse trim was made of white fur. The hussar sash was dark blue with silver cords.
Trousers: Blue pants with silver decorations.
Armament: The sabretache was covered with dark blue cloth and had a silver decorative edging. In the middle was the royal coat of arms shield with the gilt cypher. Light cavalry saber with silvered *portepée*.
Saddlecloth: Dark blue shabraque like for the light cavalry with silver braid edging and initials with a crown in pointed corners.

Page in undress uniform – daily uniform, 1810–1812
Watercolor by Henri Boisselier,
Musée de la Figurine historique,
Compiègne, photo: Paul Meganck.

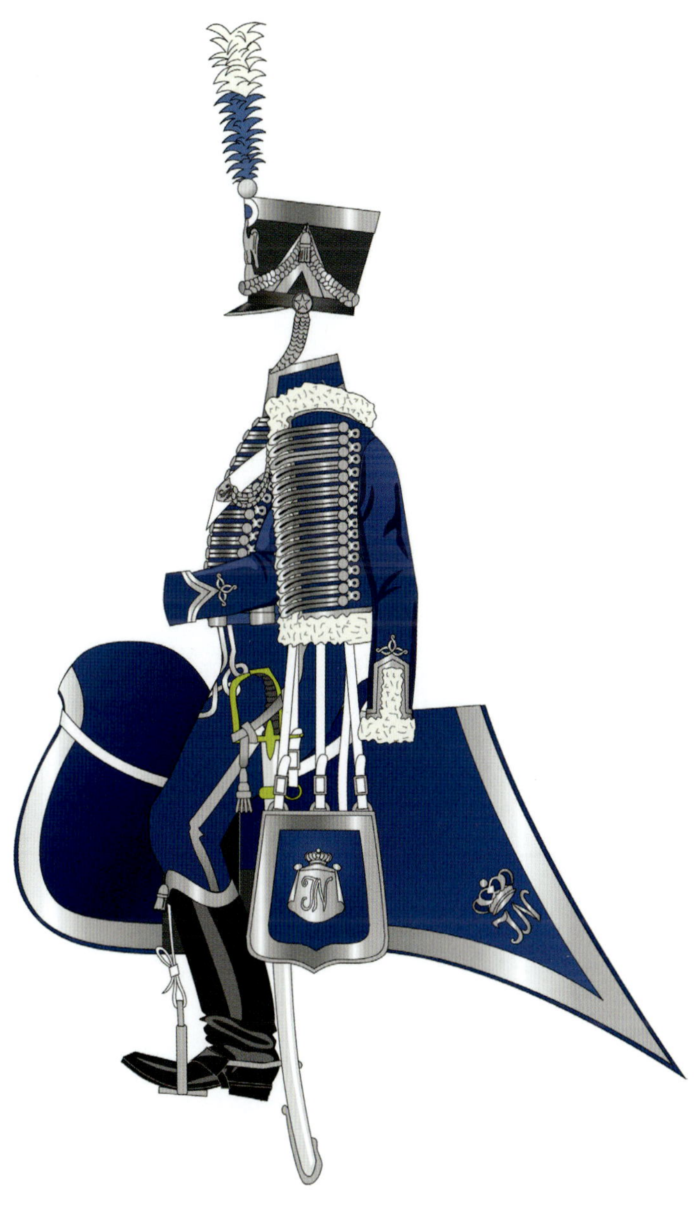

Page in the uniform for the 1812 campaign
Source: *nach den Memoiren von Lehsten-Dingelstädt, Am Hofe König Jérômes: Erinnerungen eines westfälischen Pagen und Offiziers.*

GARDE DU CORPS

The creation of this personal bodyguard unit for the King was ordered as early as 27 April 1808. It had the strength of a company and was supposed to exclusively undertake ceremonial tasks. In that, it was to be the army's most prestigious unit. It carried out guard duty in the internal areas of the palace and on campaigns in the King's headquarters. When the royal family made excursions, it provided the escort.
Napoleon rejected the establishment of this prestigious unit as too costly and useless. But Jérôme asserted himself against his brother.
The Garde du Corps was to be comprised of the sons of wealthy and respected families. Entry was voluntary. The candidate had to be over 18 years old and obligate himself for five years. The corps was also supposed to serve as a place to train officers. After two years most were assigned with ranks in the army. The unit's members received higher ranks in the army than their grade in the company. The rank of "*Gardist*" corresponded to a junior lieutenant (*Sous-lieutenant*) in the army.
The Polish *Lanciers*, who had accompanied the King at the end of 1807 at his entry into Kassel, provided a further small, but experienced part of the unit.
The company was stationed in the capital, Kassel.

ORGANIZATION (DECREES OF 1808 AND 1810)

Senior Staff *(Oberstab)* (9 men with 25 horses)	**Lower Staff *(Unterstab)*** (43 men with 12 horses)	**Company** (154 men)
1 Captain 4 Lieutenants 1 Senior Surgeon *(Chirurg-major)* 1 Quartermaster *(Quartiermeister)* 1 Instructor *(Bereiter)* 1 Veterinarian *(Veterinär)*	4 Staff Trumpeters *(Stabstrompeter)* 6 Trumpeters 2 Handworkers *(Handwerker)* 2 Blacksmiths *(Schmiede)* 2 Drivers *(Fuhrknechte)* 30 Stable Hands *(Stallknechte)* *Starting 1813* 1 Kettledrummer *(Kesselpauker)*	1 Sergeant Major *(maréchal des logis chef/Oberwachtmeister)* 4 Sergeants *(marchaux des logis/Wachtmeister)* 1 *Fourier* 8 Brigadiers 8 Sub-Brigadiers (*sous-brigadiers)* 132 Guards *(Guardsmen [Gardisten])*

The theoretical total strength was 206 men with 185 horses.
In November 1811 the actual strength was 120 men. It first reached full company strength in 1812.
Starting in May 1813 an additional company was formed, so that the Garde du Corps grew to squadron strength with 286 men.
A the end of October 1813 were there were only 114 men still present. On 1 November 1813 the last 30 men of the Garde du Corps were released in Cologne by the King.

COMMANDERS

1808: Capitaine-Général Erbprinz zu Salm-Salm, **1809**: Capitaine-Général Eblé, **1811**: Colonel Wolff

Helmet and breastplate for officers 1810–1813
The "JN" cypher below the crown in the center of the breastplate device was subsequently switched for a rosette, which indicates its later use in in the Kurhessian Army after 1814.
Original pieces, Schloss Friedrichstein (Bad Wildungen), Museumslandschaft Hessen-Kassel.

Officer, Royal Westphalian Garde du Corps, 1809
Weiland, C. F.: *Représentation des uniformes de l' armée impériale royale française et des alliés*, Weimar, 1807 and 1812, 148 colored engravings, Weimar, 1807 and 1812; of them 10 on Westphalian units.

Guardsman, Royal Westphalian Garde du Corps, 1810
Weiland, C. F.: *Représentation des uniformes de l' armée impériale royale française et des alliés.*

ACTIONS

1809
In April in Dresden in the King's headquarters.

1812
5 April: Marched off to participate in the Russian campaign (6 officers, 146 men)
16 August: Return to Kassel with the King who took no further part in the campaign.

1813
29. September: 80 men accompanied the King during his first flight from Kassel.
15 October: Returned to Kassel with the King.
26 October: The King finally left Kassel with his Garde du Corps.
1 November: The King released the last of his remaining 30 Garde du Corps members in Cologne.

UNIFORMS, 1808

PRIVATES

Headgear: A tall bicorn with gilt cords and tassels served as the headgear. A white plume with medium blue base was attached over the loop and cockade.
The forage cap *(bonnet de police)* was white with black piping and a yellow braid on the edge of the cap. A small yellow grenade was affixed to the front.
Coat: The dress *(Gala)* coat was white. It had long tails. The collar, lapels and cuffs were black with red piping; all decorated with golden laces. Red turnbacks decorated with golden grenade devices. The horizontal flaps on the coattail pockets were piped red and also decorated with laces. Golden epaulets without fringes were attached to the shoulders. The Westphalian eagle and the royal initials were stamped onto the yellow buttons.
A single-breasted, white coat with short coattails served for the undress uniform. It had golden laces on the collar and cuffs that were black with red piping. Black turnbacks decorated with golden grenades. Black piping ran along the chest seam. A golden aiguillette was worn on the right shoulder.
A white waistcoat with coattails (*Schoßweste*) was worn for internal and stable duty. The Garde du Corps was the only unit to use this pattern vest with tails. The collar and cuffs were piped black.
Trousers: White pants with tall black straight-legged boots for wear with the dress coat. Otherwise grey, leather-reinforced overalls were worn.
Armament and equipment: The privates wore a bandolier made of black leather with golden edging over the left shoulder. On it, at chest level was a rectangular shield badge with the royal initials under a crown. The cartridge pouch had gilt edging and a rhombus-shaped badge with the Westphalian coat of arms.
The waist belt was also black with golden edging. The belt buckle was gilt copper with an oak leaf wreath and the royal monogram with a crown in the center. In the early days the Kurhessian *Pallasche* (straight sabers) with a brown scabbard and iron fittings were still used. Then a straight *Pallasch* with an iron scabbard. The hilt and hand guard were of brass with a round basket on which the royal monogram was visible. White sword-strap. For mounted duty a carbine was also fastened to the saddle.
Saddlecloth: Black cloth shabraque with yellow border; holsters the same. Round black valise (*Mantelsack*) with yellow piping.

NCOs *(Unteroffiziere)*

The NCOs wore the uniform like for the privates. Their ranks were shown with golden or yellow braids on the sleeves.

Uniforms, 1808

1: Guardsman - dress uniform; **2:** trumpeter - dress uniform; **3:** guardsman - undress uniform; **4:** guardsman - dress uniform; **5:** guardsman - undress uniform; **6:** guardsman work and garrison duty; **7:** trumpeter - dress uniform; **8:** trumpeter - undress uniform; **9:** trumpeter - work and garrison duty.

Sources: 1 – S. Hahlo; 2 – O. Norie; 3 – R. Forthoffer; 4, 5, 6, 9 – H. Knötel, pattern in WGM, Rastatt;
7 – R. Forthoffer, W. Hewig; 8 – H. Boisselier, Darbou..

1
2
3
4
5
6
7
8
9

OFFICERS *(Offiziere)*

The uniform also corresponded to that of the privates and differed in its more expensive make and the golden fringed epaulets as rank insignia. Gold *portepée*. Leader belting decorated with golden laces and edged in red.

Shabraque and holsters like for privates, but all the trim was gilt. Double edging for higher-ranking officers.

TRUMPETERS

Headgear: Bicorn with white plumage and red plume. The sources show golden or red edging and cords.

The forage cap had blue piping and a red braid on the caps rim.

Coat: The trumpeters' dress (Gala) coat was white with black distinctions like for the trooper's coat. However, the piping and the turnbacks were medium blue and the coat was trimmed with red braids. Golden fringed epaulets. One source (R. Forthoffer) shows red bordering at the seams along the sleeves and red trefoil epaulets.

The white undress coat was single-breasted with medium blue coattails and piping. The collar and cuffs were black with medium blue piping and red lace trim. Golden aiguillettes were worn.

The trumpeter's vest with tails (*Schoßweste*) had blue piping.

Trousers: Like for the privates.

Trumpet: The trumpet cording was white and blue mixed. For gala events a trumpet banner made of sky blue cloth with golden fringe edging was attached. The national coat of arms was on the banner and a decorative grenade was visible in each corner.

Saddlecloth: Like for the privates.

Guardsman in dress uniform, 1808–1809
Copy by W. Hewig from Manuscrit du Canonnier Hahlo, 1807–1808.
Collection of Edmund Wagner

Private's helmet, 1810–1813
Original, Schloß Friedrichstein (Bad Wildungen), Museumslandschaft Hessen-Kassel.

UNIFORMS, 1809

PRIVATES

Headgear: The bicorn remained unchanged. The forage cap received red piping.
Coat: The dress coat remained unchanged. The undress coat received red distinctions; the collar and cuffs getting white piping. The golden braid trim and the aiguillettes remained unchanged. The piping on the vest with tails became red.

Saddlecloth: Shabraques and holsters became red with yellow edging. Also the shape of the holsters changed.

TRUMPETERS

Headgear: The bicorn remained unchanged. The forage cap became red and received white piping.
Coat: In 1809 the trumpeters received new red coats. The dress coat had a white collar, lapels, cuffs and turnbacks, all decorated with golden laces. Instead of the normal epaulets it then got trefoil epaulets.

The undress coat also received white distinctions with golden lace trim, plus wide gold laces were added to the chest.
The vest with tails was completely red with white piping.

Officer's Pallasch
Original, Schloß Friedrichstein (Bad Wildungen), Museumslandschaft Hessen-Kassel.

Uniforms, 1809

1: Guardsman - dress uniform; **2:** trumpeter - dress uniform; **3:** guardsman - undress uniform; **4:** guardsman - dress uniform; **5:** guardsman - undress uniform; **6:** guardsman work and garrison duty; **7:** trumpeter - dress uniform; **8:** trumpeter - undress uniform; **9:** trumpeter - work and garrison duty.

Sources: 1 – S. Pinhas; 2, 3 – R. Forthoffer; 4 – S. Hahlo; 5, 6, 8, 9 – H. Knötel, schemas in WGM

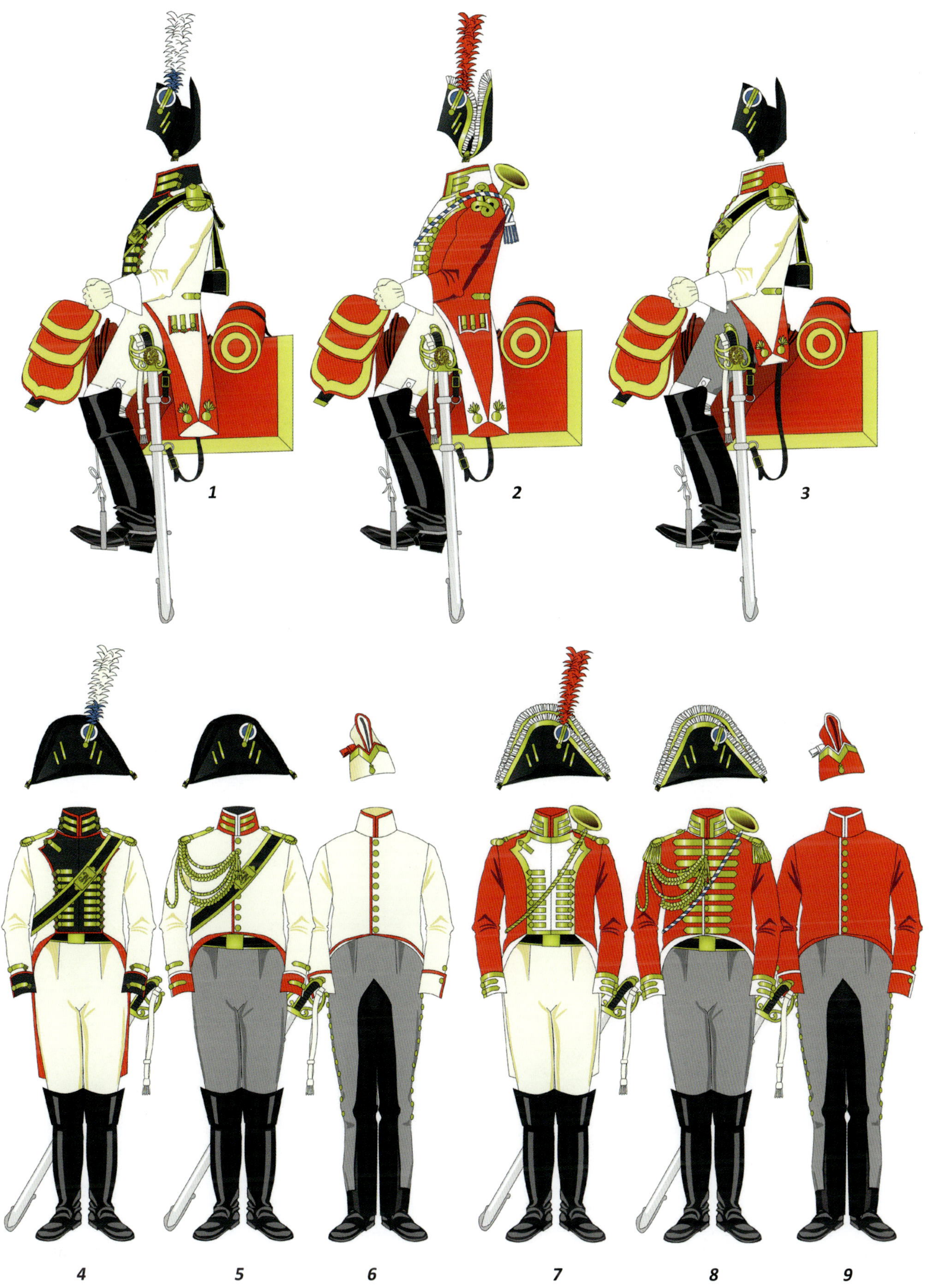
1
2
3
4
5
6
7
8
9

Guardsman attired for escort duty, 1810
Sauerweid, Alexander Iwanowitsch: *Uniformen der Königlich Westphälischen Armee*, Dresden 1810.

Colonel attired for escort duty, 1810
Sauerweid, Alexander Iwanowitsch: *Uniformen der Königlich Westphälischen Armee,* Dresden 1810.

UNIFORMS, 1810

PRIVATES

Headgear: In the beginning of 1810 a helmet of polished iron with a caterpillar crest was introduced. The fittings as well as supporting metal crest were of gilt copper. The fitting on the helmet's globe depicted a symbolized oak leaf. On the front was a metal fixture curving upward to a point. Black fur caterpillar made of bearskin. A white plume was attached on the left side. Brass chin scales.
The bicorn remained in use for service in the palace or for off duty.
The forage cap dark blue with red piping and yellow braid.
Coat: According to the Decree of 25 December 1810 the facing color of the gala/dress uniform changed to dark blue. Turnbacks and piping changed to red. Continued golden lace trim on the lapels, collar, cuffs and flaps of the coattail pockets.
The undress coat was changed to dark blue with a red collar, cuffs and turnbacks. The collar was piped in blue. Suhr, as a source, shows the aiguillettes as being mixed gold and red.
The vest with tails was also changed to blue. Starting in 1811 the vest received red piping and turnbacks. In 1812 the turnbacks were supposed to be changed back to blue again.
Trousers: The pants remained unchanged. However, along with the grey pants for the undress uniform, blue pants also show up.
Greatcoat: The greatcoat was made of white cloth with a cape on the shoulders. The collar was dark blue with red piping. The inside lining was of red cloth. On the front side of the cape there were three wide yellow braids.
Armament and equipment: Starting in 1810 a breastplate half-cuirass of polished steel was introduced. The border, fittings and the scales on the straps were of brass. In the middle of the cuirass was a sun-shaped plate in the center of which the King's monogram with a crown was attached. The inner lining was of red cloth and its outer edge had gold colored piping. The cuirass was only worn with the undress coat.
The armament, leather belting and equipment remained unchanged.
Saddlecloth: The shabraques were changed to dark blue in 1810. The border remained yellow but got red piping on the outer edge. The royal initials and a crown were sewn onto the rear corner of the shabraque. Initially a black fleece was laid over the saddle and the pistol holsters, which were done away with again in 1811. Holsters that matched the saddlecloth were reintroduced. Blue valise (*Mantelsack*).

OFFICERS

Headgear: The officers' helmet had a gilt dome and crest. The fittings were silvered.
Otherwise the officer's uniform corresponded to that of the other grades, as was previously the case. It was only more richly executed and of better quality. The ranks were shown by the golden epaulets.
Equipment and armament: The lining of the officers' cuirass was additionally trimmed along the exterior seams with golden oak leaf embroidery.
Saddlecloth: The shabraque with holsters was dark blue and embroidered with the royal monogram and crown.

Dress Uniforms, 1810

1: Colonel; **2:** trumpeter; **3:** guardsman – dress uniform, 1811; **4:** trumpeter – dress uniform (for duty in the palace); **5:** guardsman - dress uniform (for duty in the palace); **6a**: *Pallasch* saber, **6b**: button, before 1812, **6c**: cartridge pouch; **7:** trumpeter – dress uniform, 1812; **8:** guardsman – dress uniform.

Sources: 1 – C. F. Weiland; 2 – F. Neumann, R. Knötel; 3, 8 – A. Sauerweid, S. Pinhas; 4 – H. Knötel;
5,6 – from original artifacts in Schloss Friedrichstein , 7 – H. Knötel's schemas in WGM, Rastatt.

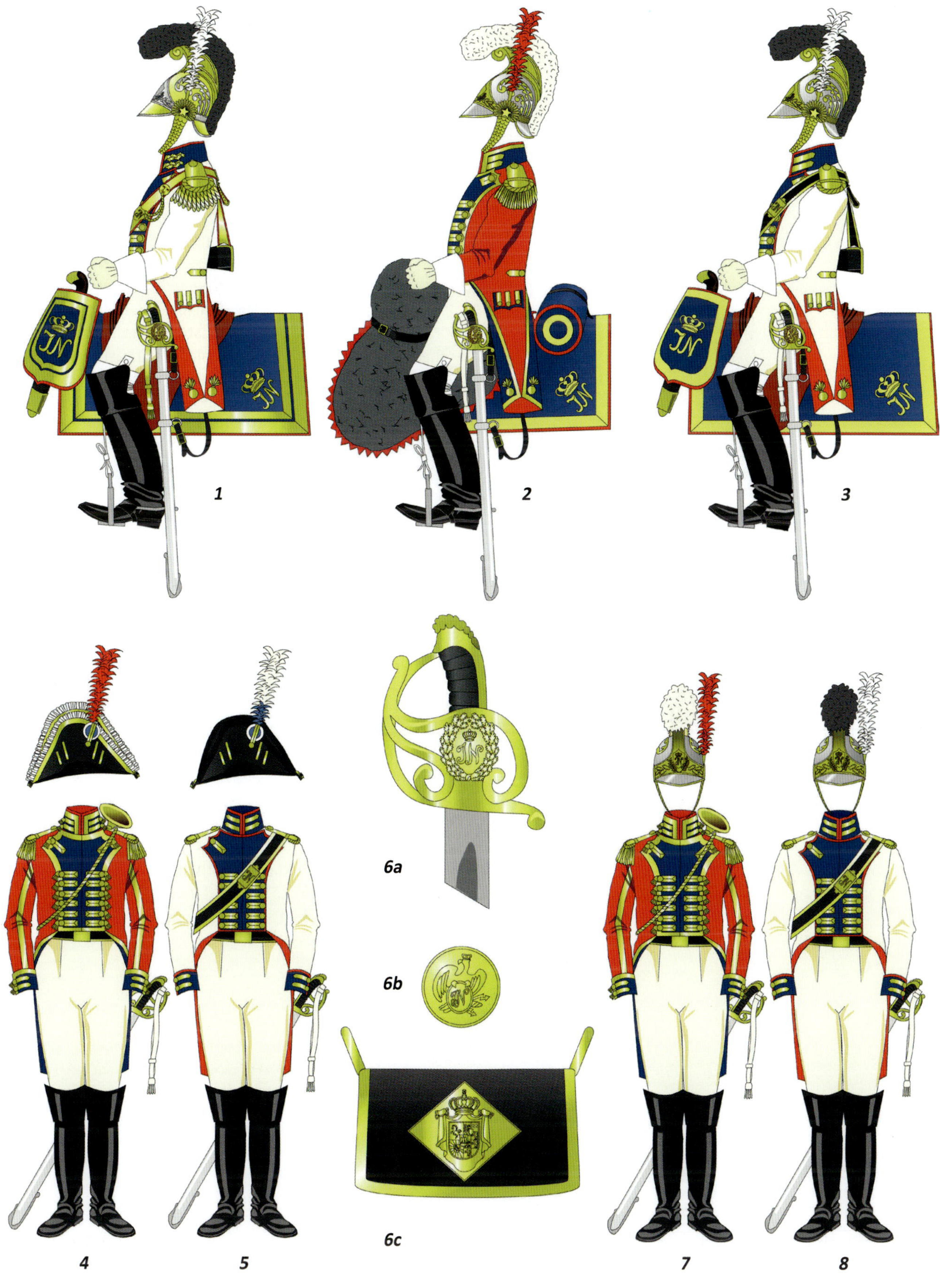
1
2
3
4
5
6a
6b
6c
7
8

Officer, guardsman and trumpeter in "second" uniform, 1812
Christoph Suhr: *Album du Bourgeois de Hambourg*, 1806–1815,
Kommerzbibliothek Hamburg, photo: Markus Stein.

Undress Uniforms, 1810

1: Colonel, **1a:** belt buckle; **2:** trumpeter – undress uniform, **2a:** privates's cuirass plate; **3:** guardsman – undress uniform with cuirass (for escort duty); **4:** colonel; **5:** trumpeter – undress uniform; **6:** guardsman – undress uniform with cuirass (escort duty); **7:** guardsman, undress uniform without cuirass; **8:** guardsman in the greatcoat; **9:** guardsman – work and garrison duty.

Sources: 1, 3, 4, 6 – A. Sauerweid; 2, 5 – H. Knötel; 7 – C. Suhr, H. Knötel; 2a, 8 – R. Forthoffer; 9 – H. Knötel's patterns in WGM.

1
2
3
1a
2a
4
5
6
7
8
9

TRUMPETERS

Headgear: Helmet with white caterpillar crest and red plume.
The red forage cap with blue piping.
Coat: The trumpeters' coats (dress and undress coat) also received dark blue facings. The trim with golden laces was retained unchanged. Additionally the turn-backs were edged with golden lace. In 1811 the seams along the sleeves were also decorated with laces.
The vest with tails had blue piping on the collar and cuffs.
Trousers: For the undress coat the pants initially remained grey, but starting in 1811 they were changed to dark blue.

Trumpeter in field uniform, 1813
Watercolor by Herbert Knötel,
Anne S.K. Brown Military Collection, Brown University Library.

Garde du Corps trumpeters' helmet
Deutsches Historisches Museum Berlin [GOS-Nr. MI007097/Inv. No. U 470].

UNIFORMS, 1813

In 1813 a new uniform was fixed by a decree of 1 February. Whether the new uniform was actually introduced is uncertain.

The individual changes were: The dress uniform coat was changed to blue with red facings. The lace trim on the lapels was changed to 8 plus 1 on each side. The buttons were stamped with a flaming grenade.

Blue pants were worn with the undress coat. The grey pants were abolished.

Sword strap was made of black leather with golden edging.

A black fleece was laid over the saddle again. The royal monogram was removed from the shabraques.

2nd Company

The Garde du Corps' 2nd company raised in 1813 wore the same uniform as for the 1st company, but all buttons, trim and lace were silver instead of gold.

Types of Garde du Corps Uniforms

For special duty events, special uniforms were worn:

Tenue de gala au palais (gala, dress uniform for duty in the palace): Hat with a plume, dress uniform coat, white pants with boots.

Tenue de gala hors palais (dress uniform for duty outside the palace): Same attire but with the helmet and attached plume.

Tenue d'escorte (dress Uniform for parade and escort duty): Helmet with the plume, undress uniform coat with aiguillettes, cuirass, white pants with boots.

Tenue ordinaire/Tenue de campagne (second uniform, normal uniform for daily duty, field duty): Hat, later helmet without plume, undress uniform coat with aiguillettes, no cuirass, grey pants with boots.

Uniforms, 1813

1: Trumpeter – dress uniform; **2:** guardsman – dress uniform; **3:** guardsman – undress uniform; **4:** button, 1813; **5:** guardsman – dress uniform.

Sources: 1, 2, 3, 5 – W. Hewig and H. Knötel's patterns in WGM; 4 – sketch by W. Hewig.

2nd Company Uniform, 1813

1: Officer – dress uniform; **2:** guardsman – dress uniform; **3:** trumpeter – dress uniform; **4:** button 1813; **5:** guardsman – dress uniform; **6:** trumpeter – dress uniform; **7:** guardsman – undress uniform with cuirass (escort duty); **8:** trumpeter – undress uniform; **9:** guardsman – undress uniform; **10:** guardsman – work and garrison duty.

Sources: 1-7 – F. Lünsmann, R. Forthoffer, 8, 9 – H. Knötel.

Tenue d'exercise (training and stable duty): *Bonnet de police*; vest with tails (*Schoßweste*), grey pants with boots.
Petite tenue (undress uniform, garrison duty): *Bonnet de police*, vest with tails, grey overalls.

Tenue société (social events): Bicorn, undress uniform coat with aiguillettes, breeches, stockings, and shoes with buckles.

Stable Hands *(Stallknechte)* and Grooms *(Pferdeknechte)* (Tartaren)

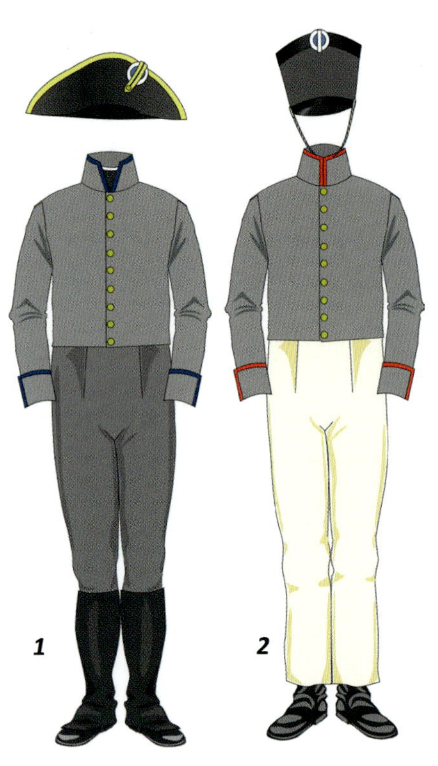

Headgear: 1810 bicorn with yellow border and loop. In 1813 the shako was decorated with only the Westphalian cockade.
Coat: Blue-grey, single-breasted stable jacket without tails and with dark blue piping on the collar and cuffs. In 1813 the jacket got red piping.
Trousers: Dark grey pants with gaiters. When on mounted duty grey overalls with leather reinforcing were worn. For stable duty they wore white cotton pants.

1: Stable hand 1812; **2:** stable hand 1813

Sources: 1,2 – H. Boisselier.

Uniform Coat Cuts, 1808–1813

1: 1808 Privates: gala dress uniform, "second" uniform – normal uniform; vest with tails – work and garrison; **2:** 1808 trumpeter: gala-dress uniform, gala variants; "second" uniform- normal uniform; vest with tails – work and garrison; **3:** 1809 privates: gala-dress uniform, "second" uniform/undress uniform; vest with tails; **4:** 1809 trumpeter: gala-dress uniform, "second" uniform/normal uniform; vest with tails; **5:** 1810–1812 privates: gala-dress uniform, "second" uniform/normal uniform, vest with tails 1810, vest with tails 1811–1812, vest with tails, 1813; **6:** 1810–1812 trumpeter: gala-dress uniform 1810; gala-dress uniform 1811–1812; "second" uniform/normal uniform, 1810–1813; vest with tails, 1810; **7:** 1813 privates and trumpeter: gala-dress uniform; **8:** 1813 2nd company – privates and trumpeter gala-dress uniform, "second" uniform/normal uniform, respectively.

Sources: 1-8 – H. Knötel's pattern sheets in WGM, Hewig, Guard Decrees of 1810 and 1813.

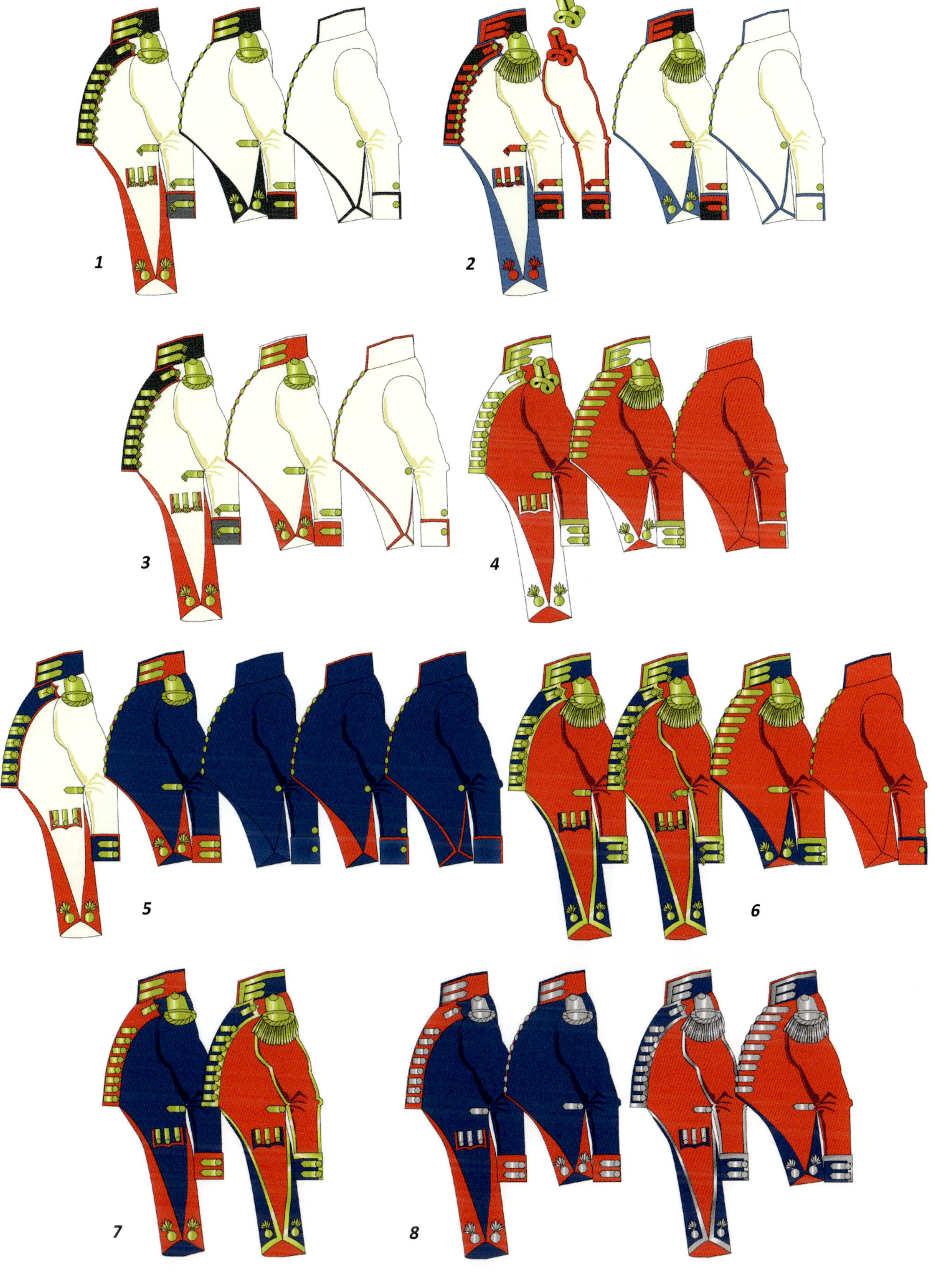
1
2
3
4
5
6
7
8

Guard Grenadiers ca. 1810
Sauerweid, Alexander Iwanowitsch: *Uniformen der Königlich Westphälischen Armee*, 1810, Dresden.

GRENADIER GUARDS *(GRENADIER-GARDE)*

The battalion was formed per the Decree of 10 April 1808. It was supposed to be composed of experienced soldiers from the former Elector Prince's army, selected grenadiers from the Line infantry regiments and selected recruits. Its establishment could not be ended until December 1808. The capital Kassel was chosen as its garrison. In peacetime the battalion performed the sentry tasks at the royal court and in the palaces.

ORGANIZATION

The Battalion (according to the Decrees of 27 Apr. 1808, 26 Dec. 1810 and 1 Feb. 1813) consisted of the staff, six companies of grenadiers and one depot company. The nominal structure counted 843 men, but between 1808 and 1813 the battalion reported fluctuations with an average strength of ca. 1,000 men.

Staff (8 men)	**Subordinate Staff** (23 men)	**Per Company** (116 men)
1 Colonel or *Major* 1 *Chef de Bataillon* 1 Haberdasher Captain *(Capitane d'habillement)* 1 Senior Adjutant *(Adjutantmajor)* 1 Senior Surgeon *(Chirugienmajor)* 1 Senior Surgeon's Aid *(Chirugien aidemajor)* 1 Quartermaster *(Quartiermaitre)* 1 Pay Officer *(Officierpayeur)*	2 Adjutants 1 Drum major *(Tambourmajor)* 1 Drummer Corporal *(Corporaltambour)* 1 Band Master *(Chef de musique)* 15 Musicians *(Musiciens)* 3 Foremen *(Maitreouvries/ Arbeitsmeister/Handwerker)*	1 Captain *(Capitaine)* 1 Lieutenant *(Premier)* 2 Lieutenants *(Second)* 1 Sergeant Major *(Sergantmajor)* 4 Sergeants 1 *Fourier* 8 Corporals 96 Grenadiers 2 Drummers

The Depot Company had the same organization, but in addition a paymaster and a clothing officer were attached. Sappers are not mentioned but in the pictorial depictions they are documented. Their existence can probably be assumed like in the other Guard units.

COMMANDERS

April 1809: *Bataillonschef* von Borck, **September 1809 until 1810**: Colonel Baron v. Langenschwarz, **July 1810 until January 1811**: Colonel Zinck, **January 1811 until September 1811**: Major von Plessmann, **September 1811 until May 1812**: Colonel Baron Legras, **May 1812 until September 1812**: Major Müldner, **October 1812 until January 1813**: Major von Ries

ACTIONS

1809: Campaign against Austria – assigned to the 1st Westphalian Guard Division with a strength of ca. 600 men (in the X Reserve Corps). Stationed north of Hanover. In June advanced to Saxony to defend against the Austrian attack. In July 1809 return to Kassel.
1812: Campaign against Russia - In the 1st Brigade of the 24th Division; General v. Ochs, VIII Corps with a strength of ca. 833 men. On 7 September 1812 participated in the Battle of Borodino. Until November 1812 the battalion was destroyed during the retreat.
1813: Reconstitution with a strength of ca. 1,000 men with the help of the Depot Company and the two Grenadier companies of the Queen's Regiment (*Regiment Königin/Régiment de la Reine*).
September 1813 – during the defense of Kassel the battalion rapidly ceased to exist due to desertions. Only a few grenadiers accompanied King Jérôme when he hastily left his capital.

UNIFORMS

PRIVATES

Headgear: A tall black bearskin hat without a front plate. On the left side was a red plume, under which was the cockade on a yellow cloth loop. Red cords of braided wool. The cloth cap bag was red cloth with yellow border, in the middle was a stylized white cloth grenade was sewn on. The brass chin scales appear to have been added to starting in 1809. A bearskin cap without decorations was worn with the field uniform. A contemporary German sketch (in Herbert Knötel's collection) shows an additional brass grenade on the front.

Until about 1809 a shako was worn with the undress uniform and field uniform. It also had a brass plate in the shape of a grenade. And it had red cording and pompom attached.

For walking out in town, the privates also wore the bicorn. It had red stiffeners on the front and tassels on the sides. A red pompom was attached over the cockade.

The field cap (*"bonnet de police"*) corresponded to the French model. It was made of white cloth with red trimming and piping. On the cap's rim there was additional yellow trim and in the front a grenade emblem. In 1813 the shape of the field cap was changed.

Coat: The white coat had a red collar, lapels, cuffs and turnbacks. The lapels were closed down to the waist. Yellow braid trim on the collar, lapels and cuffs. The placement of the laces changed over the years. As a variation, in his series for 1810, Alexander Sauerweid shows eight braids on the lapels and a white cuff flap with three buttons, two yellow braids on the cuffs. On the long coattails were vertically arranged pocket flaps with red piping and yellow braids on the buttons. Yellow cloth grenades on the turnbacks. The buttons were stamped with the Westphalian eagle emblem with the coat of arms shield on which was the "JN" royal monogram. Red fringed epaulets with a retaining button on the collar side were attached on both shoulders.

Grenadier Guards, Dress Uniform, 1808 until 1813

1: Officers' gorget, button variations, 1812–13 and 1808 until 1812; **2:** staff officer – colonel, 1810; **3:** company-grade officer; **4:** drummer, 1811 until 1812; **5:** NCO-(sergeant), 1812; **6, 7:** grenadiers, 1811–1813, the cuff flaps have been changed to those in Herbert Knötel's patterns.

Sources: 1 – original artifact in Musee l' Armee Paris, buttons: Fallou's former collection and Wilhelm Hewig's patterns in WGM;
2 – from A. Sauerweid 1810; 3 – S. Pinhas 1811; 4 – from Dr. Lienhart, R. Humbert and R. Forthoffer;
5 – reconstruction from contemporary picture, Braunschweigisches Landesmuseum; 6–7 – from A. Sauerweid.

2
3
4
5
6
7

Grenadier Guards
Copy by W. Hewig after *Manuscrit du Canonnier Hahlo*, 1807/08.
Collection of Edmund Wagner

Until 1811 a single-breasted, white coat was worn as an undress uniform (*"zweite Garnitur"*). It was closed with nine buttons; its collar, cuffs and turnbacks were red, and had yellow grenade emblems on the coattails. Double braid trim on the collar and cuffs.

The white waistcoat became single-breasted and was closed with nine buttons. The collar and the cuffs red. The collar had double braid trim. Starting in 1813 the cuffs also received three braids, and in return the pockets were eliminated.

Trousers: For parades or for sentry duty it consisted of white close-fitting breeches. Depending on the season and the event, black or white cloth gaiters were worn.

Long and wide trousers, in white, light brown or grey, were worn with the undress and field uniform. They were often decorated with red stripes on the sides.

Greatcoat: A grey greatcoat with two rows of buttons was worn in bad weather. The epaulets were attached to the greatcoat. The red collar was trimmed with two braids on each side.

Armament and equipment: The saber and cartridge box were suspended on white crossed bandoliers over both shoulders. The saber (french Model an IX) had a brass basket and a red sword-strap. In the middle of the cartridge box was a rhombus-shaped brass plate and in each corner was a grenade. Per the decree of 1808 there was only a stamped brass grenade.

The Westphalian-produced 1777/AN IX musket was the additional weapon.

The backpack was made of calfskin.

Grenadier Guards 1808–1813, undress uniform

1: Company-grade officer, 1809. The black bandolier and the chamois pants are not per regulation, usually these items were acquired privately; **2:** drummers, 1808–1811; **3, 4:** grenadiers in the 1809 campaign. Two variations of the headgear are depicted in contemporary source. The grenade badge on the front side of the fur cap is a distinctive feature; **5:** grenadier in greatcoat; **6:** officer in redingote, 1813; **7:** NCO – caporal in walking-out/city uniform; **8:** grenadier in fatigue uniform, 1808–1812; **9:** grenadier in fatigue uniform, 1813; **10:** sapper in undress uniform until 1808–1811.

Sources: 1, 3, 4 – from a contemporary picture in H. Knötel's estate in WGM; 2 – reconstruction from H. Knötel, patterns in WGM;
5 – from H. Boisselier and W. Hewig; 6, 8, 9 – from H. Knötel; 7 – from R. Forthoffer;
10 – from H. Knötel, picture from the 1924 publication of *Kaskett*

1
2
3
4
5
6
7
8
9
10

NCOs

Uniform like for the privates but with the normal rank insignia on the sleeves. Red epaulets and hat cording with gold worked through them for the more senior NCO ranks.

OFFICERS

Headgear: Bearskin cap like the privates, but with gilt cords.
The more senior staff officers wore a white plume.
For the undress and field uniform, but also for the walking out uniform, the bicorn with and without a plume and gilt decoration served as the headgear. The bicorn could be covered with a black waxed cloth to protect it. The field cap had a golden lace trim instead of the other ranks' yellow braids.
Coat: Coat like for the privates, but all the trim gilt. The more senior officers wore more extensive laces with additional tassels on the ends. The buttons were of gilt copper and decorated with the royal initials and crown; on the rim was the inscription "GARDE ROYALE."
As rank insignia golden fringed epaulets. An officers' rank insignia was a gilt gorget. Its silver-plated shield shaped badge displayed the royal coat of arms. Under the coat of arms was a curved silver-plated ribbon with the inscription "GARDE DU ROI."
A single-breasted coat with golden laces on the collar and cuffs served as the undress uniform.
Trousers: White pants. Either white or black cloth gaiters with brass buttons were worn with them. Knee-high black stovepipe boots were also worn. Tall cuffed boots were worn by senior ranks who were mounted.
For the field uniform they wore grey or white trousers, also close-fitting pants, with leather reinforcing and sometimes with trouser-straps. Hungarian style boots with gilt trimming or alternatively also "Hessian" boots with smooth cuffs.
White breeches, stocking and shoes with buckles were worn for the walking out uniform.
Greatcoat: White redingote closed with two rows of buttons and having a turned down red collar. The edge was piped with white. The epaulets were attached to the greatcoat.
Armament: Sword on the white shoulder bandolier or waist belt, gilt *portepée*. In the field sabers and black bandoliers were also used.
Saddlecloth: For the mounted staff officers, a red rectangular shabraque and pistol holsters with gilt trim and a crowned monogram.

Gorget for officers, 1808–1813
Original piece, Musée l'Armée Paris, photo: Markus Gaertner.

Grenadier in dress uniform, 1810
Weiland, C. F.: *Représentation des uniformes de l'armée impériale royale française et des alliés.*

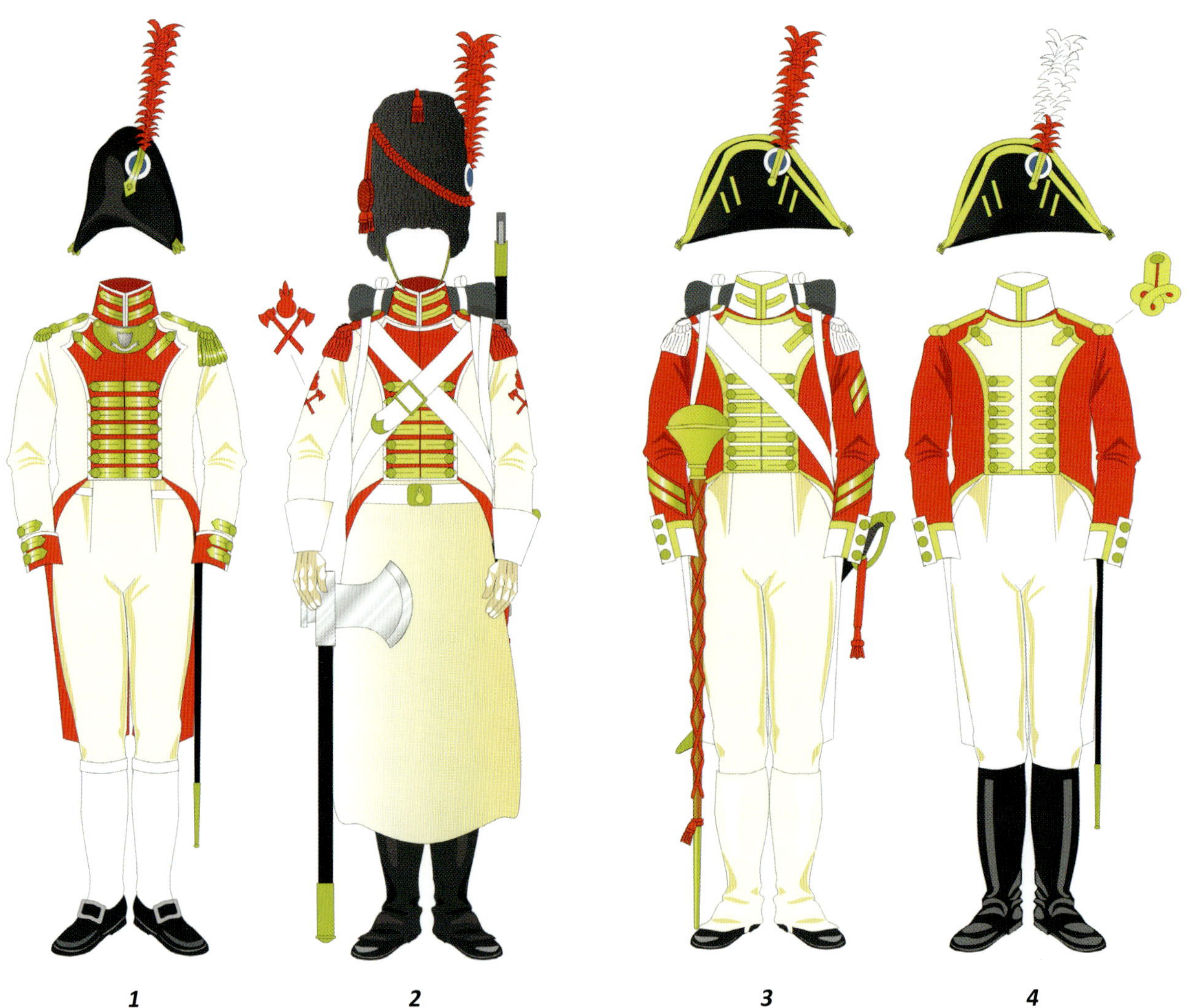

Head of Column and Coat Schemas, 1808–1813

1: Officer in the 1810–1812 full dress uniform *(Gesellschaftsanzug)*, the attire worn for social events,; **2:** sapper in dress uniform, 1808–1812; **3:** drum major, 1810, the drummers' reversed colors were standardized; **4:** musician, 1810–1812; **5:** coat schema, 1808–1810, cuff variation from A. Sauerweid; **6:** coat schema, 1811–1812, officer's coat for ranks of major and colonel with tassel trim on the laces; **7:** coat schema, 1813; **8:** coat schema undress uniform *(zweite Garnitur)*, 1808–1810/1811; **9:** badge and cartridge box with emblems.

Sources: 1 – from Lienhart and Humbert; 2 – from W. Hewig's schema in the *Zeitschrift für Heereskunde*; 3, 4 – from F. Kieffer's paper soldiers in Strasbourg; 5, 6, 7, 9 – from H. Knötel, patterns in WGM and coat patterns by W. Hewig; 8 – from A. Sauerweid, rear view of a Guard Grenadier 1810..

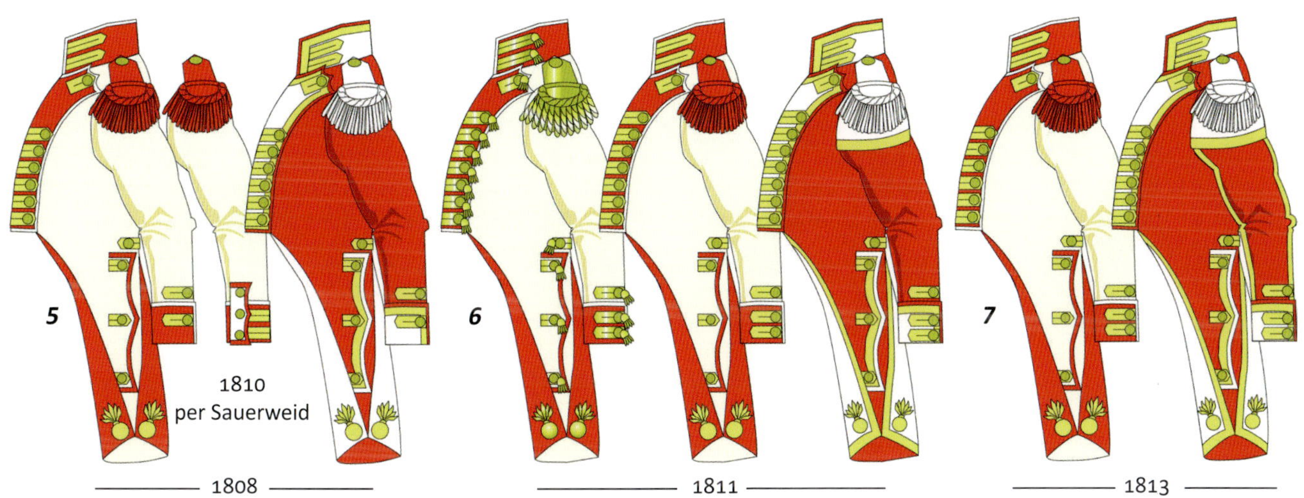
5
6
7
1810
per Sauerweid
1808
1811
1813

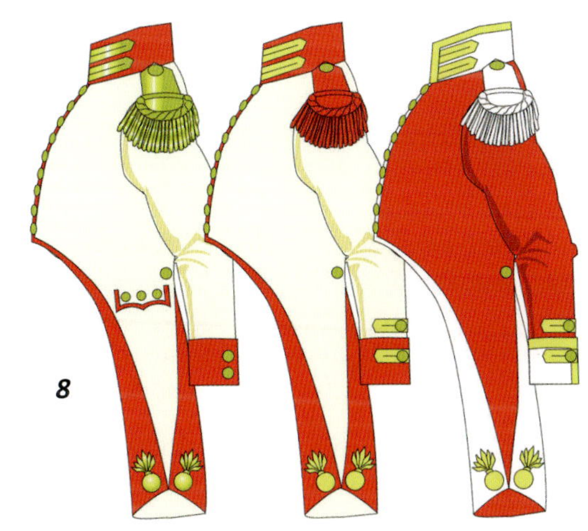
8

9

DRUMMERS

Headgear: The musicians also wore bearskin hats. According to R. Forthoffer from 1808 to 1810 the 1st Company wore a white bearskin hat for parades.
Coat: The drummers wore coats in reversed colors – red with white distinctions. Braid trim like for the privates. In addition there was yellow lace stripes on the collar, on the lapels, the coattail pockets and the cuffs. White fringed epaulets with red retaining strap. After 1811 also yellow braid – edging for the coattails and the swallow's nests. In 1813 yellow braids were also added on the seams along the sleeves.
Greatcoat: The greatcoat had a white collar like on the coat.
Otherwise the drummer's uniform was like those of the other privates.
Drum decorations: White leather belting with a brass grenade emblem in the front at breast level.
The drum shell was of brass. Light blue drum rims and white tighteners. A variation, according to Roger Forthoffer, also shows the rims painted with light blue triangles pointing down and white ones pointing upward.

SAPPERS

The strength could have been like for the Line, i.e., for each battalion one caporal with eight sappers. It was characteristic for these cadres to wear a wide and long full beard.
The uniform was like for the privates with the following differences:
Red crossed axes made of wool were sewn onto both upper arms. A leather apron was typical for sappers; on top of it they wore a leather waist belt with a brass buckle. They carried a heavy axe with its shaft painted black and a brass cap on its bottom. The armament consisted of a light cavalry carbine along with a short saber. White gauntlets with extra-long cuffs.
The field uniform also had the single-breasted coat and long pants.

DRUM MAJOR *(Tambour-Maitre)*

Nothing is known about the appearance of this cadre from a contemporary source. Only the Collection Fritz Kieffer (*Strasbourger Papiersoldaten* – Strasbourg paper soldiers) shows how the Tambour-maitre and also the musicians in the regiment's band possibly looked.

Headgear: Bicorn with yellow loop and lace trim and a red plume.
Coat: Like for the drummers, but only one lace on the collar and white flaps on the cuffs. White fringed epaulets.
Armament and equipment: Baton with red cording. Saber with red sword-strap on the shoulder bandolier.

MUSICIANS

Headgear: Bicorn with gilt loop and braid band. White plume with red base.
Coat: like the drummers, but with yellow trefoil epaulets. No laces on the collar, instead white cuff flaps.
Trousers: White pants with Hungarian boots without trim.
Armament: Sword on the waist belt.

Company-grade officer and grenadier in campaign dress, 1809
Watercolor by Edmund Wagner after a drawing by
Herbert Knötel, collection of Markus Gaertner.

Undress coat – Guard Grenadiers' "second" uniform until 1810
Original piece, Musée Royal de l'Armée et d'Histoire Militaire, Bruxelles,
© War Heritage Institute, Nr Inv WHI: 300294
photo: Luc Van de Weghe.

NCO, 1812
Schloß Friedrichstein (Bad Wildungen).
Museumslandschaft Kassel
Photo: Markus Gaertner.

Carabinier of the Jaeger Guards, 1808
Source: copy by W. Hewig from *Manuscrit du Canonier Hahlo*, 1807/08.
Collection of Edmund Wagner.

JAEGER GUARDS *(JÄGER-GARDE)*

They were created by a Decree of 20 April 1808. Its personnel were recruited like the Guard Grenadier Battalion from former Hessian and experienced soldiers who voluntarily returned to service, as well as selected recruits and men from the voltigeur companies of the Line infantry. The prescribed height was from 5'5" to 5'8" (1,65 to 1,73 m). The missions corresponded to those of the Grenadier battalion. It was also stationed in Kassel.

ORGANIZATION

According to the Decree of 27 April 1808 the battalion should have had a strength of 486 men with 4 companies and a staff (positions in French are italicized).

Senior Staff *(Oberstab)* (5 men)	**Lower Staff *(Unterstab)*** (5 men)	**Per Company** (119 men)
1 *Chef de Bataillon*	1 Adjutant	1 Captain
1 *Adjutantmajor*	1 Senior Bugler (cornetmajor)	1 *Premier-Lieutenant*
1 Quartermaster *(Maitre de quartier)*	1 Tailor *(Ouvriertailleur)*	2 *Seconde-Lieutenant*
1 Senior Surgeon *(Chirugienmajor)*	1 Shoemaker *(Ouvriercordonier)*	1 Sergeant Major
1 Surgeons' Chief Aid *(Chirugien aidemajor)*	1 Armorer *(Ouvrierarmurier)*	4 Sergeants
		1 *Fourier*
		8 Corporals
		99 Chasseurs (Jaegers)
		2 Buglers (Cornets)

With the decree of 25 December 1810, it was strengthen to six companies, now with a complement of 843 men, including the depot. A colonel's position was officially added. At the end of November 1811 the battalion had a strength of 975 men.

Drummers replaced the buglers. Unofficially there were also sappers. According to the 1810 structure along with a drum major there were also a master musician (*Musikmeister*) with musicians. Until 1813 the 1st Company functioned as an "Elite" or carabinier company.

In the beginning of 1813 six companies were raised again and with additional personnel from the two voltigeur companies of the Queen's Regiment *(Regiment Königin)* as well as selected conscripted personnel, it reached a strength 840 men.

COMMANDERS

April 1808 until the end of 1808: Colonel de Sahla, **May 1808 to 1809:** Colonel Freiherr (Baron) von Dornberg, **from 1809 to 1810:** Colonel Meyronnet de Saint Marc, **1810:** Major Bernard, **1811 to 1812:** Colonel von Lossberg, **1811 to the end of 1812:** Major von Picot, **1812:** Major Bödicker

ACTIONS

1809: Participation in the campaign in Saxony in the X Corps/1st Brigade with one battalion with 602 men.
1812: in Russia in the 23rd Division/1st Brigade, strength in June 836 men. 7 September 1812 Participation in the Battle of Borodino, 28 November 1812 wiped out completely at the Berezina River.
1813: in the September fighting around Kassel, where the troops simply dissolved.

UNIFORMS

PRIVATES

Headgear: French design shako made of black felt and leather reinforcing. A white metal semicircular shield plate with an eagle above it as an emblem. In the center was a hunting horn as an emblem and below it the inscription "GARDE ROYALE." The national cockade had a white loop. The attached, flat pompom displayed the company number in its center. In the center was the company's number in black. The cords were made of white wool. The rim of the visor as well as the chinscales were of white metal. For special occasions a green plume with a yellow tip was added.
Until about 1811 the "Elite Company" wore a bearskin cap made of black bearskin. The cords and plume were as before. The top of the cap was yellow with white edging and a hunting horn emblem in the middle.
Coat: War made of dark green cloth and cut the same way as for the Grenadier Battalion. The collar and the cuffs were yellow, each with two white laces with points toward the back and secured with buttons (according to S. Pinhas). The lapels were the color of the coat with yellow piping. They were decorated with seven laces on each side. The turnbacks were yellow decorated with white or green (according to R. Forthoffer) hunting horn emblems. There was a lace on the yellow cuff and anther one above it, and after 1811 two laces on the cuffs and after 1813 another one on top of them.
The pockets at the waist had yellow piping. There were three horizontal laces underneath the buttons. At the waist in the back were buttons with white pointed laces. The buttons were pewter.
According to W. Hewig, starting in 1812 they were changed to brass and respectively gold colored for officers. That information is not confirmed by contemporary sources.
The vest was green or white depending on the season. Different versions of the fringed epaulets have been indicated: green with yellow crescent, according to Hahlo for 1808-09, green with green crescent; according to A. Sauerweid for 1810-1811 and finally according to S. Pinhas for 1811-1812 a lighter green than the coat.
Trousers: In the same color as the coat and with white Hungarian knotting and piping on the seams in the same color. Short black Hungarian-style gaiters, i.e., a "v" cut out in the front and decorated with white edging and a tassel.
Greatcoat: Light grey closed with one row of buttons. The collar was yellow with green lace edging and double laces. The epaulets were attached.
Armament and equipment: White leather bandoliers. The cartridge box had a white metal hunting horn as its badge. Short saber with green sword-strap. The muskets were the shorter model used by the light Infantry.

Button for privates, 1812
Artifact from the Berezina River, Private collection of Paul Meganck, Brussels, photo: Markus Gaertner

Guard Jaegers Dress Uniform and Coat Patterns, 1808–1813

1: Caporal-drummers until 1812; **2:** musician, 1808–1812; **3:** major, dress uniform; **4:** officer's dress uniform coat pattern; **5:** privates's dress uniform coat pattern, sleeve braid trim, 1808, 1810 and 1813; the dress uniform's green collar piping is not shown in all the sources; **6:** coat pattern for drummers with variations starting, 1812; **7:** surtout for officers, 1808–1810; **8:** undress uniform for privates until 1810; **9:** undress uniform for drummers.

Sources: 1, 2 – F. Kieffer's Strasbourg paper soldier collection; 3 – from H. Knötel and A. Sauerweid; 4–9 – from H. Knötel's patterns in his estate in WGM.

1
2
3
4
5
6 1812
7
8
9

Jaeger Guards coat for privates, 1813

Right: front view; above: rear view, detail of lapel laces and cuff flap.
Musée de L'Empéri, Invenory No. 4615 B; Salon en Provence.

Commandant of the Jaeger Guards, 1810
Sauerweid, Alexander Iwanowitsch: *Uniformen der Königlich Westphälischen Armee*, Dresden, 1810.

Jaegers, 1810
Sauerweid, Alexander Iwanowitsch: *Uniformen der Königlich Westphälischen Armee*, Dresden, 1810.

FIELD UNIFORM

Until ca. 1810 a single-breasted coat, closed with 9 buttons and with colored facings and piping on the seams, was worn as a 'second uniform' (*"zweite Garnitur"*) for daily duty and in the field. White lace trim on the collar and on the cuffs.

Instead of the plume, the shako had a green cylindrical pompom or a disk pompom with the company number in the center.

GARRISON DUTY

Headgear: Until 1812, the forage cap made of green cloth with yellow piped point and tassel in the same color. The rim of the cap was piped in yellow with an additional white trim. In the front was a white hunting horn emblem. Starting in 1813 the *Pokalem*-Model was used.

Vest: It was made of dark green cloth, single-breasted, and closed with eight buttons. It had a yellow collar and cuffs, and lace trim only on the collar.

Trousers: Long grey pants with yellow seams on the sides.

NCOs

Silver epaulets backed with yellow, and silver cords on the shako.

OFFICERS

They wore essentially the same uniform, but made with finer cloth.

Headgear: The officers' shakos had silver trim, and for higher ranks in embroidered form. The plates, chin-scales, cording as well as the cylindrical pompom were silvered. The company grade officers wore a feather plume, in colors like for privates, stuck on the pompom. But majors and higher had a white plume.

Coat: It was cut like for the privates, but with long coat-tails and finer cloth and all the lace trim was silvered.

C.F. Weiland presents a variant of the coat, e.g., only single-breasted closed with 8 buttons for 1807 to 1811. On each side of the button was a pair of white laces.

The higher-ranking officers wore more expensively crafted laces, i.e., with additional tassels on the ends. The buttons were of silver-covered copper with the royal initials and eagle. On the outside edge was the lettering "GARDE ROYAL." Silvered fringed epaulets as rank insignia. Additionally the officers wore the gorget. This was silvered and had a gilt coat of arms shield in the middle. Under the badge, which was also gilt, was a curved ribbon with the motto "GARDES DU ROI" (King's Guard).

Trousers: The outfit was completed with green pants expensively worked Hungarian cording. Either Hungarian boots with silver edging or knee-high black straight boots were worn with this attire.

Armament and equipment: A saber serves as armament, on a white leather bandolier over the right shoulder. For higher-ranking officers the sword was worn on the waist belt; silver portepée.

Greatcoat: Grey or beige-brown and closed with two rows of buttons and with epaulets attached. Starting in 1812 there was also the redingote in green with a yellow turned down collar.

Carabinier Company *(Compagnie d' Elite)* **Dress Uniform, 1808–1812**

1: Drummers; **2:** NCO – corporal; **3, 4:** carabiniers; **5:** sapper.

Chasseur Companies (Center Companies)

6: officer; **7:** drummers; **8:** NCO – sergeant; **9, 10:** chasseurs.

Sources: 1 – F. Kieffer's Strasbourg paper soldier collection; 2–5, 7 – from S. Hahlo and from H. Knötel's schema in WGM; 6, 8-10 – from C. F. Weiland 1807, A. Sauerweid 1810 and S. Pinhas 1811–1812.

1
2
3
4
5
6
7
8
9
10

FIELD UNIFORMS

Headgear: As headgear the bicorn or shako with and without plume and gilt decoration. Usually a black waxed cover was worn over the bicorn or shako for its protection.

Coat: The single-breasted surtout with colored collar and cuffs, both decorated with silver laces, was often worn in the field.

In the *Freiburger Bilderhandschrift* an officer is depicted with a green long Überrock – cut like a *Litewka*. Coat green with yellow collar without trim; yellow piping on the coat as well as around the sleeves.

Trousers: Close-fitting chamois pants were worn along with the grey or white trousers, but then Hungarian style boots with gilt trimming or alternatively also "Hessian" boots were worn with them. As trousers, long grey or green trousers with wide or silver stripes on the sides.

Armament and equipment: The bandoliers were black lacquered leather with an oval badge.

City Walking Out (*Stadtausgang) and Gala:*

The dress uniform coat was worn with white breeches, silk stockings and shoes with buckles. Then the sword was suspended on the white waist belt.

Grey greatcoat closed with two rows of buttons, with a turned down collar in the distinction color and it was piped in white.

Saddlecloth: Shabraque and holsters were yellow or green with silvered trim and a crowned monogram on the holsters and the blanket.

1: Shako plate; **2:** buttons for privates and officers; **3:** gorget.

Sources: 1 – from an original artifact excavated in Russia; 2, 3 – W. Hewig's patterns, WGM

Officers and Privates in Field Uniforms (Undress Uniforms)

1: Officer, 1808–1810, the only depiction with a single-breasted coat and wide laces on the chest; **2:** officer in the *Überrock*, 1813; **3:** officer in the surtout until 1812; **4:** officer in redingote, 1812 until 1813; **5:** sapper; **6:** drummer; **7:** chasseur, 1808–1810; **8:** chasseur in the greatcoat; **9:** fatigue uniform, 1808–1812; **10:** fatigue uniform, 1813.

Sources: 1 – from C. F. Weiland; 2 – from *Freiberger Bilderhandschrift 1813*; 3–10 – from H. Knötel's schema in WGM.

5 6 7 8 9 10

DRUMMERS

Headgear: Like for the privates, but with the body covered with yellow felt. For parades they wore man a version with white leather reinforcing and top (according to H. Knötel). For that, a green spherical pompom and the plume were attached, the plume having a green base and yellow tip.
The Elite company wore a white bearskin hat for parades, according to R. Forthoffer.
Coat: It and the lace trim were like for privates, but in reversed colors, e.g., yellow with green facings and piping, plus white braid on the collar lapels, cuffs as well as on the coattails' pockets
From 1808 to 1811 the epaulets changed to white. From 1811 to 1813 silver epaulets, worked through with dark green with added swallow's nests in the facing color. These had white trim under the epaulets. Starting in 1813 there was additional white lacing on the sleeve seams.
Second set: Vest like that for privates. Greatcoat like for privates, but with green collar.
Armament and equipment: Short saber. Drum with light blue rims.

SAPPERS

Headgear: Bearskin hat in the shape for the carabiniers, with white cording and plume.
Coat: Like for the privates: Crossed yellow axes, with a white hunting horn over them, were sewn on both upper arms.
Armament and equipment: Apron and fittings like for axe sheath were made of white leather. Sapper's saber and carbine.
Axe with black shaft and brass fittings.
Field uniform: Shako, single-breasted coat, long grey pants with yellow stripes on the sides.

HEADS OF THE COLUMNS *(Téte de Colonne)*

According to the force structure in the Guard Decree (*Garde-Dekret*) of 1810, a drum major (*Tambourmajor*), a drummer corporal (*tambour-maitre*) as well as a bandmaster (*Musikmeister*) together with music are listed. Nothing is known about the appearance of the drum major or the bugler from contemporary sources. Only the collection from Fritz Kieffer, *Papiersoldaten Strasbourg* shows the possible appearance of a *Korporal -Tambour* and a musician (*Hautboisten*):

MUSICIANS (per the Kieffer collection)

Headgear: Shako with yellow and white plume.
Coat: Like for the privates, but with wide white edging on the lapels. The same on the collar and cuffs a braid in the same color. Silvered trefoil epaulets.
Trousers: Green with white Hungarian knotting.
Armament: Sword on the waist belt.

DRUMMER CORPORAL *(Korporal-Tambour/Tambour-Maitre)*

Headgear: Colpak/busby with yellow cap bag. White cording, plume like for privates.
Coat and Trousers: Like for musicians above.
Armament: Short saber with green sword-strap.
Drumsticks with brass fittings and gilt cords.

MUSICIANS

(Variation based on a contemporary picture in the Museum Schloss Fiedrichstein)

Headgear: Shako like for the privates, but with a white trim on the top band.
Coat: Like for the privates, but no laces on the cuffs. Green swallow's nests with fastener, that with silver trimming.
Trousers: Like for the privates with lacing; worn with short Hungarian boots.
Armament: Bandolier over the right shoulder with a short saber.

Drummer in dress uniform, 1810
Watercolor by Herbert Knötel,
Anne S.K. Brown Military Collection, Brown University Library.

Captain in dress uniform, 1811-1813
Pinhas, Salomon: *Recueil de planches représentant les troupes des différentes armes et grades de l'armée Westphalienne*, 1811–1813.

GUARD LIGHT HORSE *(CHEVAULEGERS-GARDE)*

ESTABLISHMENT

A squadron of Guard Light Horse (*Garde-Jäger zu Pferd; Chasseurs a cheval*) was already formed in January 1808, whose first company consisted of former soldiers from the Vistula Legion. Four hundred fifty men had reported by December 1808.

At the end of 1810 the regiment was completely established with three squadrons for the first time. Proven privates from the elite companies of the line cavalry and selected recruits were accepted into the unit. The regiment performed its duties in the Prince's palace and shared the escort duty with the Garde-du-Corps for the royal family. The garrison was in Kassel.

In October 1811 the regiment was reinforced by an additional squadron, now with a total strength of 38 officers and 670 men, and received lances as armament. Thereupon in November 1811 the unit's name was changed to "*Chevaulegers Lanciers de la Garde.*" After the unit's destruction in Russia, the regiment was formed anew in the beginning of 1813 from the depot and existing cadres of the 2nd Line Chevauleger Regiment. The unit was already complete again on 1 February 1813.

ORGANIZATION

A decree of 25 Dec. 1810 established the regiment's structure. It was composed of three squadrons with two companies each. There was also a depot company. The total strength was supposed to be 680 men including the regiment's staff.

Senior Staff *(Oberstab)* (16 men)	**Subordinate Staff *(Unterstab)*** (11 men)	**Per Company** (94 men)
1 Colonel	3 Adjutants	1 *Rittmeister* (Captain)
1 Major	3 Veterinarian's Assistant *(Pferdearztgehilfen)*	1 *Premier-Lieutenant*
2 Squadron Cdrs (3 starting in 1811)	1 Staff Trumpeter	2 *Seconde-Lieutenant*
1 Captain (Supply)	4 *Handwerker*	1 Senior Sergeant Major (*Oberwachtmeister*)
2 Adjutant-Majors		4 Sergeant Major *(Wachtmeister)*
1 Senior Surgeon		1 Quartermaster Corporal *(Fourier)*
2 Senior Surgeon's Assistants		8 Brigadiers
1 Quartermaster		3 Trumpeters
1 Paymaster		72 privates
1 Instructor		1 Blacksmith *(Schmied)*
1 Veterinarian		
2 Surgeons 3rd Class		

The depot company additionally had more than three drivers *(Fuhrknechte)*.

On the 1st of February 1813 the unit had a strength of four squadrons and a depot company with a strength of 913 men and 998 horses (W. Hewig).

COMMANDERS

1808: Colonel Baron Lepel von Grambow, **1808**: Major Bastineller, **1809**: Colonel Baron von Wolff, **1810**: Colonel Müller, **1812**: Major Lallemand, **1813**: General von Wolff, Colonel Berger, Major Szmauch

Chevauleger and trumpeter in undress uniform until 1812; standard bearer in dress uniform, 1810.
Watercolor by Edmund Wagner after a sketch by Herbert Knötel, collection of Markus Gaertner.

Chevauleger 1809 and officer in undress uniform 1810.
Watercolor by Edmund Wagner after a sketch by Herbert Knötel, collection of Markus Gaertner.

Officer's cartridge pouch, original
Schloß Friedrichstein (Bad Wildungen), Museumslandschaft Hessen-Kassel.

Cartridge pouch, original, detail of badge
Original Schloß Friedrichstein (Bad Wildungen), Museumslandschaft Hessen-Kassel.

Chevauleger in dress uniform, 1810–1812
Sauerweid, Alexander Iwanowitsch: *Uniformen der Königlich Westphälischen Armee,* ca. 1810, Dresden.

Colonel in dress uniform, 1810–1812
Sauerweid, Alexander Iwanowitsch: *Uniformen der Königlich Westphälischen Armee,* ca. 1810, Dresden.

ACTIONS

1809: Campaign in Saxony in March in the 1st Division (Garde) under Major General Reubell; at the end of June with the King in Leipzig. Three squadrons with 550 men under the command of Colonel von Wolff. No engagements during this campaign.

1812: At the beginning of the year a cavalry brigade for the (Westphalian) VIII Army Corps (Junot) of the *Grande Armée* was created for the upcoming campaign against Russia. The Chevaulegers (4 squadrons with 31 officers and 592 men) together with Garde du Corps formed the brigade. After the King's and the Garde du Corps' return to Kassel, the Chevaulegers were assigned to the Brigade Hammerstein (24th Cavalry Brigade) on 21 July. Its strength in August was four squadrons with 34 officers and 379 men.

Participated in the Battles of Valutina-Gora (19 August), Borodino (7 September) and Krasnoi (18 November).

1813: On the 1st of January in Thorn (Torun) with forty men returning from Russia. The new establishment of the unit took place on the 1st of February 1813. Starting in August it was ordered to the XII Army Corps (Marshal Oudinot). Three squadrons of the regiment together with the Hessian Chevaulegers formed the 1st Brigade under General Wolff (29th Light Cavalry Brigade Beaumont).

Advance on Berlin against the Prussian Northern Army, participation in the Battle of Dennewitz on 6 September. There the Chevaulegers covered the retreat of the French Army; on 24 Sep. they were at the Battle of Altenburg. Then they retreated to Torgau.

In October the regiment took part in the Battle of Wartenburg in the IV Army Corps (Brigade Beaumont) with a squadron (8 officers, 158 men). On 18 October at Liebertwolkwitz/Leipzig. After the Battle of Nations at Leipzig on 19 October, 48 men were still available for duty.

In Eberfeld they had their last review before the King with 3 officers and 40 men.

In October a squadron and the depot, as part of the von Zandt Brigade, fought against a Russian corps at Kassel. Shortly thereafter the remaining privates disbanded the unit.

Guard Chevauleger Uniforms, 1809–1810

1: Officer-*Rittmeister*, dress uniform reconstruction; **2:** trumpeter, dress uniform; **3:** chevauleger, dress uniform; **4:** officer, dress uniform; **5:** trumpeter, dress uniform, 1808; **6:** trumpeter, 1809, dress uniform, variation; **7:** Ober-*Wachtmeister*, dress uniform, reconstruction; **8, 9:** chevauleger – dress uniform.

Sources: 1, 4, 7 – from H. Knötel; 2, 3, 5, 8, 9 – H. Knötel's patterns in WGM; 6 – Forthoffer

1
2
3
4
5
6
7
8
9

UNIFORMS, 1808–1810

PRIVATES

Headgear: Initially a French model shako. Yellow or yellow and red mixed cording and a green plume. The metal plate was rhombus-shaped and the sources show different variants. For example, with an eagle holding an oval or heart-shaped shield with the "JN" royal cypher with a crown above it.

In 1809 a helmet made of black leather had already been introduced. The shako remained the headgear worn with the service dress.

The helm plate, like the ridge, side straps and visor rim, were of brass. Black fur caterpillar crest. Red plume. The contemporary sources (Weiland, Sauerweid, Pinhas) show the helmet with curved side straps and without a rear visor. On the other hand the later secondary sources show a helmet with straight side straps and a rear visor like for the chevaulegers of the Line.

The forage cap was made of green cloth with red decorations.

Coat: The uniform coat corresponded to that of the French chasseurs a cheval. It was dark green with long coattails, and had red pointed lapels. collar, cuffs and turnbacks. According to Herbert Knötel, the 1st Company could have worn red lapels in the beginning. It had yellow lace trim on the collar and on the cuffs. It had yellow trefoil epaulets on both shoulders and yellow aiguillettes on the right one. There were yellow cloth grenades as emblems on the coattails.

A Hungarian style red vest with yellow knotting was worn under the coat.

A green, single-breasted coat with red distinctions and short coattails served as the undress uniform. It had yellow lace trim on the collar, the pointed cuffs and on the chest. The yellow shoulder straps were also worn on the undress coat as Guard unit distinctions.

A dark green vest with red piping on the collar and the cuffs was worn for stable and work duties.

Trousers: Dark green pants with yellow Hungarian knotting and piping on the sides. Hussar boots with yellow trim and tassel.

For daily duty and in the field, long dark green or grey overalls with leather reinforcing on inside of the legs, and yellow stripes on the sides and button trim.

Greatcoat: Long, white cavalry greatcoat with a caped overcoat collar. Probably like that of the Garde du Corps.

Chevauleger in undress uniform, 1808
Copy by W. Hewig nach *Manuscrit du Canonnier Hahlo*, 1807/08
Collection of Edmund Wagner.

Guard Chevauleger Uniforms, 1810–1812

1: Colonel; **2:** chevauleger, dress uniform; **3:** trumpeter, dress uniform, 1812; **4:** officer – captain, dress uniform; **5:** trumpeter, dress uniform; **6:** NCO – reconstruction; **7, 8:** chevauleger, dress uniform, 1812; **9:** sapper, 1812.

Sources: 1, 2 – A. Sauerweid; 3 – E. Fort; 4 – S. Pinhas; 5 – T. Carl, *Elsässer Papiersoldaten*, Strasbourg; 6 – from H. Knötel's patterns in WGM; 7 – C.F. Weiland; 8 – F. Neumann; 9 – F. Lünsmann.

1
2
3
4
5
6
7
8
9

Equipment: The leather belting was made of light, pale yellow leather. Rectangular brass plate with the badge with the initials "JN" on the carbine bandolier. The black cartridge box was decorated with a rhombus-shaped yellow metal badge.
Leather gauntlets.
Armament: At first the regiment was equipped with old Kurhessian dragoon sabers, which were adapted by attaching the royal, initials "JN" on the hilt. They were soon exchanged for the French model light cavalry saber. The sabers had a brass- hilt, iron scabbard and a sword-strap made of light brown leather. The supplementary armament consisted of a carbine and two pistols (on the saddle).
Saddlecloth: White fleece shabraque with green wolves teeth edging. Dark green valise (*Mantelrolle*). On the ends was a yellow circle in the center and red piping on the sides.

NCOs

Uniform was like for the privates. On the sleeves rank insignia in the French system. The aiguillettes were interwoven yellow and red or gold and red. The NCOs were not armed with carbines.

TRUMPETERS

Headgear: In 1808 a shako initially served as the headgear like for the other soldiers. It had a white plume, yellow and red interwoven cording and was trimmed on the upper band with a yellow braid.
In 1809 the trumpeters received busbys (*Kolpaks*) as new headgear instead of the helmets. They had a white plume; yellow or yellow and red cording, red hat bags and brass chin-scales.
Coat: The trumpeters wore coats in reversed colors and with additional yellow braid decorations. The plates show two variations of the trumpeter's uniform that differ in their details.
Trousers: Like for the privates.
Saddlecloth: Like for the privates.
Brass trumpets with tassels and cords made of white and blue wool.

OFFICERS

Uniform like for the other ranks but of better quality. All decorations and the epaulets were gilt. For the staff officers white plume on the shako and helmet and extra tassels on the ends of the lace trimmings. The pants had golden lace trim on the front corresponding to the rank.

Guard Chevauleger Uniforms, 1808–1812

1: Chevauleger, dress uniform, 1808; **2:** chevauleger, undress uniform, 1808–1810; **3:** trumpeter, undress uniform, 1808–1810, reconstruction; **4:** chevauleger, undress uniform, 1808–1810; **5:** trumpeter, field uniform, 1810–1812; **6:** chevauleger, field uniform (in the beginning also with the shako), 1810; **7:** chevauleger in the greatcoat, 1810–1812, reconstruction; **8:** chevauleger in the vest for work and garrison duty.

Sources: 1 – R. Forthoffer; 2 – S. Hahlo; 3 – from W. Hewig; 4, 8 – H. Knötel's schema in WGM; 5, 6 – H. Knötel; 7 – from H. Knötel and H. Boisselier, Darbou.

1
2
3
4
5
6
7
8

UNIFORMS, 1810–1812

PRIVATES

Headgear: The helmet was now also worn with the undress uniform. The shako was discontinued.
Coat: The chasseur style coat with long tails was abolished. The former undress coat became the dress uniform. The following minor changes were made to the coat: Introduction of pockets on the coattails, and a straight cut to the cuffs. The sources Weiland and Sauerweid show additional buttons on the ends of the laces on the chest. The aiguillettes continued to be worn. The sources show them on both the right or left shoulder to that no system is recognizable. The chevaulegers armed with lances probably wore the aiguillettes on the left shoulder. Yellow metal buttons with the Westphalian eagle carrying an oval shield with the royal monogram. The new undress coat no longer had lace trim and no coattail pockets. The aiguillettes were still worn, but now on the left shoulder.
Trousers: As before, but the overalls had yellow stripes on the side and were without leather reinforcing.
Greatcoat and equipment: remained unchanged.
Armament: Initially unchanged.
In 1811 the lance was introduced as the new weapon. According to Fritz Lünsmann only the 1st squadron received this armament. Therefore the effected soldiers had to give up their carbine, but they retained the carbine bandoliers, and a pistol was hung on its hook.
Saddlecloth: Dark green cloth shabraque, coming to a point in the rear with yellow braid and red piping on the outer edge and with the royal initials in the corners.

Chevauleger in dress uniform, 1810-1812
Weiland, C. F.: *Représentation des uniformes de l' armée impériale royale française et des alliés*, Weimar, 1807 and 1812.

NCOs

The changes were the same as for the privates.
The NCOs had neither lances nor carbines.

TRUMPETERS

Headgear: The trumpeters still wore a colpak/busby as headgear.
Coat: The trumpeters' coats were worn in reversed colors. The extra yellow braid decorations on the collar and cuffs disappeared.
Trousers: Like for the privates.
Saddlecloth: Like for the privates.
Brass trumpets with tassels and cords made of mixed white and blue wool.

OFFICERS

Headgear: The helmet corresponded to that of the other ranks. For the undress uniform, for the social and walking out uniform or for off duty a bicorn was often worn in place of the heavy helmet.
Additionally the officers also had a field cap.
Coat: Dress and undress uniform coat corresponded to the other ranks. All the braid decorations were gilt. The chasseur style coat with long tails was also worn by offi-

Guard Chevauleger Officers, 1810–1812

1: Dress uniform, 1811–1813; **2:** full dress uniform, 1808–1812; **3:** undress uniform, 1809–1813; **4:** officer in redingote; **5:** officer in the greatcoat, 1811.

Sources: 1 – H. Boisselier; 2 – original artifact in the Army Museum Brussels;
3 – former collection of Hollitzer, Vienna; 4, 5 – H. Boisselier and H. Knötel, patterns in WGM.

cers as the walking out and social uniform. Besides that, for daily duty, the coat had short coattails without braid trim on the chest was in use.
Trousers: Green pants with golden decorations.
White pants with stockings and shoes with buckles were worn for the social uniform. Along with the green pants, leather pants were worn with the undress uniform.

Greatcoat: The officers' greatcoat was made of green cloth and with a caped collar. It was trimmed with golden lace and edged with a red piping.
Furthermore a green surtout (*Überrock* or redingote) with red collar was worn for undress duty. The epaulets were attached to the surtout coat.

SAPPERS

Although sappers are not specified in the structure before 1813, secondary sources like Fritz Lünsmann described the regiment as having four sappers.
Headgear: Colpak/busby with red cording and cap bag. White plume.
Coat: Red uniform coat with green facings, like for the trumpeters but with red or crimson trefoil epaulets and aiguillettes.
Trousers: Like for the privates.
Equipment: Brown leather apron; axe.
Saddlecloth: Like for the privates.

UNIFORMS, 1813

At the beginning of 1813 the regiment was completely newly raised with the help of the depot company and the 2nd Chevauleger Regiment of the Line that was being raised after it had been destroyed in Russia.

On 1 February 1813 a new uniform decree was issued for the new raising of the unit. Whether the changes mandated in it were actually accomplished is however not known.

PRIVATES

Headgear: The helmet was retained as the headgear. Based on the circumstances of the forming of the regiment, it is probable that various helmet models had to be worn along with one another. They would have been the guard helmets from the soldiers out of the depot and the helmets from the 2nd Line Chevauleger Regiment.
Coat: The green, single-breasted coat remained almost unchanged. However, it received nine pairs of narrow lace on the chest and semicircular buttons. This dress uniform appears to have never really been introduced. Furthermore, yellow trefoil epaulets and aiguillettes, except in the field.
The undress coat without laces on the chest, and the waistcoat remained unchanged.
Trousers: On General Wolff's initiative the regiment was supposed to retain the red pants with two yellow, parallel stripes. Many officers already extravagantly wore red pants before that. But the contemporary depictions (e.g., Traugott) only show dark green or grey overalls. They are decorated with double yellow or red stripes and button trim. Pants without trim were also used.
Greatcoat: Dark grey cavalry greatcoats.
Equipment and armament: Officially the lance was abolished and replaced with the carbine. But it is likely that the squadrons in the field continued to use the lances.
Saddlecloth: Red cloth, pointed light cavalry shabraques with yellow stripes on the sided and green piping on the exterior edges. The green valise (*Mantelsack*) continued in use.

NCOs

The changes were the same as for the privates. The NCOs carried neither lances nor carbines.

Guard Chevauleger Uniforms, 1813

1: Officer, captain, dress uniform; **2:** chevauleger, dress uniform; **3:** trumpeter, field uniform; **4:** sapper, 1813; **5:** officer – Chef d'Eskadron, dress uniform; **6:** trumpeter, dress uniform; **7:** chevauleger, field uniform; **8:** chevauleger in vest, work and garrison duty, starting 1811.

Sources: 1, 3, 5, 6, 8 – H. Knötel; 2, –R. Forthoffer Collection; 4 – Decree of February 1813;
5 – R. Forthoffer; 7 – Traugott, contemporary plate.

1
2
3
4
5
6
7
8

TRUMPETERS

Headgear: The trumpeters wore still wore a colpak/busby as headgear or a helmet with a white caterpillar crest.
Coat: The trumpeters' coats were in reversed colors.
Trousers: Like for the privates.
Saddlecloth: Like for the privates.
Brass trumpets with tassels and cords made of white and blue wool.

OFFICERS

Uniform was the same as for the other ranks, but with gilt decorations rather than yellow.

Sappers

The decree of 1 February 1813 envisioned nine sappers for the regiment.
Headgear: Colpak/busby with red pompom and white plume. Brass chin-scales.
Coat: The Polish "Kurtka cut" coat had red half lapels. Three buttons on yellow braids were located underneath the lapels. Green collar with a pair of yellow braids. Red piping on the collar and seams along the sleeves. Red fringed epaulets and aiguillettes. Red cloth crossed axes under a grenade were sewn on the sleeves.
Trousers: Baggy red Marmeluk style pants.
Equipment: Brown leather apron and an axe.
Armament: Sapper's saber with sawtooth on the unsharpened side of the blade; carabine and pistols.

Kettledrummer *(Timbalier)*

Roger Forthoffer describes a kettledrummer of the regiment for 1813. But this drummer is not confirmed by the structure or a degree. For completion of the presentation he is displayed here.

Guard Chevauleger Coat Patterns, 1808–1813

1: Kettledrummer, 1813; **2:** coat pattern, 1808 – chevauleger dress uniform, trumpeter dress uniform, chevauleger undress uniform; **3:** coat pattern 1810–1812 – chevauleger dress uniform, trumpeter dress uniform; chevauleger undress uniform 1811, trumpeter undress uniform, 1811; **4:** lace braids, 1808–1813 – variations based on various sources; **5:** coat pattern, 1813 – officer, dress uniform, trumpeter dress uniform, chevauleger undress uniform, sapper; **6:** button; **7:** officers' cartridge pouch.

Sources: 1– R. Forthoffer, manuscript in Marckolsheim;
2, 3, 5 – H. Knötel, schemas in WGM and Decree of 2 Jan. 1813; 4 – S. Hahlo, C. A. Weiland, A. Sauerweid, S. Pinhas;
6 – W. Hewig's patterns; 7 – original artifact, Schloss Friedrichstein (Bad Wildungen), Museumslandschaft Kassel.

1

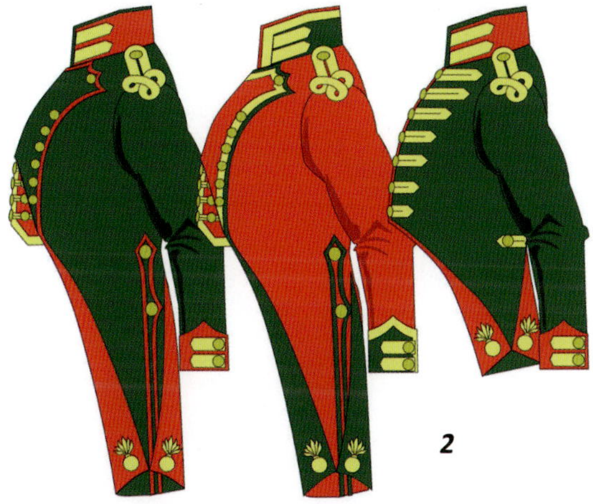

2

3

1808–1810 and 1811–1812

1810?

4

1813

Staff officers

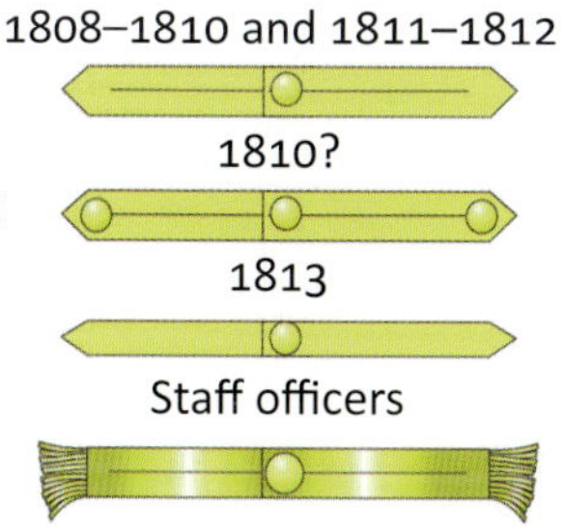

5

6

7

Officer's undress uniform coat, 1809–1813
Musée Royal de l'Armée et d'Histoire Militaire, Brussels

Photo: Luc Van de Weghe.

Helmet attributed to the Guard Chevaulegers
Musée Royal de l'Armée et d'Histoire Militaire, Brussels

WHI Inv No: 300297
Photo: Luc Van de Weghe.

Saber, Guard light cavalry
Musée Royal de l'Armée et d'Histoire Militaire, Brussels

WHI Inv No: 300291
Photo: Luc Van de Weghe.

Guard cavalry officer's saber belt
Musée Royal de l'Armée et d'Histoire Militaire, Brussels
© War Heritage Institute, WHI Inv No: 300296
Photo: Luc Van de Weghe.

Grenadier drummer, 1812
Watercolor by Herbert Knötel
Anne S.K. Brown Military Collection, Brown University Library.

GUARD FUSILIERS (QUEEN'S REGIMENT)

ORGANIZATION

On 15. August 1812 King Jérôme ordered the creation of an infantry regiment with the name *"Regiment der Königin"* (Queen's Regiment) that was to be assigned to the Guard. The strength corresponded to that of a Line regiment: two field battalions (*Feldbataillone*) each with four fusilier, one grenadier and one voltigeur company. In addition a depot battalion with four fusilier companies was formed. The structure also was the same as for the Line. Until the beginning of 1813 the unit, which was supposed to draw personnel from the Line infantry depots, only had very weak fill. The stand-up of the unit was made more difficult by having to give up the four elite companies to the Grenadier Guard Battalion and Jaeger Guard Battalion that were being recreated at this time.

On the 1st of February 1813, the regiment's organization was newly established, and the unit received the designation *"Regiment Füsilier-Garde."* After this time, the regiment consisted of two field battalions with a total of twelve fusilier companies without elite companies. The depot remained unchanged. On 25 Sep. 1813 it reported a strength of 7 officers and 160 men. The regiment was filled with privates contributed from Line regiments and selected recruits from the 1813 call-up.

COMMANDERS

August 1812: Oberst Prinz zu Salm-Salm, **Februar 1813**: Oberst von Müldner,
Mai 1813: Oberst von Benning, **Oktober 1813**: Major von Hessberg

ACTIONS

April 1813: The regiment formed a brigade with the 8th Line Regiment and the 2nd and 4th Light Infantry Battalions, plus two batteries of foot artillery as the brigade artillery.

Departure from Kassel on 1 April.

May/June 1813: Garrison in Dresden where it was assigned to the VI Army Corps.

25 June 1813: Departed for Bautzen, Goerlitz and the to Wolkersdorf in Silesia. In August the regiment was assigned to the XI Army Corps. During the autumn campaign of 1813 the regiment, in the 31st Division, took part in the following fighting and battles:

20 Aug. 1813 Ottendorf
23 Aug. 1813 Goldberg
25 Aug. 1813 Chemnitz
26 Aug. 1813 Battle on the Katzbach
30 Aug. 1813 Greiffenberg,
4 Sep. 1813 Stockkirch

In September 1813 the regiment, which had been significantly whittled down in the fighting, was consolidated into a battalion in Dresden.

An order from the Emperor to General Drouot stated: *"The Westphalian Fusilier Battalion, which is complete with 800, including the musicians; the cadre returns to Erfurt, from where it is directed to Kassel. The battalion shall be organized like the other Westphalian battalions, it will be assigned to the 2nd Guard Division."*

Beginning of October 1813 the battalion was filled with 292 grenadiers from the 2nd and 3rd Line Regiments and reinforced with an artillery battery. It was incorporated into the 2nd Guard Division:

2nd Division of the Imperial Guard
(*General de division* CURIAL)
1st Brigade:
Fusilier-Grenadier Regiment of the Guard — 2 Bns.
Fusilier-Chasseur Regiment of the Guard — 2 Bns.
2nd Brigade:
Saxon Grenadier Guards — 1 Bn.
Polish Guard Battalion — 1 Bn.
Westphalian Fusilier Guards — 1 Bn.

Westphalian Normann Foot Battery
(formerly Orges)

14 to 18 October 1813: Participation in the Battle of Nations at Leipzig with heavy losses. At the end of the battle General Curial allowed the remainder of the unit to follow the French Army or to be released from service in the homeland. The battalion decided to return to Westphalia and essentially dissolved during the march.

September 1813: The depot company stationed in Kassel was still involved with the fighting around Kassel. After the fighting ended, the unit only had about forty men remaining.

UNIFORMS

PRIVATES

Headgear: Shako with a rhombus-shaped plate made of white metal. On it was the Westphalian eagle with a shield. For the fusiliers white cording and white or blue spherical pompom. For parades a blue plume with a white tip. Grenadiers had red cording and plume. Voltigeurs had green cording and a green plume with a yellow tip. In the field a black wax cover was worn over the shako.

On garrison duty a white forage cap with dark blue piping and tassel was worn. W. Hewig shows the cap in the form of the *bonnet de police* (old style) and also in the *Pokalem* form (new style).

Coat: White coat cut like that for the Line infantry with blue lapels collar, cuffs and turnbacks. White piping for the blue parts of the coat is given in most of the sources. The number of buttons on the lapels varies in the sources from 6 and 7 on each side of the lapels. It had white braid trim on the collar, lapels, cuff flaps and coattail pockets as a Guard distinction. The white metal buttons were stamped with an eagle with the coat of arms shield. Blue wool epaulets with white crescents for the fusiliers. The epaulets of the elite companies in the appropriate colors: Grenadiers red, voltigeurs green with yellow crescents. Emblems on the coattail turnbacks: fusiliers – white stars; grenadiers - red grenades; voltigeurs – green hunting horns.

In garrison they wore a white waistcoat with a blue collar and cuffs. The sources give two different forms for the cuffs: with cuff flaps or without flaps but with braid trim directly on the cuffs.

Trousers: White pants with white, dark grey or black cloth gaiters reaching to the calf were worn for the full dress *(Grande Tenue)* uniform. Pinhas shows the voltigeurs with Hungarian style gaiters with green trim and tassel.

Long white or light grey trousers were worn in the field.

Equipment and armament: It was the same as for the Line infantry, but the fusiliers also had an infantry saber. On the cartridge box was a rhombus-shaped plate with the Westphalian coat of arms.

Greatcoat: grey greatcoat with collar like on the uniform coat. The epaulets were attached.

Königin Regiment -Fusilier Guard Dress Uniform, 1812

1: Shako plate; **2:** officers' gorget; **3:** cartridge box plate
4: Colonel Prince zu Salm-Salm; **5:** major
6: company-grade officer of the fusiliers; **7:** drummers; **8:** drummers, **9, 10:** fusiliers.

Sources: 1, 2, 3, 5, 6, 8, 9, 10 – from an original artifact and W. Hewig, Brauer-Bogen Nos. 186-188;
4 – from an original artifact belonging to Prince zu Salm-Salm.

4 *5*

6 *7* *8* *9* *10*

NCOs

Like for the privates with French pattern rank insignia:
Corporal (*Korporal*): two blue braids on each forearm.

Sergeant, *Feldwebel*: Silver braids on the forearms, silver braid on the upper shako band, shako cording, and epaulets were mixed with silver.

OFFICERS

All officers wore a silver gorget with a gold shield (Westphalia's coat of arms over the inscription "GARDE ROYALE" when on duty.

Headgear: Shako with silver decorations. For staff officers a wide and a narrow silver lace on the upper shako band and a white plume.

For off duty, inside duty and social events the bicorn was also worn.

Field cap was made of white cloth with silver edging on the band and blue piping; on the front a silver-plated emblem according to the company.

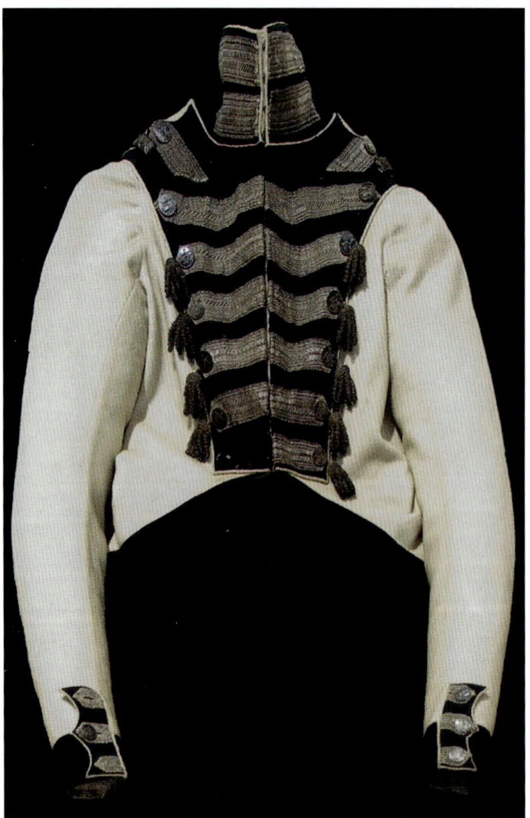

Coat: Coat with long coattails and silver-plated trim and buttons. For the staff officers, the laces on the coat had tassels added. Colonel zu Salm-Salm's parade dress coat still exists today. It had silver epaulets as rank insignia.

A single-breasted, completely blue surtout served as the undress or field uniform. Its collar and cuffs could be trimmed with laces.

Trousers: White pants in Hungarian boots with or without silver edging. The mounted staff officers could also wear tall cavalry boots.

In the field buff or blue pants were worn.

White breeches, stockings and shoes with buckles were worn for the walking out uniform.

Armament: The sources show a saber carried on the shoulder bandolier or a sword on the waist belt.

Greatcoat: Grey-blue cloth with two rows of buttons and a turned down collar. It was decorated with lace. Epaulets were attached.

Saddlecloth: Dark blue shabraque and holsters with silver trim. On the holsters and in each of the blanket's corners was the royal monogram with a crown. A variation had a crown only in the rear corner of the shabraque.

Front view of Prince zu Salm-Salm's original coat
Collection of the Prince zu Salm-Salm,
Photo Markus Gaertner from the exhibition *"Napoleon Trikolore und Kaiseradler,"* Preussen-Museum Nordrhein-Westfalen Wesel

Elite Companies, Dress Uniform, 1812

1: Grenadier officer; **2:** drummers; **3:** sergeant major; **4, 5:** grenadiers;
6: voltigeur officer; **7:** bugler/cornet; **8:** sergeant; **9, 10:** voltigeurs.

Sources: 1, 3, 8 – from S. Pinhas; 2 – from H. Knötel's watercolor in ASKB Collection;4, 5, 9, 10 – former collection of Nussbaum, Strasbourg; 6, 7 – reconstructions from information from F. Lünsmann and W. Hewig, and Brauer-Bogen.

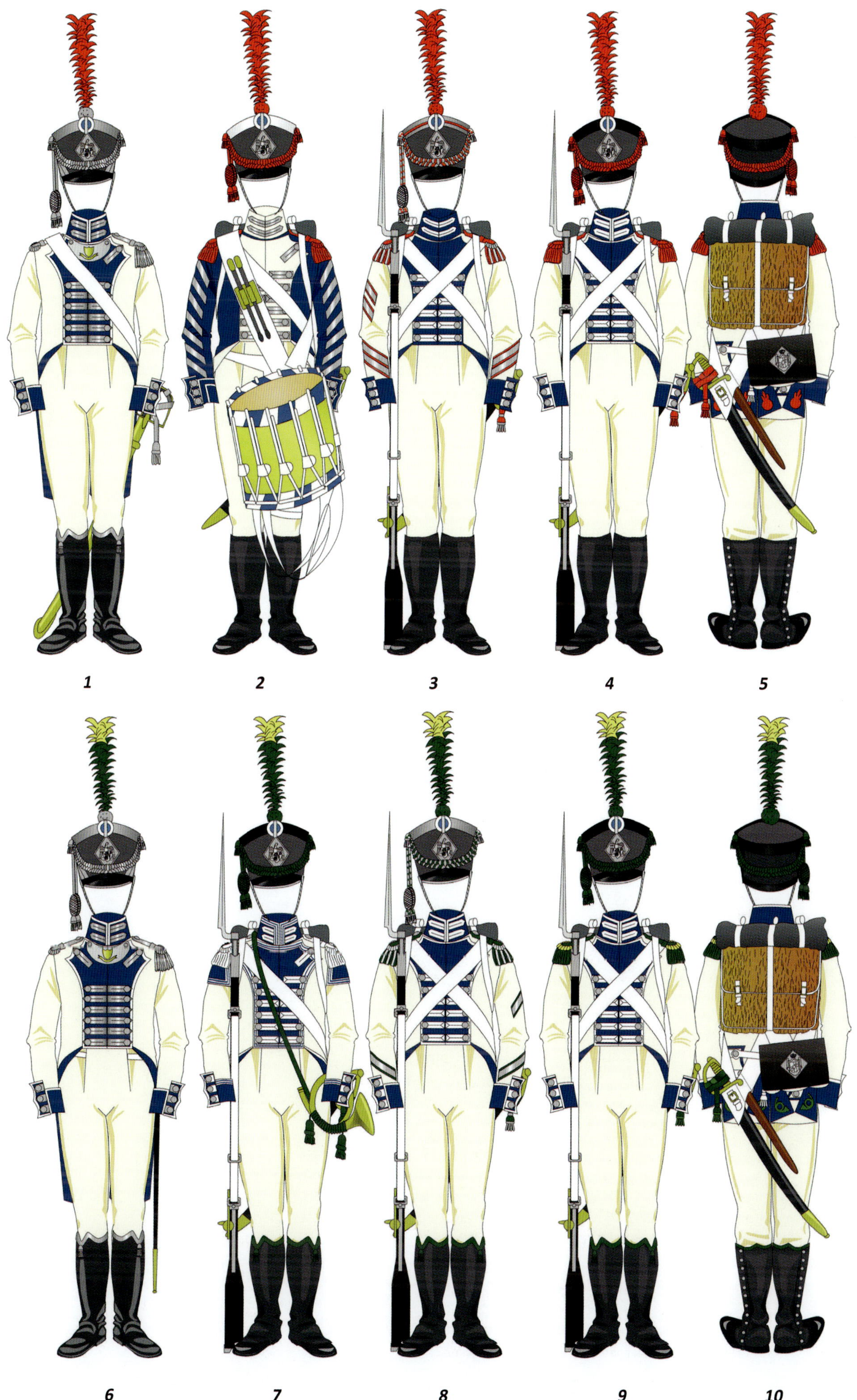
1
2
3
4
5
6
7
8
9
10

DRUMMERS

Headgear: The shako's upper band was trimmed in white.
Coat: Private´s coat with fancy additional braid trim. H. Knötel and W. Hewig show different variations of possible drummers' uniforms. All are shown in the plates. For the grenadiers, H. Knötel shows a drummer's coat in reversed colors: blue coat with white facings and silver lace trim.
Equipment: Drum decorations like for the Line. Drum rims with white and blue diagonal stripes.

BUGLERS

There is no information about the voltigeur buglers' uniforms. Using an analogy of the Line unit buglers' uniforms, we have given the buglers illustrated here the drummer's coat without the braids on the sleeves.

DRUM MAJOR *(Tambourmajor)*

H. Knötel and W. Hewig show the drum major with a bicorn, blue coat with white facings and silver lace trim. Over the right shoulder a wide, white bandolier with silver edging. The two sources differ in a whole series of details about the uniform. The plates show the variations.

SAPPERS *(Sappeure)*

Bearskin hat with a front visor; red cords and plume.
The coat had red epaulets and on the upper sleeves was a blue cloth axe emblem under a silver grenade. The cartridge box was worn in the front on the waist belt; it had a white metal badge in the form of two crossed axes. Gauntlets and a leather apron.

Coat Cuts and Drum Major, 1812–1813

1: Coat pattern for officer 1812; **2:** coat pattern for privates -fusilier, 1813; **3:** grenadier's coat pattern; **4:** coat pattern for voltigeurs; **5:** coat pattern for fusiliers, 1812; **6–9:** coat schema variations for drummers; **10:** drum major, 1812; **11:** coat pattern for drum major, variation with swallow's nest; **12:** coat cut with variation short coattail turnbacks and swallow's nest; **13:** drum major, 1813.

Sources: 1 – after an original piece belonging to Prince zu Salm-Salm; 2, 3, 4, 5, 6, 7, 10, 11 – W. Hewig, Brauer-Bogen Nos. 186-188; 8, 9, 12, 13 – based on H. Knötel's pattern sheet, WGM

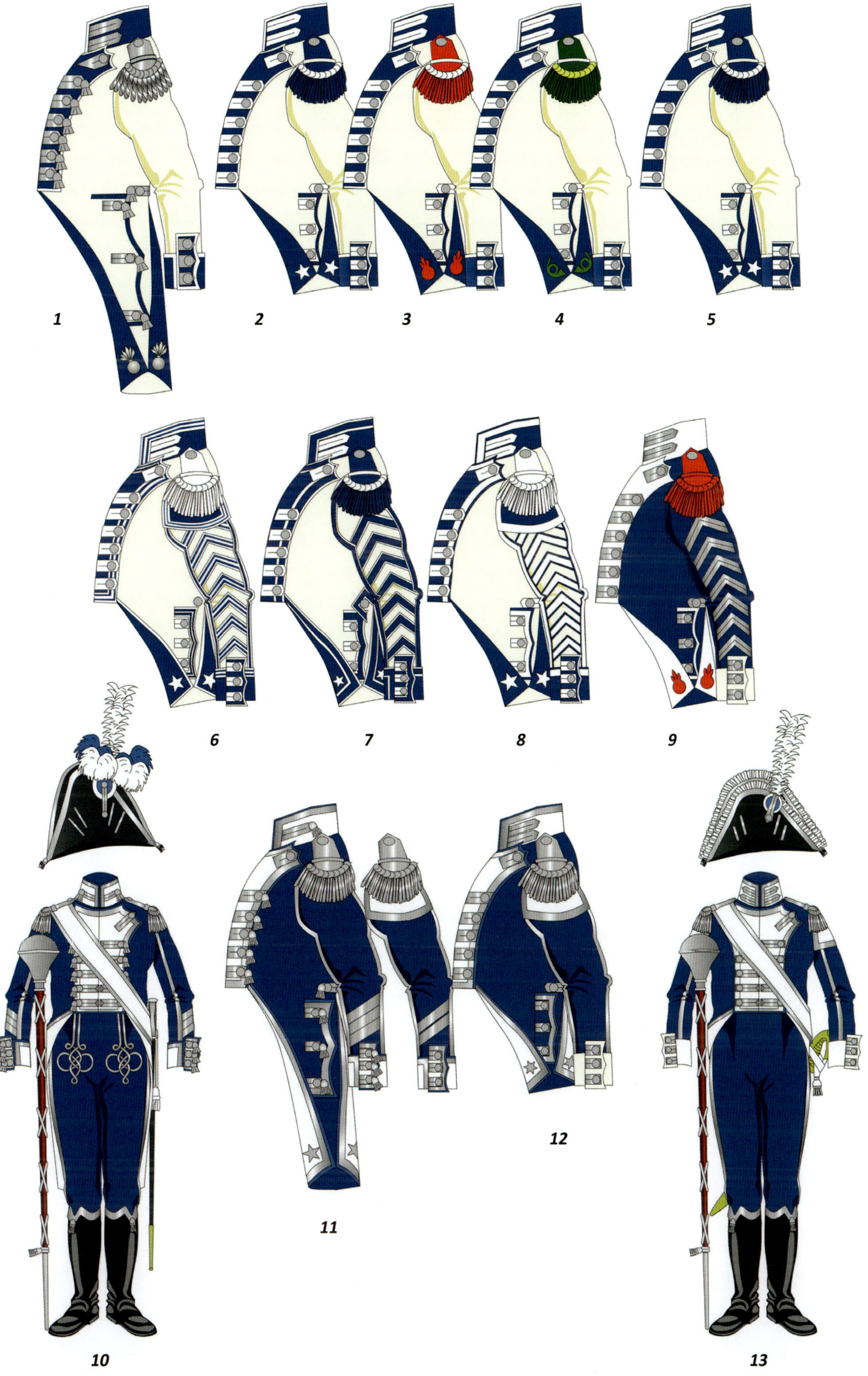
1
2
3
4
5
6
7
8
9
10
11
12
13

Fusilier, 1813
Watercolor by H. Boisselier from *Papiersoldaten* Kassel, Musée de la figurine historique, Compiègne.

Field (Undress) Uniform, 1812–1813

1: Officer in full dress uniform; **2:** officer in redingote; **3:** officer in field uniform; **4:** officer in undress uniform **5:** sapper; **6:** grenadier in field uniform; **7:** fusilier in the greatcoat; **8:** fusilier in fatigue uniform, 1812; **9:** fusilier in fatigue uniform, 1813.

Sources: 1, 2, 5, 7, 9 – from W. Hewig, Brauer-Bogen Nos. 188-189; 3, 6 – from A. Wilke, Mölkerbastei September 1951; 4, 8 – from H. Knötel's patterns, WGM.

1 2 3 4 5

Officer of the grenadiers, Königin Regiment
Pinhas, Salomon: *Recueil de planches représentant les troupes des différentes armes et grades de l'armée Westphalienne*, 1811–1813, privately owned.

Sergeant major of the grenadiers, Königin Regiment
Pinhas, Salomon: *Recueil de planches représentant les troupes des différentes armes et grades de l'armée Westphalienne*, 1811–1813, privately owned.

Colonel Brincard 1813
Watercolor by Orlando Norie, collection of Paul Meganck.

GUARD HUSSAR REGIMENT
(JÉRÔME-HUSAREN)

ESTABLISHMENT

Starting mid-1813, King Jérôme no longer felt safe in his capital Kassel. He asked his brother Napoleon for a French regiment to serve as his personal bodyguard.
With a decree of 31 July 1813, Napoleon transferred a hussar regiment to Jérôme that was assigned to the Westphalian Guard on 6 August.
The unit was composed of men contributed from all the depots of the French cavalry regiments and of recruits from the Lorraine and Italian Departments.
The first parts of the regiment were already arriving in Kassel at the beginning of August. The soldiers were only poorly equipped, not provided uniforms, and not mounted.
Horses had to be obtained from the Guard Chevaulegers' remount depots (*remonte-depots*) as well as the two disbanded hussar regiments.
The garrison was Kassel.
The regiment was sworn in to protect both King Jérôme and Napoleon.

STRENGTH

The regiment had the structure of the Line hussar regiments with four squadrons each of two companies, these each with a theoretical strength of 75 men. The squadrons were gradually formed. Starting the middle of September a depot with two companies was supposed to be formed. As a whole, during the regiment's brief existence, it was constantly undermanned.
The first company of the first squadron provided the elite company.

COMMANDERS

Colonel Brincard (from the French 4th Regiment Lancers);
starting 3 September 1813: Major Schwetz; **after 25 October 1813**: Major d´Arbeuil

ACTIONS

1813:
3 to 29 September: **The** 1st squadron, together with a squadron of chevaulegers and a jaeger-carabiniers company under General Zandt was sent in the direction of Celle in order to intercept roving Allied corps. Subsequently these forces moved to Gottingen to secure the area around there.
27 to 30 September: During the first defense of Kassel against General Czernicheff's forces the regiment lost two companies: The 8th company was captured and the 10th was surprised and destroyed in its quarters by Russian forces. King Jérôme fled from the capital with a part of his Guard, also among them a large number of Guard Hussars with horses.
7 October: The King returned to Kassel with the Guard Hussars.
27 October: During the final flight from Westphalia two companies accompany King Jérôme to Coblenz. The remainder of the regiments appears to have deserted.
The 3rd company followed him via Cologne to Aachen and provided the guard force there until the 3 December continued journey to France.
January 1814: The privates who were still present formed the core of the French Army's 13th Hussar Regiment that was newly created in Maastricht.
On 24 March 1814 this regiment was almost completely destroyed in the Battle of Frere-Champenoise. The remnants were taken into the French 5th Lancer Regiment.

UNIFORMS

Guard-Hussars in stable dress and in greatcoat
Albert Lerouix, L´armée westphalienne, series, Anne S.K. Brown Military Collection, Brown University Library.

On 5 August 1813, one day before the regiment's incorporation into the Westphalian Guard, the order regarding the uniform was issued: completely medium blue (French: *blue westphalien*) hussar uniform with yellow cording and a red shako. But due to the inadequate supplies of medium blue cloth a somewhat modified uniform was introduced.

At the end of August 1813 according to the Commander, Brincard, only the 1st Squadron was completely uniformed, equipped and armed. The 2nd Squadron wore only the undress uniform (waistcoat and riding pants), was but otherwise equipped and armed. Uniforms and equipment were expected for the 3rd and 4th Squadrons. It is not known to what extent this could actually be carried out in the course of September.

An eyewitness (Colonel Johann von Borcke) reported about the regiment's appearance:

"It remained in the process of creation, incomplete and unequipped, until the last moment. It was splendid but only partly uniformed; not only the half and poorly, without saddles, only mounted on blankets and with bridles, the men were pitiful riders because they were cobbled together from all branches and mixed with convalescents and suspended vagabonds. The regiment played a sad role, made the Kassel residents laugh, and disbanded as was its due."[1]

1 *"Es blieb bis zum letzten Augenblick in Bildung begriffen, unvollzählig and unausgerüstet. Es war prachtvoll aber nur teilweise uniformiert; nicht zur Hälfte und schlecht, ohne Sättel, nur auf Decke and Trense beritten, die Leute waren erbärmliche Reiter, da sie aus allen Waffengattungen zusammengestoppelt und mit Rekonvaleszenten und eingestellten Vagabunden vermischt waren. Das regiment spielte eine traurige Rolle, gab den Kasslern lachen und löste sich, als es galt, auf."*

PRIVATES

Headgear: The headgear consisted of a shako covered with red cloth. The upper shako band and cording were yellow. Pompoms were in the company colors and the plume was white.

The plate is depicted in several variations: Rhombus-shaped with the initials "JN" with a crown above it or shield-shaped with crowned initials.

The elite company wore a red plume on the shako to distinguish it from the other companies.

It is possible that the 3rd and 4th squadrons, which were never completely equipped, wore the shakos made of black felt with leather reinforcing and red cording and white plume.

For field duty the plume and cording were removed, and often a linen or waxed cloth cover was worn over the shako's body.

Dolman: Red dolman with blue cuffs and yellow cording. Red cuffs are also known to have existed. Red hussar sash with white and blue mixed knots.

The regiment soon got the nickname "*die Krebse*" ("the Crabs") because of the red dolmans and shakos.

Pelisse: Medium blue pelisse with yellow cording and white fur trim.

In the regiment's final phase a red pelisse with black fur trim was also approved. Which companies were actually clothed with it is unknown.

It is known that the individual squadrons had varying states of uniforms. For example, in October Colonel Brincard, the commander, confirmed that the 1st Squadron was completely armed and equipped, and only the dolman was worn in the field.

The 2nd Squadron was only equipped with blue vests and partially with greatcoats.

Private's dolman, September 1813
Schloß Friedrichstein (Bad Wildungen). Museumslandschaft Kassel.

Hussar in field uniform without pelisse, 1813
Watercolor by H. Neumann,
collection of Paul Meganck.

The companies that were raised later were already issued the red dolman.

The waist sash was red and interwoven with white and medium blue.

The single-breasted waistcoat and trousers with red stripes on the sides were worn for stable duty. The planned medium blue basic color was possibly replaced with dark blue at some point. As headgear the forage cap model *Pokalem* made of blue cloth with red piping.

Trousers: The pants in medium blue with yellow Hungarian knotting.

Dark blue or dark grey overalls with black leather inserts and red stripes on the side, often with one row of buttons, were worn in the field.

Greatcoat: **grey** cavalry greatcoat with cape over the shoulders.

Armament and equipment: The bandoliers were made of pale yellow or also white leather and had a rectangular badge with the "JN" monogram at chest level. As armament light cavalry saber, carbine and pistols.

For the sabretache there were a series of variations in the sources.

Saddlecloth: The shabraque consisted of a white fleece with blue wolves teeth trim. The valise/greatcoat roll was blue with yellow trim around the outside. The horse furniture was made of black leather.

NCOs

Wore light cavalry rank insignia on the sleeves of their uniforms.

TRUMPETERS

Headgear: Shako like for privates, the plume was white with a medium blue tip.

Dolman and Pelisse: White dolman with yellow cording and medium blue collar and cuffs piped with yellow. White pelisse with black fur trim. The sash blue with yellow buttons.

For garrisons and work duties they wore a white waistcoat without facings.

Trousers: Red pants with yellow Hungarian knotting.

Equipment: White and blue trumpet cords.

Saddlecloth: Black fleece blanket with medium blue wolves teeth.

Guard Hussar Regiment – Jérôme-Hussars, Dress Uniform

1: Staff officer, Colonel Brincard, August 1813; **2:** company-grade officer, captain *(Rittmeister/capitaine)*; **3:** trumpeter; **4:** hussar, center company.

Sources: 1 – Per O. Norie; 2 – from Rigondaud, Albert and Charrie; Pierre, plate U 37; 3 – from C. Brun and Colonel Titeux; 4 – from W. Hewig.

1
2
3
4

OFFICERS

The officers' uniform was the same as for the other troops but made from better quality cloth. All the trim, buttons and cording were gilt. The sash was red with golden buttons. The ranks were recognizable by the number of laces on the dolman's cuffs, on the pelisse sleeves and by the trim of the pants. The number and width of the laces were according to the rank.

Undress Uniform (*Interimsmontur*): For daily duty, the officers wore a blue or red "*interim*" (undress) pelisse *(Interims-Pelisse)*. On the chest were five rows of yellow cording each with three buttons. The fur trim was black or white. With it they wore long blue pants with yellow stripes on the sides.

Armament and equipment: For the dress uniform the sabretache was medium blue with a gilt border and initials. For daily use the sabretache was made of black leather with brass badges.

The suspension for the saber and the cartouche bandolier were completely gilt or made of red leather with gold edging. It had a shield-shaped badge with a small chain or a rectangular shield with the royal monogram at chest level.

Saddlecloth: Staff officers had a pointed red cloth shabraque with gold bordering and initials in the corners. The company-grade officers had medium blue shabraques, also with gilt bordering.

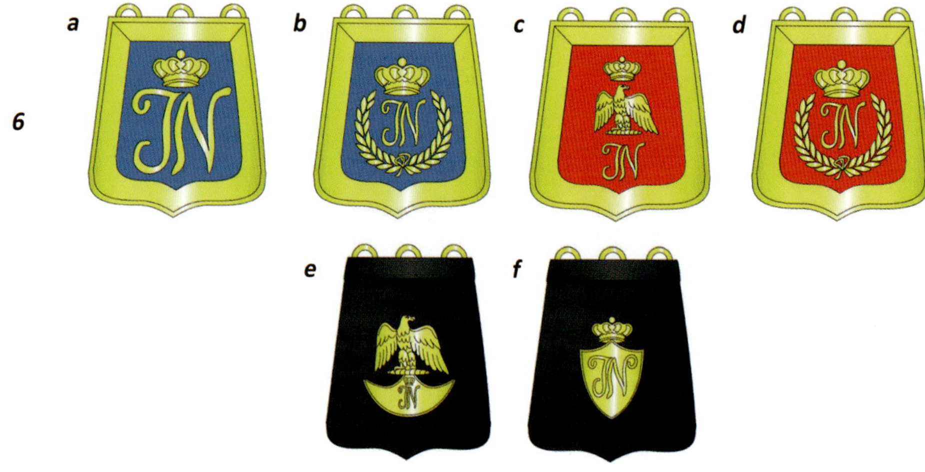

Hussar Regiment of the Guard – Jérôme-Hussars, Dress Uniform

1: Hussar, projected uniform of August 1813; **2:** company-grade officer, captain *(Rittmeister/capitaine);* **3:** trumpeter; **4:** NCO (Brigadier); **5:** hussar der elite company (red plume distinction), September 1813; **6:** sabretache variations – **a:** officers, **b:** trumpeter, **c:** hussars, **d:** variations for trumpeter, **e and f:** undress model for field duty; **7:** projected dolman; **8:** dolman according to the decree of August 1813; **9:** dolman from September to October 1813.

Sources: 1, 4 – from Cdt. Bucquoy; 2 – from Rigondaud, Albert and Charrie; Pierre; 3 – from Charles Brun; 5 – from Cdt. Dupry; 6 – from W. Hewig and Dr. Klietmann; 7 – reconstruction from W. Hewig.

1 2 3 4 5

Officer, trumpeter and hussar
Albert Leroux, Serie: *L'armée westphalienne*,
Anne S.K. Brown Military Collection, Brown University Library.

Hussar Regiment of the Guard – Jérôme Hussars, Undress, Field and Dress Uniforms

1: Hussar, starting August 1813; **2:** hussar in the red dolman without pelisse, 1813 until the beginning of 1814; **3:** hussar, stable dress; **4:** officer in undress dolman, September 1813 variant; **5:** officer (major) full dress uniform; **6:** officer in undress pelisse, first version August 1813; **7:** trumpeter, sleeved vest; **8:** hussar, sleeved vest; **9:** hussar in the greatcoat.

Sources: 1, 4, 6, 7, 8 – from W. Hewig; 2, 9 – from R. Darbou and H. Boisselier; 3, 5 – from Cdt. Bucqouy.

1
2
3
4
5

6
7
8
9

Chasseur Carabinier, 1811–1813
Pinhas, Salomon: *Recueil de planches représentant les troupes des différentes armes et grades de l'armée Westphalienne*, 1811–1813, privately owned.

JAEGER CARABINIERS *(JÄGER-CARABINIERS)*

The battalion was formed by the Decree of 13 April 1808 and was supposed to be composed on gamekeepers, trained riflemen and sons of foresters of the royal properties. The unit did not belong to the Guard but was only attached to it. However it took part in the Guard's actions in all the campaigns from 1809 to 1813.

The battalion represented a kind of forestry school (*Försterschule*). After two years of service in the unit the soldiers were granted the right to a position with the Royal Forestry Directorate (*königlichen Forstdirektion*). The actual service consisted of monitoring the forest properties and the detection and arrest of poachers and above all of deserters. The garrison was Marburg.

The battalion's four companies were filled in December 1808. The total strength was 424 men. In 1809 a fifth company was raised. By the middle of 1811 the unit had grown to 843 men in six companies. And by the end of 1811 the battalion reached its highest manning with 28 officers and 975 men.

From 1810 to 1812 there was also a band of 28 musicians with a drum major.

King Jérôme formed a so-called 'hunting company' (*"Compagnie de Chasse"/"Jagdkompanie"*) from the most reliable and best shooters. It was the 1st company and formed an elite within the battalion (source: *Minerva* 12/1845).

When the entire battalion was granted the *"d'élite"* status around 1812, the 1st company lost its special status (source: W. Hewig).

After the losses in the Russian campaign the battalion was raised again in 1813 with a strength of four companies with 424 men. After this point in time the unit was only supposed to be employed inside the national borders. Due to a shortage of suitable applicants drafted recruits also had to be inducted. In September 1813 the entire battalion still only numbered 103 men.

ORGANIZATION

(Per Decrees of 13 April 1808 and 5 March 1813)

Battalion Staff (6 men)	**Subordinate staff** (6 men)	**Company** (103 men)
1 Battalion Commander *(Chef de Bataillon)* 1 *Capitaine d'habillement* 1 Quartermaster *(Quartiermeister)* 1 Senior Adjutant *(Adjutant-major)* 1 Senior Surgeon *(Chirugien-major)* 1 Surgeons' Senior Aid *(Chirugien-aide-major)*	2 Adjutant-sous-officiers 1 Senior Bugler *(Cornet-major/Stabshornist)* 1 Armorer *(Maitre armurier/Büchsenmacher)* 1 Tailor *(Maitre tailleur/Schneider)* 1 Shoemaker *(Maitre cordonnier/Schuster)*	1 Captain *(Capitaine)* 1 Lieutenant 1 Sub Lieutenant *(Sous-Lieutenant)* 1 Sergeant Major 4 Sergeants 1 *Fourier* 6 Caporals 2 Buglers *(cornets/Hornisten)* 86 Carabiniers (jaegers, certainly also sappers)

COMMANDERS

1808: Chef de Bataillon von Füllgraf, **1809**: Colonel von Dörnberg, **1810**: Colonel Prinz v. Hessen-Philippsthal, **1810**: Major Bergeron, **1810**: *Chef de Bataillon* von Rauschenplatt, **1812**: Major Müldner, **1813**: *Chef de Bataillon* von Hessberg

ACTIONS

1809 Originally intended for the operation in Spain, but the battalion was ordered by King Jérôme to go from Metz back to the homeland.
Campaign in Saxony with the 1st Guard Division.
1812 Russian Campaign with the 27th Westphalian Division in the 1st Brigade with 700 men (1st company and the depot remained in the homeland),
17-18 August: Battle of Smolensk
19 August: the Battle of Valutina-Gora
7 September: the Battle of Borodino
By November, wiped out during the retreat.
1813 September: Active in Westphalia during the fighting to defend Kassel; after two companies deserted the remainder of the unit disbanded on 29 September.

UNIFORMS

A first uniform is only confirmed by the Decree of 13 April 1808, Article 5. It seems it was never introduced, as contemporary sources for 1808 (Manuscript of Samuel Hahlo and the memoirs of Götting) show another uniform already for 1808.

The projected Uniform should have consisted of a shako with hunting horn-emblem, green coat with lapels as the dress uniform and single-breasted coat as the undress uniform; the facings were black; the metal buttons white; green pants; black leather belting; artillery saber and rifle.

1808–1811

PRIVATES

Headgear: Shako with mixed red and green cording (completely red according to Weiland) and dark green plume with a red tip. Plume on top of a green spherical pompom (per Weiland) or a disk-shaped pompom in green with red Roman numeral company number (per Hahlo). The pompom's color probably reflected to which company it belonged. (See chapter on Infantry). The national cockade was fixed with a red loop. A brass hunting horn-emblem in the front. Brass chin-scales and visor edging.
Green forage cap with red piping and a yellow hunting horn emblem in the front.
Coat: Green coat with black collar and cuffs. Deviating from the other sources, Weiland shows pointed instead of the straight cuffs. Shoulder straps and the turnbacks on the short coattails are green. Everything piped red. Red grenade emblems on the turnbacks. The coat was closed with one row of nine yellow metal buttons. A hunting horn and the royal initials JN were stamped on the buttons.
Green, single-breasted waistcoat with black collar and cuffs.
Trousers: Green pants with red, Hungarian knotting and piping on the sides. Short gaiters with red piping.
Long white or grey trousers were worn for inside duty and in the field.
Greatcoat: Of greyish brown cloth with two rows of buttons that were covered in colored cloth.
Equipment and armament: Black leather belting. Instead of a backpack, a grey sealskin hunting bag (*Jagdtasche*) was worn on a shoulder bandolier. The cartridge pouch for 20 cartridges was also stored In this bag.
Armament was a rifle. The powder horn was attached with a red and green (red according to Weiland) cord, on whose end were two tassels.
Additional armament was a large hunting knife (*Hirschfänger*) with a brass grip. It could also be attached to the rifle as a bayonet.

NCOs

The NCOs' rank insignia followed the French pattern and was in the button color of yellow or gold. All NCOs were armed with rifles and hunting knives *(Hirschfänger).*

Colonel Commandant of the Chasseurs Carabiniers
Sauerweid, Alexander Iwanowitsch: *Uniformen der Königlich Westphälischen Armee*, Dresden 1810.

Metal Devices

1: Bandelier-badge Model 1811; **2:** shako plate Model 1811; **3:** gorget starting 1811; **4:** gorget Model 1808–1811; **5:** gorget variation with the royal monogram, 1808 until 1811, probably during the period as a hunting company; **6:** button for privates.

Sources: 1 and 2, 6 – from an original pieces excavated in Russia 2013; 3 to 5 – -from W. Hewig's patterns, WGM.

Jaeger Carabiniers (Projected Uniform), 1808

1: company-grade officer; **2, 3:** jaegers in field uniform (undress uniform); **4:** Chef de Bataillon in Jaeger Carabiniers undress uniform

Jaeger Carabiniers, 1808 until 1811

5: Company-grade officer in dress uniform; **6:** bugler/cornet, only identifiable as a signaler by the gold braid on the shako; **7, 8:** jaegers in dress uniform; **9:** jaeger in field uniform with white (summer-) overalls.

Sources: 1, 2, 3, 4 – from Decree of 13 April 1808 and from H. Knötel's patterns in WGM;
5, 6 – from S. Pinhas; 7, 8, 9 – reconstructions and Minerva magazine, December 1840.

1
2
3
4
5
6
7
8
9

BUGLERS/CORNETS

Buglers wore the privates' uniform. According to S. Pinhas they were only distinguished by a red plume and a gold braid on the shako. The horn's cords and tassels were red and green mixed.

OFFICERS

Headgear: Shako with golden decorations and cording. The bicorn was also worn for daily duty and in the field.
Coat: Green coat with long coattails. The black facings were made of velvet. Gilt epaulets as rank insignia. On duty a gilt gorget with silvered eagle emblem in the middle was worn.
A green surtout was worn for the undress uniform. For this the collar and cuffs could have been black or green. According to a contemporary portrait, the officers also wore a coat with lapels, open at the bottom, as a dress uniform. The lapels were in the coat's color and piped red. Gilet white. The knee-length pants with silk stockings also white. Black shoes with buckles.
Trousers: Green pants with more or less elaborated gold braid decorations according to rank. Hungarian boots with gilt trim and tassel.
Green trousers with golden or grey trousers with green stripes on the sides were also worn for the undress uniform or in the field.
Greatcoat: The *Überrock* (redingote, overcoat) was made of dark green cloth with black, turned back collar and red piping, and had two rows of gilt buttons. The epaulets were attached. In the field the overcoat often was rolled and put over the left shoulder.
Grey or green greatcoats like for the privates are depicted also.
Armament: The saber with gilt *portepée* was carried on the black leather shoulder bandolier. A gilt, shield-shaped badge was attached to the front of the bandolier. The sword for daily duty was suspended on the black-leather waist belt.
Saddlecloth: The mounted staff officers' rectangular shabraques were made of green cloth with golden braid trim.

Carabiniers 1808
Copy by W. Hewig from *Manuscrit du Canonnier Hahlo*, 1807/08.
Collection of Edmund Wagner.

Royal Westphalian Jaeger Carabinier
Weiland, C. F.: *Représentation des uniformes de l´armée impériale royale française et des alliés,* Weimar, 1807 and 1812.

Elite Company

The 1st company wore bearskin caps with visors, cording and a plume instead of shakos like the other companies. As elite unit distinctions they had two red laces on the collar and the cuffs, as well as light green fringed epaulets with red crescents. The laces were in gold for the NCOs and officers.

As headgear the buglers wore the colpak/busby with red plume and pompom and green cap bag piped with red. The breast of the coat was decorated with golden laces. The officers wore the bearskin hat but also the colpak/busby as headgear. Herbert Knötel shows an officer in a parade coat with broad golden lace trim on the chest.

Pair of epaulets of the Jaeger-Carabiniers d'élite, 1811–1813
Schloß Friedrichstein (Bad Wildungen), Museumslandschaft Hessen-Kassel.

Jaeger Carabiniers Elite Company, 1808–1811

1: Officer in dress uniform, instead of the tall fur cap, the busby was often used as headgear; **2:** bugler/*cornet* in dress uniform; **3:** sergeant major; **4, 5:** jaeger carabinier; **6:** jaeger, 1809, variation from Weiland with pointed cuffs; **7:** variation of a company-grade officers with fur cap; **8:** company-grade officer in field uniform; **9:** jaeger-carabinier in field uniform, starting 1811, with backpack.

Sources: 1-5, 7 – from H. Knötel's patterns and Westphälische Studie, WGM; 6 – from C. F. Weiland, 1809 edition; 8 – from H. Boisselier; 9 – reconstruction from information from Braunschweigisches Magazin, July 1845.

1 *2* *3* *4* *5*

6 *7* *8* *9*

1811–1813

The entire battalion received elite status and the difference between the first and other companies were eliminated.

The following changes to the uniform went into effect:

Headgear: Shako for all ranks had the new brass plate that bore the inscription: "CHASS^{R} CARABIN^{RS} D´ELITE." For 1811, Pinhas - the only source - shows an additional yellow pompom on the green spherical pompom topped by the plume. Probably the yellow pompom served as a company distinction?

In 1813 a new *Pokalem* type forage cap with a flat round top was introduced.

Coat: All companies received red laces (gold for NCOs and officers) on the collar and cuffs and the light green epaulets for decoration. Red laces were also added as backing on the buttons.

According to Herbert Knötel the buglers received golden lace trim on the chest, collar and cuffs.

The waistcoat received green collar and cuffs (Knötel).

Equipment: In 1811 a brown calfskin backpack of the usual pattern of the period replaced the grey hunting bag and a cartridge box with hunting horn-badge was introduced. The cartridge box and hunting knife (*Hirschfänger*) were worn on the crossed bandoleers. The cartridge box-bandoleer had a shield-shaped brass badge.

SAPPERS

Tall bearskin cap as headgear, white leather apron and gauntlets.

As armament sapper's (*Zimmermann*'s) saber and carbine. A belt made of black leather with two holsters for pistols was worn around the waist. Sappers hatchet.

Officer and rifleman, Chasseurs Carabiniers
Untitled manuscript in
Anne S.K. Brown Military Collection,
Brown University Library.

Heads of Column and Elite Jaeger Carabiniers, 1811–1813

1: Musician (*Hautboist*/oboist) 1812; **2:** drum major in dress uniform 1812; **3:** *chef de bataillon* in dress uniform, 1812; **4:** company-grade officer, dress uniform; **5:** bugler/*cornet*, 1812; **6:** sergeant major; **7, 8:** elite jaeger carabiniers.

Sources: 1 and 2 – from F. Kieffer' Strasbourg paper soldier collection;
3, 5, 6, 8 – from H. Knötel and R. Forthoffer's patterns and sketches in the estate in WGM; 4 and 7 – from S. Pinhas.

1
2
3
4
5
6
7
8

MUSICIANS

There is no contemporary evidence for the *Téte de Colonne*. The "Collection Kiefer" of paper soldiers, Strasbourg, presents a number of possible types that are depicted here.

DRUM MAJOR

Colpak/busby with gilt cording and red bag, green ostrich feathers, green plume with a red tip.
Green coat with lapels with long coattails. Lapels red; collar green; white vest; green pants. All parts of the uniform were richly trimmed with golden laces. Golden epaulets.
Black gauntlets with wide gilt trim on the cuffs. The drum major's baton had silver cords.

MUSICIANS *(HAUTBOIST)*

They wore the privates's uniform with following distinctions: golden lace trim on the collar, cuffs and pants; golden trefoil (*Trèfle*) epaulets; sword on the waist belt.
Chef de musique: Musician's uniform with doubled lace trim on the collar; rank insignia of a sergeant major on the sleeves.

Elite jaeger carabinier bugler, 1808–1811
Watercolor by Herbert Knötel,
Col. Elting collection, Anne S.K. Brown Military Collection, Brown University Library.

Coat Patterns from 1808 to 1811, and Officers and Sapper

1: Coat pattern for privates, dress uniform, 1808; **2:** coat pattern for privates's undress uniform, 1808; **3:** coat pattern privates, 1808–1809; **4:** coat pattern for the elite company, 1808–1813; **5:** coat pattern for buglers; **6:** coat pattern for officers; **7:** officer in full dress uniform/walking out dress; **8:** officer in redingote; **9:** sapper, 1810; **10:** company-grade officer in field/undress uniform, 1812; **11:** jaeger in fatigue uniform.

Sources: 1 to 6 – from H. Knötel's patterns, WGM; 7 – from a contemporary. portrait, former collection of Maitland; 8 – from R. Darbou; 9 – from F. Kieffer's Strasbourg paper soldier collection; 9 and 10 – from H. Knötel, Todd's watercolor collection and patterns in WGM.

1
2
3
4
5
6
7
8
9
10
11

Officer in dress uniform, 1810
Weiland, C. F.: *Représentation des uniformes de l' armée impériale royale française et des alliés*, Weimar, 1807 and 1812.

GUARD ARTILLERY COMPANIES

MOUNTED COMPANY *(BERITTENE KOMPANIE)*

When the Artillery Regiment was created in 1808, the mounted company was detached, together with a train company, to the Guard. The Guard status was not definitively applied until 1812, nevertheless the unit often is titled the Mounted Guard Artillery (*Garde-Artillerie zu Pferde*) for the whole period. Until 1813 the personal and the ordnance were subordinated to the Administration of the Grenadier Guards. The company was the only unit of artillery that was always organized as a battery. That means it was equipped with cannon and horse teams all the time. The garrison was Kassel.

STRUCTURE

The structure corresponded to the one of the line companies (1812-1813)

1 Captain
1 *Kapitän en second* (second captain)
1 *Premier-Leutnant* (first lieutenant)
1 *Seconde-Leutnant* (second lieutenant)
1 *Wachtmeister/maréchal des logis chef* (sergeant major)
3 *Sergeanten* (*maréchal des logis*) (sergeants)
1 *Fourier* (senior corporal)
3 *Korporale/brigadier* (corporals)
2 Trumpeters
1 *Feuerwerker/Artificier* (artillery sergeant)
30 *Ober-Kanoniere/canoniers 1ere classe* (gunner 1st class)
45 *Kanoniere/canoniers 2ème classe* (gunner 2nd class)
2 *Handwerker (Sattler)* (saddlers)

Total strength: 92 men

In 1810 the strength was increased by two officers and 92 men and by the middle of 1812 by another 4 officers with 110 gunners with 113 horses. After the annihilation in Russia in 1812 a reorganization was ordered with an additional foot company.
After 6 August 1813 the formation of a foot battery in Kassel was ordered. It was supposed to be part of the guard. The strength was 3 officers, 14 NCOs and 87 gunners with six 6-pounder guns.

ORDNANCE

The battery consisted of four 6-pounder cannons, Model 1808 Allix, and two 7-pounder howitzers, Model 1808. They were supplemented with twelve ammunition wagons and a forge. About 1809 the number of guns was raised to eight. All the cannon were lost during the 1812 campaign in Russia.

COMMANDERS

1808: Unknown, **1810**: Captain Kersting, **1812**: Captain Grüning, then Captain Lemaître, then Captain Brünig

Officer – captain, Guard Horse Artillery, 1810
Sauerweid, Alexander Iwanowitsch: *Uniformen der Königlich Westphälischen Armee,* 1810.

Gunner, Guard Horse Artillery, 1810
Sauerweid, Alexander Iwanowitsch: *Uniformen der Königlich Westphälischen Armee,* 1810.

ACTIONS

1809 – Campaign in Saxony
With the 1st Guard Brigade of the 1st Division (X Army Corps)

1812 - Campaign in Russia
With the VIII Army Corps. Until July with the Guard Cavalry Brigade, after the 21 July transferred to 24th Light Cavalry Division (General von Hammerstein). On 23 August the battery counted 5 officers and 167 privates with 192 horses.
In the course of the campaign the entire unit perished. On 9 November all the cannon had to be abandoned due to severely icy conditions.

***Maréchal des logis*, Guard Horse Artillery, 1811**
Pinhas, Salomon: *Recueil de planches représentant les troupes des différentes armes et grades de l'armée Westphalienne,* 1811.

Guard Mounted Artillery Company, Dress Uniforms, 1808–1810

1: Officer (lieutenant); **2:** gunner; **3:** gunner in undress uniform; **4:** officer; **5:** trumpeter variation as staff trumpeter; **6:** trumpeter; **7:** NCO – *maréchal des logis*; **8:** gunner.

Sources: 1, 4 – from C. F. Weiland 1809 and A. Sauerweid 1810; 2, 3, 6, 7, 8 – reconstructions based on the patterns in H. Knötel's estate in WGM and W. Hewig; 5 – from R. Forthoffer's information and H. Knötel's sketch.

1
2
3
4
5
6
7
8

UNIFORMS

1808–1811

The uniforms, their development, as well as the changes after 1811 mainly corresponded to those of the line companies. Being part of the guard was shown by their wearing yellow aiguillettes with the dress uniform.

Particular Uniform Variations

Officer in gala dress *(tenue de société)* 1808–1812 according to W. Hewig
Bicorn with gilt decoration in the front and tassels on the corners. Red pompom (for company officers). The coat was like for the dress uniform with long coattails. Tight white pants with knee-length silk stockings and with buckled shoes. Sword suspended from a waist belt.
Officer in walking dress *(tenue de ville)* 1811 according to R. Forthoffer
Bicorn with red plume.
The coat was the same as the dress uniform, but with lace trim on the collar and the pointed cuffs. Dark blue close-fitting trousers with yellow, v-shaped Hungarian knotting.
Trumpeter 1811 according to R. Forthoffer
Colpak made of black fur with mixed yellow and red cords, and a red pompom topped with a white plume. Red bag with yellow piping.
The coat corresponded to the dress uniform depicted for 1808-1810, but with elaborate gold lace trim. Dark blue epaulets with yellow crescents.

1811–1812

The uniform changes followed those of the line artillery. Additional crimson braids on the collar and on the cuffs were attached to the coat. The yellow aiguillettes continued to worn with the dress uniform
In 1811 the Guard Company got dark blue cloth saddlecloths with red border lace.

1813

The Guard company, projected for 1813, should have worn coats of the 1808 uniform pattern (according to W. Hewig). Available old depot stores could possibly have been used again. The uniform coats should have been decorated with yellow braids on the collar and cuffs. The turnbacks had yellow grenade devices.
Since the mounted Guard company was never actually raised, this uniform never was issued.

Guard Mounted Artillery Company, 1811–1813

1: Officer in dress uniform; **2:** trumpeter; **3:** gunner; **4:** officer in dress uniform; **5:** trumpeter; 6, **7:** gunners; **8:** gunner in projected uniform for 1813.

Sources: 1, 2, 3, 4, 5, 7, 8 – reconstructions based on the patterns in H. Knötel's estate in the WGM; 6 – based on S. Pinhas 1811.

1
2
3
4
5
6
7
8

Guard Mounted Artillery Company Coat Patterns and Officers, 1808–1813

Dress uniform 1808–1811 – 1: company-grade officer; **2:** gunner; **3:** trumpeter, undress uniform until 1811; **4:** gunner; **5:** trumpeter.
Dress uniform 1811–1813 – 6: officer; **7:** gunner; **8:** trumpeter, undress uniform Guard model 1811–1813; **9:** gunner; **10:** trumpeter; **11:** officer in the full dress uniform or tenue de société, 1808–1812; **12:** officer in the city dress *(Stadtanzug/tenue de ville)*, 1811.

Sources: 1, 2 – from A. Sauerweid; reconstructions based on the patterns in H. Knötel's estate in WGM and information from W. Hewig; 11 – from W. Hewig, 12 – from R. Forthoffer

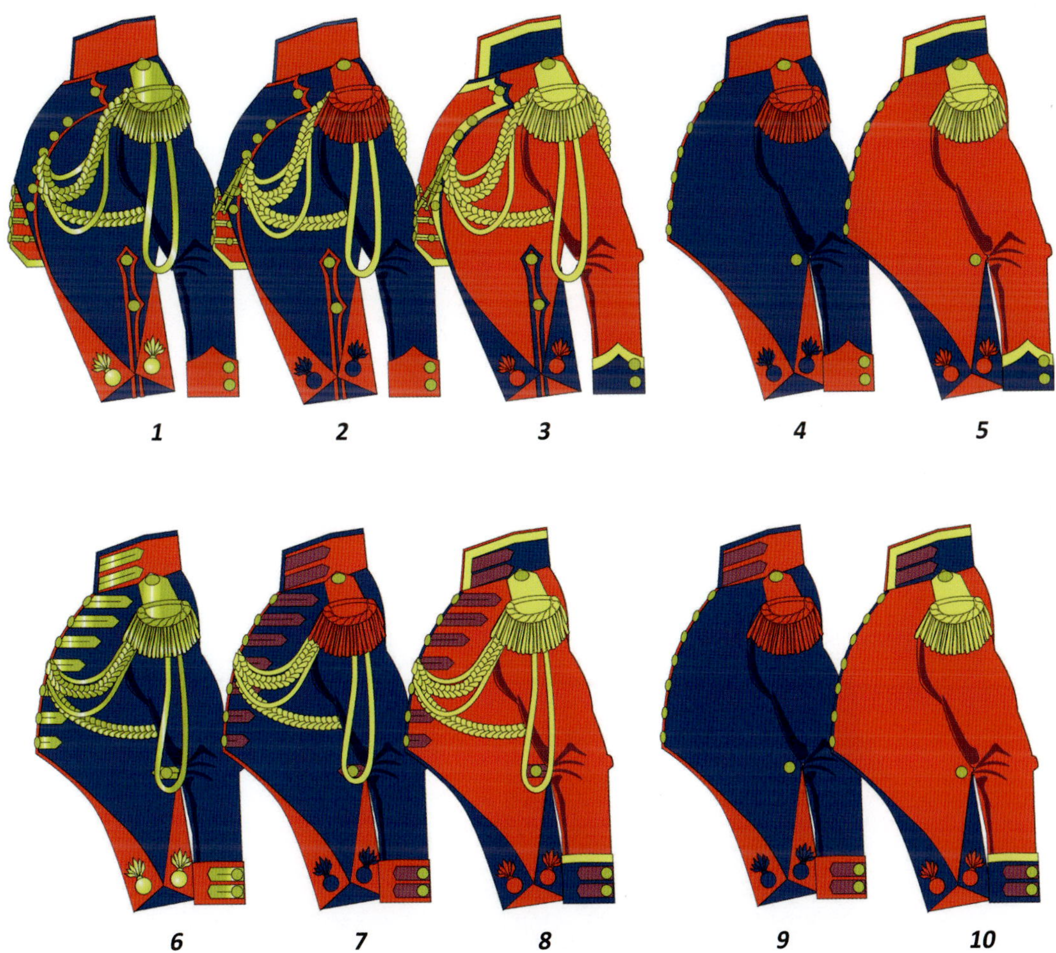
1
2
3
4
5
6
7
8
9
10

1 2 3 4 5 6

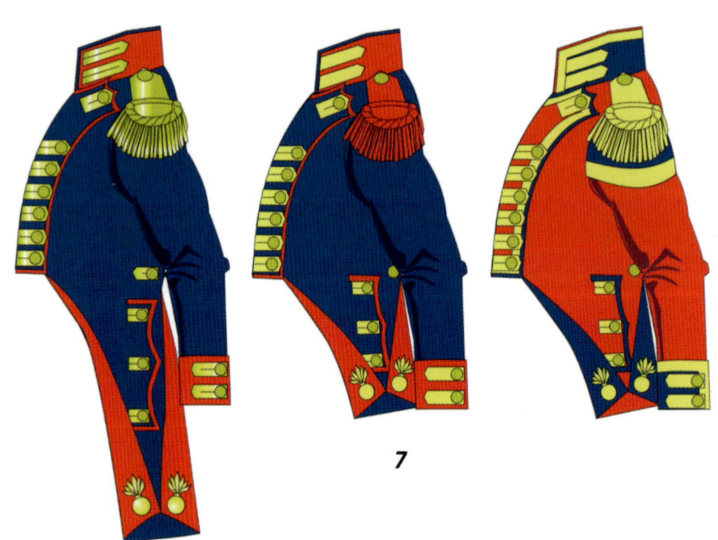

Guard Foot Artillery, 1813

1: Officer – captain in dress uniform; **2:** drummer dress uniform; 3, **4:** artillerymen; **5:** artilleryman in the greatcoat; **6:** artilleryman in garrison and fatigue uniform; **7:** coat patterns for officer, artilleryman, drummer.

Sources: 1–7 – reconstructions based on the patterns in H. Knötel's estate in WGM and information from W. Hewig.

FOOT ARTILLERY COMPANY

(ARTILLERIE KOMPANIE ZU FUSS/COMPANIE D'ARTILLERIE À PIED)

On 6 August 1813, the formation of a Guard Foot Artillery Company on was ordered. The formation was finally carried out and the battery was engaged on 28 September 1813 at the defense of Kassel.
The armament consisted of six 6-pounder cannon.

STRUCTURE

3 officers
14 NCOs
87 Cannoneers

COMMANDERS

1813: Captain Heinemann, then Captain Wille

UNIFORMS

The uniform corresponded to that of one of the line companies but had additional yellow braids on the collar, lapels, cuffs and flaps of the coattail pockets.

Gunner, Foot Artillery of the Royal Guard
1813
Watercolor by Herbert Knötel,, Anne S.K. Brown Military Collection, Brown University Library.

1
2
3
4
5
6
7
8

TRAIN COMPANY OF THE GUARD

Starting in 1810 a train company was permanently attached to the Guard. The company that was newly raised in 1813 provided the horse teams for the Foot Company of the Guard.

UNIFORMS

PRIVATES

Coat: Until 1810 the coat corresponded to that of the line companies. In 1810 the train adopted the light cavalry style dress of the mounted artillery company but of iron grey color with red facings. The buttons were white metal and white grenade ornaments were placed on the coattails. As a guard distinction it had white aiguillettes on the left shoulder.
According to R. Forthoffer additional white guard laces were attached to the collar and the cuffs in 1812. H. Knötel shows the guard company in 1813 wearing the single-breasted coat with crimson lace trim, and the white guard laces on the collar and on the straight cuffs as the dress uniform. Probably the single-breasted coat with the appropriate distinctions was the only coat that was worn at that late period.
The single-breasted coat was also worn for daily duty and in the field. It had a red seam along the buttons in the front. A variant had shoulder straps or epaulets. In the field the aiguillettes were removed.
The waistcoat was grey with red piping like for the line companies. In 1813 it also had laces on the collar and cuffs.
Trousers: The pants were in coat color with red Hungarian knotting and side stripes. For daily duty long grey overalls with leather inserts and red stripes and buttons on the sides. 1813 white Hungarian knotting was added. The stable duty trousers were brownish grey.
Equipment and Armament: Pale yellow leather bandolier over the shoulder with a cartridge pouch with a white metal shield-shaped "JN" plate at chest level on the bandolier. Light cavalry model saber with a pale yellow leather sword strap.
Saddlecloth: Brown leather saddle with a grey blanket on top. For the NCOs a white fleece blanket with red wolves teeth, grey valise/greatcoat roll with red edging.

Train Company of the Guard, 1810–1812

1: Officer, dress uniform; **2:** driver, dress uniform; **3:** driver, undress uniform, field duty; **4:** officer, dress uniform, 1812; **5:** trumpeter, dress uniform, 1812; **6:** driver, dress uniform, 1812; **7:** driver, undress uniform, 1812; **8:** driver, field uniform, 1812.

Sources: 1, 2, 3 ,7, 8 – reconstructions; 4, 5, 6 – from R. Forthoffer and H. Knötel's notes and watercolor in his estate in WGM.

OFFICERS

Headgear: They wore the shako or the bicorn with a red plume and silver trim. Cording was added for the dress uniform.
Coat: Like the privates but with silver trimming. Silver aiguillettes were worn with the dress uniform.
With the reorganization of 1813 only the single-breasted coat with straight cuffs and short coattails was worn.
Equipment: **The** cartridge pouch bandoleer silvered with red leather trim and a badge in the front with royal monogram. Silver *portepée*. Pale yellow leather gauntlets.
Saddlecloth: The grey cloth shabraque with pointed ends was edged in silver and had the royal monogram in the corners.

TRUMPETERS

Headgear: Colpak/busby with a red pompom and white plume. The cording was white and red intermixed. Red busby bag with white piping and tassel.
Coat: in reversed colors, and with additional white border trim distinction on the collar, cuffs and lapels. These were decorated with laces. White epaulets and aiguillette.
Starting in 1813 the single-breasted coat was also in red with light grey distinctions and white laces. On the chest seam were white rectangular laces ending in points to the outside.
Saddlecloth: Black fleece blanket with red wolves teeth.

Train Company of the Guard, 1813

1: Officer, dress uniform; **2:** trumpeter, dress uniform; **3:** NCO, dress uniform; **4:** driver, dress uniform; **5:** driver, undress uniform; **6:** driver, dress uniform, in projected 1813 uniform; **7:** driver in the greatcoat; **8:** driver in fatigue uniform, 1810–1812; **9:** driver, fatigue uniform, 1813.

Sources: 1, 5, 7 – reconstructions; 2, 3, 4 , 6, 8, 9 – from H. Knötel's patterns in his estate in the WGM and watercolor, collection of Col. Elting.

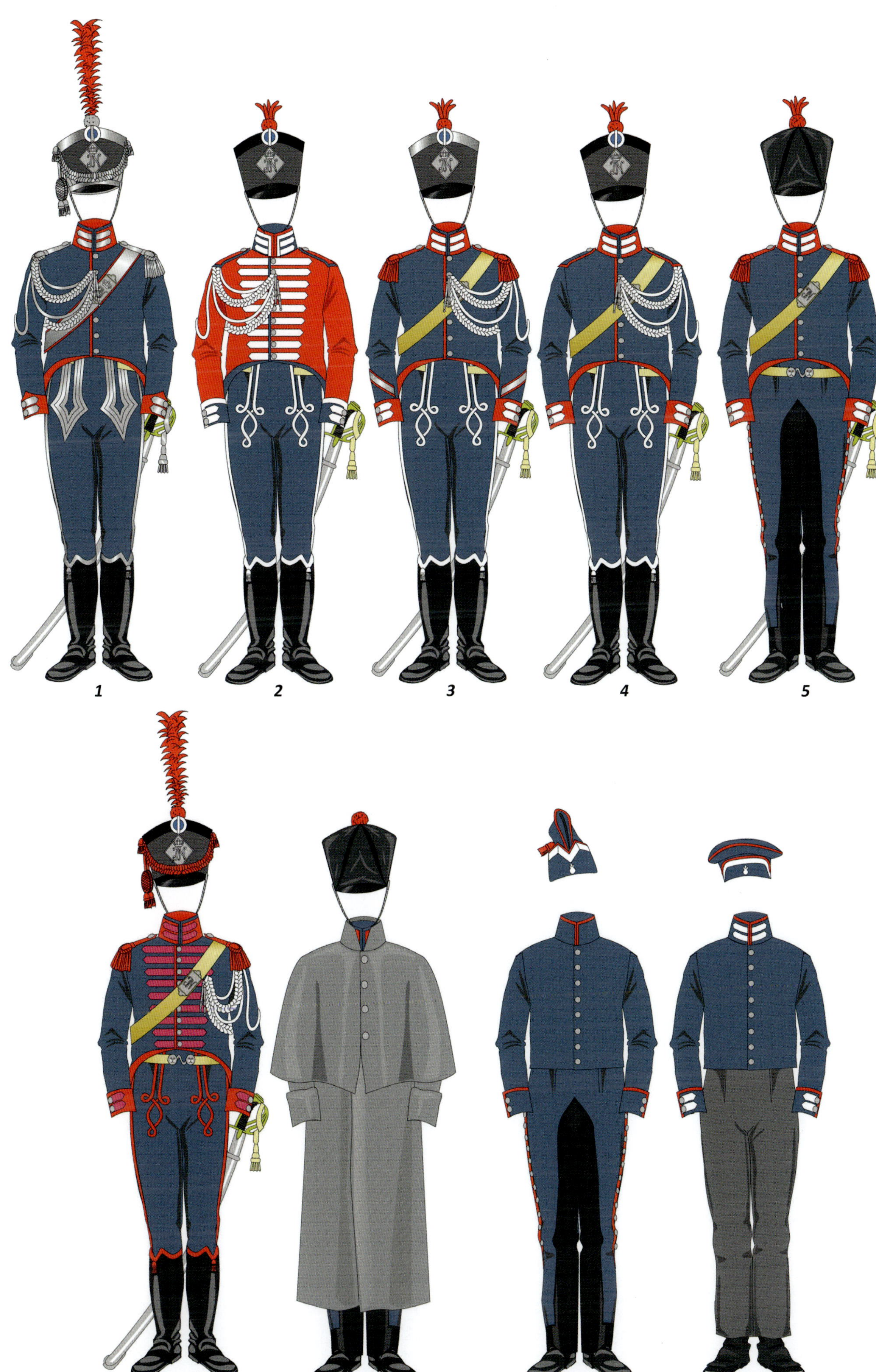
1
2
3
4
5
6
7
8
9

Driver, Guard Train, 1813; projected uniform
Watercolor by Herbert Knötel,
John R. Elting Collection, USA.

Train Company of the Guard 1810–1813 Coat Schemas

Dress uniform 1810 until 1812	**1:** officer; **2:** driver; **3:** trumpeter
Undress uniform until 1812	**4:** driver; **5:** trumpeter
Dress uniform, 1812	**6:** officer; **7:** driver; **8:** trumpeter
Undress uniform, 1812	**9:** driver; **10:** trumpeter
Uniforms, 1813	**11:** officer; **12:** driver with aiguillette; **13:** driver with variation of the epaulets; **14:** trumpeter dress uniform; **15:** driver dress uniform corresponding with Guard Artillery

Sources: 1 to 5, 10 – reconstructions; 6, 7, 8 – from R. Forthoffer's notes; 9, 12, 13, 14 – based on the patterns in H. Knötel's estate in WGM; 15 – from a H. Knötel watercolor, collection of Col. Elting.

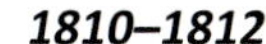

1810–1812

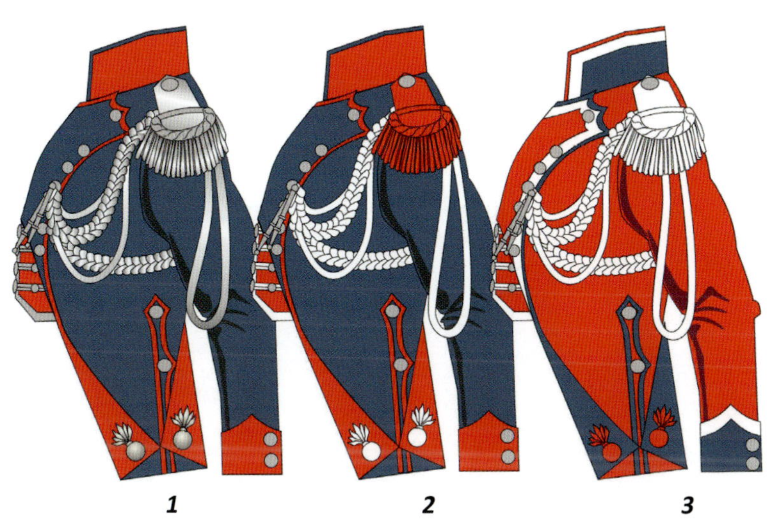

1 2 3 4 5

1812

6 7 8 9 10

1813

11 12 13 14 15

R. Knötel

GENERAL OFFICERS

General Staff of the Guard

General Staff of the Line

Generals

Chief of a General Staff

Staff Officer *(Adjoint)*

Adjutants

Guides of the General Staff

1812: "The bridle, head-stall and uncomfortable gold-plated bit introduced for the Westphalian General Staff was put on the Saxon cavalry horses, which were used to light harnesses, [the horses] bucked and threw off their riders ... the Westphalians did not want to get back on again, but preferred to mount the Polish guides' farm horses, which however appeared, to the great amusement of the onlookers, very adventurous ..."

From: *"Tagebuch des Leutnants von Wolfferdorff"* [The Diary of [Saxon] Lieutenant von Wolfferdorf] in: Baumgarten-Crusius, Die Sachsen 1812 in Russland, 1912.

From left to right:
Orderly officer to the King; adjutant, General Staff of the Guard (mounted); adjutant to a Guard general; major general, Captain General of the Guard (mounted); brigadier general of the Guard; *Revueinspekteur* (Military Administration)
Richard Knötel, *Uniformenkunde Band IV*, plate 7.

Generals' epaulets
Schloss Friedrichstein (Bad Wildungen), Museumslandschaft Hessen-Kassel, photo: Markus Gaertner.

General's shabraque
Schloss Friedrichstein (Bad Wildungen), Museumslandschaft Hessen-Kassel, photo: Markus Gaertner.

GENERAL OFFICERS

At the beginning of the kingdom, to a large extent the generals were comprised of senior French officers to support the stand-up of the army. They had received Napoleon's approval to enter Westphalian service for a specified length of time. Along with these officers, a number of officers who came from disbanded armies (Kurhessen, Hanover) were employed with leadership tasks during the creation of the Kingdom of Westphalia. On the French model there were only two generals ranks, i.e., the major general (*Général de Division*) and the brigadier general (*Général de Brigade*).

The number of active generals changed over the years:

	Generals, total	Major Generals (*Général de Division*)	Brigadier General (*Général de Brigade*)
1808–1809	7	5	2
1810	14	4	10
1812	15	3	12
1813	18	7	11

The generals were named and approved by the king. They usually had no independent commands in the army, but in wartime received changing duties or commanded field units whose compositions were mostly newly established for the campaigns. A portion of the general officer corps was subordinate to the leadership of the Military Divisions (*Militärdivisionen*). These administrative districts were primarily important for organizing and managing the conscription system.

GENERAL STAFF OF THE GUARD

From the major generals, three (in 1813 two) were named as Captain Generals of the Guard (*Generalkapitänen der Garde*). This was not a rank but rather a special function. They were inspectors of the branches of the line units. The Captain General who had duty at a given time carried out his duties in the immediate vicinity of the King. He was simultaneously the commanding general of the Guard under the command of the King and passed along the King's daily orders. Each Captain General was supported by three *Adjutanten* (aides de camp, ADC). They were one *Chef d´escadon*, one captain and one lieutenant.

Two brigadier generals of the Guard (*Brigadegenerale der Garde*) commanded the Guard Infantry and Guard Cavalry.

The General Staff of the Guard was the only staff in the Westphalian Army that was continuously filled. The Chief of Staff was a brigadier general or colonel. He was assigned four *Adjutanten* (captains or lieutenants). Additionally the staff had two officers (*Adjunkten*, *Adjoints*, deputies). They were in the grades of *chef de bataillon/ chef d'escadron* or captain.

The staff personnel were chosen from the entire army, i.e., also from the Line units.

GENERAL STAFF OF THE LINE

In case of war, the major generals or brigadier generals formed the staffs, which they supported in the leadership of their subordinate contingents. The Chief of Staff was assigned a varying number of officers (adjutants).

Major general
Pinhas, Salomon: *Recueil de planches représentant les troupes des différentes armes et grades de l'armée Westphalienne*, 1811–1813.

Brigadier general of the Guard in dress uniform
Pinhas, Salomon: *Recueil de planches représentant les troupes des différentes armes et grades de l'armée Westphalienne*, 1811–1813.

Captain General of the Guard
Sauerweid, Alexander Iwanowitsch:
Uniformen der Königlich Westphälischen Armee, ca. 1810, Dresden.

Generals, 1808 to 1813

1: Dress uniform coat pattern for a major general, plus details of brigadier general's collar and cuff embroidery; **2:** undress uniform coat pattern for a major general, plus detail of collar and cuff embroidery for a brigadier general; **3:** shabraque for a major general's dress uniform, plus detail for a brigadier general; **4:** shabraque for a major general's undress uniform, plus detail for a brigadier general; **5:** Captain General of the Guard in dress uniform; **6:** major general in dress uniform; **7:** major general in undress uniform; **8:** brigadier general in dress uniform; **9:** brigadier general in dress uniform, in greatcoat (redingote)

Sources: 1–9 – Patterns by Herbert Knötel, WGM; 1–9 – *Décret Royal portant Organisation de la Garde Royale* of January 1811 and of February 1813; 1, 2, 7, 9 – Salomon Pinhas; 5 – Alexander Sauerweid, *L'armée westphalienne* 1810; 9 – Henri Boisselier.

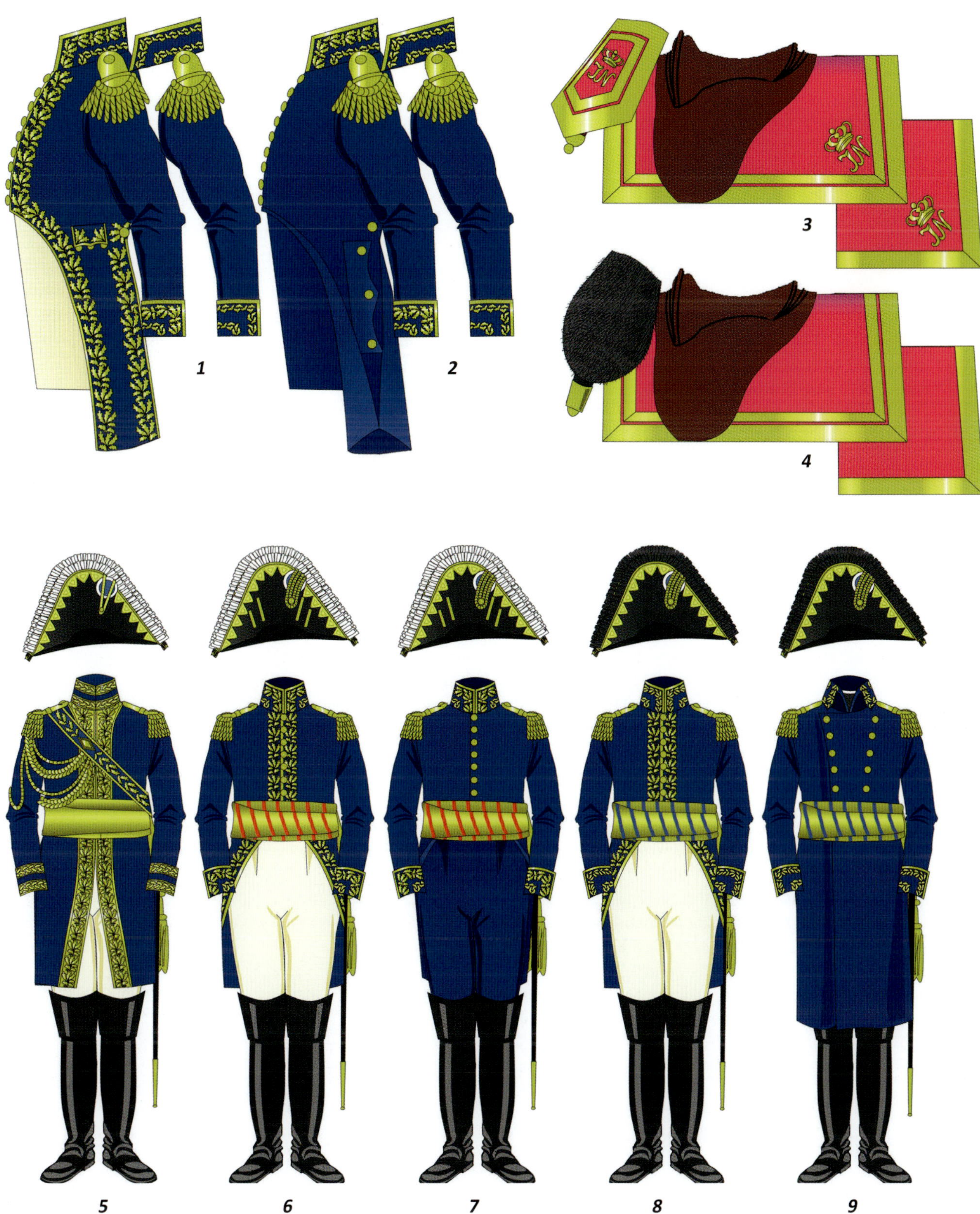

This applies for all of the following uniform descriptions: All ranks/functions wore a dress and an undress uniform. The Guard uniforms corresponded to that of the Line. Their only difference was a golden aiguillette on the right shoulder for the Guard officers. A sword was carried for duty on foot, while a light cavalry saber was worn for mounted duty.

CAPTAIN GENERALS *(GENERALKAPITÄNE)*

There were three uniform variations for the *Generalkapitäne*:

- Dress uniform (*Große-* or *Gala-Uniform*)
- Middle uniform (*Mittlere Uniform*)
- Undress uniform (*Kleine Uniform*).

The *Mittlere* and the *Kleine* uniforms corresponded exactly to the general's dress and undress uniforms and are presented there.

DRESS UNIFORM *(GROSSE UNIFORM)*

Headgear: Bicorn, trimmed with golden, scalloped embroidery on the edge and white plumage.
Coat: Blue frock coat, on which the coattails were not turned back. The lapels, the collar and the cuffs were decorated with wide golden braid embroidery. It was closed with nine buttons in the front.

The uniform included major general's gold epaulets (thick bullions, three stars on the slider retining strap), gold aiguillettes and a sash. The sword was worn on a blue shoulder bandolier that was extensively decorated with gold embroidery.
Pants: White pants with heavy cavalry boots; white breeches with stockings and shoes with buckles were worn for duty at the royal court.
Saddlecloth: Saddlecloths like for the major general.

GENERALS

Headgear: **B**icorn, decorated with golden, scalloped embroidery on the edges. White plumage for major generals, black for brigadier generals.
Coat: Blue, single-breasted coat with blue collar, cuffs and turnbacks. The dress uniform coat did not have turnbacks. Collar, cuffs, coattail pockets and the edges of the coattails were adorned with gold oak leaf embroidery. The major general's (turned up) collar embroidery consisted of one wide (3cm of 1¼ inches) and one narrow (2cm or ¾ inch) braid; the brigadier general's had two narrow (2cm or ¾ inch) braids. The undress uniform coat was embroidered on the collar and cuffs.
Gold general's epaulets. The major generals (*général de division*) wore three stars, the brigadier generals two stars on the epaulets retaining straps). The golden sash was worked through with red for the major generals and with light blue for the brigadier generals.
Pants: White pants for the dress uniform, blue pants for the undress uniform; heavy cavalry boots were worn with it.

Greatcoat: Like all army officers, the generals could also wear a greatcoat with a long cape-like collar or an Überrock (light greatcoat, a so-called redingote). All were blue with the appropriate embroidery for the rank on the cuffs and collar.
Saddlecloth: Crimson saddlecloths and pistol holster covers with embroidered royal initials and gold edge trim. Along with the brigadier general's 6cm or 2½" wide edge braid, the major generals had an additional 2cm or 3/4" wide braid. For duty in the undress uniform, a simpler saddlecloth was used. It did not have the royal initials and the holster covers were made from fur.

Chief of a Staff from 1807 until 1813

1: Dress uniform coat pattern for a colonel as a chief of staff, 1811. Starting 1813, nine buttons with embroidery on the chest; **2:** undress uniform coat pattern for a colonel as a chief of staff, 1813. Before 1813 only seven buttons on the chest; **3:** colonel in dress uniform, mounted; **4:** colonel in dress uniform, 1811; **5:** colonel in undress uniform, 1813; **6:** colonel of the General Staff of the Guard, 1813. The officers of the Guard wore aiguillettes for all types of uniforms.; **7:** colonel in the overcoat (*Überrock*/redingote).

Sources: 1–7 – Schema by Herbert Knötel, WGM; 1, 2, 3, 4, 5, 6 – *Décret Royal portant Organisation de la Garde Royale* of January 1811 and of February 1813; 1, 3, 4 – Wilhelm Hewig.

1
2
3
4
5
6
7

CHIEF OF A GENERAL STAFF

The Chief of a Staff was either a brigadier general or a colonel. A general continued to wear his normal uniform. A colonel in the chief of staff position wore a special uniform:

Headgear: Bicorn with black plume with a yellow tip.
Coat: Single-breasted, completely blue coat closed in the front with seven buttons (in 1813: nine buttons). Gold oak leaf embroidery around the buttons. The collar was embroidered on the right and left with two braids and the cuffs with three braids each. The turnbacks were edged with gold. The undress uniform coat only had the embroidery on the collar and cuffs.
Gold epaulets of a colonel.

STAFF OFFICERS *(ADJOINTS)*

Adjutant Supérieur du Palais
(Officer of the General Staff of the Guard in dress uniform) 1810–1811
Sauerweid, A. I.: *Uniformen der Königlich westphälischen Armee*, ca. 1810, Dresden.

Headgear: Bicorn with black plume with a yellow tip.
Coat: Staff rank officers (Colonel, Major) wore the dress coat like the Chief of Staff. According to H. Knötel the only difference was a modified embroidery on the cuffs (two loops arranged horizontally). It should be noted that this embroidered uniform variation is not mentioned in the royal decree on the organization of the Guard.
Chefs d´escadron/de bataillon or captains wore the single-breasted coat without embroidery on the chest or cuffs. For the captain the turnbacks were not trimmed with gold.
A blue frock coat with pointed lapels was worn for the undress uniform. Its collar, cuffs and pocket flaps were piped red; red turnbacks; red vest. The cuffs for the colonel and major were decorated with loops that the other ranks did not have.
Pants: White pants for the dress uniform, blue ones for the undress uniform.
Greatcoat: Blue redingote or greatcoat with embroidery on the collar and cuffs.
Saddlecloth: Blue cloth shabraque with gold edge braid. The width of the braid depended on the rank (Colonel and major: 5cm or 2 inches, for the *Chef d´escadron/de bataillon* 4,5 cm of 1¾ inches and for the captain/*Hauptmann* 4cm or 1½ inches). The shabraque was edged in red.

General Staff Officers *(Adjoints d´Etat-Major)*

1: Dress uniform coat pattern for a colonel or major. The difference between the two ranks was the epaulets (colonel gold epaulets, major gold epaulets with a silver backing); **2:** coat pattern dress uniform of a *chef de bataillon* and *chef d'escadron*. The same for a captain's dress uniform, but here captain's epaulets and no gold piping on the turnbacks; **3:** coat pattern of a colonel or a major's undress uniform. Plus detail: cuff for *chef de bataillon/d'escadron* and captain; **4:** colonel in dress uniform; **5:** major of the Guard in undress uniform; **6:** *chef de bataillon* in dress uniform; **7:** captain *(Hauptmann)* in undress uniform; **8:** captain in undress uniform and in the greatcoat with forage cap

Sources: 1–8 – H. Knötel's schema in WGM; 6 – Alexander Sauerweid; 8 – H. Boisselier.

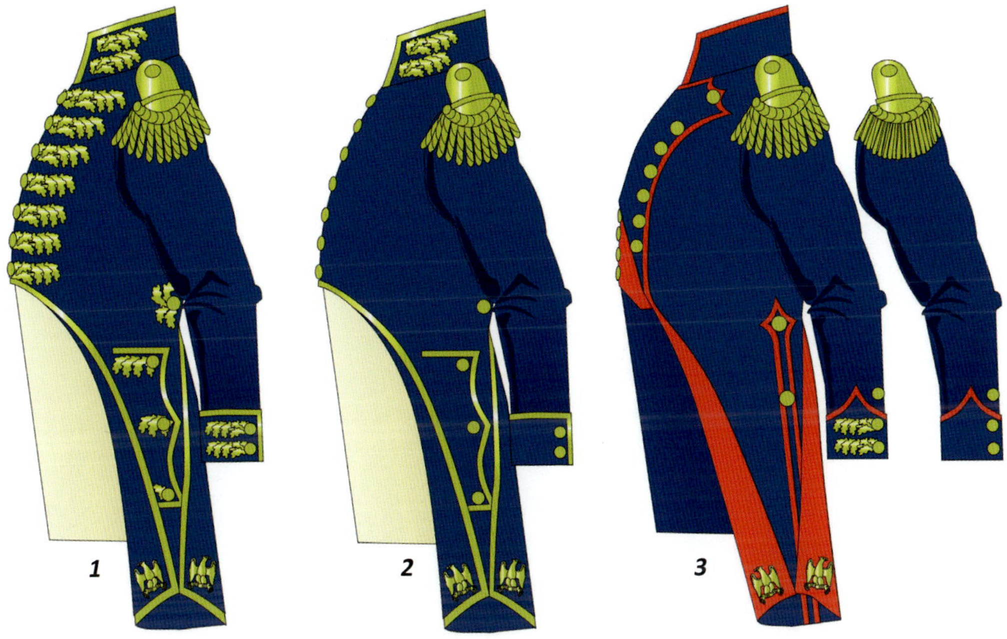

1 *2* *3*

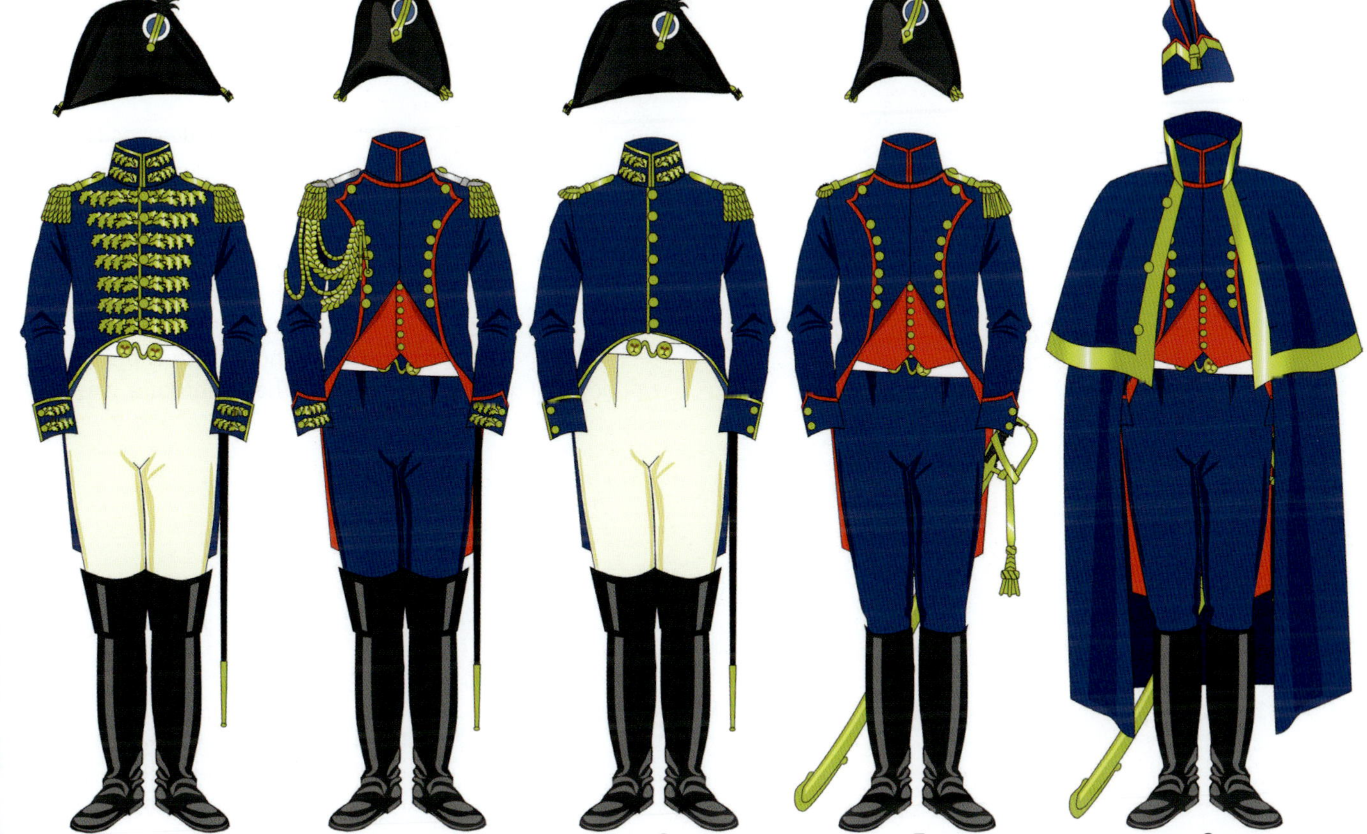

Officer of the General Staff
Sauerweid, Alexander Iwanowitsch: *Uniformen der Königlich Westphälischen Armee,* 1810.

Adjutant to a Captain General of the Guard
Sauerweid, Alexander Iwanowitsch: *Uniformen der Königlich Westphälischen Armee*, 1810.

ADJUTANTS

The adjutants for the Captain Generals have to be distinguished from those of the other staffs.

ADJUTANT to a CAPTAIN GENERAL

Gold aiguillettes were worn for all versions of the uniform.

Headgear: Bicorn with a yellow plume; in 1813 the plume was white with red tip.
Coat – 1809-1810: Blue frock coat with pointed lapels and cuffs. The collar, cuffs, turnbacks and the piping on the lapels and coattail pockets were yellow. The collar and cuffs were decorated with gold embroidery. A red vest with gold cording was worn under the frock coat. For the undress uniform, a simple vest without cording was exchanged for the expensive one with cording. The frock coat itself remained unchanged.
Coat – 1811-1812: In 1811 the coat became single-breasted and closed with seven buttons. The cuffs took on a straight shape. The embroidery on the collar and cuffs were eliminated. The vest was no longer visible. A gold and blue sash was put on for the dress uniform. For the undress uniform the coat remained unchanged, but the sash was not worn.
Coat – 1813: The golden embroidery on the collar and cuffs was reintroduced. Furthermore the coat was closed with nine buttons on the chest. The uniform's frock coat from 1808 was worn again as the undress uniform. The sash was only worn with the dress uniform.
Pants: White pants with tall cavalry boots for the dress uniform; blue pants and hussar boots for the undress uniform.
Greatcoat: Blue redingote or greatcoat with yellow collar and cuffs.
Saddlecloth: A French saddle with rectangular, blue saddlecloth was used for the dress uniform. The saddlecloth had gold braid edging and was decorated with the king's initials. The width of the braid depended on the rank: Staff officers' braid was 5cm or 2 inches wide, captains' 4cm or 1½ inches, and lieutenants' 3cm or 1¼ inches. The pistol holsters on the saddle were covered with black bearskin.
For the undress uniform a pointed blue cloth shabraque with golden braid edging. The shabraques were piped with blue on the outside edge. In 1813 the piping was changed to yellow.

ADJUTANT on a STAFF

The staff adjutants wore the same uniform as the *General-Kapitäns* but with the following differences:

As a distinction the adjutants wore an armband on the left upper arm. It was made of gold silk with red stripes (adjutant for a major general) or with light blue stripes (adjutant for a brigadier general). No sashes were worn. The coats were never decorated with embroidery. The yellow plume on the bicorn also remained unchanged in 1813.

Adjutants for Captain Generals

1: Adjutant in dress uniform, 1809; **2:** adjutant in dress uniform, 1811; **3:** adjutant in undress uniform, 1811; **4:** adjutant in dress uniform, mounted, 1811; **5:** adjutant in dress uniform, 1813; **6:** adjutant in undress uniform, 1813; **7:** adjutant (overcoat with forage cap *(Feldmütze/bonnet de police)*, 1813; **8:** adjutant in undress uniform, mounted, 1813.

Sources: 2, 3, 4 – *Décret Royal portant Organisation de la Garde Royale* of January 1811; 2, 4 – A. Sauerweid; 5, 6, 8 – *Décret Royal portant Organisation de la Garde Royale* of February 1813; 1-8 – patterns by Herbert Knötel, WGM.

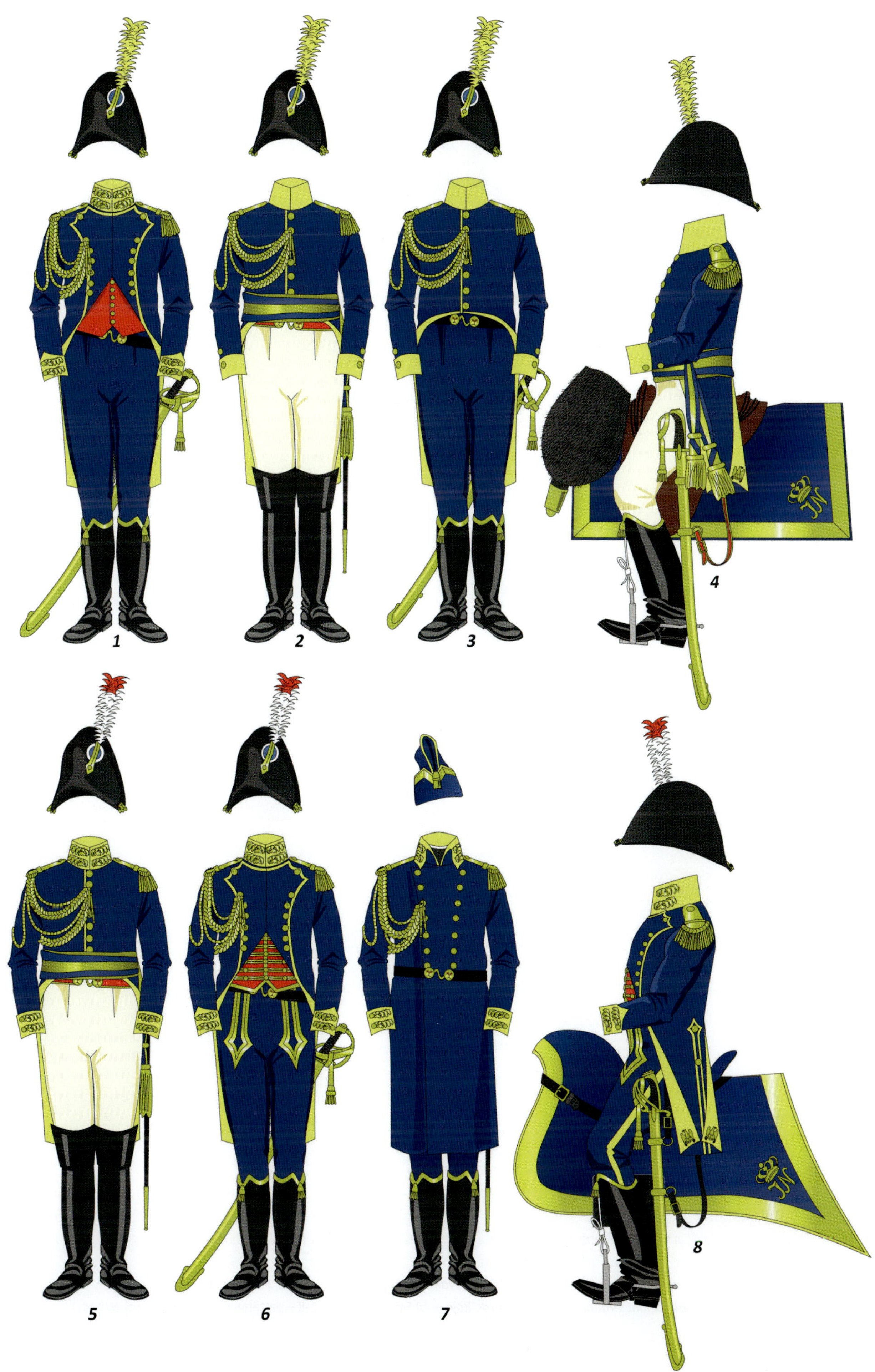

JN
1
2
3
4
5
6
7
8
JN

Adjutant, 1809
Weiland, C. F.: *Représentation des uniformes de l'armée impériale royale française et des alliés*, 1807 and 1812.

Adjutants (of a Staff) – *Aides de Camp d'Etat-Major*

1: Dress uniform coat pattern of an adjutant, 1809; **2:** adjutant's dress uniform coat pattern, 1811; **3:** adjutant in dress uniform, mounted, 1809; **4:** adjutant in dress uniform, 1809; **5:** adjutantin undress uniform, 1809; **6:** adjutant in dress uniform, 1811; **7:** adjutant in undress uniform, 1811; **8:** adjutant in an overcoat (*Überrock*, redingote).

Source: 1–8 – patterns by H. Knötel in WGM, and W. Hewig; 3 – C. F. Weiland 1st Edition 1809; 5 – S. Pinhas.

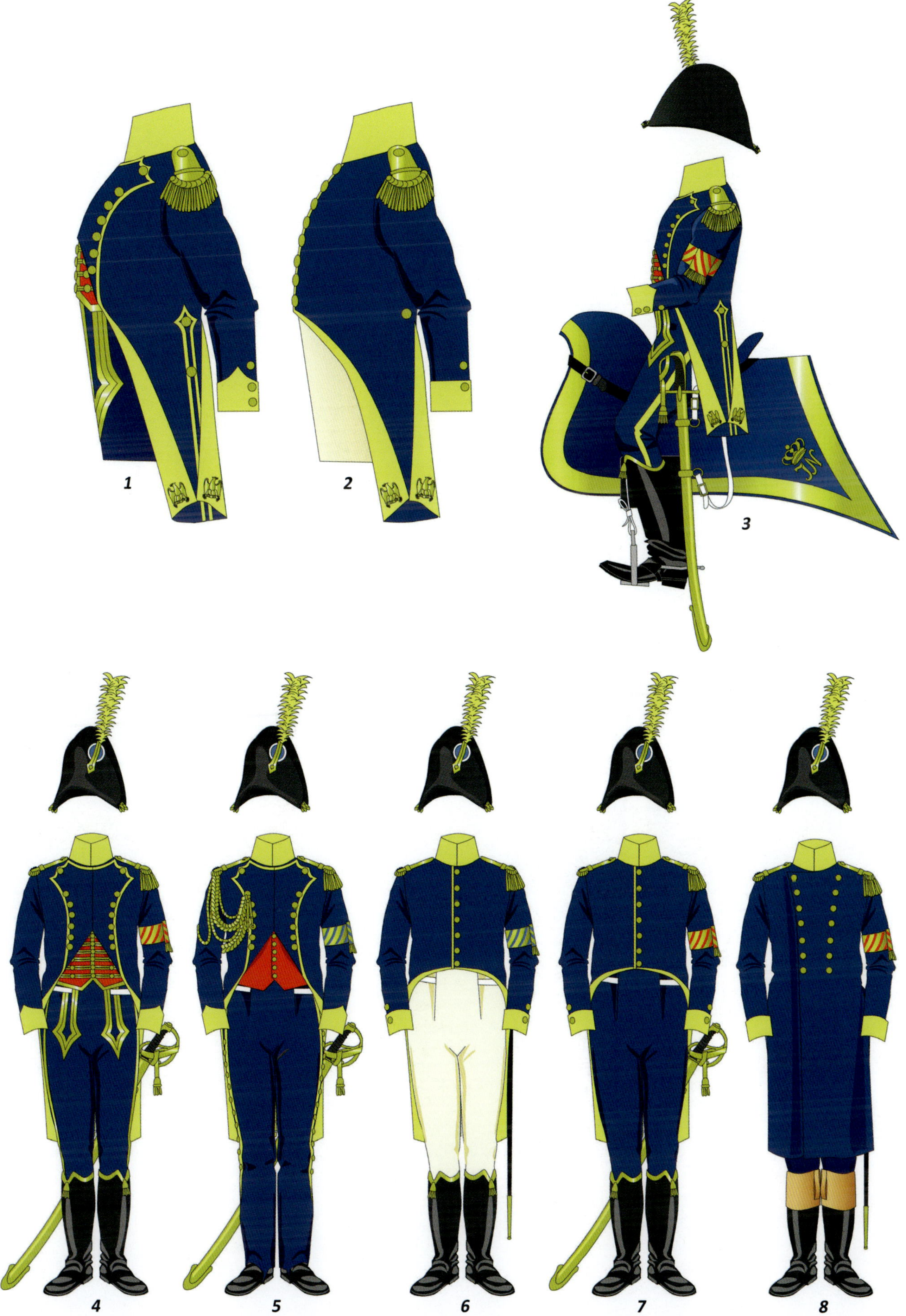
1
2
3
4
5
6
7
8

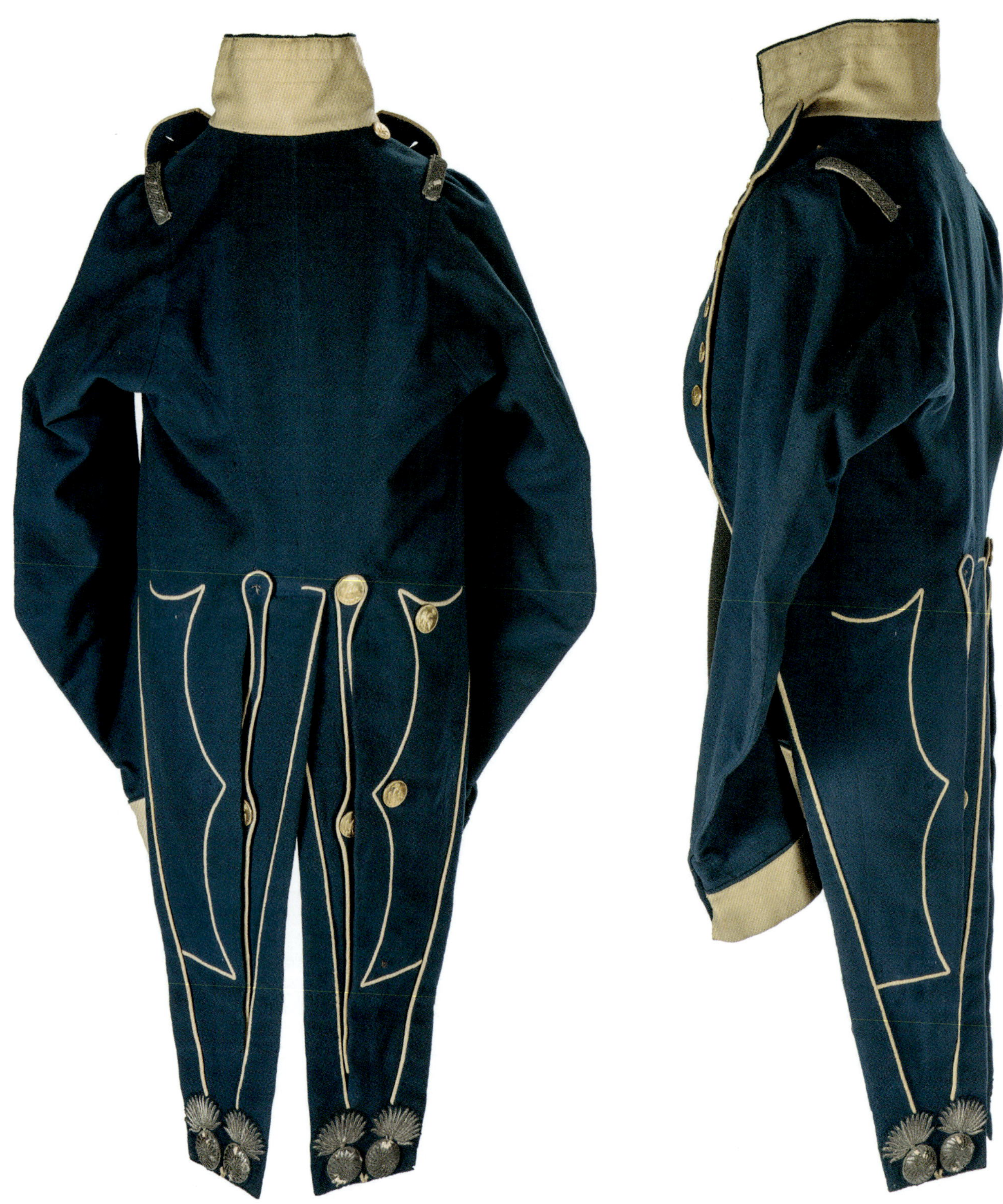

Adjutant's coat, 1809
Original piece in the Musée Royal de l'Armée et d'Histoire Militaire

Photo: Luc Van de Weghe.

Staff Guide, 1812

Watercolor by Herbert Knötel, Westphälische Studie, WGM.

GUIDES OF THE GENERAL STAFF

From 1808 until 1813 a small unit of guides is said to have existed that was employed to deliver messages for reconnaissance tasks as were done in France. The official documents from 1808-1813 do not mention this unit. A description of their uniform is given by Roger Forthoffer in his description of the Westphalian Army and in Herbert Knoetel's illustrations.

Headgear: Colpak/busby with a green bag piped white. Light blue plume with a white tip.

Coat: Pattern given by Forthoffer:

Green coat with lapels and short tails. Lapels, collar, cuffs and turn-backs light blue. White buttonhole lace attached to the lapels. White fringed epaulets.

Pattern given by Knoetel:

Green coat with short tails. The coat was closed with a single row of seven buttons. White horizontal button lace on each button. Collar, cuffs and turn-backs light blue. White fringed epaulets. White bugle horn ornaments on the turnbacks.

Trousers: Green trousers with white Hungarian knots and side stripes. Hussar boots with white trim.

Equipment:

Light cavalry saber. Light blue sabretache with the white royal initials or the Westphalian crest. Carbine and white cartridge pouch belt.

Saddlecloth: Shabraque of green cloth with light blue trim.

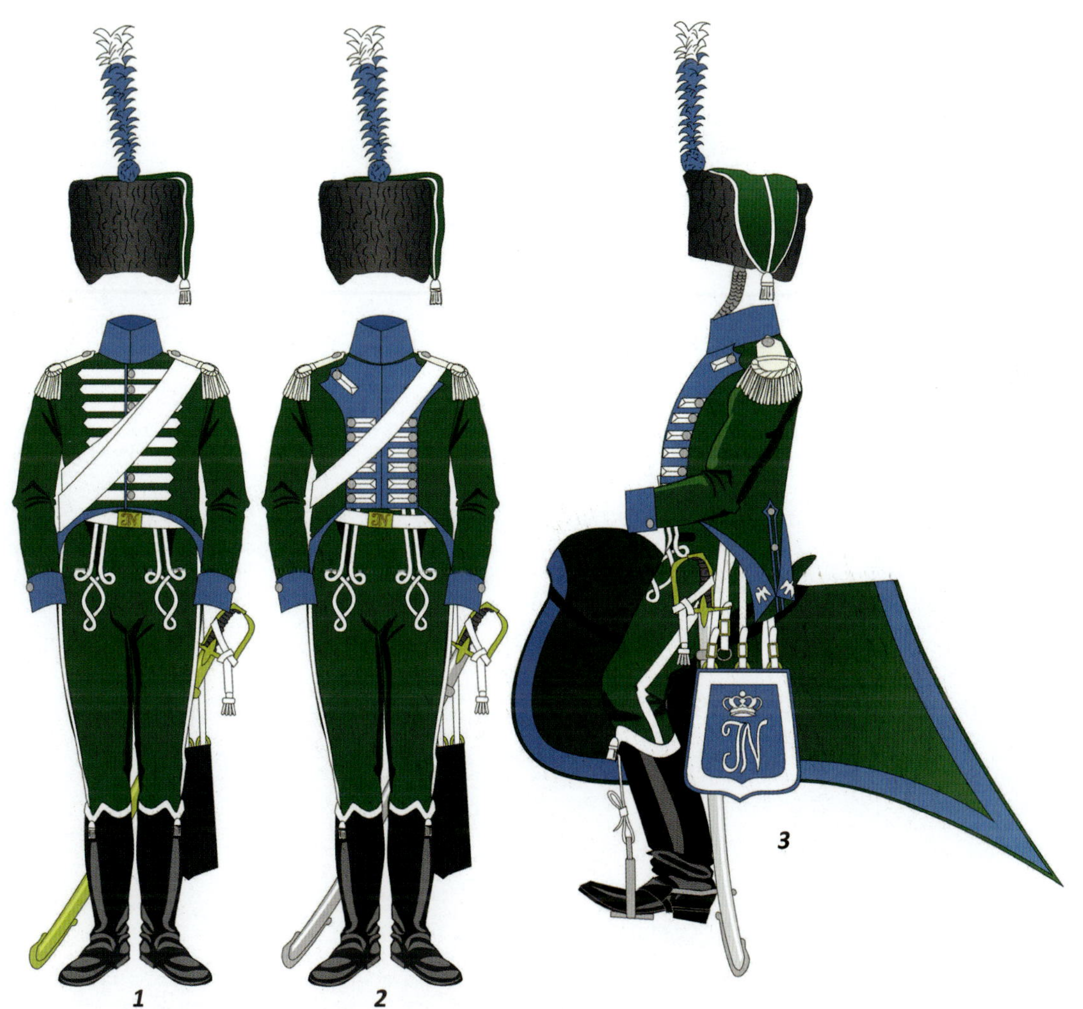

Guides of the General Staff

1: Guide; **2:** guide; **3:** mounted guide.

Sources: 1 – Uniform per H. Knötel; 2–3 – uniforms per R. Forthoffer.

THE LINE FORMATIONS

Infantry of the Line

Light Infantry

Cavalry of the Line

Artillery and Technical Troops

"At the very beginning, the battalion's uniform was changed and improved in that instead of the former green, now received brick red collar and cuffs, whereby it is more noticeable and became more tasteless, because the light blue basic color of the coat and trousers remained unchanged. The first time I put on the uniform, I had to laugh to myself."

"Gleich zu Anfang wurde die Uniform des Bataillons verändert und dadurch verbessert, dass sie statt der bisherigen grünen, nun ziegelrote Kragen und Aufschläge erhielt, wodurch sie noch auffallender und geschmackloser wurde, weil die hellblaue Grundfarbe des Rockes und der Beinkleider bestehen blieb. Als ich zum ersten Mal diese Unifrom anzog, musste ich selbst lachen."

From: Borcke, J. v., Kriegerleben des Johann von Borcke (Berlin, 1888

Officer and fusilier1812 – Line infantry of the Westphalian Army
Untitled manuscript, Anne S.K. Brown Military Collection, Brown University Library.

5th Regiment 1809–1812, drummer, drum major, standard bearer and fusiliers in Hamburg
Suhr, Christoph: *Album du Bourgeois de Hambourg*, 1806–1815, Kommerz-Bibliothek Hamburg, photo: Markus Stein.

INFANTRY OF THE LINE *(LINIENINFANTRIE)*

ESTABLISHMENT

The infantry of the line regiments formed the backbone of the Army. The organization, drill manuals and the internal structure completely corresponded to the French model. The mass of the soldiers were assigned through conscription and call-ups.

When the army was created, many officers coming from foreign militaries were incorporated. Naturally there were also applicants especially from the disbanded armies of Westphalia's predecessor states: Hesse-Kassel, Brunswick and Hanover. Additional officers were to be obtained from graduates of the new Westphalian military. The graduates of the new Westphalian military academies were expected to secure the further replacement of officers.

ORGANIZATION

Each regiment had two field battalions (*Feldbataillone*) and a depot.

The battalions consisted of a grenadier company, a voltigeur company and four fusilier companies. The tallest soldiers were consolidated in the grenadier companies. The smallest soldiers formed the voltigeurs, who were specially trained for the dispersed fighting to the front of the battle lines. They were also armed with lighter muskets. The grenadiers and the voltigeurs were considered the elite companies. Each grenadier company was provided with four grenadiers as sappers (*Zimmerleute*) with special equipment. The depot consisted of four fusilier companies. Its main task was to train the new conscripts before they were send to the field battalions. The regiment's major was the depot's commanding officer.

One battalion had a strength of circa 840 men. In theory an infantry regiment had a total strength of 2,284 men including the depot and staff personnel.

A pool of eight wagons for ammunition and equipment transport also belonged to a regiment.

After 1808 it was planned to reinforce the regiments with a third field battalion. Until the 1812 Russian campaign this was accomplished only for the 2nd and the 7th Regiments.

STAFF

Senior Staff *(Oberstab)* (13 men)	**Lower Staff *(Unterstab)*** (31 men)	**Per Company** (140 men)
1 Colonel	4 Adutants (*Adjudanten*)	1 Captain
1 Major	1 Drum Major (*Tambourmajor*)	1 First Lieutenant (*Premier-Lieutenant*)
2 Battalion Commanders (*Bataillonschefs*)	1 Corporal Drummer (*Korporal-Tambour*)	1 Junior Lieutenant (*Unter-Lieutenant*)
1 Quartermaster (*Quartiermeister*, in the Depot)	1 Master Musician (*Musikmeister*)	1 Sergeant Major (*Feldwebel* or *Sergent-major*)
1 Paymaster (*Zahlmeister*)	22 Musicians (*Musiker*)	4 Sergeants (*Sergenten*)
1 Clothing Captain (*Bekleidungskapitän, Depot*)	2 Gunsmiths (*Büchsenmacher*)	1 *Fourier*
1 Senior Surgeon (*Oberchirurg*)		8 Corporals (*Korporale*)
2 Surgeons 2nd Class		121 Privates
3 Surgeons 3rd Class		2 Drummers (Voltigeur company: buglers/*cornets*)

THE UNIFORMS 1808–1812

PRIVATES

Headgear: The infantry wore the French Model 1806 shako made of black felt with leather reinforcing. A brass rhombus-shaped plate was attached on the front side. There were known to be different variations of the plates for the individual regiments. The white and blue cockade, and for the fusiliers a spherical pompom, was attached above the plate. The pompoms were colored differently by company: 1st fusilier company had light blue, the 2nd company white, the 3rd company yellow, and the 4th company dark green. After 1810 different types of pompon were in use at the same time. White disc shaped pompoms with company colored border and the company number painted in the center are confirmed. Brass chin scales. White woolen cords for fusiliers. On campaign the shakos were protected by oil cloth covers. In Spain linen covers of various colors (brown, light brown, green) were used. The company numbers were often painted on those covers.
The voltigeur shakos had green cords and green plumes with a yellow tip fixed atop a green of yellow pompom. When the grenadiers wore shakos while marching or on campaign the shakos were decorated with red cords and plumes. The actual headdress of the grenadiers was a bearskin following the French standard. The Westphalian grenadier caps had a leather front visor and red plumes and cords. The cap's rear patch was red with a white grenade ornament.
For garrison duty they wore a white field cap with piping and tassel in the regimental color. The elite companies had their company insignias (grenade, hunting horn) attached to the front.
Coat: The coat of 1808 was white and had lapels closed to the waist. The tails were short with turn-backs and pocket flaps placed vertically. There is no certainty if all regiments had coattail pockets. The turnbacks had white stars for fusiliers, red grenades for grenadiers and green hunting horns for voltigeurs. Depending on the source, the number of buttons on the lapels were six or seven per side. The collar was closed. Two pattern of cuffs are quoted in the sources: round cuff with two buttons placed directly on the cuff or a cuff with a cuff flap with three buttons attached. Both variations were probably in use at the same time. The buttons were made of brass for all regiments and bore the regiment´s number. The fusiliers had white shoulder straps piped in the regimental color. For the elites woolen epaulets in their representative colors red or green or yellow. Until 1811 two regiments each shared a common regimental color applied differently on the coat.
Besides the dress coat with lapels, a single-breasted coat without lapels was worn as service dress or second dress until 1810. Collar, cuffs and piping were in the facing color. A white waistcoat was worn beneath the coat. It served as service dress when the second coat was discontinued in 1810.
Trousers: White pants with short, black gaiters. For the voltigeurs, Hungarian style gaiters with colored piping were possible. For special occasions and parades white gaiters could have been worn.
In 1810 white wide trousers worn over the gaiters were introduced for summer time. Grey trousers, with blue side stripes for the fusiliers and red ones for grenadiers, were worn in the winter.
Greatcoat: The greatcoat corresponded to the French model and was made of greyish brown wool and was usually closed with one row of brass buttons. The elite companies wore their epaulets with the greatcoat.
Armament and equipment: The armament and equipment corresponded to the French Army's standards.
The muskets were mostly of French manufacture. The fusiliers did not carry the "*sabre-briquet*" model infantry saber. The sword-straps for the grenadiers were red, for the voltigeurs green, and possibly with a yellow tassel.
The leather equipment was white. The scabbard for the bayonet was also attached on the fusiliers' cartridge box bandoleer
The elite companies wore their bandoliers for the cartridge box and saber/bayonet crossed across the chest. A metal badge was attached to the cartridge box cover: for the grenadiers in the form of a flaming grenade; for the voltigeurs a hunting horn. The fusiliers' cartridge boxes were without any badge. It appears that the cartridge box badges were only introduced in the 1st Regiment. The forage cap was rolled up and attached under the cartridge box with two straps.
The backpack was carried on two white leather straps. The greatcoat was rolled and buckled onto the backpack; in the field additional utensils like a haversack (*Brotbeutel*), canteen (*Feldflaschen*) and cooking utensils in varied arrangements were carried.

Shako plate, 3rd Regiment
Deutsche Historisches Museum, Berlin.

Shako plate, (probably) Grenadier officer's
Musée l'Armee, Paris.

NCOs

The NCOs wore the uniform of the privates but with their particular rank distinctions. The upper shako band was covered with gold lace for sergeants and sergeant majors (double lace for sergeant majors). In the fusilier companies the NCOs were armed with sabers.

SAPPERS

The sappers were provided by the grenadier companies (1 corporal sapper and 4 sappers). They wore the grenadier uniform and bore the typical pieces of equipment of their special function: apron, axe and gauntlets. The sappers were armed with a light carbine and had a special pattern saber.

DRUMMERS/BUGLERS

Headgear: They wore the shako or colpak of their companies. Sometimes the upper band of the shakos was covered with white or yellow braid.

Coat: The drummers and buglers wore colorful coats that were different for every regiment. Collar, lapels and cuffs had decorations with regimental lace. Some regiments also had lace chevrons on the sleeves. Variations of coats for drummers/buglers are quoted for some units. The buglers had yellow collars as a general rule because they belonged to the voltigeur companies.

Armament and equipment: The drum bandolier and the drum apron were worn on the left leg were of white leather. The drumsticks were inserted in a brass holder on the front of the bandolier. Brass drums had hoops of various colors. The fusilier drummers were armed with sabers. The brass bugles had green, yellow or green and yellow woolen cords.

OFFICERS

Headgear: The upper shako band was covered with a gold lace. Its width differed according to rank. In addition, the shako's sides were decorated with gold chevrons pointing upward. The number of the chevrons indicated the rank. Gold shako plate and cords. The company officers had a gold pompom and a plume in the company color. The grenadier officers wore the bearskin cap with a red plume. Senior officers had white plumes attached to a tulip-shaped socket. A bicorn hat was worn for undress.

Coat: The officers' uniform coats had long tails. On the coat all the buttons and decorations were gilt. Gold gorget with a silver badge.

A dark blue coat without lapels (surtout) was worn for undress. It was closed with a row of nine buttons in the front. White, blue or leather trousers were worn along with this coat.

A white single-breasted surtout was worn for social events like balls. The collar, cuffs and turn-backs were in the facing color. White breeches, stockings and silk vest accompanied the uniform.

Greatcoat: The greatcoat was dark blue with two rows of buttons. In Spain it could have also been brown. The epaulets were attached to the greatcoat.

Equipment and armament: The armament consisted of a sword for the fusilier- and voltigeur officers, while he grenadier officers carried a saber. Usually the sidearm was worn on a white waist belt. But on campaign a shoulder bandoleer was used. The leather was white, but black is also documented.

Saddlecloth: The mounted senior officers' rectangular shabraque and the pistol holster covers were cloth in the facing color and were decorated with gold border lace. The width of the lace was according to rank. The royal cypher was in the back corner. Saddlery in black leather.

Line infantry, voltigeur corporal, 1811–1813
Pinhas, Salomon: *Recueil de planches représentant les troupes des différentes armes et grades de l'armée Westphalienne*, 1811–1813, privately owned.

HEAD OF THE COLUMN *(Téte de Colonne)*

DRUM MAJOR *(Tambour-Major)*

Headgear: For parades a bicorn with gold trim and four vertical stiffeners was worn. A tassel on each corner of the hat. Feathers of plumage and plume were different for the various regiments.

For daily duty a simple pattern bicorn was used.

Coat: The drum major of each regiment had a special uniform richly adorned with gold lace for parades. The drum major´s rank was sergeant major (*Feldwebel*).

A single-breasted coat with long tails in the color of the parade dress was worn for daily duty and on campaign.

Trousers: White or colored trousers with Hungarian style gold trim.

Equipment: A broad white or colored bandolier, probably with gold trim, was worn over the right shoulder. A brass badge with slings for the drumsticks was attached in the front. A sword was the armament.

MUSICIANS *(Hautboisten)*

Headgear: A bicorn with tassels on the corners and gold stiffeners and trim was worn in most cases. The musicians of the 3rd Regiment wore shakos.

Coat: Single-breasted surtouts with long coattails. Single-breasted surtouts with long tails. The color of the coat mostly corresponded to the color of the drum major´s coat. Gold lace decorations on collar and cuffs. On the shoulders were gold colored trefoil or clover-shaped (*trèfle*) epaulets, which was backed with a cloth strip in the facing color.

Trousers: White or colored pants with low Hungarian boots. These had gold colored tassel and edging. For the pants for Regiments Nos. 3, 4 and 8, Hungarian knots are quoted in sources.

Over the right shoulder a white leather bandolier with a sword.

Equipment: A white leather belt suspending a sword was worn over the right shoulder.

Grenadier, 1st Regiment, 1808
Copy by W Hewig from *Manuscrit du Canonier Hahlo,* 1807/08.

1st Regiment, drum major in dress uniform, 1811
Pinhas, Salomon: *Recueil de planches représentant les troupes des différentes armes et grades de l'armée Westphalienne,* 1811–1813, privately owned.

1st REGIMENT

Formed: 21 January 1808
Garrison: Marburg, later Halberstadt.

COMMANDING OFFICERS

1808: Colonel von Schmidt, **1809**: Colonel Vauthier, **1810**: Colonel Legras, **1812**: Colonel von Plessmann

STRENGTH

1808: Initially 487 men from the Regiment of the Hessian Legion, then 2 battalions with 6 companies each: 1,200 men; **1811:** 2,289 men in November; **1812:** 43 officers and 1,439 men

ACTIONS

1809: In April in the 2nd Westphalian Division of the X Army Corps under King Jérôme. On May 5, engaged at the combat of Dodendorf with four elite companies. Casualties were 6 officers and 160 men. In June active at the combat of Oelper.
1811: With the French X Army Corps, in April detached to reinforce the garrison of Danzig.
1812: The regiment was sent to join the *Grande Armée*. Deployed along with the Prussian Auxiliary Corps in Courland.
1813: Garrison of Danzig again from January 5. Capitulation of the besieged fortress in November. The remnants of the regiment were 16 officers and 280 men. They were taken into Prussian service and formed the new 27th Prussian Infantry regiment together with other units.

UNIFORMS

Shako plate: Eagle over regiment´s number.
Facing color: Blue.
Drummers/Buglers: Blue coats with crimson facings. The lace was yellow with two longitudinal red stripes. Variations of the uniform are documented.
Drum major: Blue frock coat with crimson facings. Gold lace decorations. White trousers.
Musicians: blue frock coat with crimson facings. Gold lace decorations. White trousers.

1st Infantry Regiment Fusiliers

1: Drum major, 1811; **2:** musician; **3:** officer; **4:** staff officer – colonel; **5:** drummer; **6:** drummer – variation; **7:** sergeant major; **8, 9:** fusilier, pompoms, 1st–4th companies.

Sources: 1 – S. Pinhas; 2 – H. Knötel; 3 – Vinkhuijzen Collection, Public Library, New York; 4 – F. Kieffer; 2, 5 – R. Forthoffer; 8, 9 – reconstruction.

1
2
3
4
4.
3.
2.
1.
5
6
7
8
9

1st Infantry Regiment Grenadiers and Voltigeurs

Grenadiers – 1: company-grade officer – captain; **2:** drummer; **3, 4:** grenadiers, dress uniform; **5:** drummer 1810–1812; **6:** grenadier 1808.
Voltigeurs – 7: company-grade officer- captain; **8:** bugler; **9, 10:** voltigeurs; **11:** sapper.

Sources: 1, 2, 3, 8, 9 – reconstructions; 3, 4 – Fr. Lünsmann; 5 – F. Neumann from S. Pinhas; 6 – S. Hahlo; 7, 10, 11 – H. Knötel.

?
7
8
9
10
11

Officer in undress uniform
Watercolor by F. Neumann, collection of Paul Meganck, Brussels.

1st Infantry Regiment Officers' and Camp and Field Uniforms

1: Officer in the full dress uniform, 1811; **2:** officer in the surtout, undress uniform; **3:** officer in the greatcoat (redingote); **4:** shako plate until 1811, cartridge pouch badge, attributed to the 1st Regiment, gorget for officers and variations; **5:** sergeant major of the grenadiers in drill uniform; **6:** fusilier in the work attire; **7:** fusilier in undress uniform until 1810, shako plate variation and pompom for grenadiers and voltigeurs; **8:** fusilier sergeant in the greatcoat; **9:** grenadier in the greatcoat with attached epaulets.

Sources: 1 – H. Boisselier; 2, 6, 7, 8, 9 – reconstructions; 3 – W. Hewig; 4 – from original artifacts and sketches by W. Hewig; 5 – F. Neumann.

1
1 REGIMENT DE LIGNE
1
2
3
4
5
6
7
8
9

2nd REGIMENT

Formed: 14 March 1808,
Garrison: Braunschweig, later Kassel

COMMANDING OFFICERS

1808: Major Broeske, **1810** Colonel von Bosse, **1811**: Colonel von Füllgraf, **1813**: Colonel Picot

STRENGTH

1808: 2 battalions with 6 companies each: 1,200 men; **1811:** Introduction of a 3rd battalion, 3122 men in November
1812: 67 officers and 2,400 men, formation of an artillery company

ACTIONS

1809: In Spain with two battalions in the 1st Brigade, 2nd Division under General Morio;
May to December at siege of Gerona

1812: Russian campaign with the 23rd Division of the VIII Army Corps
1813: Campaign in Saxony, garrison of Dresden, disarmed in August

UNIFORMS

Shako plate: 1st and 2nd Battalion: Rhombus plate with initials "JN" and regiment´s number under a crown; 3rd Battalion: Eagle with wings spread, holding shield showing "JN" above regiment´s number.
Facing color: blue.

Drummers/Buglers: red coats with blue facings. The lace was blue edged orange. Variations of the uniform are documented.
Drum major: No information is available on the uniform.
Musicians: blue frock coat with red facings. Gold lace decorations. White trousers.

2nd Regiment, 3rd Battalion, shako plate Model 1811
Original artifact found in Russia, 2012,
Photo: Markus Gaertner.

2nd Infantry Regiment

1: officer; **2:** fusilier drummer; **3:** fusilier, dress uniform; **4:** grenadier drum major; **5:** fusilier drummer; **6:** voltigeur bugler; **7:** voltigeur bugler – variation starting 1811; **8:** sapper; **9:** musician; **10:** shako plate, 1808.

Sources: 1 – reconstruction; 2, 6 – R. Forthoffer; 3 – *Elsässer Papiersoldaten*, Strasbourg; 4, 5, 7, 9 – F. Kieffer's paper soldiers; 8 – H. Knötel; 10 – original artifact.

1
2
3
4
5
6
7
8
JN
2
10
9

2nd Regiment, 1808–1811, shako with plate with JN monogram and crown
Schloss Friedrichstein (Bad Wildungen), Museumslandschaft, Hessen Kassel.

3rd Regiment 1811, NCOs' shako
Schloss Friedrichstein (Bad Wildungen), Museumslandschaft, Hessen Kassel.

6th Regiment, shako for Fusilier Company
Forum 1813 - Museum zur Geschichte der Völkerschlacht, Leipzig.

3rd REGIMENT

Formed: 10 March 1808
Garrison: Paderborn and Bielefeld

COMMANDING OFFICERS

1810: Colonel Hereditary Prince of Hohenzollern-Sigmaringen,
1810: Colonel Zinck, **1812**: Colonel Bernard, **1813**: Colonel von Hille

STRENGTH

1808: 2 battalions with 6 companies each; 1,200 men
1811: 2,189 men in November
1812: 43 officers and 1,634 men

ACTIONS

1809: in Spain with two battalions in the 2nd Brigade, 2nd Division
May to December siege of Gerona
1812: Russian campaign with two battalions in the VI Army Corps in Lithuania
1813: Campaign in Saxony; Battle of Dennewitz (6 September 1813); one battalion defected to the Prussians.

UNIFORMS

Shako plate: Eagle with wings spread, holding shield showing "JN" above the regiment´s number.
Facing color: Light blue.
Drummers/Buglers: Yellow coats with light blue facings. The lace was white with light blue lozenges.
Drum major: Yellow frock coat with light blue facings. Gold lace decorations. Light blue trousers.
Musicians: Yellow frock coat with light blue facings. Gold lace decorations. Light blue trousers.

Grenadier, 3rd Regiment, 1808
Copy by W. Hewig from *Manuscrit du Canonier Hahlo*, 1807/08
Collection: Edmund Wagner.

3rd Infantry Regiment

1: Fusilier drummer; **2:** fusilier sergeant major; **3:** fusilier, field uniform; **4:** shako plate until 1811; **5:** staff officer, mounted; **6:** grenadier, dress uniform; **7:** voltigeur bugler ; **8:** voltigeur, dress uniform; **9:** drum major; **10:** musician, 1808–1811.

Sources: 1, 9, 10 – R. Forthoffer; 3 – H. Knötel and Grangie, Strasbourg; 4 – from an original artifact; 5, 8 – reconstructions, 6 – S. Hahlo; 7 – H. Knötel.

1
2
3
4
5
6
7
8
9
10

4th REGIMENT

Formed: 10 March 1808
Garrison: Magdeburg, later Brunswick

COMMANDING OFFICERS

1810: *Colonel* von Lossberg, **1812**: *Colonel* von Rossi, **1813**: *Colonel* Bork

STRENGTH

1808: 2 battalions with 6 companies each; 1,200 men
1811: 2,198 men
1812: 48 officers and 1,638 men

ACTIONS

1809: in Spain with two battalions in the 1st Brigade, 2nd Division
May to December siege of Gerona
1812: Russian campaign with the 24th Division of the VIII Army Corps; after the 1st of November detached to the 34th Division (XI Army Corps). On December 9, the remainder of the regiment was annihilated at Vilnius.
1813: newly raised from a "march" battalion. After February it was garrisoned in the fortress of Kustrin *(Kostrzyn nad Odra)* along with the 5th Regiment.

UNIFORMS

Shako plate: Eagle with wings spread, holding shield showing "JN" above the regiment´s number.
Facing color: Light blue.
Drummers/Buglers: Light blue coats with white facings. The lace was yellow edged red.
Drum major: Light blue frock coat with white facings. Gold lace decorations. White trousers.
Musicians: Light blue frock coat with white facings. Gold lace decorations. Light blue trousers.

4th Infantry Regiment

1: Fusilier drummer; **2:** fusilier, dress uniform; **3:** drum major; **4:** drum major, field uniform, 1808–1810; **5:** musician until 1812; **6:** grenadier-officer, captain; **7:** grenadier drummer; **8:** grenadier, dress uniform; **9:** shako plate until 1811; **10:** voltigeur bugler; **11:** voltigeur; dress uniform; **12:** voltigeur in undress uniform until 18045

Sources: 1, 5, 9 – R. Forthoffer; 2 – Strasbourg paper soldiers; 3 – W. Hewig; 4, 8 – H. Knötel and L. Scharf; 6, 7, 11 – reconstructions; 9 – from an original artifact; 12 – F. Neumann.

1
2
3
4
5
4
9
6
7
8
10
11
12

5th REGIMENT (FIRST FORMATION 1809)

Formed: End of February 1809
Garrison: Magdeburg, later Muhlhausen.

COMMANDING OFFICERS

1809: Colonel von Meyronnet

STRENGTH

Two battalions and a depot with a total strength of 2,600 men.

ACTIONS

1809: In Halberstadt in July, annihilated in street fighting against the Black Band of the Duke of Brunswick with 200 men killed and more than 1,500 taken prisoner.

UNIFORMS

Shako plate: Letters "JN" with crown over regiment´s number.
Facing color: Green.
Drummers/Buglers: Green coats with white facings. The lace was red edged white.
Drum major: Green frock coat with red facings. Gold lace decorations. Red trousers.
Musicians: Green frock coat with red facings. Gold lace decorations. White trousers.

Grenadier in dress uniform, 5th Line Regiment until 1811
Watercolor by Herbert Knötel, ASKB Collection, Providence

5th Infantry Regiment

1: Fusilier-officer, captain; **2:** fusilier drummer, dress uniform; **3:** fusilier; **4:** drum major; **5:** musician; **6:** grenadier drummer; **7:** bugler, dress uniform; **8:** voltigeur; **9:** shako plate; **10:** officer in field uniform; **11:** grenadier in undress uniform; **12:** voltigeur in field uniform.

Sources: 1, 2, 7 – reconstructions; 3, 8, 12 – H. Knötel; 4, 5, 6, 11 – R. Forthoffer; 9 – original artifact in the Musee l' Armee Paris; 10 – R. Knötel.

1
2
3
4
5
6
7
8
9
10
11
12

5th REGIMENT (SECOND FORMATION 1809)

Formed: November 1809
Garrison: Magdeburg, later Muhlhausen

COMMANDING OFFICERS

1809: Colonel von Meyronnet, **1811**: Colonel von Gissot; **1813**: Colonel von Göben

STRENGTH

1811: 2,289 men
1812: 47 officers and 1,716 men

ACTIONS

1810: After May guard duties at the North Sea coastline
1812: Russian campaign with two battalions in the 24th Division of the VIII Army Corps.
1813: newly raised from a marching battalion and garrisoned in the fortress of Kustrin along with the 4th Regiment.

UNIFORMS

Shako plate: Letters "JN" and crown over regiment´s number.
Facing color: Yellow.
Drummers/Buglers: Light blue coats with yellow facings. The lace was red edged yellow.
Drum major: Light blue frock coat with yellow facings. Gold lace decorations. White trousers.
Musicians: Light blue frock coat with yellow facings. Gold lace decorations. Light blue swallow nests with gold decorations. Light blue trousers.

Grenadier epaulets, 1808–1813
Schloss Friedrichstein (Bad Wildungen). Museumslandschaft, Hessen Kassel.

5th Infantry Regiment

1: Fusilier drummer; **2:** drummer variation; **3:** fusilier, dress uniform; **4:** drum major, dress uniform; **5:** drum major, field uniform, 1810-1812; **6:** grenadier drummer; **7:** grenadier, undress uniform; **8:** officer's shako plate; **9:** voltigeur bugler; **10:** bugler-variation; **11:** voltigeur in dress uniform.

Sources: 1, 3, 4, 5 – C. Suhr; 2, 6, 8 – R. Forthoffer; 9 – H. Knötel; 7, 10 – reconstructions.

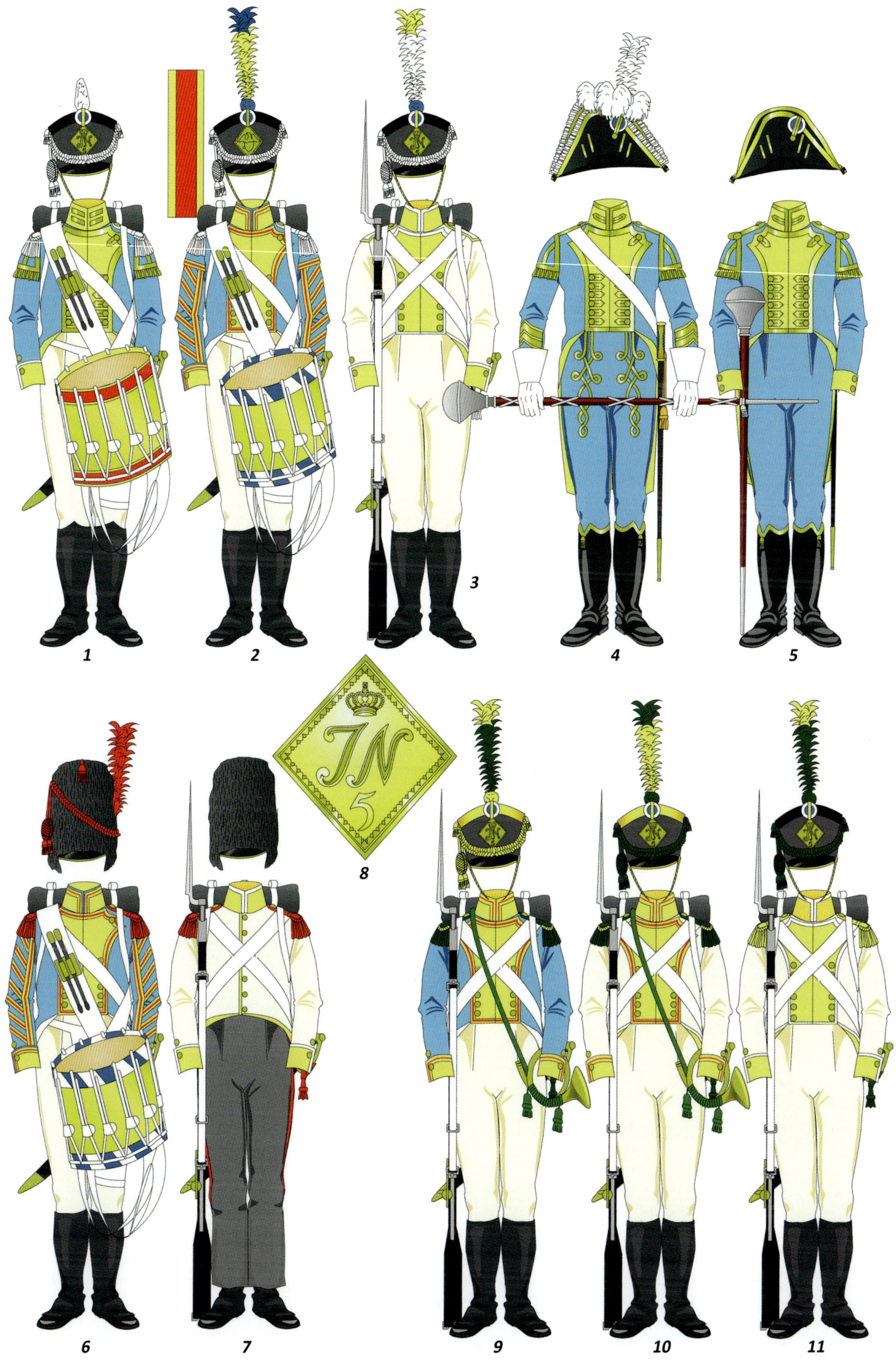
1
2
3
4
5
6
7
8
9
10
11
JN
5

6th REGIMENT

Formed: June 1809
Garrison: Magdeburg, then Hersfeld

COMMANDING OFFICERS

1809: Major von Bosse; interim: von Borstell. **1810**: Colonel Ruelle

STRENGTH

1809: 44 officers and 1,522 men in June, **1811**: 2,289 men.

ACTIONS

1809: in the 2nd Brigade of the X Army Corps. In June involved in the combat at Oelper
1812: Russian campaign with the 24th Division of the VIII. Army Corps. Attacked and annihilated by superior Russian forces at Vereya on 10 October. Two officers and 49 men killed. 370 men were taken prisoner. One battalion flag lost. King Jérôme ordered that the regiment not be reorganized due to its poor performance.
The depot company served as a reinforcement of the 5th Regiment in 1813.

UNIFORMS

Shako plate: Eagle with wings spread, holding shield showing "JN" above regiment´s number.
Facing color: Yellow.
Drummers/Buglers: Yellow coats with white facings. The lace was medium blue with black borders and white areas with black, both framed with black.
Drum major: No information is available on the uniform.
Musicians: Yellow frock coat with white facings. Gold lace decorations. White trousers.

Fusilier, 6th Regiment, 1808–1811
Weiland, C. F.: *Représentation des uniformes de l'armée impériale royale française et des alliés*, privately owned.

6th Infantry Regiment

1: Fusilier officer, captain; **2:** fusilier drummer's dress uniform; **3:** fusilier; **4:** shako plate; **5:** staff officer, major in dress uniform, mounted; **6:** grenadier drummer; **7:** grenadier, dress uniform; **8:** voltigeur bugler; **9:** voltigeur in undress uniform; **10:** musician.

Sources: 1, 5, 9 – reconstructions; 3 – from C. F. Weiland; 2, 6, 7, 8, 10 – R. Forthoffer; 4 – from an original artifact.

6
4
1
2
3
5
6
7
8
9
10

7th REGIMENT

Formed: The order to raise the regiment was issued on July 23, 1809. Only one battalion formed until June 1810. Augmented to fill three battalions in 1811.
Garrison: Hanover, later Eschwege.

COMMANDING OFFICERS

1810: Battalion Commander (*Chef de bataillon*) Bechthold, **1811**: Colonel de Chabert; **1812**: Colonel Lageon

STRENGTH

1811: three battalions with 3,125 men; **1812:** 67 officers and 2,252 men.

ACTIONS

1812: Russian campaign with the 23rd Division of the VIII Army Corps

1813: In garrison within the kingdom; dispersed during the fighting around Kassel in September.

UNIFORMS

Shako plate: Eagle with wings spread, holding shield showing "JN" above the regiment´s number.
Facing color: Black.
Drummers/Buglers: Red coats with black facings. The lace was white decorated with light blue eagles.

Drum major: Red frock coat with black facings. Gold lace decorations. White trousers.
Musicians: Red frock coat with black facings. Gold lace decorations. White trousers.

Grenadier's cartridge box
Forum 1813 - Museum zur Geschichte der Völkerschlacht, Leipzig.

7th Infantry Regiment

1: Fusilier drummer; **2:** fusilier, dress uniform; **3:** drum major; **4:** musician; **5:** grenadier drummers; **6:** grenadier, dress uniform; **7:** shako plate; **8:** voltigeur bugler; **9:** voltigeur.

Sources: 1, 3, 4 – R. Forthoffer; 2 – H. Knötel; 5, 6; 7, 8 – reconstructions; 9 – Neumann.

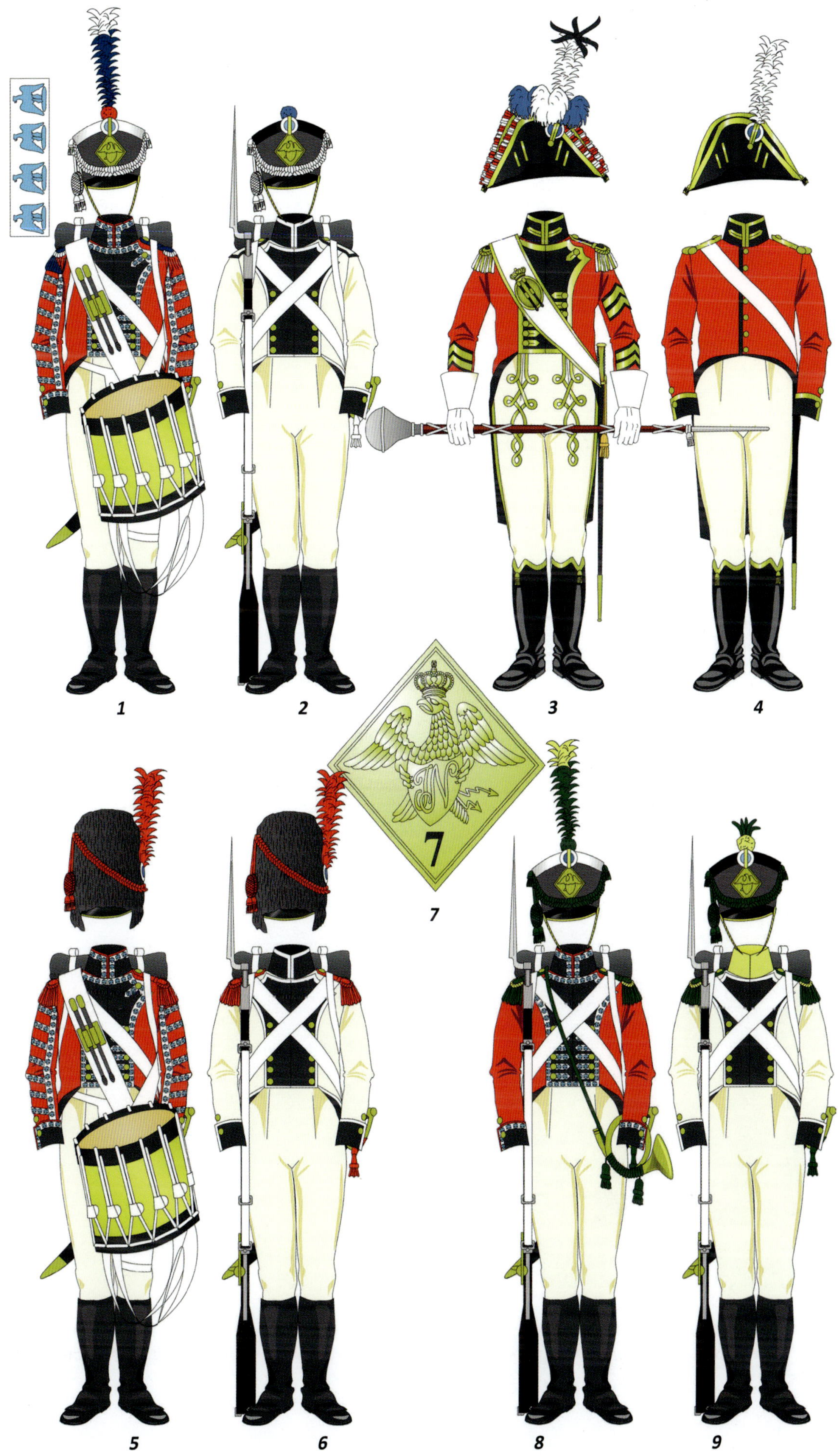
1
2
3
4
7
5
6
7
8
9

8th REGIMENT

Formed: June 1810
Garrison: Hanover, then Quedlinburg

COMMANDING OFFICERS

1809: Colonel Danloup-Verdun, **1812**: Colonel Bergeron

STRENGTH

1810: one battalion with 47 officer positions; **1811:** two battalions with 2,278 men.

ACTIONS

1811: in August 1811 moved to Danzig to reinforce the garrison.

1812: End of September 1812 transferred to the VIII Army Corps. Strength was two battalions with 1,950 men.
1813: campaign in Saxony with the 31st Division of the XI Army Corps at Leipzig.

UNIFORMS

Shako plate: Eagle with wings spread, holding shield showing "JN" above the regiment´s number.
Facing color: Black.
Drummers/Buglers: Light blue coats with white lapels and black facings. The lace was orange with black borders.
Drum major: Light blue frock coat with black facings. Gold lace decorations. Red trousers.
Musicians: Black frock coat with red facings. Red swallow's nests with gold trim. Gold lace decorations. White trousers.

8th Regiment, fusilier in field uniform, 1809–1812
Watercolor by H. Boisselier after H. Knötel, Musée de la Figurine historique, Compiègne.

8th Infantry Regiment

1: Fusilier drummer; **2:** fusilier, dress uniform; **3:** shako plate; **4:** fusilier in field uniform; **5:** grenadier in undress uniform, alternative with shako; **6:** grenadier drummer; **7:** officer, captain in undress uniform; **8:** voltigeur bugler; **9:** voltigeur; **10:** drum major; **11:** musician.

Sources: 1, 7, 8, 9 – reconstructions; 2, 3, 4 ,6 – H. Knötel; 5, 10, 11 – R. Forthoffer.

1
2
3
4
5
6
7
8
9
10
11

THE INFANTRY IN SPAIN 1809–1812

The 2nd, 3rd and 4th Infantry Regiments were deployed in Spain for a couple of years. The conditions during the campaign caused a tremendous deterioration of the uniforms. The troops replaced the heavily damaged items such as trousers, greatcoats and shoes directly from the country´s resources. The use of brown cloth for trousers and greatcoats was characteristic of that period. The brown cloth was easy to obtain everywhere in Spain. Worn out shoes often were replaced with Spanish sandals. Canteens, bags and haversacks were added to the field equipment. Officers and NCOs adopted additional pistols that were stowed in holsters fixed at belts and bandoliers.

The drawings of the so-called "Frankfurt Collection" (*Frankfurter Sammlung)* display a number of examples from the period of the Spanish campaign. Some of these are presented here.

2nd Regiment, grenadier officer and grenadier in field uniform in Spain, 1809
Watercolor by H. Knötel, estate in the WGM.

2nd Infantry Regiment

1: officer; **2:** grenadier officer, 1809; **3:** grenadier; **4:** sapper; **5:** adjudant-major, 1810–1811.

3rd Infantry Regiment

6: voltigeur -officer; **7:** fusilier; **8:** voltigeur.

Sources: 1, 4, 6, 7, 8 – L. Scharf, *Frankfurter Tagebuch*; 2, 3, 5 – H. Knötel from R. Forthoffer.

1
2
3
4
5
6
7
8

Regiment 1809, drum major in field uniform *(Tenue de campagne)* in Spain
Watercolor by H. Knötel, estate in WGM.

4th Regiment 1809, voltigeur and grenadier in Spain
Watercolor by H. Knötel, estate in WGM.

4th Infantry Regiment

1: Grenadier; **2:** fusilier-corporal; **3:** grenadier; **4:** officer; **5:** grenadier; **6:** voltigeur.

Sources: 2, 3 – L. Scharf, *Frankfurter Tagebuch;* 1, 4, 5, 6 – H. Knötel from R. Forthoffer.

1
2
3
4
5
6

REGIMENTAL ARTILLERY

An order was given in May 1811 to raise an artillery company in every line infantry regiment. But this order was not carried out in all regiments. No artillery companies were formed in the 3rd, 4th and 9th Regiments. The 1st and the 8th Regiment were the first units that received their guns in 1811. Each company was armed with two 6-pounder guns. The 2nd and the 7th regiment received three guns each. A train detachment was also part of each company. The required officers and soldiers were drawn from the senior regiment. The artillery companies were deployed on the 1812 campaign and were decimated in Russia. Only the company belonging to the 2nd Regiment succeeded in saving its two guns on the retreat.
When the regiments were reorganized in the beginning of 1813, no artillery companies were raised again.

ORGANIZATION

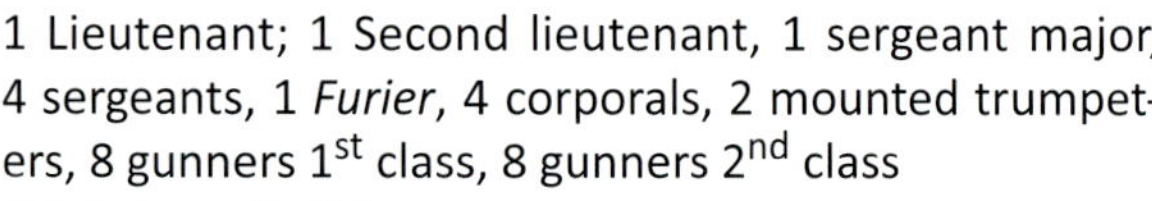

1 Lieutenant; 1 Second lieutenant, 1 sergeant major, 4 sergeants, 1 *Furier*, 4 corporals, 2 mounted trumpeters, 8 gunners 1st class, 8 gunners 2nd class
Total strength: 32 men
Train detachment: 4 Corporals, 26 train drivers with 4 wagons, 3 ammunition carriages and forge

UNIFORMS

Dress uniform *(Grande Tenue)*

The uniform corresponded to the one of the grenadiers on the senior regiment but with red collar and cuffs.

Field dress *(Petite Tenue)*

The field dress was like the field uniform of the gunners of the artillery. Shako with cover. Blue, single-breasted coat with red facings. Dark blue grenade badges were attached to the turnbacks. Grey trousers.

Officer of the Regimental Artillery of the 2nd Regiment, 1811–1812
The "3" regimental number on the shako plate is incorrect.
Watercolor by Herbert Knötel,
ASKB Collection, Providence.

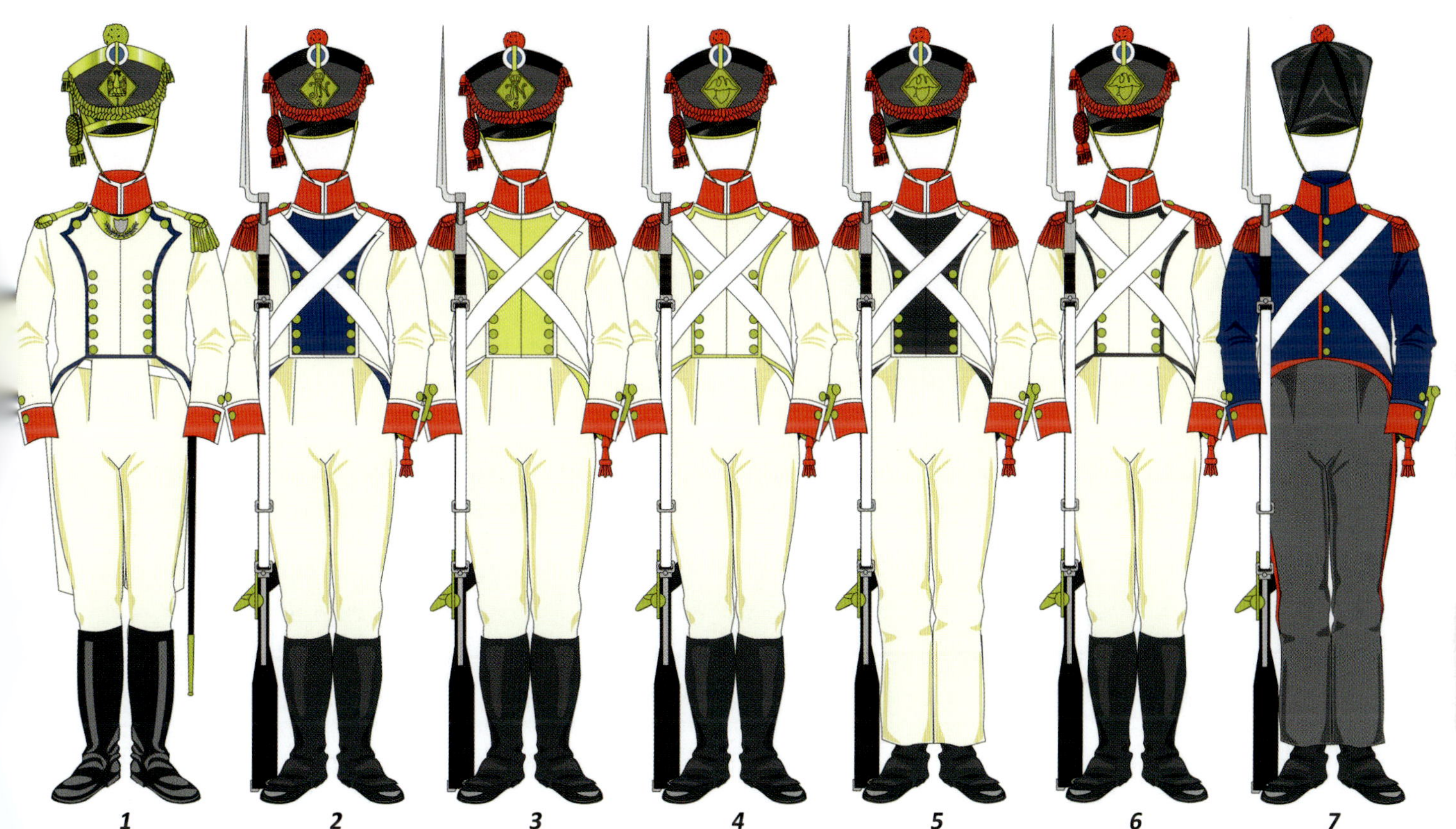

Regimental Artillery

1-6: 1st, 2nd, 5th, 6th, 7th and 8th Infantry Regiments in dress uniform; **7:** undress uniform for all regiments.

THE INFANTRY UNIFORM, 1812–1813

Headgear: The shako then became the regular headgear for grenadiers as well. It had a red plume and cords. The shako plate with the pattern showing the Westphalian eagle presenting a coat of arms shield with the royal cypher and the regimental number was introduced in general. An additional version of the plate - with an eagle holding a hunting horn with the royal cypher in the center and the regimental number in the lower edge - is confirmed for voltigeurs. A dark blue plume with a red tip was attached on the fusiliers' shakos for parades. Also red spherical pompoms with dark blue tassels were in use. Further variants were blue pompoms with a white center showing the regimental number. A field cap in the new shape (*pokalem*) was introduced.
Coat: The facings were standardized as dark blue for all the regiments. Collar, lapels and cuffs had white piping. The number of buttons on the lapels should have been increased to eight on each side but this is not confirmed for all regiments. Cuffs were without patches, but dark blue patches with white piping are confirmed for the 8th Regiment (Trojan and S. Pinhas' manuscript).
The variation with a white patch with dark blue piping has also been depicted. The coattail pockets were eliminated. The turnbacks lost their piping and the emblems on the turnbacks were white for all the companies. For the fusiliers the regimental number was sewn on the outer turnback and a star was sewn on the inner turnback. The Fusiliers received dark blue fringed epaulets with white crescents. Shoulder straps with dark blue piping were also used.
The introduction of the new model of the coat only took place slowly in the individual regiments. Only the 9th Regiment, which was created starting at the end of 1812, wore the new uniform from the beginning. Until the departure for the Russian Campaign in the spring of 1812, the old regiments - first the Regiments Nos. 2, 5 and 8 - most probably had the new uniforms, while the other regiments still wore the old outfits into 1813.
Although the undress coat was officially abolished, it appears that single-breasted coats with colored facings continued to be worn by individual regiments as a consideration.
Trousers: No changes.
It is documented that the 1st and the 8th Regiments that were serving as occupiers in Danzig (Gdansk) in 1812–1813, had dark blue trousers made as payment for their work on the defenses. The trousers had colored stripes on the sides for the elite companies: red for grenadiers and yellow for voltigeurs.
The equipment and armament remained unchanged. The fusiliers were given their regimental number in brass as a cartridge box badge.

DRUMMERS and BUGLERS

The musicians' uniforms were also standardized. The uniform coats were changed to white and the drummer´s braid became white with two blue center stripes. Some regiments probably kept their old drummers' braids (see Knoetel plate, page 262).

AT THE HEAD OF THE COLUMN *(Téte de Colonne)*

DRUM MAJOR

Headgear: Gold trimmed bicorn with white and blue feathers and plumage.
Coat: White uniform coat with long coattails and blue facings. Gold lace trim and epaulets.
Trousers: Red pants with gold Hungarian knots. Hungarian boots with gold trimming.

MUSICIANS *(Hautboisten)*

Headgear: Shako with white cords. Blue spherical pompom a blue, white and blue feather plume attached. The upper shako band was decorated with gold lace.
Coat: Blue surtout with long coattails. Collar, cuffs, turnbacks and piping along the row of buttons white. Gold trefoil or clover-shaped (*trèfle*) epaulets.
Trousers: White pants, Hungarian boots.
Over the right shoulder a white leather bandolier with a sword.
H. Boisselier gives a variation of the uniform for the 2nd Regiment's musicians:
Shako with a blue and white plume. Privates´ uniform with gold laces on the collar and gold *Trèfle* epaulets.

Line infantry, grenadiers' and fusiliers' field uniforms, 1812
Watercolor by H. Knötel, estate in WGM.

6th Regiment, fusilier in Hamburg, 1812
Watercolor by Georg Schäfer from Dr. Buck Collection, H. Knötel estate in WGM.

Infantry coat from 5th Regiment, 1811–1813
Musée Royal de l'Armée et d'Histoire Militaire, Brussels
© War Heritage Institute, WHI Inv No: 300291
Photo: Luc Van de Weghe.

9th REGIMENT

Formed: 23. September 1812
Garrison: Magdeburg

COMMANDER

Oberst von Lindern

STRENGTH

One understrength battalion and a depot.

ACTIONS

1813: The battalion participated in the fighting at Hagelberg on 27 August. In October it took part in the Battle of Möckern (Leipzig).

UNIFORMS

Shako plate: Eagle with wings spread and holding a coat of arms shield above the regimental number.
Facing color: Blue.
Drummers/Buglers: Musicians wore privates´ coats with braid trim. The braid was white with two blue longitudinal stripes. Variants of the coats are known.
Drum major: White frock coat with blue facings. Gold lace decorations. Red pants.
Musicians: Blue frock coat with white facings. Gold lace decorations. White pants. Shako as headgear.

9th Infantry Regiment and Standard Uniform *(Einheitsuniform)*, 1812–1813

1: Drum major; **2:** musician, 1811; **3:** musician variation; **4:** staff officer, colonel, mounted; **5:** company officer in dress uniform; **6:** drummer in dress uniform; **7:** drummer variation, 1812; **8:** sergeant major of the fusiliers in dress uniform; **9, 10:** fusilier in dress uniform.

Sources 1, 2 – R. Forthoffer; 4, 5, 6, 9, 10 – H. Knötel; 7 – Fr. Lünsmann; 3 – H. Boisselier; 7 – reconstruction; 8 – S Pinhas.

1
2
3
4
5
6
7
8
9
10

Line infantry 1812–1813, coat for grenadiers, Model 1812
Schloss Friedrichstein (Bad Wildungen), Museumslandschaft Hessen-Kassel.

9th Infantry Regiment and the Standard Uniform, 1812–1813

1: Grenadier, 1st Regiment, 1812; **2:** company-grade officer, captain, dress uniform; **3:** voltigeur bugler **4:** voltigeur, 8th Inf. Regiment in field uniform, 1812; **5:** fusilier in field uniform, 1813, here the King's initials as an emblem instead of the badge; **6:** fusilier in the greatcoat; **7:** fusilier in sleeved vest, 1811; **8:** fusilier in fatigue uniform, 1812; **9:** sapper, now with the grenadier shako.

Sources: 1–8 – R. Forthoffer, H. Knötel, H. Boisselier and original artifacts; 5 – *Freiberger Bilderhandschrift.*

5  6  7  8  9

Line Infantry
1st Infantry Regiment - officer; fusilier corporal and drummer, 1813
Watercolor by Herbert Knötel
Deutsches Historisches Museum, Berlin [GOS-Nr. MGR05713 / Inv. No. MGr 56/42.1].

Line infantry fusilier, 1812–1813
Weiland, C. F.: *Représentation des uniformes de l'armée impériale royale française et des alliés*, privately owned.

Light Infantry, 2nd Battalion, voltigeur, 1809–1810
Watercolor by Herbert Knötel,, Anne S.K. Brown Military Collection, Brown University Library.

LIGHT INFANTRY

PERIOD 1808–1811

ESTABLISHMENT

The light infantry were supposed to be trained for skirmishing and be tactically employed in that manner following the French model.

Just like in France, this differentiation from the infantry of the line was irrelevant because the light infantry had the same armament and also were not employed for their envisioned special missions.

ORGANIZATION

The battalions had the same organization as the infantry of the Line. Each battalion consisted of six companies: one carabinier and one voltigeur company as elite companies and four *chasseur/jaeger* companies as center companies. The battalion's strength was ca. 870 men including the staff. Plus there were another 140 men from the depot. An artillery detachment was not attached to the light battalions like it was for the Line infantry.

The 1st Battalion was raised in 1808. In following period, the light infantry was increased to four battalions. In November 1810 the existing battalions were temporarily combined as the 1st Light Infantry Regiment under Colonel von Füllgraf. In July 1811 the individual battalions became independent again.

Light Infantry 2nd Battalion,
jaeger in undress and dress uniform
Watercolor by Herbert Knötel,
estate in WGM.

Light Infantry, voltigeurs sergeant and a carabinier, 1810
Watercolor by Herbert Knötel,
estate in WGM.

1st BATTALION

COMMANDERs

1808: Battalion Commander (*Bataillonschef*) von Bongars, Major Freiherr von Heimrod, **1809 to 1810**: *Bataillonschef* von Meyern, Captain Bödicker (in Spain), **1811**: *Bataillonschef* von Rauschenplatt **1813**: *Bataillonschef* Bechthold

ACTIONS

1808: **On** 31 January it was formed from a former Hohenzollern battalion.
Strength on 1 May 1808: 600 men.
1809: Marched off to Spain. Participated in the siege and capture of Gerona with significant losses.
1810: **Three** companies were disbanded due to heavy casualties and their remaining able-bodied men were ordered back to Kassel. There, on 1 July, four new companies were raised using troops from the depot and new recruits.
The three companies that remained in Spain, together with the remnants of the infantry from the Line Regiments 2, 3 and 4, formed the so-called "Spanish Regiment."
1811: The battalion raised anew in Westphalia with 6 companies with a total strength of 23 officers and 975 men. It was garrisoned in Marburg.
The weak remnants that were still located in Spain received the new designation of "*4. Bataillon*" (4th Battalion).
1812: Russian Campaign.
In VIII Army Corps (Jerôme/Junot), 24th Division (Ochs), 1st Brigade (Legras).
Strength at the beginning of the campaign on 25 June.
1812: 19 officers and 795 men.
1813: Newly formed with a strength of seven companies. Starting in July participation in the campaign in Saxony. The battalion returned to the field with six companies.

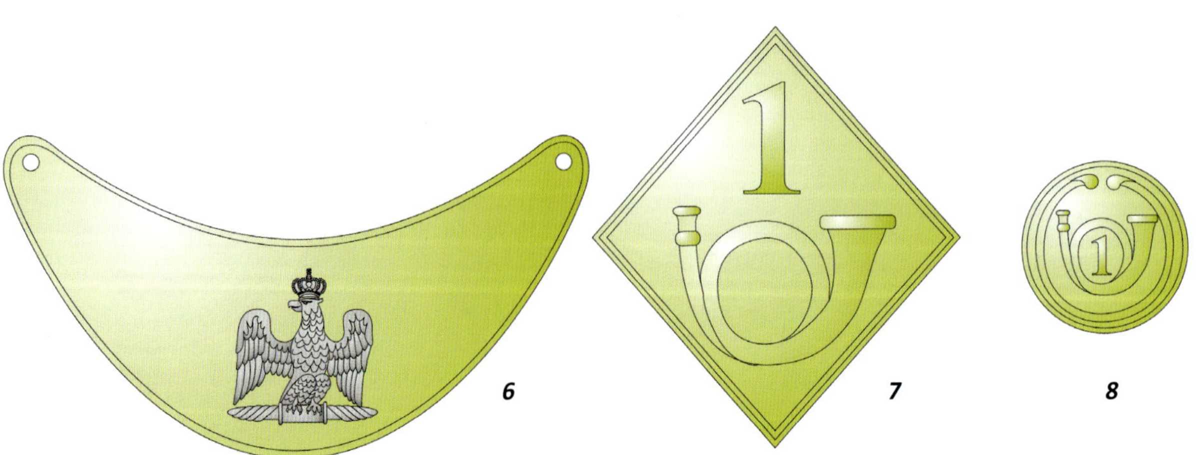

1st Battalion, Light Infantry, 1808 until 1810 (1)

1: Jaeger in dress uniform, 1808; **2:** 1808 dress uniform coat pattern; **3:** officer's dress uniform coat pattern, emblems for carabiniers and voltigeurs; **4:** jaeger's dress uniform coat pattern, emblems for carabiniers and voltigeurs; **5:** jaeger's undress uniform coat pattern; **6:** gorget with Westphalian eagle, for voltigeur officers with a hunting horn as the emblem; **7:** shako plate; **8:** uniform button; **9:** drum major's dress uniform. In the original drawing of the drum majors, the buttons and trim are shown in silver. Here the buttons have been changed to gold; **10:** musician in dress uniform; **11:** staff officer in dress uniform.

Sources: 1–2 – L. Scharf from von Borcke's memoirs; 3–5 – H. Knötel, watercolor, estate in WGM; 6–8 – W. Hewig, Studie Embleme, H. Knötel's estate; 9–10 – H. Knötel from R. Forthoffer, WGM; 11 – reconstruction from H. Knötel and H. Boisselier.

1
2
3
4
5
9
10
11

UNIFORMS, 1808–1811

PRIVATES

Headgear: Shako like for the Line regiments. The plates and chin-scales were initially made of brass, but later made of white metal like for the other battalions.
The plate had a rhombus shape and displayed a hunting horn with the battalion's number above or inside it as the emblem. Variations with the Westphalian eagle in the center of the plate or the royal monogram "JN" are also confirmed.
For the center companies the cording was made of white or green wool. The attached pompoms displayed the respective company colors. A white plume was worn for parades. The carabinier companies wore bearskin caps with red cording and a plume. The cap bag was light blue with a white cross sewn onto it.
The voltigeur shakos were decorated with green or yellow cording and plumes. A cover made of black waxed cloth was used in the field.
The forage cap in the shape of the French *bonnet de police* was made of light blue cloth and had orange piping.
Coat: First a single-breasted light blue coat was designed. It was closed in the front with a row white buttons; dark green collar, cuffs and turnbacks.
But by the beginning of 1808 a coat like for the line regiments with closed lapels and short coattails was introduced. The basic color of the uniform remained light blue. But the collar, lapels, cuffs, turnbacks and piping appeared in the new orange facing color. Straight cuffs had two buttons attached. The buttons showed a hunting horn with the battalion´s number in the center. Carabiniers were distinguished by red epaulets and grenade devices on the turnbacks. The voltigeurs wore green epaulets with yellow crescents.
Besides the dress uniform a second garment existed: the "small uniform"(undress uniform). Instead of lapels it only was closed in the front with one row of buttons with colored piping.
For internal duty a light blue waistcoat with orange collar and cuffs was worn.
Trousers: Light blue pants. According to the sources, to some extent the short gaiters showed Hungarian pattern with colored trim and tassel (red for carabiniers, green for voltigeurs). Those of the chasseurs had a straight edge without trim. Light blue, white or grey trousers were worn in the field. For Spain, like for the other regiments, pants in various colors, especially brown and olive green ("*Schilfgrün*") are mentioned.
Greatcoat: **Grey** greatcoat. Variations are also shown in beige and light brown.
Equipment and armament: **During the raising of the unit,** black leather belting was planned, however very soon it was replaced with white leather. Cartridge boxes probably had brass plates for the elite companies (a grenade for carabiniers, a hunting horn for voltigeurs). Light brown calfskin backpack. A canteen, haversack and cooking utensils were part of the field equipment.
The armament consisted of a rifle with a bayonet. Sabers were only carried by the elite companies.

NCOs

NCOs' rank insignia followed the French pattern. All NCOs were armed with a rifle and a saber.

DRUMMERS – BUGLERS

The uniform coats were decorated with yellow braid on the collar and cuffs. All drummers, also those with the jaegers, were armed with sabers.

1st Battalion, Light Infantry, 1808 until 1810 (2)

1–5: Jaegers, dress uniform; **1:** company-grade officer; **2:** drummer; **3:** NCO (sergeant); **4–5:** jaegers; **6–8:** carabiniers dress uniform; **6:** drummers; **7–8:** carabinier; **9–10:** voltigeurs dress uniform; **9:** bugler; **10:** voltigeur.
The carabiniers' and voltigeurs' gaiter trim was also shown in the sources with colored edging in red or yellow.

Sources: 1, 3, 4, 5, 7, 8, 10 – H. Knötel's estate in WGM; 2, 6, 9 – reconstructions from H. Boisselier's coat patterns.

4. Kompanie
3. Kompanie
2. Kompanie
1. Kompanie
1
2
3
4
5
6
7
8
9
10

OFFICERS

Headgear: The plates and the cording on the officers' shako were gilt. The width and the placement of the lace bands, as well as the chevrons on the sides, corresponded to the Line's rank system. The shako with a cover or the bicorn was worn in the field.
The officers' field or forage cap was trimmed with golden braid.
Coat: The officer's coat had long coattails with vertically arranged pocket flaps.
All buttons, emblems and rank insignia were gilt. The gorget was gilt with a silver emblem in the center. Different variations are mentioned in the sources: e.g., a Westphalian eagle, grenade and hunting horn.
A single-breasted surtout was worn as the undress uniform.
Trousers: Light blue pants with Hungarian boots, usually with gilt trimming. Along with them, light blue trousers were in use. In Spain they also wore brown, loose-fitting pants.
Greatcoat: It was made of grey or light blue cloth with the collar in the distinction color.
The *Überrock* (redingote) was light blue. Numerous variations are known, for example closed with one or two rows of buttons or with colored piping in the front and on the cuffs. The epaulets were attached in this case.
Armament and equipment: The saber with silver *portepée* was carried on the shoulder bandolier made of black leather. For certain occasions the sword was worn on the white waist belt.
For service in Spain the officers additionally armed themselves with pistols that were stuck in a leather holster.
Saddlecloth: The mounted staff officers' rectangular shabraques were made of light blue cloth with silver braid trim

DRUM MAJOR *(TAMBOURMAJOR)*

As headgear a bicorn with white blue plumage, golden lace trim and cockade. Light blue, white and orange ostrich feathers were attached, and a white plume worked through with light blue was worn.
The coat with long tails and the pants were richly trimmed with golden laces. The rank insignia of the *Feldwebel* (double chevrons on the sleeves, bicolored epaulets) and insignia of seniority in gold and orange. Black gauntlets. Broad bandoleer of black leather with gold lace edging and gilt badge. Baton.
R. Forthoffer shows the battalion's the drum major with all silver decorations on his uniform. We changed the metal color to gold, as the yellow metal strictly belongs to the 1st Battalion.

MUSICIANS

Bicorn with gold lace trim and a white plume with light blue bottom. The uniform coat had long tails and lace trim on the collar, lapels and cuffs. Gold trefoil epaulets. As armament a sword worn on a shoulder bandolier.

2nd BATTALION

COMMANDERs

1812: *Bataillonschef* Bödicker, **1813**: *Bataillonschef* von Lepel

1st Battalion, Light Infantry, 1808 until 1810 (3)

1: Carabinier-officer dress uniform; **2:** jaeger officer in the surtout, undress uniform; **3:** officer in field uniform; **4:** staff officer in redingote *(Überrock)* with forage cap, 1809; **5:** officer in the greatcoat, 1809; **6:** carabinier undress uniform, 1809-10; **7:** jaeger drummer's undress uniform; **8:** jaeger in undress/field uniform; **9:** jaeger in sleeved vest and forage cap.

Sources: 1, 2, 3, 6, 7, 8, 9 – reconstructions from H. Knötel, H. Boisselier, Klaus Tohsche; 4, 5 – H. Knötel's estate in WGM.

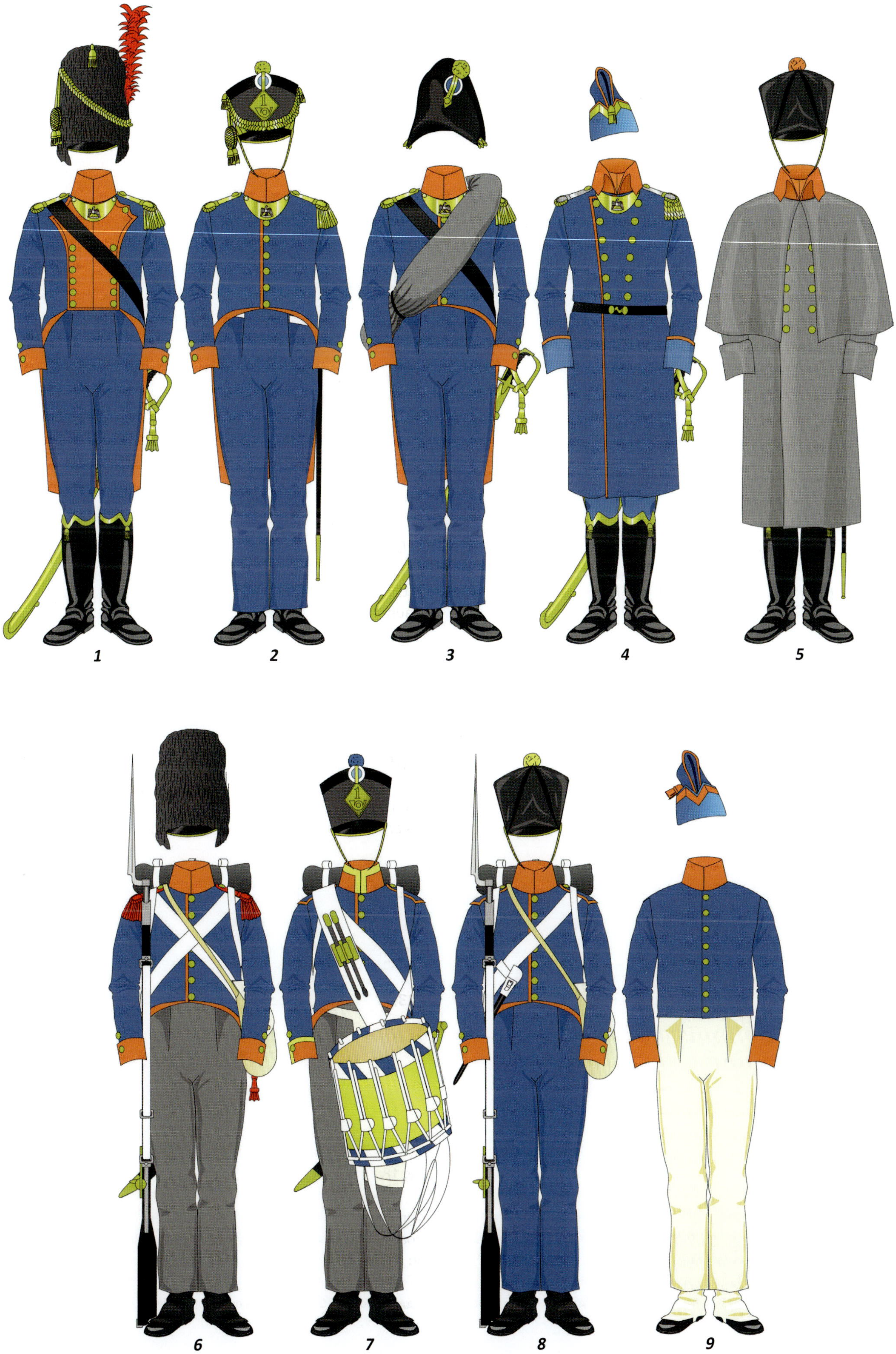

1 2 3 4 5

ACTIONS

1809: **F**irst mentioned at the end of July, but the exact date of establishment is unknown. Garrison in Ziegenhain.
1812: Russian Campaign
VIII Army Corps (Jerôme/Junot), 23rd Division (Tharreau), 2nd Brigade (Wickenberg)
Strength report in August: 20 officers and 583 men.

1813: On the 1st of April newly formed with a strength of four companies and participated in the campaign in Saxony.
In August the battalion was disbanded during the cease-fire and half of the privates were sent back to Westphalia. The remainder of the troops were taken into the 4th Battalion which was located with the X. Army Corps.

UNIFORMS, 1809–1811

The uniform, which the 2nd Light Battalion (*2. Leichte Bataillon*) received at its creation in 1809 was the same as that of the 1st Battalion with the following differences:

1. Lapels and turnbacks light blue with orange piping.
2. Silver metal color and officers' gorgets.
3. The voltigeur buglers wore orange uniforms.
4. The musicians wore orange uniforms and czapkas as headgear.
5. Drum major was probably attired like for the 1st Battalion, but with silver lace trim.

2nd Battalion, Light Infantry, 1808 until 1810 (1)

Dress uniform 1: coat pattern for officers, emblems for carabiniers and voltigeurs; **2:** coat pattern, jaeger, emblems for carabiniers and voltigeurs; **3:** coat pattern undress uniform; **4:** uniform button 2nd Battalion; **5:** staff officer; **6:** gorget for voltigeur-officers; **7:** shako plate; **8:** officer; **9:** drummer; **10:** NCO (*Feldwebel*/sergeant-major); **11, 12:** jaegers.

Sources: 1, 2, 3, 5, 8, 9, 10, 12 – H. Knötel's estate in WGM; 4, 6, 7 – W. Hewig, *Studie Embleme,* estate of H. Knötel;
11 – from S. Hahlo's manuscript. 1807/08

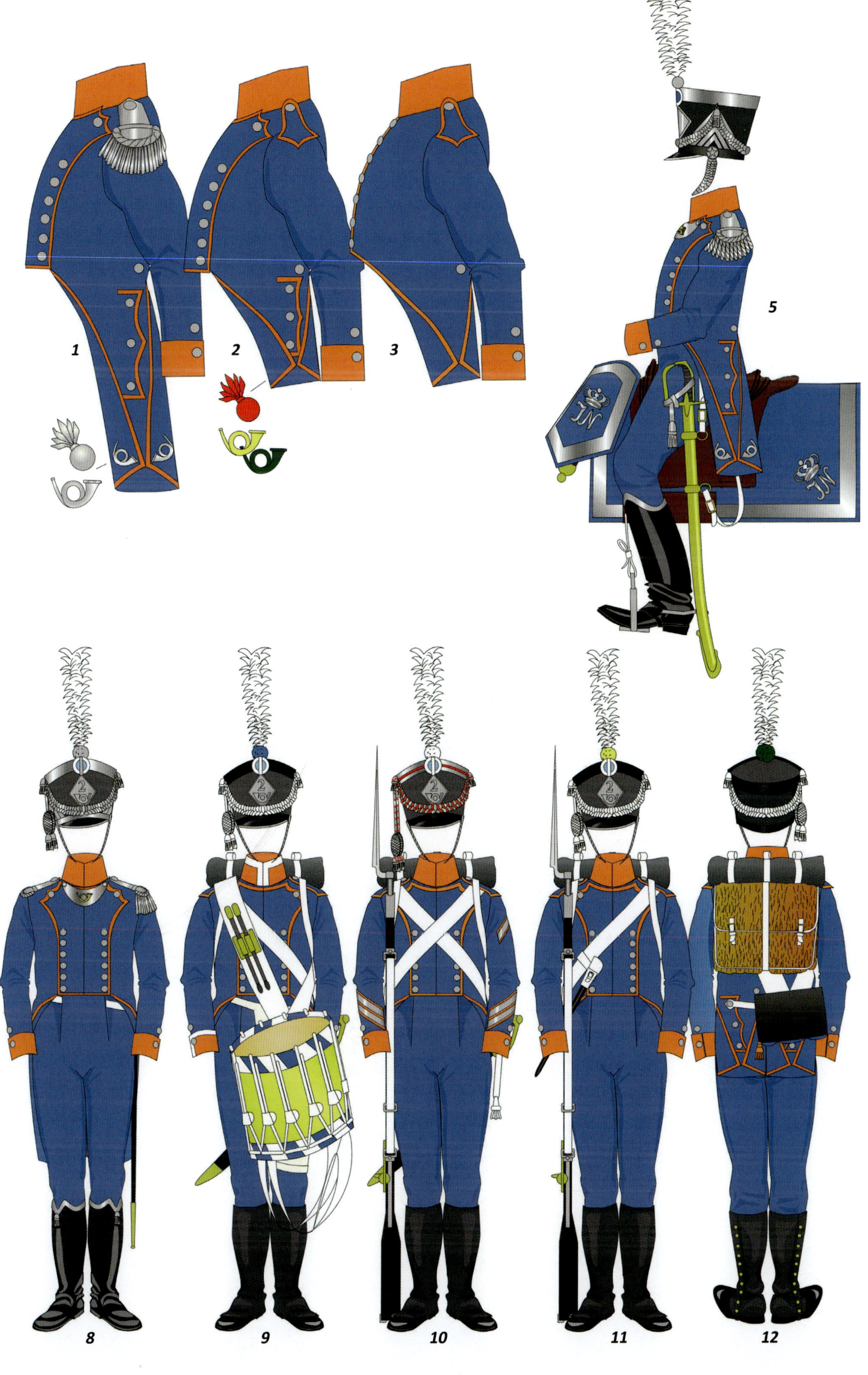
1
2
3
5
8
9
10
11
12

PERIOD 1811–1813

3rd BATAILLON

COMMANDERS

1811: *Colonel* Füllgraf, Major Humbert-Verneuil, **1812**: *Bataillonschef* von Hessberg, **1813**: *Bataillonschef* Vigelius

ACTIONS

1811: Probably formed in February, more detailed information is not known. Garrison in Paderborn.
1812: Russian Campaign, VIII Army Corps (Jerôme/ Junot), 23rd Division (Tharreau), 1st Brigade (Damas)

1813: When newly raised in April it received the title "4. Leichtes Bataillon" (4th Light Battalion). In September it was wiped out during the defense of Kassel.

Light infantry, jaeger
2nd Battalion, 1809
Copy by W. Hewig from *Manuscrit du Canonier Hahlo*, 1807/08. Collection: Edmund Wagner.

2nd Battalion, Light Infantry, 1808 until 1810 (2)

1–5: Dress uniform **1:** carabinier drummer **2:** carabinier **3:** voltigeur bugler **4–5:** voltigeurs **6:** officer in surtout, undress uniform **7:** jaeger drummer, undress uniform **8:** jaeger, undress uniform **9:** voltigeur bugler undress uniform **10:** musician dress uniform.

Sources: 1, 7, 8, 9 – reconstructions, 2, 3, 4, 5, 10 – H. Knötel's estate in WGM, 6 – Vinkhuijzen Collection, NYPL.

4th BATTALION

COMMANDER

1813: Major von Winkel

ACTIONS

1810: On 1 May the so-called "Spanish Regiment" (*"spanische Regiment"*) was created in Spain from the remnants of the Infantry Regiments Nos. 2, 3 and 4 and the 1st Light Battalion.

1811: The remnants of the 1st Battalion in Spain received the new designation of the "4th Light Battalion" (*"4. Leichtes Bataillon"*).

1813: In April the unit was newly constituted from the able-bodied privates and recruits returning from Spain. The battalion then received the designation as the "3rd Battalion" (*"3. Bataillon"*).

UNIFORMS, 1811–1813

The light Infantry battalions that were newly raised starting in 1811 received a new uniform, which had already been introduced in the first two existing battalions. Because it was the same for all the battalions, in sources it is often called the *"Einheitsuniform"* (standard uniform).

PRIVATES 1818–1813

Headgear: For the jaegers and voltigeurs the headgear remained unchanged. The battalion's number was now displayed on all the shako plates. The carabiniers then also received a shako with red decorations. However, the bearskin hat seems to have remained in use for a while (possibly as a parade accoutrement).

The forage cap was made of green cloth and had light blue piping.

Coat: Dark green, single-breasted coats with light blue distinctions and piping. The cuffs became round again and were decorated with two buttons. The white metal buttons each showed the battalion's number.

The special distinctions for the elite companies were as before.

The waistcoat also became green with light blue collar and cuffs.

Light Infantry Battalions, 1811–1813 (1)

Dress uniform 1: officer's coat pattern; **2:** jaeger's coat pattern; **3:** uniform buttons of the 4 battalions; **4:** shako plate for 2nd Battalion; **5:** gorget model starting 1811; **6:** staff office, major; **7:** jaeger officer; **8–9:** jaeger; **10:** carabinier; **11:** voltigeur.

Sources: 1–2 – from H. Knötel and L. Scharf, estate in WGM, 3–5 – W. Hewig, Studie Embleme, estate in WGM, 6 – reconstruction from H. Boisselier, 7 – S. Pinhas, 8–9 – L. Scharf, 10 – C. F. Weiland, 11 – H. Boisselier.

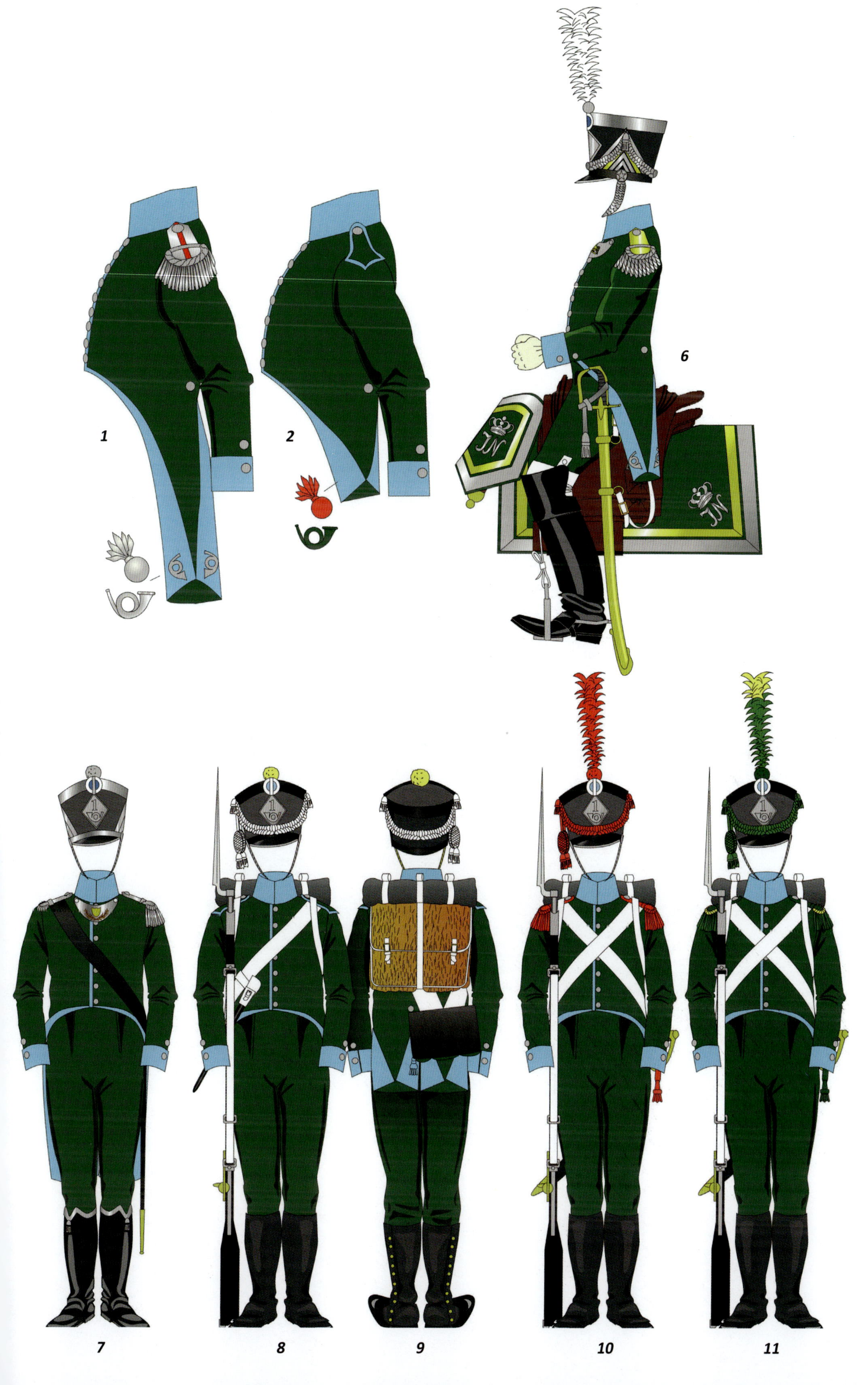
1
2
6
7
8
9
10
11

Light infantry officer, 1811
Pinhas, Salomon: *Recueil de planches représentant les troupes des différentes armes et grades de l'armée Westphalienne*, 1811–1813.

Light Infantry carabinier, 1812
Weiland, C. F.: *Représentation des uniformes de l'armée impériale royale française et des alliés*, 1807 and 1812.

Trousers: The pants were dark green. Black gaiters reaching to just under the knee. Some of the elite still wore the Hungarian style gaiters with colored trim and tassels. Grey or (in the summer) white overalls were in use in the field. As peculiarities, baggy pants in varying colors of grey, brown to olive green (*schilfgrün*) are mentioned in Spain.
Greatcoat: Unchanged.

Equipment and armament: The sources show white as well as black leather belting. Whether the color can be attributed to specific battalions or assigned to certain periods of time is unknown. Otherwise the equipment remained unchanged.
Starting in 1811 the jaegers were equipped with infantry sabers.

NCOs

Unchanged.

OFFICERS

Shako: Shako with silver decorations.
Coat: Coat with long tails. All buttons, emblems and rank insignia were in silver. The silver gorget had the royal emblem in the center. Variations were possible, e.g., for the 1st Battalion had a gilt hunting horn; for the 2nd Battalion a gilt Westphalian eagle. For the carabinier officers, the grenade was possible as an emblem.
Trousers: Green pants with Hungarian boots with silver trim. Additionally trousers in varied colors were in use, e.g., in Spain frequently brown baggy pants.
Greatcoat: Grey greatcoats and green surtouts *(Überröcke).*

Armament and equipment: The saber with silver *portepée* was worn on the black leather shoulder bandolier. At the chest height was a shield-shaped badge with the royal initials. For special occasions the sword was worn on a white waist belt. For service in Spain the officers equipped themselves with pistols that were worn stuck in a holster made of leather.
Saddlecloth: The rectangular-cut shabraques for the mounted staff officers were made of green cloth and had silver braid trim.

DRUMMERS – BUGLERS

The privates´ coat had braid trim on the collar and cuffs. The braid was white with light blue rhombuses or rectangles.
The drum rims were depicted with variations: light blue and white triangles, light blue and white bars or completely light blue.
In the sources there are still special uniforms for the drummers and buglers of the individual battalions:
1st Battalion – *Grenadier-Tambour* according to H. Knötel:
Bearskin hat with red decorations; uniform completely light blue with green distinctions. The coat also has green lapels! The lapels, collar and cuffs were bordered with a white braid with light blue vertical stripes.
2nd Battalion – *Chasseur-Tambour* according to the *Papiersoldaten Kasseler Papierfiguren*, in the estate of H. Knötel:
The green coat was edged on the collar and cuffs with a yellow braid with green rectangles. On each sleeve were five braid stripes.
3rd Battalion – *Chasseur-Pfeiffer* according to R. Forthoffer:
Shako with green pompom, light blue plume with red tip and light blue cording with red *raquettes* on the right side. Light blue uniform like for the grenadier drummer of the 1st Battalion. Light blue epaulets with red crescents.
4th Battalion – *Chasseur-Tambour* according to R. Forthoffer:
The green coat is decorated on the collar, cuffs and on the chest with white braid with light blue rhombuses. Light blue epaulets with white crescents.

Light Infantry Battalions, 1811–1813 (2)
Head of Column / *Tetes de Colonne*

1: Carabinier drummer, 1st Battalion; **2:** drummer, 1st Jaeger Battalion; **3:** drummer, 2nd Jaeger Battalion; **4:** drummer, 3rd Jaeger Battalion; **5:** drummer, 4th Jaeger Battalion; **6:** voltigeur bugler; **7:** drum major drummer corporal; **8:** musician 2nd Battalion 1810–1813; **9:** musician 3rd Battalion; **10:** musician 4th Battalion.

Sources: 1, 4, 5, 8, 9, 10 –pictures series by R. Forthoffer, H. Knötel's estate in WGM; 3 – Strasbourg paper soldiers, H. Knötel estate WGM; 2, 6, 7 – H. Boisselier from Collection Fritz Kieffer, Elsässische Papiersoldaten; 10 – C. F. Weiland; 11 – H. Boisselier.

1
2
3
4
5
6
7
8
9
10

DRUM MAJOR

The drum majors' uniform of this period is unknown.

MUSICIANS

The musicians of the individual battalions wore special parade uniforms according to R. Forthoffer:

1st Battalion: Uniform is not known.
2nd Battalion: Shako the body covered in green. White trim bands on the upper and lower edges. Cording and pompom white, and above it a white plume with a green base. Orange coat with long coattails. Collar, lapels and cuffs were dark green. Everything was trimmed with silver braid. Silver trefoil epaulets. Green pants; Hungarian boots with silver trim. Sword on the white shoulder bandolier as armament.

3rd Battalion: Bicorn with silver edging and a white plume with a green base. Light blue surtout with green distinctions. Silver braid trim on the collar and cuffs; silver trefoil epaulets. Light blue pants with Hungarian boots. The sword was carried on a white shoulder bandolier.
4th Battalion: Bicorn with silver edging and a white plume with a blue tip. Green surtout with light blue distinctions. Silver trefoil epaulets. White pants with Hungarian boots. The sword was worn on a white shoulder bandolier.

Light Infantry – officer, jaeger and drummer, 1811.
Deutsches Historisches Museum, Berlin [GOS-Nr. MGR05714/Inv. No. MGr 56/42.2].

Light Infantry Battalions, 1811–1813 (3)

1: Officer 2nd Battalion in dress uniform; **2:** officer in redingote; **3:** officer field dress; **4:** drummers undress uniform; **5:** jaeger, field dress; **6:** jaeger in fatigue uniform with sleeved vest and forage cap; **7:** officer, Spain, 1811–1813; **8:** carabinier, Spain, 1811–1813.

Sources: 1 – O. Norie, sketches; 2 – H. Boisselier; 3 – S. Pinhas, – from F. Kieffer's Strasbourg paper soldier collection; 5 – H. Boisselier; 6 – reconstruction analogous Line infantry; 7 – L. Scharf; 8 – H. Knötel.
The pointed lapels are among the peculiarities of this depiction. According to W. Hewig, the coat with lapels is possible, perhaps as a dress uniform or a battalion-specific unique feature. However, this is not corroborated by other sources.
Regarding 8, also with the bearskin cap292. For Spain possible, because the old equipment was worn until it wore out.

1
2
3
4
5
6
7
8

Heavy cavalry: cuirassier and officer of the 1st Regiment
Suhr, Christoph: *Album du Bourgeois de Hambourg*, 1806–1815, Kommerz-Bibliothek Hamburg, photo: Markus Stein.

CAVALRY OF THE LINE
CUIRASSIERS *(KÜRASSIERE)*

King Jérôme established two cuirassier regiments. He did this contrary to the express wishes of his brother Napoleon. In Napoleon's opinion the heavy cavalry's equipment was too expensive for the Kingdom of Westphalia.

A regiment consisted of four field squadrons (*Feld-Eskadronen*) with two companies each. There was no special elite company.

ORGANIZATION

Upper Staff ***(Oberstab)*** (11 men)	**Lower Staff** **(*Unterstab*)** (12 men)	**Company** (85 men)
1 Colonel	4 Adjutants	1 Captain
1 Major	2 Surgeons 3rd Class	1 *Premier-Lieutenant*
2 Squadron Commanders (*Eskadronschefs*)	1 Veterinarian	1 *Seconde-Lieutenant*
2 *Adjudants Majors*	1 Horse Doctor's Aid (*Pferdearztgehilfe*)	1 *Oberwachtmeister*
1 Paymaster Officer (*Offizierzahlmeister*)	1 Foreman (*Arbeitsmeister*)	2 *Wachmeister*
1 Quartermaster	2 *Handwerker*	1 *Fourier*
1 Instructor		8 *Brigadiers*
1 Senior Surgeon (*Oberchirurg*)		2 Trumpeters
2 Surgeons 2nd Class		66 Cuirassiers

In addition, there was a depot company that was led by the major and the clothier captain (*Bekleidungskapitän*). Assisting them were also the quartermaster (*Quartiermeister*), the "instructor" (*Bereiter*), a surgeon 3rd class and a foreman (*Arbeitsmeister*) with the two workers (*Arbeitern*). Additionally a train section with four baggage wagons and 16 horses, driven by eight train soldiers (*Trainsoldaten*), from the Train Company were attached.

Kurhessian *Pallasch* saber with royal monogram, ca. 1808
Museum Schloss Friedrichstein (Bad Wildungen), photo: Markus Gaertner.

1st CUIRASSIER REGIMENT *(1. KÜRASSIER-REGIMENT)*

Beginning on 10 March 1808 a first cuirassier regiment was raised as a heavy cavalry unit. The peacetime strength with the depot was established as 735 men. However, the number of troops varied greatly.

The recruiting for this unit proceeded only in fits and starts and until the end of 1808 the 1st Regiment reached a total strength of just 471 men. At the end of 1811 the strength of 30 officers and 640 men was confirmed.
The 1st Regiment's garrison was at Brunswick (Braunschweig), then Aschersleben and Ziegenhain.

COMMANDERS

1808: Colonel K. F. Klösterlein, **1809**: Colonel F. von Wurthen, **1812**: Colonel Eitel von Gilsa, Colonel von Wolff, **1813**: Colonel Lallemand, Major Darbaud

ACTIONS 1809–1812

1809: – *April* – 1st Squadron against the Dörnberg uprising – *July* – in the 2nd Westphalian Division in North Germany – *1 August* – Battle of Oelper
1810: Return to Garrison in Aschersleben
1812: Russian Campaign
IV Cavalry Corps (Latour-Maubourg), 7th Division (Lorge), 2nd Brigade (Lepel)
Strength in June 1812: 538 men

7 September: the Battle of Borodino, Colonel v. Gilsa was fatally wounded and died of his wounds on 12 September in Mohaisk.
October in Moscow, retreat with heavy losses. Assembly location at Thorn (Torun, Poland), where only about 60 men from the two cuirassier regiments arrived by year's end.

UNIFORMS

PRIVATES

Headgear: Metal helmet with brass crest and black or dark brown fur caterpillar. The front of the crest ended in a shield-shaped badge which was decorated with the royal initials "JN". The lower part of the helmets dome was covered with sealskin. The visor was leather had a brass rim. Brass chin-scales. For parades a red plume was attached on the left side.
The forage cap corresponded to the infantry's model and until ca. 1811 was white, after that dark blue. Both models were piped in the distinction color and had a grenade emblem or the regiment's number on the front.

Coat: White uniform coat with crimson red distinctions. In the various sources the crimson varies from dark rose to red. The lapels were closed. The coat had short tails without coattail pockets. The turnbacks were decorated with white grenade devices. Until 1811 the cuffs had cuff flaps. The metal buttons were white. Red fringed epaulets.
A white coat without lapels was worn for the undress uniform. It was closed with one row of seven buttons.

1st Cuirassier Regiment, 1808–1810

1 and 4: officer, Colonel in full dress (grande tenue), 1808-1809. At the Regiment's early phase, a coat with French-style open lapels was worn as the undress coat; **2 and 5:** trumpeter in dress uniform until 1810;
3 and 7: cuirassier, in dress uniform had a plume added; **6:** NCO, *maréchal des logis chef* in dress uniform.

Sources: 1, 4 – from the painting *"Das Gefecht bei Oelper,"* Braunschweig; 2, 5 – from R. Forthoffer, *Fiches documentaires* plate 172; 3, 7 – from Christoph Suhr *Bourgeois de Hambourg*; 6 – reconstruction from R. Forthoffer.

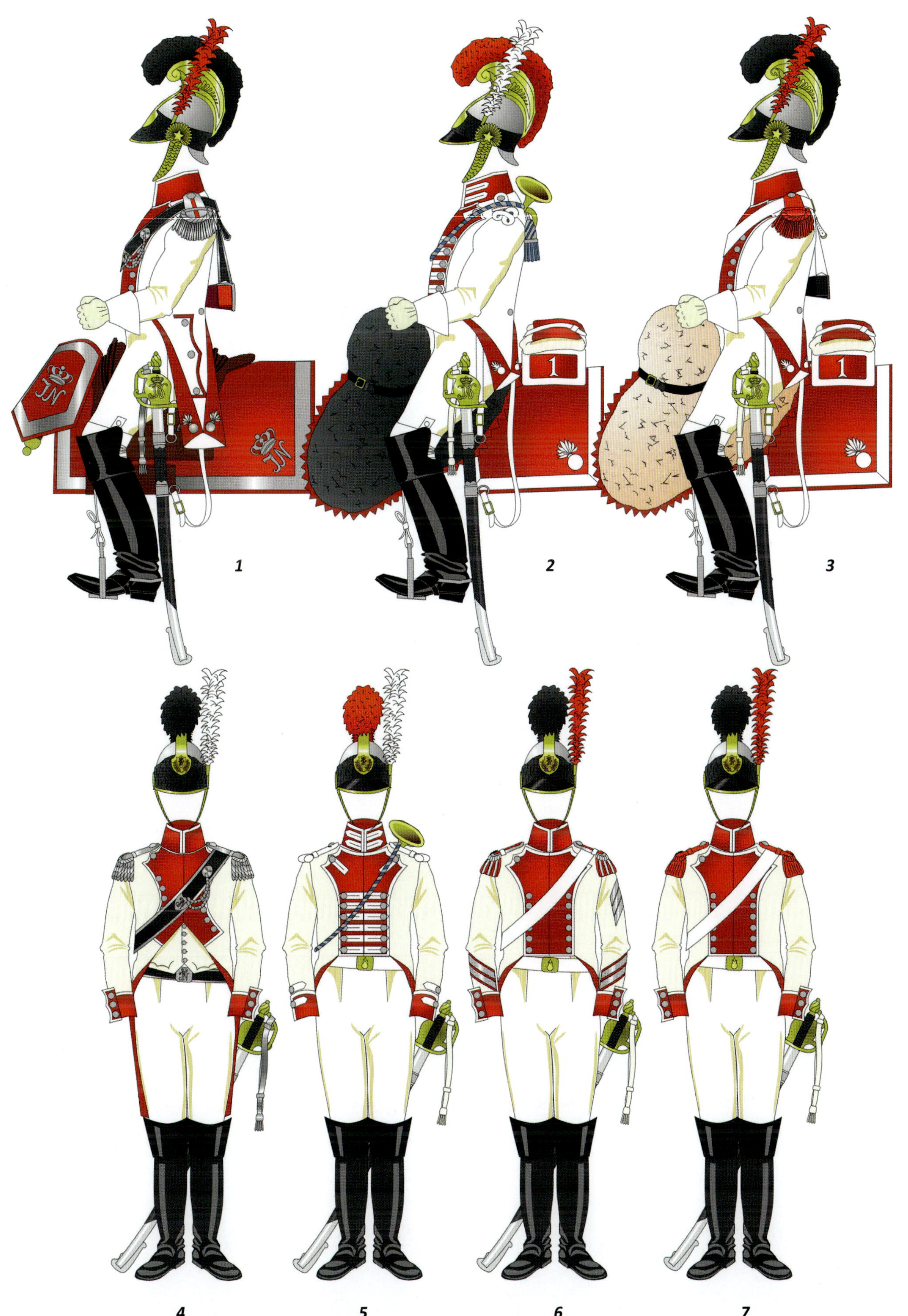
1
2
3
4
5
6
7

In 1810, the coat with lapels was discontinued and the undress coat – now with eight buttons in front and coat-tail pockets – was worn.

For inside and stable duty a grey waistcoat was worn. Its collar and cuffs had crimson piping.

Pants: White pants for the parade dress uniform with tall cavalry boots. Grey or brown riding trousers, with crimson stripes on the sides, were worn for daily duty and in the field. There were also grey overalls with a row of buttons at the sides and with leather reinforcing on the leg´s inside. They were pulled over the boots. Grey cloth pants and shoes for stable duty.

Greatcoat: The white greatcoat had a facing-colored collar.

Equipment: When the regiment was created in 1808 it did not receive cuirasses. Around 1810 the first company was equipped with full cuirasses of polished steel. In the remaining companies only the officers were issued cuirasses at that point. Only in 1812 were cuirasses provided for the whole regiment.

It also seems that in the beginning, cuirasses of a different pattern, which consisted of a black frontal plate only, were issued.

For field dress, the cuirassiers who did not have cuirasses wore the greatcoat rolled up over the shoulder for protection from saber blows.

White leather belting. The black leather cartridge pouch had no decorations.

Armament: In the beginning, the old Hessian sabers, which had a lightly curved blade, were still in use. But later French Model AN II straight swords with metal scabbards were introduced. The armament was also supplemented by two pistols on the saddle.

Saddlecloth: The saddlecloth was the same as the French heavy cavalry model. It consisted of a white fleeces with crimson wolves teeth on the edge. It was on top of a rectangular saddlecloth of crimson cloth with white edging trim and white grenade devices. It had a rectangular valise/greatcoat roll marked with the number "1".

NCOs

The NCOs wore the same uniform as the privates but with French rank insignia in the form of braids on the coat sleeves. The more senior NCOs *(Wachtmeister)* probably had mixed silver and red epaulets.

OFFICERS

The helmet's caterpillar crest was made of black bearskin. Staff officers had a white plume.

For the undress uniform and internal duties the helmet could have been exchanged for a bicorn.

Uniform: Coat with long coattails, which had vertical pocket flaps with red piping.

A single-breasted frock coat (surtout) without lapels was worn for undress.

Until the middle of 1809 the officers also wore a coat with open and pointed lapels. All decorations, buttons and badges and the rank insignia were silvered.

Along with the French model polished cuirass, the officers also appeared with black breastplates. They were decorated with a gilt sun-shaped plate.

Black bandoliers for the cartridge pouch with silvered edging. The sources show various patterns for officer's cartridge pouches. The saber belt was also made of black leather with silver edging.

Tenue de ville et société* (walking out and social dress):* A bicorn as headgear. White or dark blue surtout with red piping.

The pants made of calico and knee high silk stockings. Black, low cut shoes with metal buckles. Sword on the waist belt.

Saddlecloth: cloth shabraque with pistol holsters. On both parts the royal cypher "JN" and edging trim in silver.

1st Cuirassier Regiment, 1808–1810

1: Officer in the 1808 full dress uniform, the attire worn for social events. For this, the bicorn was worn as the headgear and instead of boots, half-high shoes with silk knee socks were worn; **2 and 7:** cuirassiers in undress uniform; **3:** cuirassier in the field uniform until 1811; **4:** cuirassier in the stable-/work dress with forage cap and sleeved vest; **5:** coat pattern dress uniform for privates until 1810; **6:** coat pattern for trumpeters, 1808–1810; **7:** coat pattern for privates's undress uniform; **8:** front badge for metal helmet and button with the regiment's number.

Sources: 1 – from H. Knötel and R. Forthoffer, *Fiches documentaires* plate 173; 2, 7 – from H. Knötel; 3 – reconstruction from H. Knötel; 4 – from W. Hewig; 5, 6, 7 – from R. Forthoffer, *Fiches documentaires* plate 172; 8 – from C. F. Weiland and W. Hewig's patterns.

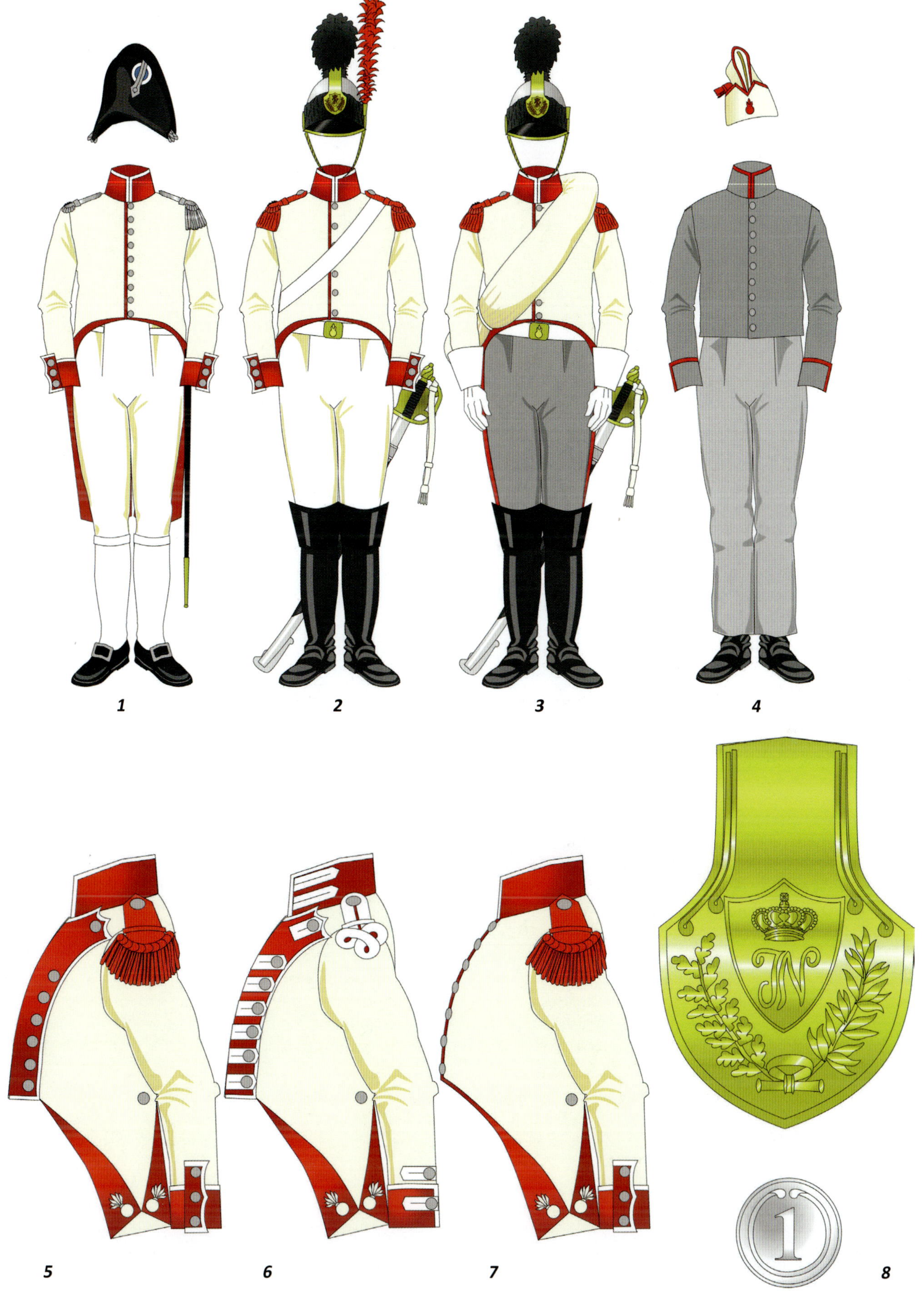

1
2
3
4
5
6
7
8

1st Cuirassier Regiment, 1809
Suhr, Christoph: *Album du Bourgeois de Hambourg*, 1806–1815, Kommerz-Bibliothek Hamburg; photo: Markus Stein.

Officer, 1st Cuirassier Regiment, 1809
Weiland, C. F.: *Représentation des uniformes de l' armée impériale royale française et des alliés, 1807 und 1812.* Lipperheide Kostümbibliothek, Berlin.

Half cuirass for 1st Regiment, 1808–1812
Photo: Markus Gaertner.

1st Cuirassier Regiment, 1810–1812

1 and 3: Officer in dress uniform with French model full cuirass and variation with half cuirass based on an original artifact. From Herbert Knötel's Westphälische Studie and patterns in WGM; **2, 4 and 5:** cuirassiers of the 1st company with full cuirass and undress uniform. From Herbert Knötel's patterns, WGM collection; 3a: detail of sun badge on officer's cuirass. From an original photo, collection by Herbert Knötel; **6:** cuirassier in stable and work dress with sleeved vest, 1812. For the Russia campaign, the cuirassiers supposedly wore the sleeved vest and grey overalls as the uniform on the march. For body protection, the full cuirass made of steel, the cartouche bandolier as well as waist belt made of black leather. For armament, a straight Pallasch with a brass hilt, on which was a round badge with the royal "JN" monogram . The shabraque of black fleece with crimson border and round valise with the numeral "1".

Sources: 1, 2, 3, 4, 5 – from H. Knötel's patterns; 3a – from an original photo, collection H. Knötel;
6 – from R. Forthoffer, *Fiches documentaires* plate 174.

1
2
3
3a
4
5
6
1
1

TRUMPETERS

1808–1810:
Headgear: Helmet with red caterpillar and white plume.
Coat: The trumpeters wore the coat like for the privates but with additional white lace trim on the collar and on the lapels; white trefoil epaulets on both shoulders.
Trumpet cords and tassels were mixed white and blue.
The trumpeters did not carry a cartridge box. The saddlecloth was like for privates but with a darker fleece cover.

1810–1812:
Headgear: Helmet with a white caterpillar crest and plume.
Coat: **Coat in reversed colors** – crimson red with white distinctions. The collar did nnot have the lace trim; instead the collar, lapels, cuffs and coattails were decorated with a wide silver braid. Crimson red grenade devices on the turnbacks. White or silver fringed epaulets.
Undress (*Kleine*) Uniforms*:* As headgear a colpak/busby made of dark brown or black fur with a red bag and white metal chin-scales. On the left side was the cockade.
Single-breasted, crimson coat with 7 horizontal white or silver laces on the chest. Lace edging on the collar and cuffs. Epaulets made of white wool.
Grey pants with wide crimson stripes on the sides.

7

1st Cuirassier Regiment, 1810–1812

1 and 2: trumpeter in dress uniform, 1811–1812; **3:** trumpeter in undress uniform; **4:** coat pattern for cuirassier, 1810; **5:** coat pattern for trumpeter. dress uniform until 1811; **6:** coat pattern for trumpeter. undress uniform until 1811; **7:** officer's cartridge pouch variations.

Sources: 1, 2 – from R. Forthoffer, *Fiches documetaires* plate 172; 3 – from H. Knötel, *Westphälische Studie*; 7 – from C. F. Weiland; 8 – from an original photo, collection H. Knötel.

1
2
3
4
5
6

Officer, 1st Cuirassier Regiment, 1811
Pinhas, Salomon: *Recueil de planches représentant les troupes des différentes armes et grades de l'armée Westphalienne,* 1811–1813, in privately owned series.

Officer, 2nd Cuirassier Regiment, 1811
Pinhas, Salomon: *Recueil de planches représentant les troupes des différentes armes et grades de l'armée Westphalienne,* 1811–1813, in privately owned series.

2nd CUIRASSIER REGIMENT

1811–1812

Forming the 2nd Cuirassier Regiment began in 1811. The unit was ready for the 1812 Russian Campaign and was deployed along with the 1st Cuirassier Regiment. Its garrison was in Hanover.

1

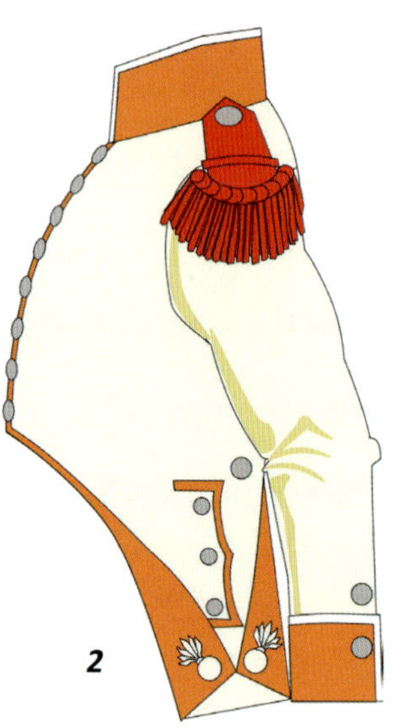

2

2nd Cuirassier Regiment, 1809–1811

1: Front plate for the helmet with the emblem for 2nd Regiment, uniform button; **2:** coat pattern for privates for the uniform until 1811. The coat now had 8 small buttons forward on the chest, modified cuffs and pockets on the coattails;
3 and 5: officer dress uniform; **4 and 6:** cuirassier in dress uniform. Saddle variation in the first color given – orange – for the 2nd Regiment; **7:** duty uniform without cuirass; **8:** NCO (*maréchal des logis*) in the walking out dress (surtout).

Sources: 1 – From an original artifact in the Deutsches Historisches Museum, Berlin and a sketch by W. Hewig;
2 – from patterns by H. Knötel, WGM; 3, 5, 8 – from R. Forthoffer's manuscript;
4, 6 – from sketches by von H. Knötel, WGM; 7 – R. Forthoffer, *Fiches documentaires* plate 173.

3
4
5
6
7
8

COMMANDERS

1811: Colonel Carl G. von Bastineller, **1813**: Colonel Scheffer

UNIFORMS

PRIVATES

Headgear: Polished iron helmet with a black caterpillar crest like for the 1st Regiment. It had its own shape of the brass plate in the front.
Coat: White, single-breasted uniform coat like for the 1st Regiment but with orange facings.
This uniform was possibly only projected; the regiment had already gotten the blue uniform when it was raised, which is descripted below under 1813. Pinhas' series of illustrations show an officer of the regiment in a blue uniform coat.

Pants: White pants for the parade dress uniform with tall cavalry boots. Grey cloth pants and shoes for stable duty.
Equipment: Steel cuirass. White leather belting. The cartridge box was made of black leather decorated with a brass grenade emblem.
Armament: *Pallasch* straight saber and pistols like for 1st Regiment.
Saddlecloth: The heavy cavalry saddlecloth with fleece over the saddle. Until 1812 orange cloth shabraque and valise (*Mantelsack*) with white edging. After that blue shabraque. Valise (*Mantelsack*) was round on the ends.

NCOs

The NCOs wore the privates's uniform with French rank insignia in the form of braids on the coat sleeves. More senior NCOs *(Wachtmeister)* probably had mixed silver and orange epaulets.

OFFICERS

For the officers,the coat had long coattails. The attire was otherwise the same as for the 1st Regiment.

2nd Cuirassier Regiment, 1809–1812

1 and 2: trumpeter, dress uniform, 1809–1810; **3:** trumpeter, dress uniform, 1810–1812; **4:** trumpeter, dress uniform, 1812; **5:** trumpeter undress uniform; **6:** trumpeter's coat, 1810; **7:** trumpeter's coat dress uniform, 1812; **8:** trumpeter's coat undress uniform, 1811.

Sources: 1, 2 – from O. Norie; 3, 4, 5, 7, 8 – from H. Knötel's *Westphälische Studie*; 6 – from W. Hewig.

2
4
1
3
6
7
8
5

TRUMPETERS

1811:
Headgear: Helmet with red caterpillar crest and white plume.
Coat: White privates's coat with orange facings, with white lace trim on the collar, lapels, and cuffs. Silver trefoil epaulets on both shoulders and white aiguillettes on the left.
Saddlecloth: Shabraque like for the privates, but with black fleece.
1812:
Headgear: Colpak/busby with an orange bag and white cording and plume. The helmet with a red caterpillar crest was also continued to be worn.
Coat: Orange coat with blue facings with white braid trim on the collar, lapels and cuffs. White fringed epaulets.
For the undress uniform they wore a single-breasted, dark blue coat with seven white laces on the chest and white edging around the collar and cuffs. It had red fringed epaulets.
Pants: White pants and high cavalry boots. In the field close-fitting grey pants with wide orange stripes on the sides. Long overalls were also possible.
Saddlecloth: Orange cloth shabraque like for privates. Round valise/greatcoat roll dark blue with white trim and the numeral "2" on the side.

STARTING IN 1813

With the end of the Russian campaign both Westphalian cuirassier regiments were nearly annihilated. The regiments were reorganized with the privates from the depots and new recruits. By the middle 1813 the two units reached a strength of about 600 men each. In mid-September they were combined in a brigade and stationed in the area around Berka. During the subsequent assault by the Allies on Kassel on 28 September 1813, the cuirassiers, who were scattered in various villages around Kassel, dissolved due to desertions.

UNIFORMS

PRIVATES

Headgear: French model cuirassier helmet. However, instead of the hanging horsetail, a black caterpillar plume was attached.
The dark blue *Pokalem* style undress cap had orange piping and a white grenade emblem in the front.
Coat: Dark blue, single-breasted coats with orange distinctions. The coattail emblems were blue. Red fringed epaulets.
For stable duty a dark blue waistcoat that was closed in front with 9 buttons. The collar and cuffs were piped in the distinction color.
Pants: White pants with tall straight boots. In the field long grey or light brown overalls with or without leather reinforcement were also worn. The pants were usually trimmed with wide crimson red stripes along the seams
Greatcoat: grey cavalry greatcoat.
Equipment: White leather belting. The black leather cartridge box had a brass grenade badge.
Armament: French cuirassier's straight saber with a metal scabbard. The sword-strap was made of white leather. Two pistols were housed in the holsters on the saddle, completing the armament. The cuirassiers were probably not armed with carbines.
Saddlecloth: The heavy cavalry saddlecloth with fleece cover over the saddle. Cloth shabraque in the blue basic color. A round valise (*Mantelsack*).

1st and 2nd Cuirassier Regiments, 1813

1 and 3: Officer in dress uniform; **2 and 5:** cuirassier in dress uniform. Greatcoat variations as differences between the regiments; **4:** NCO – *maréchal des logis* in dress uniform; **6:** cuirassier without cuirass in the undress uniform.

Sources: 1, 2, 3, 4, 5 – from H. Knötel's patterns; 6 – from W. Hewig, and notes in H. Knötel's estate.

1
2
3
4
5
6

NCOs

The NCOs wore the privates's uniform with French rank insignia in the form of braids on the coat sleeves. More senior NCOs *(Wachtmeister)* probably had silver and red mixed epaulets.

OFFICERS

Coat like for the other ranks. Otherwise the dress was unchanged.

TRUMPETERS

Headgear: Helmet with white caterpillar crest and plume. For the undress uniform colpak/busby with white cording and plume.
Coat: Single-breasted, dark blue coat like for the privates. White braid trim on the buttonholes. Collar and cuffs with edged with white braid. White grenade emblems on the turnbacks.

Saddlecloth: Saddlecloth like for cuirassiers but with dark fleece over the saddle.

Trumpeter's helmet, 2nd Cuirassier Regiment
Deutsches Historisches Museum, Berlin.
photo: Peter Bunde.

1st and 2nd Cuirassier Regiments 1813

1 and 2: Trumpeter in dress uniform 1813; **3:** trumpeter in undress uniform; **4:** cuirassier in field uniform; **5:** cuirassier in the greatcoat. According to Salomon Pinhas, 1811–13; **6:** cuirassier in stable dress; **7:** coat pattern for cuirassier's dress uniform; **8:** trumpeter's dress uniform coat pattern; **9:** uniform buttons – the two regiments only differed in the embossing on the buttons.

Sources: 1, 2, 8 – from R. Forthoffer, Manuscrit de Marckolsheim; 3, 4, 7 – from H. Knötel; 5 – from Salomon Pinhas; 6 – reconstruction; 9 – from W. Hewig's patterns.

1
2
3
4
5
6
7
8
9
1
2

***Chef d'Escadron* 1st Chevauleger Regiment, 1812, after Salomon Pinhas**
Watercolor by Edmund Wagner, collection of Markus Gaertner.

CHEVAULEGERS

The organization was identical to that of the cuirassiers. But the 1st company of the 1st squadron was distinguished with the title *"Elite-Kompanie"* (elite company).

1st CHEVAULEGER REGIMENT

The 1st Regiment was raised on 10 March 1808 in Osnabrück with former Hessian, Prussian and other generally experienced cavalrymen. In September 1808 it was ordered to march out to the Spanish theater. To rapidly fill out the number of horses the regiment needed for Spain, 200 horses were transferred from the Guard Chevaulegers. When the unit departed, the effective strength of the four squadrons was 632 men (including the depot). Due to the conditions of the campaign in Spain, the strength of the unit was subject to strong fluctuations (in 1810 with new replacements it increased to 814 men; but in November 1811 only 300 men remained).

The regiment's depot was stationed in Wolfenbüttel.

COMMANDERS

1808: Colonel Girard, **June 1808 to 1809**: Colonel Hans Georg E. von Hammerstein, **1809 to 1811**: Major von Heßberg, **1811 to 1813**: Colonel von Stein

ACTIONS 1808–1813

1808: 12 September – The regiments departed for Spain with 59 officers and 500 men, marching via Wesel, Luxemburg and Orléans to Bayonne.

12 December – Grand Review in front of Napoleon in Madrid.

Combined with the French 5th Dragoon Regiment into a cavalry brigade under Brigadier General Maupetit.

1809: Numerous engagements in Spain.

28 July – two squadrons fought at the Battle of Talavera.

1813: The remains of the decimated regiment marched back to the homeland. A squadron remained operating in Spain and was disarmed by French forces in December.

A planned new raising of the regiments in 1813 in Kassel did not occur.

Privates´ helmet, 1810
Side view, original piece, Schloß Friedrichstein (Bad Wildungen), Museumslandschaft Hessen-Kassel.

Privates´ cartridge pouch
Schloß Friedrichstein (Bad Wildungen), Museumslandschaft Hessen-Kassel.

Privates´ helmet, 1810

Original piece, Schloß Friedrichstein (Bad Wildungen), Museumslandschaft Hessen-Kassel.

UNIFORMS

PRIVATES

Headgear: Shakos were issued when the regiment was activated. A rhombic, brass plate with the Westphalian eagle was attached below the cockade. Dark green plume over an orange pompom, and white cording. Brass chin scales. Very soon a crested black leather helmet replaced the shako. The helmet was richly decorated with brass trim and it was like the type of helmet worn by the Guard Chevaulegers.
The forage cap was made of green cloth and had orange decorations. Its shape changed around 1813 following the French pattern.
Coat: A dark green coat with orange distinctions and cutout, pointed lapels was introduced as the dress uniform. It was the same as the coat of the French mounted chasseurs (*habit à la chasseur*). An orange vest with white braid was worn under the coat.
A single-breasted coat with short coattails, closed with seven white metal buttons served as the undress uniform. The facings were also orange. In 1809 this coat became the dress uniform. The *habit à la chasseur* was discontinued. Some minor changes to the coat occurred in 1812: Nine buttons, vertical coattail pockets à la soubise. The sources show pointed and also straight cuffs. All buttons were of white metal with the regimental number. The shoulder-straps were dark green with orange piping. The coattails had stylized dark green eagle ornaments.
A dark green waistcoat without tails was worn for stable and internal duty. Only the collar and cuffs had orange piping. The vest took on a grey basic color in 1813.
Trousers: Dark green pants with white Hungarian knotting. Hungarian boots with white trim and tassel.
Green overalls were introduced for field duty. They were buttoned at the sides without decorations but had leather reinforcing on the inside. For Spain, grey or brown riding trousers are known. According to the memoirs of Carl von der Bussche the regiment also wore blue trousers in January 1809.
Greatcoat: Long, grey cavalry greatcoat with sleeves and cape-like collar.
Equipment: The leather belting was made of light, pale yellow leather. In Spain white leather belting was also used later. The black cartridge box was decorated with a rhombus-shaped plate made of white metal.
Armament: At first the regiment was equipped with old Hessian dragoon sabers which were adapted by attaching the royal initials "JN" on the hilt. They were soon exchanged for the French model light cavalry saber. The saber had a brass hilt, iron scabbard and a sword-strap made of light brown leather. The supplementary armament consisted of a carbine and two pistols (on the saddle).
The lance was first introduced into the regiment in 1811. The lance pennant was white with a light blue triangle like for the Guard Chevaulegers.
Saddlecloth: Light colored fleece blanket edged with dark green wolves teeth. Dark green valise/greatcoat roll with orange piping and white regimental number on the sides.

1st Chevauleger Regiment, 1808–1809

1: Officer in dress uniform; **2:** trumpeter in dress uniform 1808; **3:** chevauleger in dress uniform; **4:** officer in dress uniform; **5:** trumpeter in dress uniform 1809; **6:** trumpeter in undress uniform; **7:** NCO in dress uniform; **8:** chevauleger in dress uniform, in the 1808 stand-up phase with shako.

Sources: 1–8 – W. Hewig, *Heer and Tradition, Brauer-Bogen* Nr. 193-196. Schema H. Knötel, WGM; 8 – Manuscrit du Canonier Hahlo, 1807–08

1
2
3
4
5
6
7
8

NCOs

The NCOs wore the privates's uniform with French pattern rank insignia. They were not armed with either carbines or lances.

OFFICERS

The officer's uniform was essentially the same as for the other ranks. The helmet plates were gilt. Silver eagle emblems on the coattails.

A bicorn with silver decorations, white breeches andh shoes with buckles were worn for the walking out and social uniform.

4

Trousers: Green pants with silver stripes on the sides. Hussar boots with the upper edge braids and tassels in silver. Hussar-style silver braids were applied to the upper thigh, serving as rank insignia along with the epaulets.
Greatcoat: The officers wore a light green overcoat (redingote) for daily duty or a heavy grey greatcoat with cape collar during poor weather conditions.
Equipment: The officer's cartridge pouch was covered with red leather and its lid was adorned with a silver badge. The cartridge pouch bandoleer is depicted in different ways: completely covered with silver lace or black leather with silver borders or red leather with silver lace edging.
Armament: The armament consisted of a saber and pistols. When the unit was being established, the officers used a dragoon saber of Kurhessian origin, like the other ranks. It was replaced by the French light cavalry Model AN-XI saber.
Saddlecloth: Dark green pointed cloth shabraques of the light cavalry pattern with silver border lace and orange piping. In the rear corner were either the "JN" royal initials with a crown in silver or a badge in the shape of a sun with two crossed lances superimposed. In the center was the regimental number as a Roman numeral, and everything was topped by a crown. The valise had silver trim.

1st Chevauleger Regiment, 1810–1813

1: Officer in dress uniform, 1812; **2:** emblem an officer's shabraques; **3:** uniform button; **4:** helmet badge with royal monogram; **5:** officer in dress uniform, 1810; **6:** NCO in field uniform with overalls, 1810; **7:** chevauleger in dress uniform and in field uniform with overalls, 1812; **8:** chevauleger in dress uniform, 1812.

Sources: 1–8 – W. Hewig, *Heer and Tradition, Brauer-Bogen* Nr. 193-196;
1, 5 – S. Pinhas; *Recueil de planches*; 7, 8 – C. Suhr, *Bourgeois de Hambourg*.

1
2
3
5
6
7
8

Officer, 1st Chevauleger Regiment, 1811–1813
Pinhas, Salomon: *Recueil de planches representant les troupes des differant armes et grades de l'armée westphalienne,* 1811.

1st Chevauleger Regiment, 1812–1813,
Watercolor by Herbert Knötel, Anne S.K. Brown Military Collection, Brown University Library.

TRUMPETERS

Many variations for the trumpeters' uniform are presented in the sources.

Headgear: Black colpak/busby with green bag with white piping and a white pompom. Its chin-scales were brass. White cording and a white plume were added for the dress uniform.

Coat: In the beginning, the coat, with long tails à la chasseur with pointed lapels, was worn as the dress uniform. It was light blue with green facings. White braid trim on the collar and cuffs, white epaulets. A red vest with white braid was worn under the coat. Herbert Knötel gives two variations of the uniform that differ in details. The single-breasted coat with short coattails was worn for undress. It was light blue with green distinctions and white braids on the collar and cuffs.

When in 1809 the previous coat of the undress uniform became the dress uniform, it got additional white braid trim in the front. Herbert Knötel presents variations of the dress here too.

The waistcoat for stable duty was light blue for the trumpeters.

Trousers: As for the privates.

Greatcoat: As for the privates.

Equipment: The belt was made of light, pale yellow leather. Trumpet cords and tassels were white or mixed white and light blue.

Armament: The armament with a saber was the same as for the privates. The trumpeters carried neither lances nor carbines.

Saddlecloth: As for the privates. Apparently, no black sheepskin saddle cloths were used for the trumpeters as it often was usual in the period.

1st Chevauleger Regiment, 1810–1813

1: Officer in the full dress uniform with hat, shoes with buckles, and light sword; **2:** officer in redingote; **3:** chevauleger in the greatcoat; **4:** chevauleger in the stable dress, 1808–1811; **5:** chevauleger in stable dress, 1812; **6:** trumpeter of the 2nd to 9th companies in dress uniform, 1810; **7:** trumpeter of the 2nd to 9th companies in dress uniform, 1811; **8:** trumpeter of the 2nd to 9th companies in dress uniform, 1812; **9:** trumpeter of the 2nd to 9th company in dress uniform, 1810.

Sources: 1–9 – W. Hewig, *Brauer-Bogen* 196 and H. Knötel, WGM;
8 – C. Suhr; *Bourgeois de Hambourg* and E. Fort; Bibliothèque Nationale, Paris.

6 *7* *8* *9*

ELITE COMPANY

H. Knötel and W. Hewig give some details on the elite companies after 1809.

PRIVATES

Headgear: Red plume on the left side of the helmet.

Coat: The dress uniform probably was a green coat with orange lapels. Besides this, a single-breasted coat without lapels, like for the center companies, served as the undress uniform.

OFFICERS

The officer's uniform was essentially the same as for the other ranks.

Headgear: Helmet with a red caterpillar crest. The officers also used a black colpak/busby with an orange bag with silver piping. A silver shield and a crown were attached in the front. The shield showed the royal initials. Silver cording and pompom as well as a red plume.

Coat: Like for the privates, but with silver eagle emblems on the coattails and silver piping on the cuffs.
Saddlecloth: Red, pointed cloth shabraques like the light cavalry with silver edging lace and green piping, or leopard-skin shabraques.

4

1st Chevauleger Regiment, 1810–1813

1: Dress uniform coat pattern 1808; **2:** undress uniform coat pattern, 1808 and dress uniform, 1810; **3:** dress uniform coat pattern 1812 with round cuff variant; **4:** cartridge pouches *(gibernes)* for officers and privates; **5:** officer in Spain starting 1808; in the field the epaulets were removed and the bicorn was worn as headgear; **6:** chevauleger in Spain in field uniform; **7:** chevauleger in Spain in field uniform. The overcoat was worn rolled up over the shoulder to protect from saber blows. Dark blue pants were acquired in January 1809 according to the memoirs of Carl von dem Bussche. **8:** Chevauleger in Spain in field uniform.

Sources: 1-4 – W. Hewig, *Heer and Tradition, Brauer-Bogen* Nr. 195 u. 196; 5, 6 – L. Scharf, sketches in H. Knötel's estate in WGM; 7 – from C. v. d. Bussche: *"Auf Pferderücken durch Europa"*; 8 – W. Hewig, *Heer and Tradition, Brauer-Bogen* Nr. 194.

1
2
3
5
6
7
8

TRUMPETERS

Headgear: White colpak/busby with an orange bag piped with white and with a red pompom and plume. Brass chin scales. Cording also red.

Coat: A single-breasted orange coat was worn as the dress uniform. The collar and cuffs green had white borders. The braid was trimmed with light blue lozenges. The turnbacks were also green. White braid trim on the breast. Red epaulets with white crescents.

The undress coat probably had no braid in front and only simple shoulder-straps.

For parades a trumpet flag was attached to the Instrument. The trumpet cords and tassels were red.

Trumpeter of the Elite Company, 1st Chevauleger Regiment, 1812
Watercolor by Herbert Knötel, Anne S.K. Brown Military Collection, Brown University Library.

1st Chevauleger Regiment – Elite Company, 1810–1813

1: Officer in dress uniform; **2:** trumpeter in dress uniform; **3:** officer in duty uniform; **4:** officer in duty uniform; **5:** trumpeter in dress uniform; **6:** trumpet banner; **7:** dress uniform coat pattern, 1811; **8:** chevauleger in dress uniform, 1811; **9:** chevauleger with single-breasted coat, 1811.

Sources: 1-5 – from watercolor H. Knötel, WGM; 1-7 – from schema by W. Hewig, *Heer and Tradition, Brauer-Bogen* Nr. 193; 8 – reconstruction from W. Hewig's schema; 9 – from H. Boisselier, *La Giberne* No. 6.

1
2
3
HN
6
4
5
7
8
9

2nd CHEVAULEGER REGIMENT

The creation of a second regiment was ordered in December 1809. But the regiment was not stood up at this time. Only in October 1812 was a new order postulated to gather appropriate privates from all the cavalry depots. Transfers of officers to the new regiment are documented. Nevertheless the unit only existed for a short period. By 15 January 1813 the cadre was integrated into the newly raised Guard Chevaulegers Regiment. Only the depot maintained a strength of 60 men and it was garrisoned in Kassel.

COMMANDER

1812: Colonel Mauch

ACTIONS 1812

1812: The Regiment was formed in the autumn of 1812

UNIFORMS

The uniform of the 2nd Chevaulegers Regiment corresponded to that of the 1st Regiment with the following differences:

1. The crest of the helmet was not brass but made of white metal.
2. The uniform´s facing color was chamois.
3. The lance pennant was white with a black triangle.
4. The regimental number was in white on the ends of the valise. Chamois piping.
5. Trumpeter: Straw yellow coat with red facings and white hussar braiding. Colpak/busby.

The 2nd Regiment's Trumpeter Corps (*Trompeterkorps*) was composed of personnel provided by their units. Christopher Suhr shows trumpeters in the *Trompeterkorps* that are still wearing the light blue uniform of the 1st Chevauleger Regt. and the rose uniform of the 2nd Hussar Regt.

Whether an elite company existed and whether it had special distinctions is unknown.

2nd Chevauleger Regiment, 1812–1813

1: Officer in dress uniform; **2:** chevauleger in dress uniform; **3:** trumpeter in dress uniform; **4:** officer in dress uniform; **5:** NCO in dress uniform; **6:** uniform button; **7:** dress uniform coat pattern; **8:** trumpeter in dress uniform; **9:** chevauleger in dress uniform.

Sources: 1–4, 8, 9 – C. Suhr, *Bourgeois de Hambourg*; 5-9 – W. Hewig, *Heer and Tradition, Brauer-Bogen* Nr. 195.

1
2
3
4
5
7
8
9

Téte de Colonne
Head of column of the 2nd Chevauleger Regiment with the various trumpeters' uniforms, ca. 1812, Suhr, Christoph: *Album du Bourgeois de Hambourg,* 1806–1815.

Richard Knötel: *Uniformenkunde, Band XIV, Blatt 43.*

2nd Chevauleger Regiment, 1812
Suhr, Christoph: *Album du Bourgeois de Hambourg,* 1806–1815,
Kommerz-Bibliothek Hamburg; photo: Markus Stein.

Officers, 1st Hussar Regiment, 1810–1813
Watercolor by Edmund Wagner after a sketch
by Herbert Knötel, WGM, Rastatt.

HUSSARS

In the second half of 1810, two hussar regiments were raised with volunteers in the territories of the former Electoral Principality of Hanover.

ORGANIZATION

The organization followed that of the heavy cavalry. The 1st company of the 1st squadron was given the title of elite company.
In the beginning of 1811 both regiments were complete with four squadrons with two companies each. The 9th company was the depot. Including the staff, each regiment had a strength of 670 men. Each regiment also had a regimental band of 12 musicians.

The garrisons were in Hanover for the 1st Regiment and in Aschersleben for the 2nd.

ACTIONS 1811–1813

Both regiments formed a brigade and were nearly always deployed together.

1812 Russian Campaign

VIII Army Corps (Jérôme, later Junot), Corps Cavalry under Brigadier General *Graf* (Count) von Hammerstein along with the Guard Chevaulegers
Strength of 1st Hussar Regiment:
On 25 June 1812: 38 officers and 579 men.
On 23 Aug. 1812: 30 officers and 408 men.
Strength of 2nd Hussar Regiment:
On 25 June 1812: 39 officers and 585 men.
On 23 Aug. 1812: 28 officers and 428 men.

19 August: The 2nd Regiment took part in the Battle of Valutina-Gora.
17 September: the Battle of Borodino, employed there in the attack on the redoubts.
28 November: The few remnants of the unit reached the Berezina River.

1813

Both regiments were reestablished with the forty survivors from Russia and new recruits. The regiments again formed a brigade under Brigade General Graf von Hammerstein (II Army Corps Marschall Victor)
Strength of thee 1st Hussar Regiment:
On 5 July 1813: 10 officers and 222 men
Strength of the 2nd Hussar Regiment:
On 5 July 1813: 12 officers and 215 men

22-23 August: Both regiments almost completely went over to the Allies (the Austrians) at Freiburg in Saxony. Then the regiments were officially disbanded in the Westphalian Army and their standards that were stored in the depot were burned.
September: Both regiments were taken into Austrian service and formed the cavalry of the Austrian-German Legion *(Österreichischen–Deutschen Legion).* The brigade was disbanded after the 1814 campaign in France.

1st HUSSAR REGIMENT *(1. HUSAREN-REGIMENT)*

REGIMENT COMMANDERS

1811: Colonel von Zandt, **1812**: Colonel von Zandt, Major von Pentz, **1813**: Colonel von Hammerstein

UNIFORMS

PRIVATES

Headgear The center companies' shakos followed the French model. The plate was made of brass until 1811. It was shield-shaped and showed the initials "JN" under a crown. For the period after 1811–1812 the Westphalian eagle is depicted in white metal over a semi-circular plate. Chin-scales and edge of the front visor were white metal. The cording and plume were white at first, but changed to dark green in 1812. In the field the shako usually was covered by black oilcloth.

For the elite company the colpak/busby was made of black fur and had a green bag, white cording and red plume. Brass chin-scales.

The forage cap (*bonnet de police*) was made of dark green cloth with white piping.

Dolman and Pelisse: They were dark green. Until 1812 the dolman's collar and cuffs were red. After that the distinctions were green. All the piping and cording was white. The cording on the dolman and the pelisse each was decorated with 15 pewter buttons in three rows. Black fur trim on the pelisse. The sash had white and crimson knots.

In the field the pelisse was probably not worn.

For internal and stable duty a waistcoat in the regiment's colors was worn (similar to the other units).

Pants: Green with white Hungarian knotting in a number of variations.

In the field, grey or green overalls with black leather reinforcing on the inside. They were often trimmed with colored stripes and buttons on the sides. Hussar boots with white trim were worn for parades.

Equipment and armament: Two black leather bandoliers with white metal badges for the carbine and for the cartridge box were worn over the left shoulder. When the unit was reconstituted in 1813 the leather belting was changed to white.

The light cavalry model saber with an iron scabbard and brass hilt was the armament. White or black *portepée*. The sabretache was made of black leather. The numeral "1" stamped out of white metal was attached as a decoration on the sabretache cover.

Saddlecloth: White fleece shabraque with dark green wolves teeth border. Horse furniture was made of black leather. The green valise/greatcoat roll with the regimental number on the sides was tied to the rear of the shabraque.

1st Hussar Regiment, 1810–1813

1: Trumpeter of the center company in dress uniform; **2:** officer 1810 until 1811 – lieutenant – in dress uniform with red distinctions until 1812 and sabretache per Orlando Norie; **3:** hussar in dress uniform, 1812; **4:** officer's dolman, 1811, rear view; **5:** hussar's dolman, rear view.

Sources: 1 – reconstruction from R. Forthoffer, *Fiches documentaires*; 2 – reconstruction from H. Boisselier and S. Pinhas; 3 – from O. Norie and F. Neumann; 4, 5 – reconstructions from an original artifact in Schloss Friedrichstein.

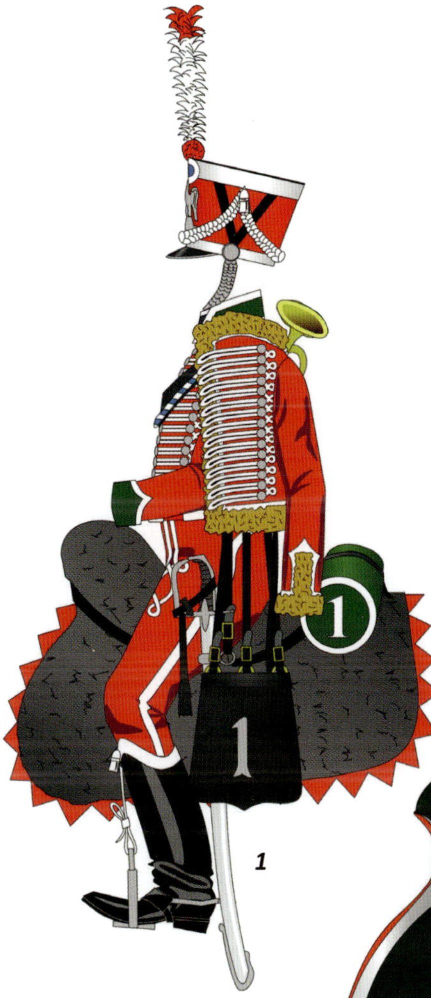

1

3

2

4

5

NCOs

Wore the light cavalry rank insignia on their uniform sleeves.

OFFICERS

The rank was recognizable from the numbers of laces on the dolman's cuffs, on the pelisse's sleeves and on the trim on the pants. The number and width of the laces were according to the rank.

Headgear: The upper shako band and cording were in silver. Silver chevrons on both sides indicated of rank. In the field, the shako was usually worn with a cover or the colpak/busby was worn without decoration.
The source, Orlando Norie, shows an officer with a shako with the body of red cloth and with a red plume.
The forage cap had silver trim and piping with further red piping around the turned up portion.
Dolman and Pelisse: All trim, piping and cording were silver. Five rows of buttons with braiding on the chest. The sash was silver with dark red knots.
According to the *Freiberger Bilderhandschrift*, the undress pelisses were adorned with only five rows of cording with three buttons each. Variations of this source also show the pelisse as grey.

Pants: Along with the dark green pants, the officers also wore versions in red or chamois with or without rank insignia.
On campaign, they wore overalls, which according to the sources were depicted in red, brown or grey. Some of the pants were decorated on the sides with silver trim.
Equipment: Leather equipment was decorated with silver lace. The cartridge belt's shield-shaped plate was at chest level and bore the royal monogram. The sabretache was in red with decorations and the royal monogram in silver. Silver *portepée*.
Saddlecloth: Pointed shabraques were made of dark green cloth with silver bordering trim with red edging. The royal monogram in the corners was also silvered.

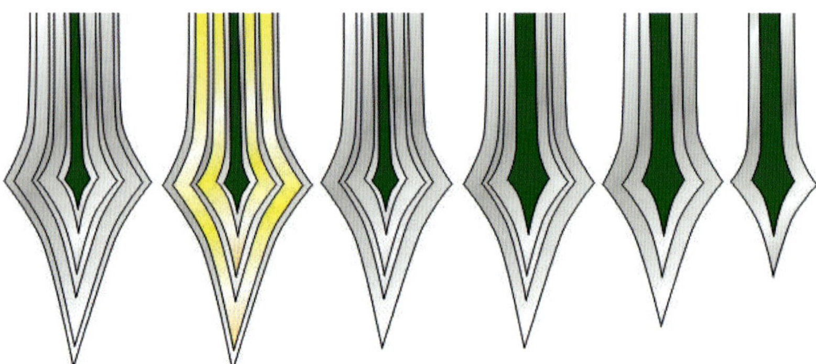

Hussar Officers' Rank Insignia

Colonel, major, *Eskadronschef*, captain, first lieutenant, second lieutenant.

1st Hussar Regiment, 1810–1813

1: Hussar 1810; **2:** officer, captain of the elite company; **3:** trumpeter, 1811; **4:** hussar of the elite company, dress uniform, 1811; **5:** officer – captain – in dress uniform, 1812; **6:** trumpeter of the center company; **7:** NCO – *maréchal-des-logis*; **8:** hussar in dress uniform, 1812–1813.

Sources: 1 – from R. Forthoffer, *Fiches documentaires*, plate 152; 2 – from S. Pinhas and H. Knötel;
3 – from H. Boisselier, F. Kieffer's paper soldier collection; 4 – from H. Boisselier, *Westphalen, Armee von Jerôme Napoleon* series in private ownership; 5 – from S. Pinhas; 6 – reconstruction from O. Norie and R. Forthoffer;
7 – reconstruction from R. Forthoffer, *Fiches documentaires*; 8 – from S. Pinhas and Neumann.

1
2
3
4
5
6
7
8

Officer,
1st Hussar Regiment 1812
Pinhas, Salomon: *Recueil de planches representant les troupes des differant armes et grades de l'armée westphalienne*, privately owned series.

1st Hussar Regiment, 1810-1813

1: Officer, captain, 1811. The "JN" royal monogram, crown and edging braid on the sabretache all in silver; **2:** officer, 1813. The pants are also depicted in dark brown as a variation; **3:** officer; **4:** officer, 1812 in the duty uniform with the *bonnet de police*; **5:** elite company trumpeter in field attire, 1812–1813; **6:** center company hussar in field uniform; **7:** hussar in fatigue/stable uniform.

Sources: 1 – from O. Norie; 2 – from *Freiberger Bilderhandschrift*; 3, 4 – from H. Knötel, Westphälische Studie; 5 – from H. Knötel and colored sketch by R. Forthoffer; 6 – reconstruction from S. Pinhas and *Freiberger Bilderhandschrift*; 7 – reconstruction from description in text.

1 *2* *3* *4*

TRUMPETERS

Headgear: Red shako with white decorations. White plume with red tip. The elite company's trumpeter wore a busby with a red bag, white cording and a red plume with a white tip.

Dolman and Pelisse: The trumpeters wore the uniform in reversed colors, i.e., red dolman and pelisse. Dark green collar and cuffs on the dolman. The pelisse had white or light brown fur trim.

Pants: Red with white trim and cording. In the field green overalls with red side seams with brass buttons along them.

Saddlecloth: The shabraque was made of black sheep's fleece, trimmed with red wolves teeth.

Trumpet made of brass; cord in silver interwoven with medium blue (*bleu westphalien*) threads.

1

2

1st Hussar Regiment, 1810-1813

1: shako plate, 1810; **1:** Shako plate, 1812–1813.

Source: 1, 2 – from W. Hewig.

1st and 2nd Hussar Regiments
Untitled manuscript in
Anne S.K. Brown Military Collection, Brown University Library.

Hussars, 1812

Officer, 1st Hussar Regiment; officer, 2nd Hussar Regiment; hussar, 1st Hussar Regiment

Knötel, Richard: *Uniformenkunde.* Vol. VII.

Hussars, 1813

Trumpeter and hussar, Hussar Regiment Jerôme Napoleon; officer, 1st Hussar Regiment winter service uniform; officer, 2nd Hussar Regiment winter service uniform.

Knötel, Richard: *Uniformenkunde*. Vol. XVII.

2nd HUSSAR REGIMENT *(2. HUSAREN-REGIMENT)*

REGIMENT COMMANDERS

1812: Colonel von Hessberg, **1813**: Colonel von Berger, **1813**: Major Czernizky

UNIFORMS

PRIVATES

The uniform corresponded to that of the 1st Hussar Regiments, but had a different set of colors. It had sky blue with red as its regimental colors, then later – starting in 1812 – rose distinctions.

Headgear: Shako with a red plume with a light blue base, mounted on a red spherical pompom. Shield-shaped rhomboid plate of white metal with the royal cypher. Starting in 1812 the plume was rose-colored and there was a new shield-shaped plate: Westphalian eagle with a semicircular shield and the royal monogram.

Dolman and Pelisse: Were sky blue with red collar and cuffs. All piping and cording were white. The pelisse's fur trim was initially light brown, later black. The sash with white and crimson cording.

Pants: Sky blue pants with white cording. According to R. Forthoffer, red pants were also worn from the beginning until 1811. Otherwise, grey overalls with black leather reinforcing were worn in the field.

For inside and stable duty, a light blue waistcoat and light grey overalls were worn.

Equipment and armament: Like for the 1st Regiment; but the number "2" in white metal on the sabretache.

Saddlecloth: Like the 1st Regiment; but with light blue wolves tooth trim and a light blue valise.

2nd Hussar Regiment, 1810–1813

1: Officer, dress uniform; **2:** officer – captain – in field uniform, 1812; **3:** hussar, elite company, in field attire; **4:** officer's dolman, 1811, rear view; **5:** privates's dolman, rear view; **6:** hussar in dress uniform, 1811.

Sources: 1 – from F. Neumann, Serie in NYPL Vinkhuijzen Collection and G. Leroux, series in der ASKB;
2 – from R. Forthoffer, *Fiches documentaires*, plate 155;
4, 5 – from an original artifact in Schloss Friedrichstein; 3, 6 – from R. Forthoffer, manuscript.

1
2
3
4
5
6

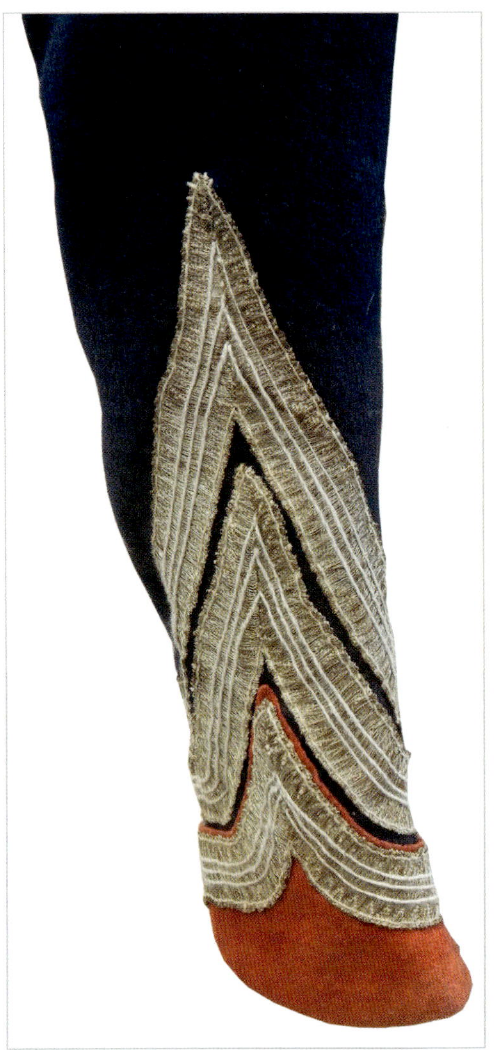

Officer's dolman, 2nd Hussar Regiment:
collar
cuff with rank chevrons
back of the pelisse
Schloß Friedrichstein (Bad Wildungen),
Museumslandschaft Hessen-Kassel.

Officer's dolman, 2nd Hussar Regiment
Schloß Friedrichstein (Bad Wildungen), Museumslandschaft Hessen-Kassel.

Hussar's dolman, 2nd Hussar Regiment
Front and side views with left and right sleeves.
Schloß Friedrichstein (Bad Wildungen), Museumslandschaft Hessen-Kassel, photo: Markus Gaertner.

Hussar's dolman, 2nd Hussar Regiment
Front of the colla.
Schloß Friedrichstein (Bad Wildungen), Museumslandschaft Hessen-Kassel, photo: Markus Gaertner.

Officer (captain), 2nd Hussar Regiment 1812
Pinhas, Salomon: *Recueil de planches representant les troupes des differant armes et grades de l'armée westphalienne.*

Officer, 2nd Hussar Regiment, field dress
Watercolor by Herbert Knötel, WGM, Rastatt.

OFFICERS

Same as for the 1st Regiment.

The sources show following special campaign dress:

Lieutenant 1812 (according to Roger Forthoffer): shako covered with red cloth and a braid chevron on the sides to show the rank. Light blue pelisse with light grey fur; bandolier of red leather with silver trim and a heart-shaped plate. Red, long pants with silver trimming.
Lieutenant 1813 (according to the *Freiberger Bilderhandschrift - BH*): shako covered with black waxed cloth, pelisse with five rows of frogging; black leather bandolier with silvered trim. Long red pants.

Lieutenant 1813 (according to the *Freiberger BH*): Busby with neither cording nor a busby bag. Light blue pelisse. grey overalls with leather reinforcing and trim reaching to below the knee – as a kind of "false boot" ("*falsche Stiefel*"); light blue trim along the outside seam.
Saddlecloth: Sky blue cloth shabraques with silvered edging. In the corners either the royal monogram or a "2" as the emblem.

***Rittmeister* (captain)**
2nd Hussar Regiment
Portrait, private collection

2nd Hussar Regiment, 1810–1813

1: Officer, elite company (reconstruction); **2:** brigadier, elite company in field uniform; **3:** hussar, elite company, 1812; **4:** officer, lieutenant 1812; **5:** *maréchal des logis*; **6:** hussar in dress uniform, 1812.

Sources: 1 – from S. Pinhas and R. Forthoffer; 2 – reconstruction from H. Boisselier; 3 – from H. Boisselier; 4, 6 – from S. Pinhas; 5, 6 – from R. Forthoffer, *Fiches documentaires*, plate 152.

1
2
3
4
5
6

TRUMPETERS

The 2nd Regiment's trumpeters also wore coatees in reversed colors. The sources describe the following variations:

Staff trumpeter/*trompette-major* 1811 (according to the *Memoiren von Klinkhardt*): White plume interspersed with medium blue "points" (dots). Red spherical pompom and cap bag. The busby was made of black fur. Dolman and pelisse were red, distinctions were light blue, cording was white interwoven with medium blue threads. Two silver chevrons on the forearm as rank insignia. White waist-sash with light blue sections. The pelisse's fur was light brown. The pants were light blue. The cartouche bag and leather belting were black.

Trumpeter 1812 (according to E. Fort, Bibliotheque Nationale): Busby with only a white pompom, on the front a heart-shaped metal badge with the "JN" monogram. Red close-fitting pants with Hungarian knotting.

Staff trumpeter/*Trompette major* 1812-13 (according to Herbert Knötel): As depicted above, but with the following differences: the braiding was entirely light blue. The red of the regimental facing color was more varied to a rose tint. Light brown fur trim. Light blue pants. Busby with white plume with red pompom.
White sheepskin saddle cover with light blue wolves teeth border.

Trumpeter 1813 (according to Christoph Suhr): Dolman and pants were light red tending to pink. Busby with rose bag and a white plume with a rose tip. This was attached to a rose colored pompom.

Musician 1812-1813 (according to the *Manuscrit de Marckolsheim*): Red dolman, pelisse and pants, braiding completely light blue. The facing color on the collar and cuffs was also red with light blue piping. A badge on the front of the busby. White plume mixed with light blue points. The red busby bag also had light blue piping.

Saddlecloth: Black sheepskin saddle cover with light blue wolves teeth border. Light blue valise with white trim and the number on the sides.

4

2nd Hussar Regiment, 1810–1813

1: Officer, field uniform; **2:** officer, field dress, 1813; **3:** officer, field dress, 1813; **4:** shako plate variations. Also rhombus-shaped with der numeral "2" below the eagle; **5:** hussar, 1811; **6:** hussar field dress; **7:** hussar, work and stable dress; **8:** hussar, dress uniform, 1812–1813. In 1813, according to this depiction, the distinctions must have changed to pink or rose.

Sources: 1 – from R. Forthoffer, sketch H. Knötel, WGM; 2 – from *Freiberger Bilderhandschrift*; 3 – from *Freiberger Bilderhandschrift*; 4 – from W. Hewig; 5 – from R. Forthoffer, *Fiches documentaires*, plate 152; 7 – reconstruction based on text; 8 – from S. Pinhas.

1
2
3

5
6
7
8

2nd Hussar Regiment, 1811–1813

1: Staff trumpeter *(trompette-major)*, 1811; **2:** trumpeter in reversed colors; **3:** trumpeter; **4:** staff trumpeter *(trompette-major)*; **5:** trumpeter; **6:** trumpeter; **7:** musician.

Sources: 1 – from Klinkhart and R. Forthoffer, *Fiches documentaires*, plate 152; 2 – reconstruction and from D. Lordey, Tradition Nr. 180; 3 – from H. Boisselier and *Soldats de carton*; 4 – from H. Knötel, sketch WGM; 5 – from R. and H. Knötel, Collection de Ridder; 6 – from H. C. Suhr, *Bourgeois de Hambourg*; 7 – from R. Forthoffer, *Manuscrit de Marckolsheim*.

4
5
6
7

VETERINARIANS

In the staff of each cavalry regiment and of the Artillery Regiment there were two authorized positions for veterinarians (*Veterinäre*). The senior staff had the *Artiste-vétérinaire* or *Rossarzt* (literally a "horse doctor") who in the Westphalian Army had the rank of a lieutenant (*sous-lieutenant*). He accompanied the regiment when it deployed. He was assisted by the veterinarian's assistant (*aide-artiste-vétérinaire* or *Rossarzt-Gehilfen)* in the lower staff. That individual had an NCO's rank and remained in the depot.

UNIFORMS

Almost nothing is known about the veterinarians' uniforms. They probably wore the uniform of the unit where they served, like was the custom in the French Army. In the French Army, it was only after 1812 with the enormous losses of horses in Russia that Napoleon paid more attention to veterinarian's position and that a special uniform was introduced.
Two plates by Boisselier give information about the veterinarians uniforms which were very similar to those of the French for 1813-14. For completeness, those uniforms are described here. Whether they were actually worn is, however, questionable.
Headgear: Bicorn with white edging and cockade.
Coat: Blue surtout with white buttons and white braid trim on the collar and cuffs. The trim on the cuffs was different for the *Rossarzt* and *Rossarzt-Gehilfen*.
Trousers: White pants for the dress uniform, blue pants for the undress uniform. Heavy cavalry or light cavalry boots depending on which regiment they belonged to.
Armament: The veterinarians carried the sidearms assigned to their regiments.
Furthermore, Boisselier presents two more veterinarian ranks but which are not expressly depicted in the Westphalian structure.:
Artiste-vétérinaire en chef: In June 1812 the 1st Chevauleger Regiment's veterinarian (*Rossarzt*) was promoted to "*Ober-Rossarzt*" (senior 'horse doctor") with the rank of captain. That would have been a possible equivalent. In 1813 the rank of "*Vétérinaire-inspecteur*" was created in the French Army. His duties included veterinary oversight of the large remount depot, checking on the veterinarians, and ensuring the safety and cleanliness in the cavalry stables. That would be a further explanation of this rank.
Uniform: The uniform was richly decorated with silver laces.
Vétérinaire du train In the train companies' structure there was no veterinarian (*Rossarzt*) included. Because these units' capability to perform their mission was completely dependent upon the health of the draft horses, it is possible that a qualified NCO was named to take over veterinary matters.
Uniform: Hat without a border; blue surtout with a white braid on the collar and NCO's rank insignia on the sleeves.

Veterinarians

1: *Artiste-vétérinaire en chef*; **2:** light cavalry *artiste-vétérinaire*; **3:** train veterinarian;
Coat patterns: 4: *Artiste-vétérinaire en chef*; **5:** *Artiste-vétérinaire*; **6:** *aide-artiste-vétérinaire*; **7:** train veterinarian.

Sources: all from H. Boisselier.

ARTILLERY AND TECHNICAL TROOPS

ARTILLERY REGIMENT

(ARTILLERIE-REGIMENT - REGIMENT DE L'ARTILLERIE A PIED ET A CHEVAL)

ORGANIZATION

Immediately after the founding of the kingdom in the second half of 1807, the creation of the artillery began. It was to have a strength of 1,500 men. The establishment of the individual companies initially only proceeded slowly, for example in March 1808 only 470 recruits were available.

In **1808** the Artillery Regiment consisted of:

- 3 companies of foot artillery *(Fuß-Artillerie)*
- 1 company of horse artillery *(Artillerie zu Pferd)*
- 1 Handwerker company *(Ouvriers)*
- 1 Engineer company *(Pionier/sapeur)*
- 4 train companies

The mounted artillery company and a train company were attached to the Guard. They are also discussed in detail in the chapter on the Guard.

In **1809** a fourth foot artillery company was formed.

In **1810** more companies were added and the Artillery Regiment consisted of:

- 4 companies of foot artillery
- 2 companies of horse artillery
- 2 artisan companies *(ouvriers)*
- 1 Engineer company *(Pionier/sapeur)*
- 4 Train companies
- 1 company of Train d'Equipages (for the wagons of the Army units)

The first mounted artillery company and a train company remained with the Guard.
The artillery companies were not equipped with their own cannon. The cannon were housed in the central arsenal and maintained there. They were issued for deployments and exercises and an artillery company manned a battery of four 6-pounder cannons and two 12-pounder howitzers
Only the horse artillery company assigned to the Guard was permanently equipped with cannons.
During the campaigns the artillery and the attached train companies were apportioned to the individual Army divisions.

The entire artillery and engineer system was under the command of a general directorate (*Generaldirektion*). It additionally had command of all the artillery pieces and equipment, and was responsible for the preparation of gunpowder, fortifications, construction of roads, bridges and canals as well as the construction of military buildings.

Structure and strengths at the end of **1811**:

Staff	
2 mounted companies	220 men
4 foot companies	440 men
2 companies of artisans	220 men
1 Engineer company *(Pionier/sapeur)*	110 men
5 train companies (including the baggage train)	500 men

Total strength: 42 officers and
1,535 men with 1,221 horses

1813: After the loss of the companies that had gone to Russia, creation of new units was begun in the beginning of 1813.
Two effective foot artillery companies that had returned from Spain were located in Kassel. There was also an artisan company with 207 men and the remnants of various companies. The total available strength was ca. 553 men.

Up until July 1813 the following were reestablished:

- 4 foot artillery companies
- 1 horse artillery company
- 1 artisan company
- 5 artillery train companies

Starting in August 1813 it was planned to create artillery for each Guard unit with a foot company and a mounted company. However, it was only possible to form the foot company.

STRUCTURE

The regiment had its own staff with, at any one time, two colonels (one commandant and one colonel in the staff) and two *Bataillonschefs* as battalion commanding officers. Plus there was an officer (*Kapitain-Kommandant*) for the train, who commanded there.

And the staff had another 14 men:

1 Adjudant–Major
2 Adjutants
1 Staff trumpeter or staff drummer
1 Paymaster
1 Veterinarian
1 Quartermaster (in the Depot)
1 Surgeon 1st Class (doctor's assistant)
2 Artisans (*Handwerker* – in the depot)
1 Surgeon 2nd Class
1 Drum major
1 Corporal blacksmith
1 Staff trumpeter

Foot company with a strength of 107 men:

1 Captain (commandant)
1 Sergeant major *(Feldwebel)*
1 Artificer (*Handwerker/artificier)*
1 Captain 1st class
3 Sergeants
30 Senior gunners (*Ober-Kanoniere – 1ère classe*, starting in 1811)
1 First *(Premier-)* Lieutenant
1 Quartermaster
60 Gunners (*canonniers 2ème classe*, starting in 1811)
1 Second lieutenant
3 Corporals
2 Drummers

The horse artillery company had, according to regulations, a strength of 4 officers and 86 NCOs and privates:

1 Captain (*Rittmeister* – commandant)
1 Sergeant major *(Oberwachtmeister)*
3 Artificiers (*Handwerker)*
1 Captain second class *(Rittmeister 2ème classe)*
3 Master sergeants *(Wachtmeister)*
28 Senior gunners (*Ober-Kanoniere – 1ère classe*)
1 Premier – Lieutenant
1 Quartermaster
45 Gunners 2nd class *(canonniers 2ème classe)*
1 Second Lieutenant
3 Brigadiers
2 Saddlemaker *(Sattelmacher)*
2 Trumpeters
1 Farrier *(Hufschmied)*

The train company had a strength of 105 men:

1 Captain (*Rittmeister* – commandant)
1 *Brigadier-Fourier*
2 Trumpeters
1 Second Lieutenant
6 Brigadiers
1 Farrier *(Hufschmied)*
1 Sergeant major *(Oberwachtmeister)*
28 Train drivers (1st class)
1 Saddle-maker *(Sattelmacher)*
3 Master sergeants *(Wachtmeister)*
58 Train divers (2nd class)

The structure of the sapper and artisan companies was the same as the foot artillery with the exception that only one officer commanded.

COMMANDERS

1810 to 1813: Brigadier later Major General Jaques Alcandre Francois Allix, *General-Direktor* and Commander of the Regiment, **1808**: Colonel Karl Friedrich Ludwig v. Huth, **1812**: Colonel von Pfuhl, Artillery, Colonel Ulliac, Genie-Sapeure

ACTIONS

1809: April to May: Suppression of Colonel Dörnberg's rebellion in the fighting on the Knallhütte with a platoon of foot artillery.
July: Campaign in Saxony in the X Army Corps with a foot company and a horse battery with 10 cannons in the two brigades.

1810: July to August: A company as a coastal defense brigade (under General Wellingerode) on the North Sea.

1812 Campaign against Russia: The following were assigned to the VIII Westphalian Army Corps:
2 companies foot artillery with 16 cannons/howitzers
2 mounted companies with 16 cannons/howitzers
4 train companies with 508 men
baggage train with 324 men
A detachment of 88 artillerymen was located in the reserve park under the direct command of General Allix. Plus a detachment of artisans (*Handwerker/Ouvriers*) with 1 officer and 22 men, 1 sapper company with 2 officers and 99 men as well as a train detachment with 132 men.

20 Aug. up to this time no engagements. Strength 509 men artillery and 250 men for the train with 525 horses.
29 Aug. in the Battle of Valutina-Gora two batteries saw action.
07 Sep. Battle of Borodino, here all three batteries were in the fighting.
21 July A platoon of horse artillery with 2 cannons and 40 artillerymen as well as 28 train men were assigned to the Guard Cavalry Brigade, and then assigned to the Hammerstein Cavalry Brigade (1st and 2nd Hussar Regiments). A separate howitzer battery was formed that was personally used by General Allix.
In the course of the campaign up until November 1812 all the companies were almost completely wiped out. At Smolensk on 9 December all the cannons were lost on the slippery ice due to lack of draft horses.
General Allix returned from Russia with only 4 officers, 5 NCOs and a few privates.

1809 – 1813 in Spain: In February 1809 two foot batteries with 2nd Division (Major General Count Morio) under the command of captain von Heinemann left for Spain to take part in the 1809 siege of Gerona. Later the unit formed a part of the garrison stationed there.
In the beginning of 1813 the remnants arrived back in Kassel with ca. 100 men.

1813:
1 Apr. Two foot batteries, with six cannons each, were mobilized for the campaign.
12 July another foot battery and a horse company with twelve cannons and attached train were equipped to be ready to march for the upcoming campaign to Saxony.
26-27 Aug. Battle of Dresden
16-18 Oct. Battle of Leipzig, it was heavily engaged in the fighting here with the 2nd (II) Division of the Old Guard (Major General Curial) with a foot battery of six cannon.
In the Kingdom Westphalia and around Kassel:
Summer: A platoon of foot artillery was attached to the Cuirassier Brigade (of Gen. Bastineller). In the course of the retreat, the cannons were lost in the Fulda River.
28 Sep. Fighting around Kassel – the remnants (Depot) of the foot artillery with two cannons in action. Two further cannons were taken by the Cossacks.
30 Sep. The artillery still had a strength of 209 men from the depot and 13 handworkers.

ARTILLERY PIECES AND TECHNICAL EQUIPMENT

The acceptance, distribution and use of the guns for the artillery cannot always be arranged clearly or chronologically.
At the end of 1807 the General Directorate took over the existing material from the predecessor countries:

> For example, from Kurhessen–Kassel (the system before 1807): 16 3-pounder cannon and two light cannons;
> from Hanover: 6- and 12-pounder cannons;
> and from Prussia: an unknown number of 6-pounder and 7- pounder howitzers.

In December 1807 the batteries that had been formed up until then were also equipped with Russian Arakcheev 1805 System cannons, that corresponded to the French 6- and 12- pounders.
In 1809 the regiment received 18 French tubes (6-pounder, AN XI) with suitable ammunition as a "gift." Thus the regiment could report 32 cannons.
General Allix, who was a critic of the French Gribeauval system, developed his own limber and wagon systems, which allowed various barrels to be transported on a standard carriage with three different size wheels. Plus a type of limber wagon completed the equipment. The ammunition wagons were also standardized. The system was tested in trials and approved by the King. The reequipping was accomplished by the end of 1811.
At this time the branch could report 40 cannons and 16 howitzers with an additional 400 draft horses for the train. But there were still 9 cannon barrels without carriages.
In the 1812 campaign, 26 cannons – 6-pounders – and 8 howitzers – 7-pounders – were taken along for the batteries. Plus they took four reserve barrels with them. Along with 16 ammunition wagons, another nine wagons for the sappers' material and five with bridging equipment went with them. Eleven field smiths, coal wagons and spare carriages were also listed.
The batteries were divided into three sections of two guns and were commanded by a sergeant. The howitzers remained together. Each section was supported by two ammunition wagons.
The crew for the 8-pounder cannons or 6-pounder howitzers consisted of 13 men, of them 8 were trained gunners. The 4-pounder cannons were served by 8 men, of whom 5 were specialists. A train company hauled two batteries.
The gun carriages and vehicles were painted light grey and had metal fittings that were painted black. The barrels, on the Prussian model without grips or on the French Gribeauval model with grips (according to original pieces in the Kremlin, Moscow and Borodino), were made of bronze or iron.
The French regulations were used as the basis for the training and operation of the artillery:

Initially the work about drill was *"d'Urtubie von 1791 Manuell und Regulatio"* that was later replaced by the work *"collections des lois aretes et reglements actuellement en vigeur, sur les differents service de l'artillerie,"* published in 1812.

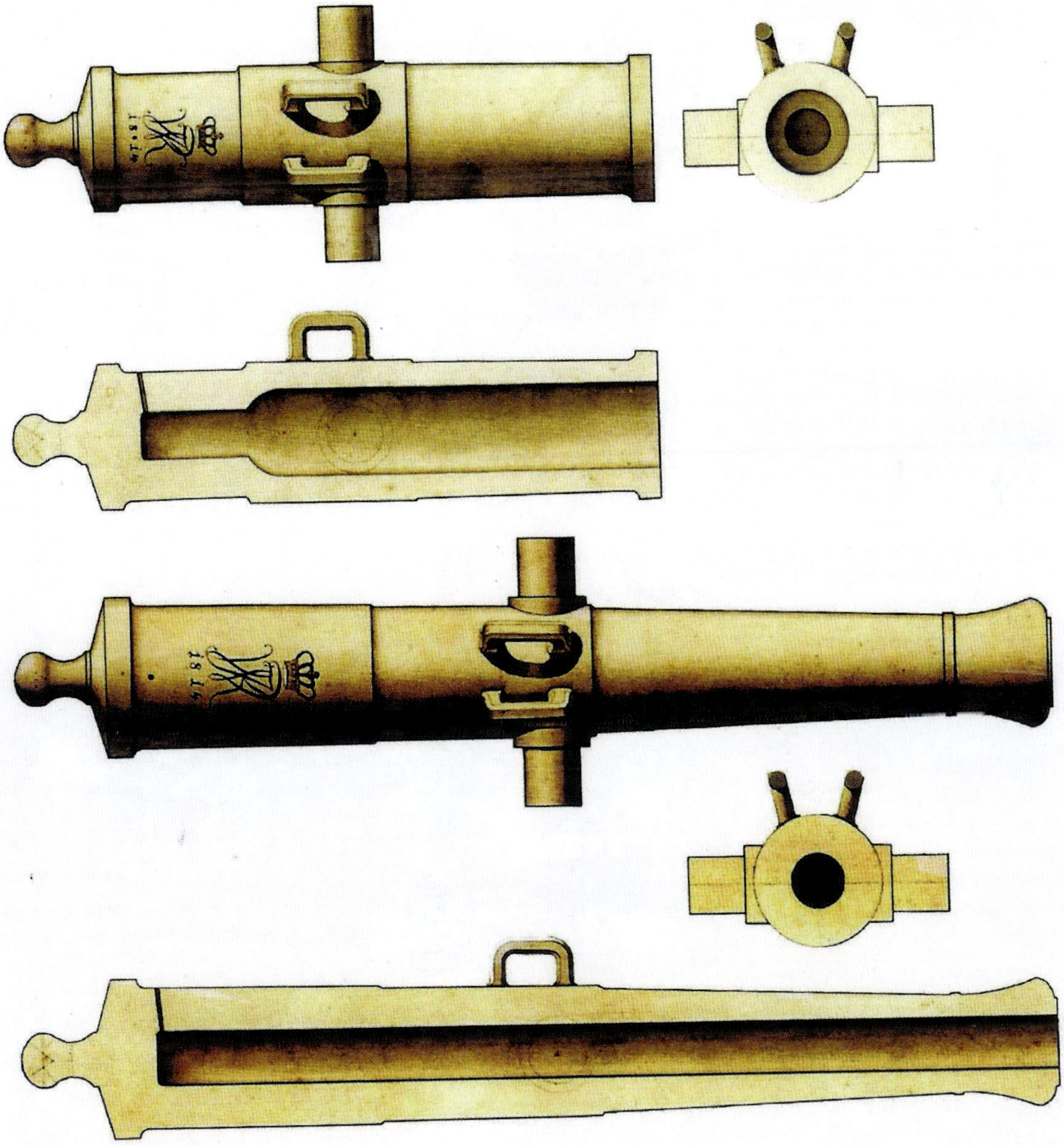

Six-pounder barrel for Model 1808 Allix and seven-pounder howitzer barrel
Drawing by Stephen Summerfield
These depict old Kurhessisan barrels (with Electoral Prince Wilhelm I's monogram).

Gunner in dress uniform, 1812
Watercolor by Neumann after Papiersoldaten Kassel, privately owned collection of Paul Meganck.

FOOT ARTILLERY *(ARTILLERIE ZU FUSS)*

UNIFORMS

PRIVATES

Gunner in dress uniform, 1810
Copy by W. Hewig from *Manuscrit du Canonier Hahlo* 1807/08.
Sammlung: Edmund Wagner.

Headgear: Shako with red cording and pompom; for parades a red plume was added. The brass rhombus-shaped plate had two crossed cannon barrels with a crown above them. A variation had a heart-shaped plate with the royal monogram on the crossed barrels in the middle. In the field they wore the shako with a cover usually made of black waxed cloth, and only the red pompom was attached. In Spain (according to the *Frankfurter Tagebuch*, L. Scharf), it had white, light grey or brown linen covers, some of which had flaps in the rear neck protection from the sun. Brass chin-scales with a grenade emblem on the securing disks.
Forage cap (*Feldmütze*) made of blue cloth with red piping.
Coat: Dark blue coat cut like for the infantry with a red collar, cuffs and turnbacks. The lapels were piped in red. Until 1810 it had blue cuff flaps with buttons and red piping or completely red cuffs. After that it had round cuffs without flaps but with a button on the cuff and a button above it. The brass buttons had a grenade emblem. Starting in 1812, vertical, red-piped pockets with three buttons at the waist. Blue cloth grenade emblems on the turnbacks. Red fringed epaulets.
A single-breasted dark blue coat with red facings served as the undress uniform until 1810.
According to the *Frankfurter Tagebuch*, the detachment in Spain still had some distinctive features: Instead of epaulets they only wore shoulder-straps and the undress coat continued to be used there.
A dark blue waistcoat with red collar and cuffs was worn for duty in garrison. Starting in 1813 only red piping on the collar and cuffs. The vest was single-breasted and closed with eight buttons.
Trousers: Blue pants with black cloth gaiters. These were often replaced with dark blue, light grey or light brown trousers with wide red trim on the sides when in the field. In Spain, ragged blue pants were mainly replaced with ones of various tones of brown.
White trousers were worn in garrison.
Greatcoat: It was made of light grey cloth and had two rows of buttons. Epaulets were worn on the greatcoat.
Armament and equipment: All companies wore the infantry saber with a red sword-strap. The cartridge box had a badge with two crossed cannon barrels or a grenade. Plus they had backpacks and the infantry muskets.

NCOs

They were uniformed and equipped like the privates but wore the appropriate rank insignia.

DRUMMERS

Headgear: Privates´ shako with yellow braid on the upper shako band.
Coat: Red coat with blue facings and yellow braid trim on the collar, lapels, cuffs as well as on the flaps on the coattail pockets. The turnbacks were dark blue with red grenade emblems. Yellow epaulets.
In 1813 blue swallow's nests with yellow braid trim under the epaulets were added. The coattail pockets also got yellow piping then.
Trousers: Dark blue like for privates.
Armament and equipment: Infantry saber.
The drum shell was of brass, the rims were medium blue.

Shako plate, 1808–1813
Original piece, artifact from Russia, privately owned.

Artillery in Dress Uniform, 1810–1813

1: Shako plate and button until 1813; **2:** staff officer; **3:** company-grade officer; **4:** drummer, starting 1812; **5:** NCO Sergeant; **6, 7:** gunners, starting 1812.

Sources: 1 – from original artifacts; – from S. Pinhas 1811; 2, 4, 7 – reconstructions based on the patterns in H. Knötel's estate in the WGM; 5 – reconstruction; 6 – from S. Hahlo.

1
2
3
4
5
6
7

OFFICERS

OFFICERS

Headgear: The trim on the shako's band and the cording were gilt. The V–shaped chevrons on the sides, as rank insignia, were also gilt.

Coat: The coat was usually made of finer cloth and had longer tails, gold-plated buttons and emblems as well as rank insignia. Another rank distinction was a gilt gorget with "JN" or an eagle over crossed cannon barrels.

A blue surtout (single-breasted coat) with red distinctions was worn in the field. The epaulets were usually not worn in Spain.

Trousers: Dark blue pants with Hungarian boots. Mounted officers had tall cuffed boots. In Spain the wide trousers were red-brown, grey or white.

Greatcoat: The grey greatcoat had two rows of buttons and was often rolled up and worn over the shoulder when in the field.

Armament and equipment: A sword, with a gold *porte-pée*, was worn on the shoulder bandolier or on the waist belt made of white leather. A variation was also having the bandolier of black lacquered leather.

For mounted staff officers, the cloth shabraque was made of blue cloth with golden edging and with the royal monogram in the corners.

Officer in the surtout in Spain, 1808–1812/13
Scharf, Ludwig: *"Frankfurter Tagebuch"* – Frankfurt Collection (manuscript) 1808–1811, former collection of H. Knötel, Rastatt.

Officer in dress uniform, ca. 1811
Pinhas, Salomon: *Recueil de planches représentant les troupes des différentes armes et grades de l'armée Westphalienne,* 1811–1813, privately owned.

Artillery in Undress and Camp Uniforms, 1808–1813

1: Company-grade officer, in the surtout, 1808–1813; **2:** drummer, until 1810; **3:** gunner, 1808–1810; **4:** gunner in Spain, 1808–1813; **5:** gunner in the greatcoat, 1808–1813; **6:** fatigue and garrison uniform 1808–1810; **7:** schema for dress uniform: coat 1808–1810; coat 1810-12; coat 1812–1813; **8:** schema drummer's dress uniform: coat 1808–1810, coat starting 1810, with swallow's nest starting 1812; **9:** schema – undress uniform: surtout for officers; undress uniform privates until 1810; coat drummer, undress uniform until 1810.

Sources: 1, 3 to 9 – based on the patterns in H. Knötel's estate in WGM and information from W. Hewig; 2 – reconstruction.

1  2  3 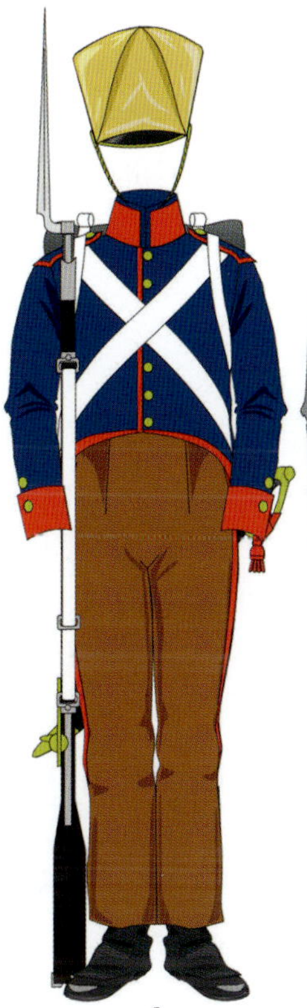 4  5  6

1
2
3
4
5
6
7

HORSE ARTILLERY *(ARTILLERIE ZU PFERD)*

UNIFORMS, 1810–1811

PRIVATES

Headgear: Shako with red cords and plume. A rhombus-shaped brass plate was attached in the front. The sources show two variations: one with the "JN" initials beneath the royal crown and the other with crossed cannon barrels beneath a crown. Brass chin-scales. In the field a waxed or oiled cloth cover was added.
The forage cap was made of blue cloth with red trim.
Coat: A dark blue coat with red distinctions with pointed lapels was introduced as the dress uniform. It was like the coat worn by the French chasseurs a cheval (*habit à la chasseur*), but had short coattails. Blue cloth grenades were sewn on the turnbacks; vertical coattail pockets. A red vest with yellow cording was worn under the coat. Red fringed epaulets.
A single-breasted coat with short coattails closed with seven brass buttons served as the undress uniform. The distinctions were also red here. There were no decorations on the turnbacks.
Trousers: Dark blue pants with yellow Hungarian knotting and piping on the sides. Hussar boots with red edging.
In the field, they wore dark blue trousers with red stripes on the sides and that were buttoned along the sides.
Greatcoat: Light grey with a cape collar.
Equipment and armament: Bandolier and belt were made of light brown leather. A brass badge with the initials "JN" was attached to the front of the bandolier. The black leather cartridge box had a brass badge in the shape of a grenade.
Light cavalry saber with light brown sword-strap. A cavalry pistol was carried on the saddle.
Saddlecloth: A fleece shabraque was part of the horse furniture. It had dark blue wolves teeth edging (per A.Sauerweid), while other sources state red (e.g., H. Knötel). Dark blue valise piped in red on the sides red and with a red grenade emblem in the center. The bridle and other leather horse gear were black.

NCOs

Like for the privates, but with the normal rank insignia.

TRUMPETERS

Headgear: Shako, decorated with a yellow upper band. Forage cap was red with blue piping.
Coat: The trumpeters wore the coat and distinctions in reversed colors. Along with the piping on the collar, lapels and cuffs, there was additional yellow braid trim. Epaulets were of yellow wool.
For work duties, a red waistcoat with blue distinctions was probably worn.
Trousers: Dark blue pants with yellow piping and cording.
Equipment: Trumpet cords with tassels were interwoven with silver and medium blue.
Saddlecloth: Trumpeters had black fleece shabraques.

Horse Artillery, 1810–1811

1: Officer in dress uniform; **2:** gunner; **3:** gunner in undress uniform; **4:** officer in dress uniform; **5:** trumpeter in dress uniform; **6, 7:** gunners.

Sources: 1, 4 – from C. F. Weiland 1809; 2, 3, 5, 6, 7 – reconstructions based on the patterns in H. Knötel's estate in WGM.

Horse artillery
Untitled manuscript in
Anne S.K. Brown Military Collection,
Brown University Library.

Horse artillery officer, 1812
Weiland, C. F.: *Représentation des uniformes de l' armée impériale royale française et des alliés*.

Horse Artillery in Undress and Camp Uniforms, 1808–1810

1: Company-grade officer; **2:** drummer until 1810; **3:** gunner, 1808–1810; **4:** trumpeter in fatigue uniform; **5:** gunner in garrison and fatigue uniform 1808–1812; **6:** gunner in the greatcoat.

Horse Artillery Coat Patterns, 1810–1813

Dress uniform 1810–1811 – 1: company – officer; **2:** gunner; **3:** trumpeter
Undress uniform 1810–1811 – 4: gunner **5:** trumpeter
Dress uniform starting 1811 – 6: officer; **7:** gunner, cuff flap – variation with flap
8: trumpeter, undress uniform; uniform 1811–1813; **9:** gunner; **10:** trumpeter.

Sources: 1–10 – based on the patterns in H. Knötel's estate in WGM and information from W. Hewig.
1–6 – reconstructions based on the patterns in H. Knötel's estate in WGM and information from W. Hewig.

1 *2* *3* *4* *5* *6*

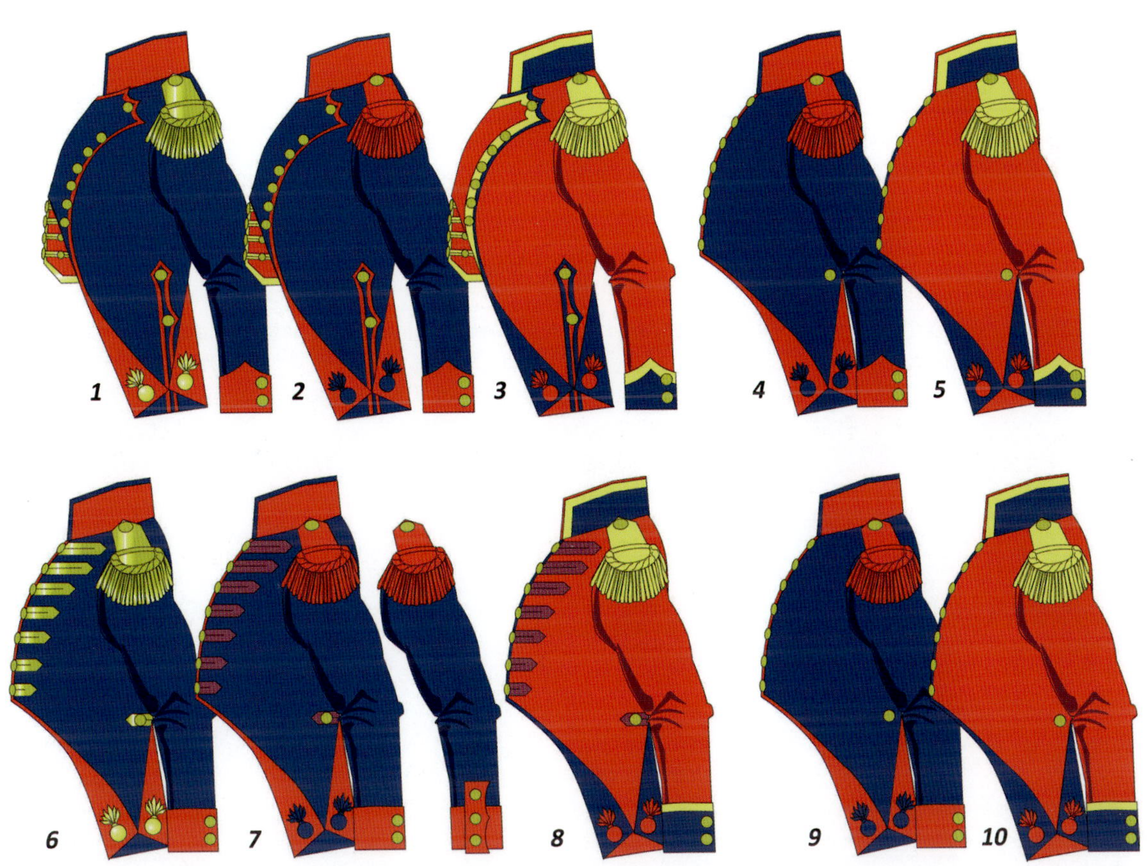

OFFICERS

Headgear: Shako with gilt cording and bands. Rank chevrons on the sides of the shako. For company grade officers a gold-colored pompom and a red plume.
Coat and Trousers: The same uniform as for the privates but with gilt decorations and rank insignia.

Equipment and armament: Gold-colored, red-edged bandolier with a cartridge pouch made of black or rot-lacquered leather. The badge had crossed cannon barrels beneath a crown, the bottom surrounded by a laurel wreath.
Saddlecloth: Dark blue cloth shabraque ending in a point with a wide gold border and crowned royal monogram in the corners.

UNIFORMS, 1811–1813

PRIVATES

Coat: In November 1811 a new coat was introduced for the dress uniform.
The coat now extended to the hips in front and was closed with one row of buttons. It had crimson lace trim around the buttons. Straight cut cuffs, although pointed cuffs are also still shown in some sources. Blue cloth grenades on the turnbacks.

Although according to regulations, the former undress coat without braid trim had been abolished, according to H. Knötel it continued to be worn as a field uniform.
For work duties they wore a dark blue waistcoat with red piping on the collar and cuffs.
Trousers: The pants received red piping.
For work duties and in the field they wore dark blue riding breeches with red stripes on the sides and trimmed buttons. The insides of the legs had leather reinforcing.

NCOs

Like the privates but with the normal rank insignia.

TRUMPETERS

The same changes as for the privates were introduced for the trumpeters. The reversed colors (red with blue facings) were retained for the coat.

The pants dark blue with red pants trim.

OFFICERS

Coat: The coat like for the other ranks, but all braid trim and the epaulets were gilt.

Trousers: Blue pants with golden decorations corresponding to the rank.
Greatcoat: Grey-beige color.

Horse Artillery in Dress Uniform, 1811–1813

1: Officer in dress uniform; **2:** trumpeter; **3:** gunner; **4:** officer in dress uniform; **5:** trumpeter; **6:** NCO – *maréchal des logis*; **7, 8:** gunners.

Sources: 1–5, 7, 8 – reconstructions based on the patterns in H. Knötel's estate in WGM; 6 – from S. Pinhas 1811.

1
2
3
4
5
6
7
8

JN
1
2
3
4
5
6
7

ARTILLERY TRAIN *(TRAIN DER ARTILLERIE)*

UNIFORMS, 1808–1810

PRIVATES

Headgear: Shako with a plate and pompom like for the artillery but made of white metal. In the field the shako was protected with a black waxed cloth cover.

Grey forage cap with red piping and tassel, on the front a white grenade emblem was visible. Starting in 1813 the *pokalem* model was used.

Coat: The uniform coat was of the same cut as that of the foot artillery but was iron grey with red distinctions and piping. The buttons were white metal imprinted with crossed cannon barrels with a crown. The turnbacks had grey grenade emblems. A variation shown by R. Forthoffer has the turnbacks in the coat's color with red piping, but without emblems.

An iron grey, single-breasted coat with red distinctions was worn for daily duty and in the field as the undress uniform.

In garrison they wore a grey waistcoat with red piping on the collar and cuffs.

Trousers: Grey pants in hussar boots.

In the field they wore long overalls with black leather reinforcing on the insides. The outside seams had red stripes decorated with buttons. The overalls could also be without the red stripes.

Additionally until 1811 they had with red stripes on the sides and buttons. After that both variations of only red stripes or only with buttons.

Greatcoat: Grey, single-breasted cavalry greatcoat with cloth-covered buttons.

Armament and equipment: infantry saber with pale yellow leather belt buckled around the waist. The cartridge box for pistol ammunition was on the shoulder bandolier.

Saddlecloth: Drivers used a rectangular leather saddle for the draft horses.

NCOs

Dressed like the privates with corresponding rank insignia. White light cavalry lambskin shabraque with red wolves teeth. Valise was light grey with red edging.

TRUMPETERS

Trumpeters wore a coat in reversed colors: red with iron grey facings. Black fleece over the saddle. Trumpet cords and tassels were white and blue.

OFFICERS

Headgear: Along with the shako with silvered cording and pompom, the busby with a red bag was worn. Red feather plume for either headgear.

Coat: Coat with long coattails and silver trimming.

Vertical coattail pockets piped with red.

For daily duty or in the field they wore the undress uniform with a single-breasted coat.

Trousers: grey pants in hussar boots with silver trim.

Armament and equipment: Light cavalry saber with silver *portepée*. The cartridge pouch bandolier was covered with silver, with a red or black leather backing. A rectangular badge with crossed cannon barrels and a crown was at chest level.

Saddlecloth: Iron grey cloth shabraque coming to a point at the back with a silver border and red piping on the edge.

Train Company, 1808–1810

1: Officer, dress uniform; **2:** trumpeter, dress uniform **3:** officer, dress uniform; **4:** trumpeter, dress uniform until 1810; 5, **6:** drivers; **7:** officer in undress uniform, in Spain 1808–1813

Sources: 2, 4, 5, 6 – based on the patterns in H. Knötel's estate in the WGM;
7 – from L. Scharf, sketch from *Frankfurter Tagebuch*; 1, 3 – reconstructions.

UNIFORMS, 1810–1812

The following changes to the uniform were introduced in the course of 1810:

Train soldier, 1812
Knötel, Richard: *Uniformenkunde*.

PRIVATES

Coat: The coat received the horse artillery pattern (per C.F. Weiland). The colors remained unchanged. A vest red with white cording and trim was worn and visible.
Trousers: The grey pants for the dress uniform got trim with white Hungarian knots.
Armament and equipment: Light cavalry saber worn on the shoulder bandolier or on the waist belt.

TRUMPETERS

Headgear: Busby with red bag piped in white. Light blue pompom with a white feather plume with a light blue tip or light blue with a white tip. The chin-scales were made of white metal.
Coat: Red coat with light blue distinctions. Red vest with light blue cording.
Trousers: Light blue pants with red trim and stripes on the sides

OFFICERS

The officers also implemented the uniform changes, plus they wore silver chevrons on the pants like for the light cavalry.

Train Company, 1810–1813

1: Officer, dress uniform; **2:** trumpeter, dress uniform until 1813; **3:** driver in undress uniform; and field duty; **4:** officer in dress uniform with busby variation; **5:** officer; **6:** trumpeter; **7:** NCO – *maréchal des logis*; **8:** driver in dress uniform.

Sources: 2, 3, 6 – from H. Knötel, watercolor in his estate in the WGM; 4 – from R. Forthoffer sketch, estate of R. Knötel; 1, 5 – from S. Pinhas 1811; 7 – from H. Boisselier, *Studie Westphälische Armee*; 8 – from C. F. Weiland, Serie 1812.

1
2
3
4
5
6
7
8

UNIFORMS, 1813

During the 1813 re-establishment, only the undress uniform, consisting of the single-breasted coat, was issued.

Driver, Artillery Train, 1812
Weiland, C. F.: *Représentation des uniformes de l' armée impériale royale française et des alliés, Weimar, 1807 und 1812.*

Officer in dress uniform, 1811–1812
Pinhas, Salomon: *Recueil de planches représentant les troupes des différentes armes et grades de l'armée Westphalienne,* 34 Blatt, 1811–1813, Cassel.

Driver and trumpeter in dress uniform, 1812
Watercolor by Edmund Wagner after a sketch by Herbert Knötel, WGM, Rastatt.

Train Company Dress and Undress Uniforms, 1808–1813

1: Officer, dress uniform 1813; **2:** trumpeter, undress uniform until 1810; **3:** driver in undress uniform and field duty until 1813; **4:** driver, undress uniform until 1813; **5:** driver in fatigue uniform until 1810; **6:** driver in the greatcoat 1808–1813.

Sources: 3, 4, 5, 6 – based on the patterns in H. Knötel's estate in the WGM; 1, 2 – reconstructions.

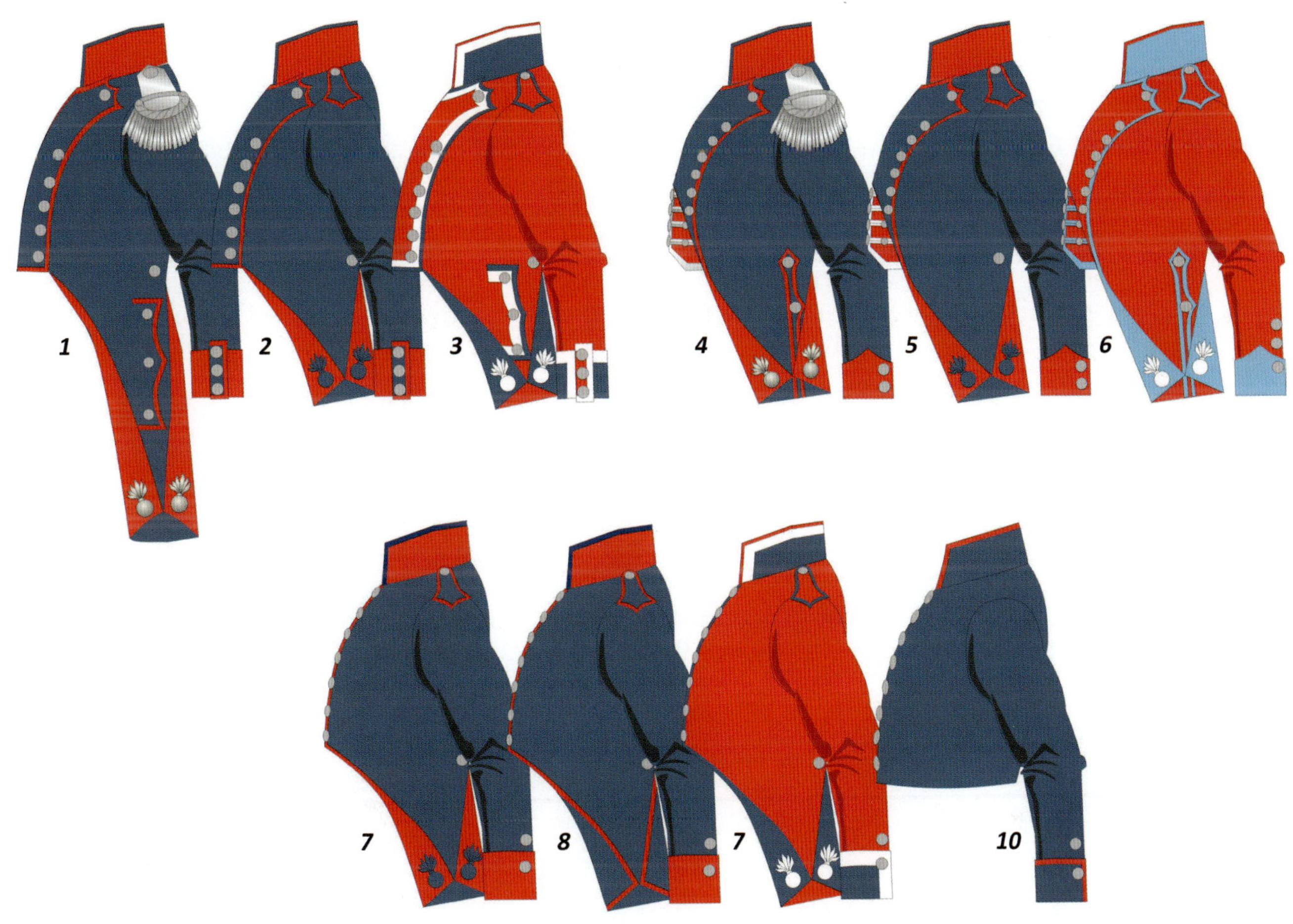

Train Company Coat Patterns, 1808–1813

Dress uniform 1808 until 1810 – 1: officer; **2:** driver; **3:** trumpeter
Dress uniform 1810 until 1813 – 4: officer; **5:** driver; **6:** trumpeter
Undress uniform – 7: driver until 1810; **8:** driver variants until 1813; **9:** trumpeter until 1810
10: fatigue uniform for privates until 1813.

Sources: 1, 2, 3, 6, 7, 10 – based on the patterns in H. Knötel's estate in WGM; 4 – from S. Pinhas 1811; 5 – from C. F. Weiland 1812; 8 – from R. Forthoffer; 9, 10 – reconstructions.

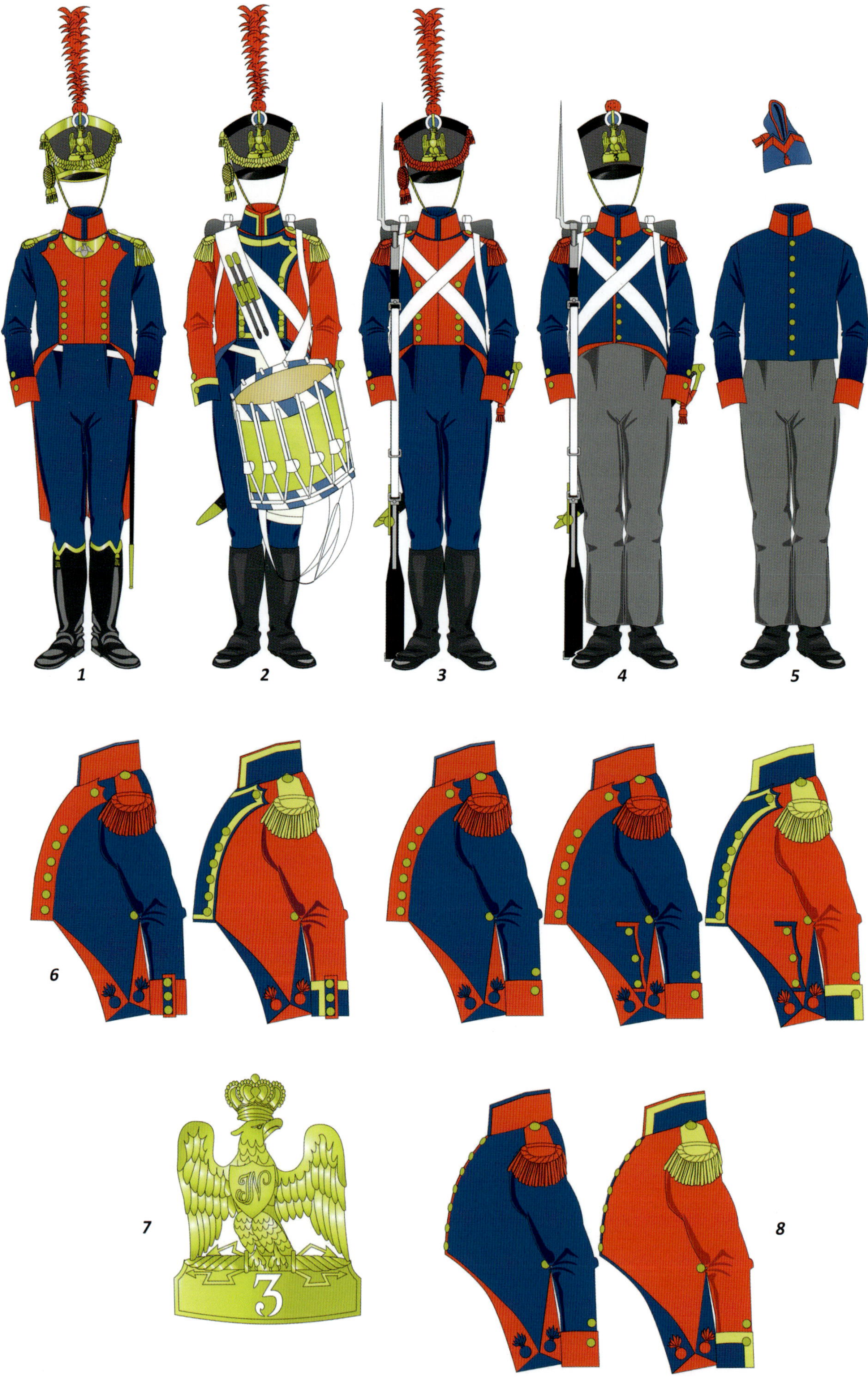
1
2
3
4
5
6
7
8

TECHNCIAL TROOPS *(TECHNISCHE TRUPPE)*

ARTISANS COMPANIES *(HANDWERKER-KOMPANIEN – OUVRIERS)*

The two Workers *(Ouvriers)* Companies were created in 1808 and 1810. After the losses in the Russia campaign, one company still existed in 1813.

UNIFORMS

The *Ouviers* Companies' uniforms corresponded to those of the foot artillery with the following differences: Red facings, special shako plate made of brass.

Worker *(Ouvriers)* Company, 1808–1812

1: Officer, dress uniform, 1810–1812; **2:** drummer, dress uniform until 1813; **3:** artisan *(Handwerker)*, dress uniform 1810–1812; **4:** artisan in undress uniform for field duty 1810; **5:** artisan in fatigue uniform; **6:** schemata – dress uniform: coat for artisan and drummer until 1810, artisan, 1810–1812, artisan 1813, drummer 1812; **7:** shako plate for 3rd company (it is the 2nd *Ouvriers*/ Workers Company. The 1st Company was the Sapper Company.); **8:** schemata – undress uniform: coat for artisan and drummer until 1810.

Sources: 2, 3, 5, 6, 8 – based on the patterns in H. Knötel's estate in the WGM;
7 – from an original artifact in the Schloss Friedrichstein (Bad Wildungen). Museumslandschaft Kassel; 1, 4 – reconstructions.

1
2
3
4
5
6
7
8
9

ENGINEER COMPANIES *(PIONIER-KOMPANIE/SAPEURS)*

The Sapper Company was created in 1808. It was destroyed during the Russia campaign. A new company was not raised in 1813.

UNIFORMS

The uniform of the Sapper Company corresponded to those of the foot artillery with the following differences: Black collar and cuffs with red piping, white metal buttons, special shako plate made of white metal.

OFFICERS AND NCOS OF THE ADMINISTRATION OF MILITARY BUILDINGS AND CASERNS, 1812–1813

Bicorn with tassels. Single-breasted surtout coat in dark blue with red seam on the chest. The distinction color was shown on the collar and cuffs. Red coattails without pockets or emblems. White vest. Dark blue pants with low boots without trim. Sword on the waist belt. Rank insignia according to grade.

Sapper Company, 1808–1813

1: Officer, dress uniform, 1808–1813; **2:** drummer, dress uniform until 1813; **3:** sapper, dress uniform, 1808-13; **4:** sapper in undress uniform until 1810; **5:** sapper in fatigue uniform 1808–1813; **6:** NCO, Administration of Military Buildings, 1812–1813; **7:** schemata – dress uniform: coat for sapper and drummer until 1810, sapper 1810 and 1813; **8:** shako plate for 1st company; **9:** schemata – undress uniform: coat for sappers and drummers until 1810.

Sources: 2, 3, 4, 5, 6, 7, 9 – based on the patterns in H. Knötel's estate in the WGM; 8 – from an original artifact in the Schloss Friedrichstein (Bad Wildungen). Museumslandschaft Kassel; 1 – reconstruction based on an original artifact.

H. BOISSELIER

OTHER FORMATIONS

Royal Gendarmerie Legion

National Guard

Honor Guards

Veterans Companies

Departmental Companies

Disciplinary Units

Gendarme, duty on foot
Watercolor by Heneri Boisselier after *Papiersoldaten* Kassel, collection of Paul Meganck, Bruxelles.

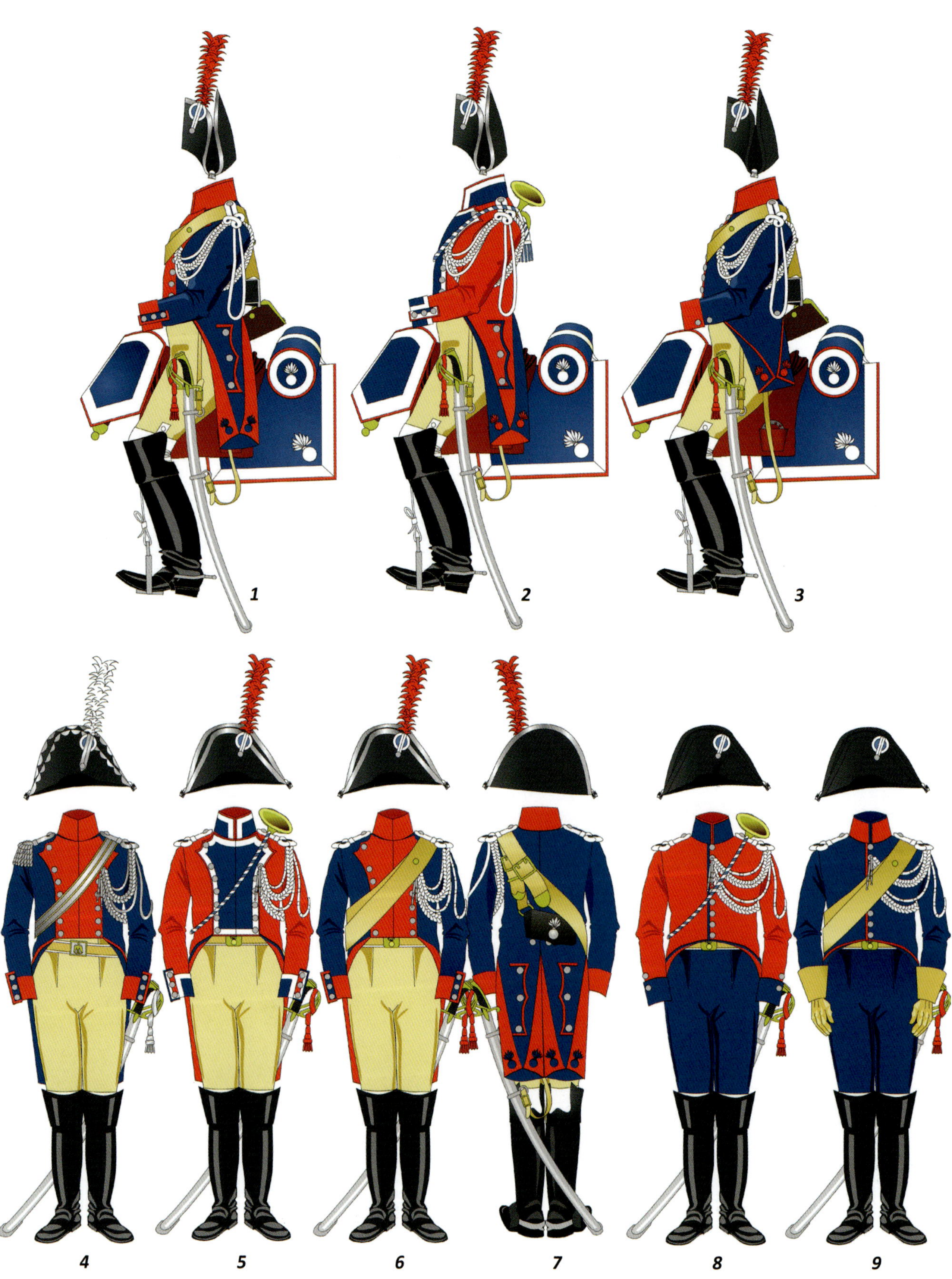
1
2
3
4
5
6
7
8
9

ROYAL GENDARMERIE LEGION
(LEGION DE GENDARMERIE ROYALE)

ESTABLISHMENT

The Royal Decree of 29 Feb. 1808 initially established a gendarmerie (military police force) in Westphalia that was composed entirely of French troops because King Jérôme wanted to create a security force that was completely loyal to him. After conflicts with Brunswick's populace in September 1808, only countrymen were still inducted. The officers and NCOs had to be married and be able to read and write German and French. The gendarmes had to be able to read and write German and have served in the army.

ORGANIZATION

In May 1810 the "Royal Gendarmerie Legion" was fully organized according to Bulletin No. 24. It consisted of a General Staff and one gendarmerie company per department.

The general staff consisted of the Legion Commander, General Bongars, and three (starting in 1810 four) squadron commanders. Each squadron commander commanded the gendarmerie of a military division. Furthermore, an *adjudant-major* in the rank of a captain, a quartermaster and a sergeant major belonged to the Legion's staff. The staff was stationed in Kassel.

The gendarmerie company was made up of a staff and mounted and foot "brigades." The staff was composed of a captain, a lieutenant, a trumpeter and a *sergeant major* per district. The trumpeter belonged to the 1st mounted "brigade" of the respective company and had the duties of a normal gendarme. A different number of mounted and foot gendarmerie "brigades" were posted in each district depending on the local requirements. A "brigade" constituted the smallest gendarmerie unit which each had four gendarmes led by a *brigadier*.

The Gendarmerie Legion developed into an elite unit that carried out its duties and tasks with zeal. But it was feared and hated by the native inhabitants especially because of it was responsible for carrying out conscriptions.

In 1811 the Gendarmerie had a strength of 25 officers and 910 NCOs and privates, assigned in 182 Gendarmerie "brigades."

Pistol, mounted Gendarmerie
Museum Schloß Friedrichstein (Bad Wildungen), photo: Markus Gaertner.

Mounted Gendarmerie, 1808–1812

1: Gendarme 1807, dress uniform; **2:** trumpeter 1807, dress uniform; **3:** gendarme, undress uniform, 1810; **4:** officer, dress uniform, 1810; **5:** trumpeter, dress uniform, 1810; **6-7:** gendarme, dress uniform, 1807; **8:** trumpeter, undress uniform, 1810; **9:** gendarme, undress uniform, 1810.

Sources: 1, 6-7 – S. Hahlo, *Manuscrit 1807/08*; 2, 5 – reconstructions based on H. Knötel's patterns; 3, 8, 9 – *Dekret vom 14. Mai 1810*; 4 – S. Pinhas, *Recueil de planche*, 1811.

UNIFORMS, 1810–1812

The Decree of 14 May 1810 about the creation of the Royal Gendarmerie Legion also established the following uniforms. Before that, the French gendarmerie uniform was probably worn. It differed from the 1810 Westphalian uniform only in the open lapels and red turnbacks

PRIVATES

Headgear: Bicorn made of black felt with a cockade and white loop. There were white tassels at the hat's ends. A red plume was attached over the cockade. The hat was edged with silver trim. A hat without the silver trim was worn with the undress uniform.

The field cap was made of blue cloth with white trim and red piping and a red tassel.

Coat: A dark blue coat with long coattails and closed lapels was worn as the dress uniform. Its collar, lapels and cuffs were red, as was the pie piping on the coattail pockets. The collar was possibly piped in blue. The cuffs were decorated with cuff-flaps. Buttons were white.

The turnbacks were shown as red in the two well-known contemporary sources (in Hahlo for 1808) or as blue with red piping (in Pinhas starting 1811-1812). Grenade devices in contrasting colors were sewn on the turnbacks. The secondary sources (Knötel, Boisselier, Forthoffer) show the turnbacks in both variants, without recognizable reference to the time. We assume that in the beginning the red turnbacks were worn like for the French Gendarmerie uniform. The decree of 1810 prescribed blue turnbacks ("lined with blue serge"), which were also introduced then (see Pinhas 1811–1812).

The mounted gendarmes wore white trefoil epaulets on both shoulders and white aiguillettes on the left shoulder. The foot gendarmes wore red epaulets with silver edging.

Undress uniform: a blue coat with short tails and closed with one row of 9 buttons served for this outfit.

The waistcoat was completely blue with red piping on the collar and cuffs.

Trousers: For the dress uniform the mounted gendarmes wore light brown chamois pants, while they had dark blue pants for the undress uniform. Tall cavalry boots. Dark blue overalls with black leather riding trim also appear in the sources.

The foot gendarmes wore light brown, long cloth pants in gaiters. They were supposed to wear short boots with the undress uniform.

Gendarme, ca. 1812
Detail from painting von Francois-Joseph Kinson; *"Serment au drapeau Westphalien,"* Chateau de Fontainebleau, photo: Markus Gaertner.

Mounted Gendarmerie, 1813

1, 5, 6: Gendarmes, 1813, dress uniform; **2-3:** trumpeter, dress uniform, 1813; **4:** *Wachtmeister*, dress uniform, 1813; **7:** gendarme in the greatcoat, 1813; **8:** gendarme in fatigue uniform with sleeved vest and forage cap, 1810.

Sources: 1, 4 – Herbert Knötel's patterns in WGM; 2–3 – reconstructions per *Dekret vom 14. Mai 1810* and Henri Boisselier; 5–8 – *Dekret vom 14. Mai 1810.*

1
2

3
4
5
6
7
8

Gendarme, 1807–1808
Copy by W Hewig from *Manuscrit du Canonier Hahlo.*
collection: Edmund Wagner.

Officer, Royal Gendarmerie, 1811–1812
Pinhas, Salomon: *Recueil de planches représentant les troupes des différentes armes et grades de l'armée Westphalienne*, privately owned series.

Gendarme of the mounted brigades, 1813
Watercolor by Herbert Knötel, Anne S.K. Brown Military Collection, Brown University Library.

Greatcoat: Long, blue cavalry cape with a piped collar for the mounted gendarmes; blue greatcoat for the foot gendarmes.
Equipment: The leather belting was made of light brown leather. The black cartridge box was adorned with a grenade shaped badge of white metal.

Armament: Infantry musket and saber for the foot gendarmes. Light cavalry model saber with a red swordstrap according to the Bulletin; in the sources they are often shown in white. The mounted gendarmes had a carbine and pistols.
Saddlecloth: Dark blue cloth shabraque with holsters and round valise, all the parts had white edging with red piping.

NCOs

Uniform like for the privates with following rank insignia:

Brigadier: a silver chevron above the cuff.
Wachtmeister: two silver chevrons above the cuff.

The aiguillettes for the mounted NCOs were silver with blue silk mixed in.

OFFICERS

The officer's uniform largely the same as for the other ranks. The aiguillettes and coattail emblems were silver. Their hat had a scalloped silver trim. Silver epaulets as rank insignia. Silver trim on the saddlecloths.

TRUMPETERS

The trumpeters wore uniform coats in reversed colors. Collar, lapels and cuffs were trimmed with white braid. White and blue trumpet cords and tassels.
No drummers were assigned to the foot gendarmerie.

UNIFORMS, 1812–1813

In 1812 the uniform was changed (per the Decree of 21 September 1812). The old dress uniform was abolished. The undress uniform worn up to that time took its place.
A bearskin cap with white cords and a red plume was introduced as the new headgear. The top in the rear was red cloth with a white grenade. According to W. Hewig the bearskin was not worn in Kassel because it was the same as the French grenadier cap and the populace was increasingly anti-French. The trumpeters' bearskin was white.

The leather belting probably received a white border then.
The saddlecloth did not have the cloth holsters. Starting in 1813 the saddle and pistol holsters were covered with a light fleece with red wolves teeth.

Coat Patterns and the Foot Gendarmerie, 1808–1813

1: Coat for mounted Brigades, dress uniform, 1807; **2:** coat for foot gendarme, dress uniform, 1810; **3:** coat for mounted gendarme, undress uniform 1810, starting 1813 dress uniform; **4:** coat for trumpeter, dress uniform, 1808; **5:** coat for trumpeter, undress uniform, 1810, starting 1813 dress uniform; **6-7:** foot gendarme, dress uniform, 1810; **8:** gendarme, undress uniform, 1810; **9:** foot gendarme in the greatcoat, 1810; **10-11:** foot gendarme, dress uniform, 1813.

Sources: 1 – S. Hahlo, *Manuscrit 1807/1808*; 2–3 – *Dekret vom 14. Mai 1810*; 4 – reconstruction per H. Knötel; patterns and *Dekret vom 14. Mai 1810*; 5 – reconstruction derived from *Dekret vom 14. Mai 1810*; 6–10 – *Dekret vom 14. Mai 1810*.

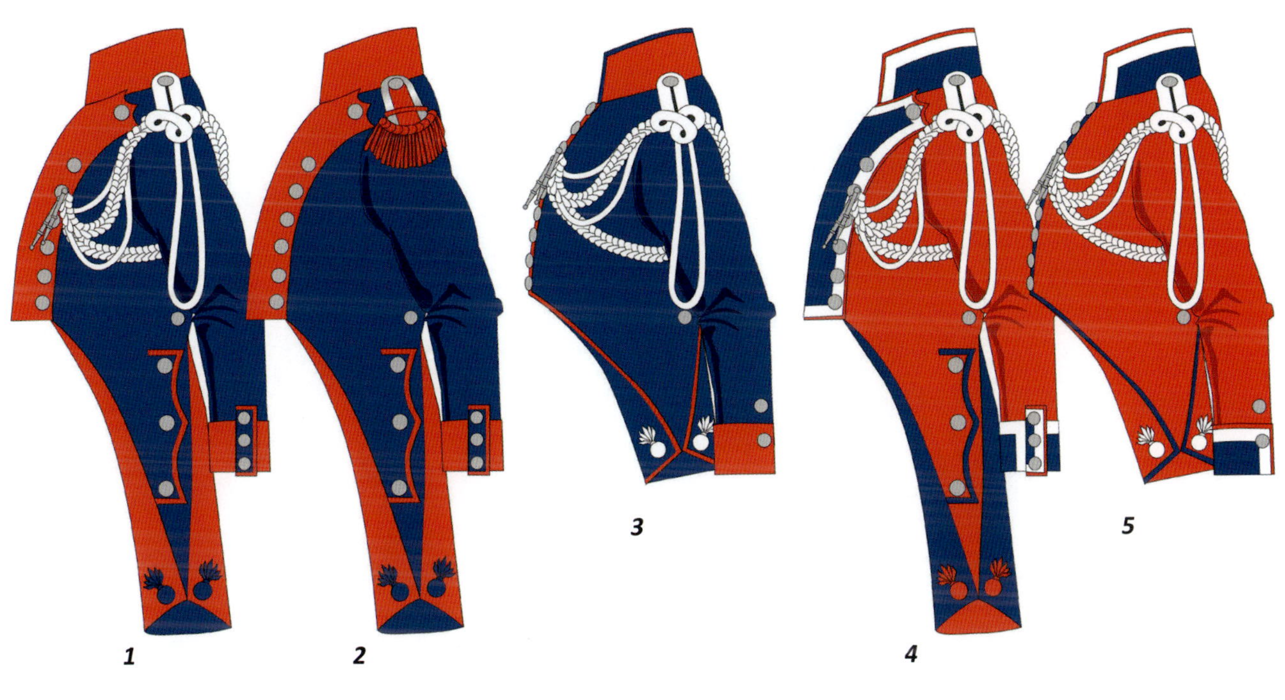
1
2
3
4
5

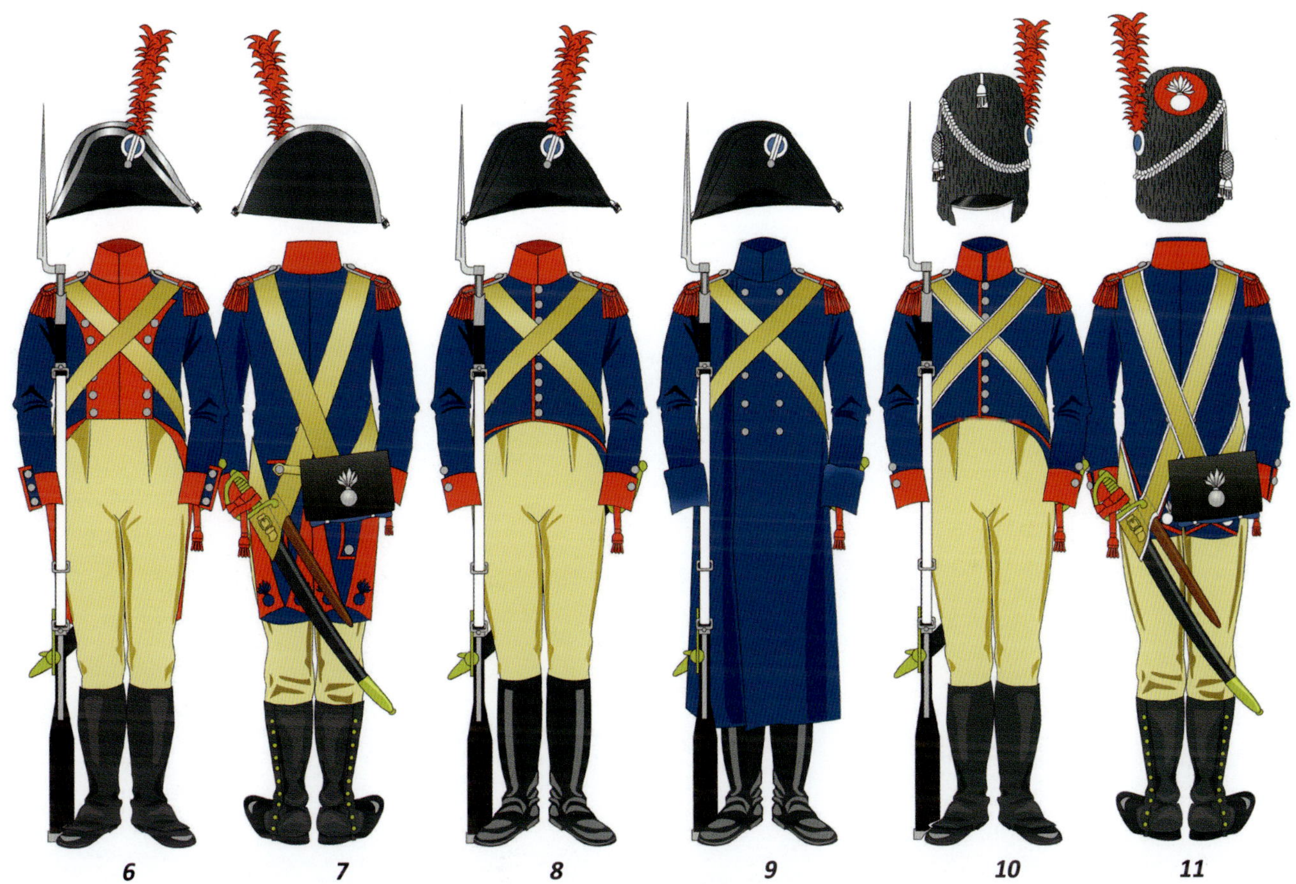
6
7
8
9
10
11

Carabinier, National Guard 1st Battalion, 1812
Pinhas, Salomon: *Recueil de planches représentant les troupes des différentes armes et grades de l'armée Westphalienne,* 1811–1813, privately owned.

Carabinier officer, National Guard 1st Battalion
Pinhas, Salomon: *Recueil de planches représentant les troupes des différentes armes et grades de l'armée Westphalienne,* 1811-1813, privately owned.

NATIONAL GUARD *(NATIONALGARDE)*

ESTABLISHMENT

In 1808 a National Guard was formed in all the larger cities of the kingdom. All well-to-do burghers and property owners between the ages of 20 and 60 were supposed to enlist. Belonging to the National Guard was a prerequisite for getting an authorization to carry out a trade. The National Guard's assigned tasks were sentry duty in the town or city and at the town or city gates and representation in the city at festive events. It was not a military unit and never took part in military actions. The local commandant (*Platzkommandant*) had command of the National Guard in his area of responsibility. The broader staff included the prefect (*Präfekt*), the police prefect (*Polizeipräfekt*) and the mayor.

ORGANIZATION

The National Guard only had a set organization in the capital, Kassel.

In November 1808, a first battalion consisting of four foot companies and one mounted company was stood up there. The battalion's guardsmen were given the designation "*Arkebusiere*" (arquebusiers). In July 1809 a second battalion was raised. It was composed of one grenadier company, four fusilier companies and one voltigeur company. The strength was supposed to be 1,232 men.

In March 1813 the National Guard in Kassel was completely organized as new. The new structure envisioned three battalions. The first two battalions each consisted of one grenadier company, four fusilier companies and one voltigeur company. The third battalion formed the depot and only had four fusilier companies. The already existing grenadier company of the 2nd Battalion was assigned to the new 1st Battalion. The voltigeur company became the grenadier company of the 2nd Battalion. The four *Arkebusiere* companies of the former 1st Battalion were converted to the two new voltigeur companies of the 1st and 2nd Battalions. The mounted company remained and was reduced to ca. 80 men.

The reorganization was never fully implemented, and in September 1813 the National Guard was disbanded without attention.

In 1809 a musicians' band was formed, but no information about its strength or composition is preserved. The National Guard from the town of Eschwege supposedly received a flag in 1812, but here there are no graphic depictions available.

STRUCTURE 1813

Staff (12 men)	**Company** (120 men)
1 Colonel 1st Class	1 Captain
1 Colonel 2nd Class	1 Lieutenant 1st Class
1 Major	1 Lieutenant 2nd Class
2 Battalion Commanders (*Bataillonschefs*)	1 Junior Lieutenant
3 *Adjudants Major*	1 Sergeant Major
3 Adjutants	4 Sergeants
1 Quartermaster (*Quartiermeister*)	1 Quartermaster Corporal (*Fourrier*)
	8 Corporals
	2 Drummers
	100 Guardsmen (*Gardisten*)

UNIFORMS, 1811–1813

The only depictions of the National Guard for the time around 1811 were in a series of pictures published by S. Pinhas. The 1813 reorganization of the National Guard, which was supposed to result in a standardization of its structure, certainly would have been accompanied by changes to the uniform. However, details are not known.

1st BATTALION – CARABINIERS *(KARABINIERS)*

PRIVATES

Headgear: Bicorn with loop and Westphalian cockade, green plume with a red base.
Coat: Dark blue coat with closed lapels and long coattails. Blue collar, lapels, cuffs with flaps; all piped with red. Red turnbacks. The buttons were brass.
Trousers: Blue pants with black or white short gaiters. For normal duty in the summer long white or beige trousers.

Equipment and armament: Infantry saber, with white sword-strap, on the black shoulder bandolier and a musket.
In addition, a gunpowder bottle on red and green cord was worn over the left shoulder.

NCOs

The NCOs' rank insignia followed the French system and were in the yellow/gold button color.

DRUMMERS

No information is available about the drummer's uniform.

OFFICERS

Gilded buttons, rank insignia and *portepée*. Dark blue pants with short boots. Shoulder bandolier made of black leather with gold-colored edging.

Gorget, for the 1st and 2nd Battalions, National Guard, 1812–1813
Museum Schloß Friedrichstein (Bad Wildungen), photo: Markus Gaertner.

National Guard 1st and 2nd Battalions, 1812

1: Officer, 1st Battalion; **2:** carabinier, 1st Battalion; **3:** officer of the fusiliers, 2nd Battalion; **4:** grenadier, 2nd Battalion; **5:** fusilier, 2nd Battalion; **6:** gorget for the 1st and 2nd Battalions of the National Guard 1812

Sources: 1, 2, 3, 5, – from Pinhas, Salomon 1811-1813, private possession; 4 – from a miniature picture in Schloss Friedrichstein (Bad Wildungen). Museumslandschaft Kassel; 6 – original in Schloss Friedrichstein (Bad Wildungen). Museumslandschaft Kassel.

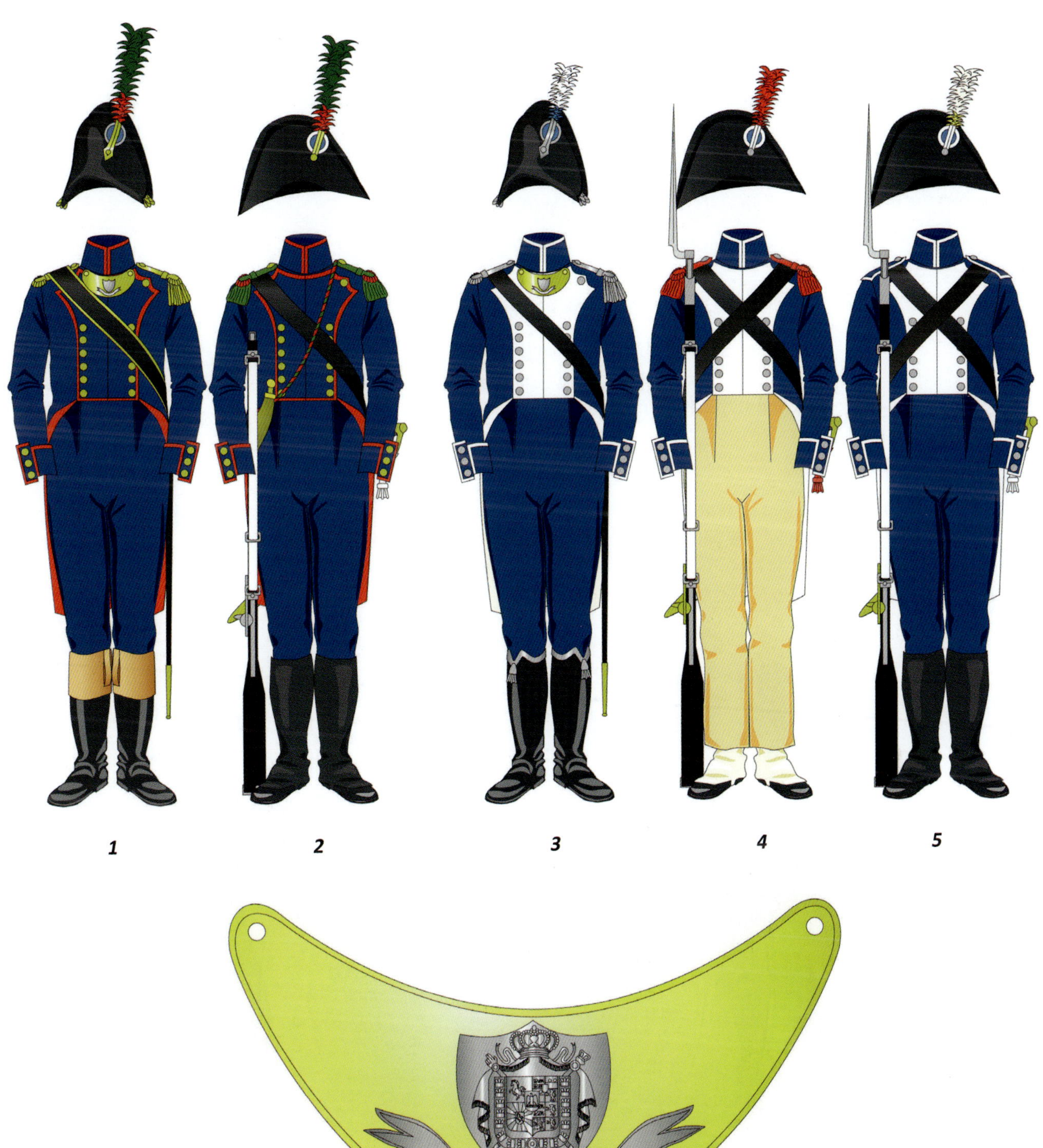

6

2nd BATTALION

PRIVATES

Headgear: Bicorn with loop and Westphalian cockade. A short feather plume with a white tip was attached to the hat. The bottom portion was probably in the company color (1st to 4th company: light blue, white, yellow, green).
Coat: Blue coat with white lapels and turnbacks. Cuffs and collar were blue with white piping. The cuffs were either decorated with blue patches (per Pinhas) or were cut in the Polish fashion (based on a painting in the Schloss Wilhelmstein). The buttons were white metal. The fusiliers had blue shoulder-straps with white piping. The grenadier's plume and epaulets were red. Voltigeurs' plume and epaulets were green.

NCOs

The NCOs' rank insignia followed the French model and were in the button color, white or silver.

DRUMMERS

There is no information about the drummers' uniforms.

OFFICERS

The uniform corresponded to that of the privates. The epaulets were in silver. Shoulder bandolier made of black leather with a sword. Gilt gorget and portepée. Hungarian boots with silver trimming.

Fusilier, 2nd Battalion of the National Guard
Pinhas, Salomon: *Recueil de planches représentant les troupes des différentes armes et grades de l'armée Westphalienne,* 1811–1813, privately owned.

Officer of the fusiliers of the 2nd Battalion of the National Guard, 1812
Pinhas, Salomon: *Recueil de planches représentant les troupes des différentes armes et grades de l'armée Westphalienne,* 1811–1813, privately owned.

Grenadier, National Guard 2nd Battalion, 1812
Museum Schloß Friedrichstein (Bad Wildungen), photo: Markus Gaertner.

MOUNTED COMPANY *(BERITTENE KOMPANIE)*

PRIVATES

Headgear: Bicorn with white plume with light blue base.
Coat: Completely blue coat in the cut of the French light cavalry. Collar, lapels and cuffs were piped in red. Red fringed epaulets.
The red hussar-style vest had yellow cording.
Trousers: Blue pants with red stripes on the sides and Hungarian knotting. Hussar boots with red trim.

Armament: Light cavalry saber. The cartridge pouch had a rhombus-shaped badge, on which was the royal coat of arms. Black leather belting.
Saddlecloth: Pointed cloth shabraque in blue with red edging.

OFFICERS

Like for the privates but with gilt epaulets and trimming and Hungarian knotting.
The shoulder bandolier and waist belt were gilt with red edging. The cartridge pouch with an emblem was worn on a gold-colored bandolier.
Saddlecloth like for privates but with golden lace trim on the edge.

TRUMPETERS

The plume was white with a light blue tip. The bicorn had yellow braid edging.
The coat was in reversed colors, in this case in red with dark blue piping. Yellow epaulets.

Variations: Coat in red with dark blue distinction color on the collar, lapels, cuffs and coattails. These parts had yellow braid edging. Fringed epaulets in yellow. Vest like for the privates.
Saddlecloth: like for the privates. A variation had holsters in dark blue and red trim.

Cartridge pouch, National Guard mounted company
Museum Schloß Friedrichstein (Bad Wildungen), photo: Markus Gaertner.

National Guard Mounted Company, 1812

1: Officer, captain; **2:** trumpeter; **3:** badge for the cartridge pouch; **4:** privates; **5:** officer; **6:** trumpeter; **7:** trumpeter variant; **8, 9:** privates.

Sources: 1, 3, 4, 7 – from S. Pinhas, Salomon 1811-1813; 2, 5, 6 – reconstructions from K.-G. Klietmann;
8 – reconstruction; 3 – original in Schloss Friedrichstein (Bad Wildungen). Museumslandschaft Kassel.

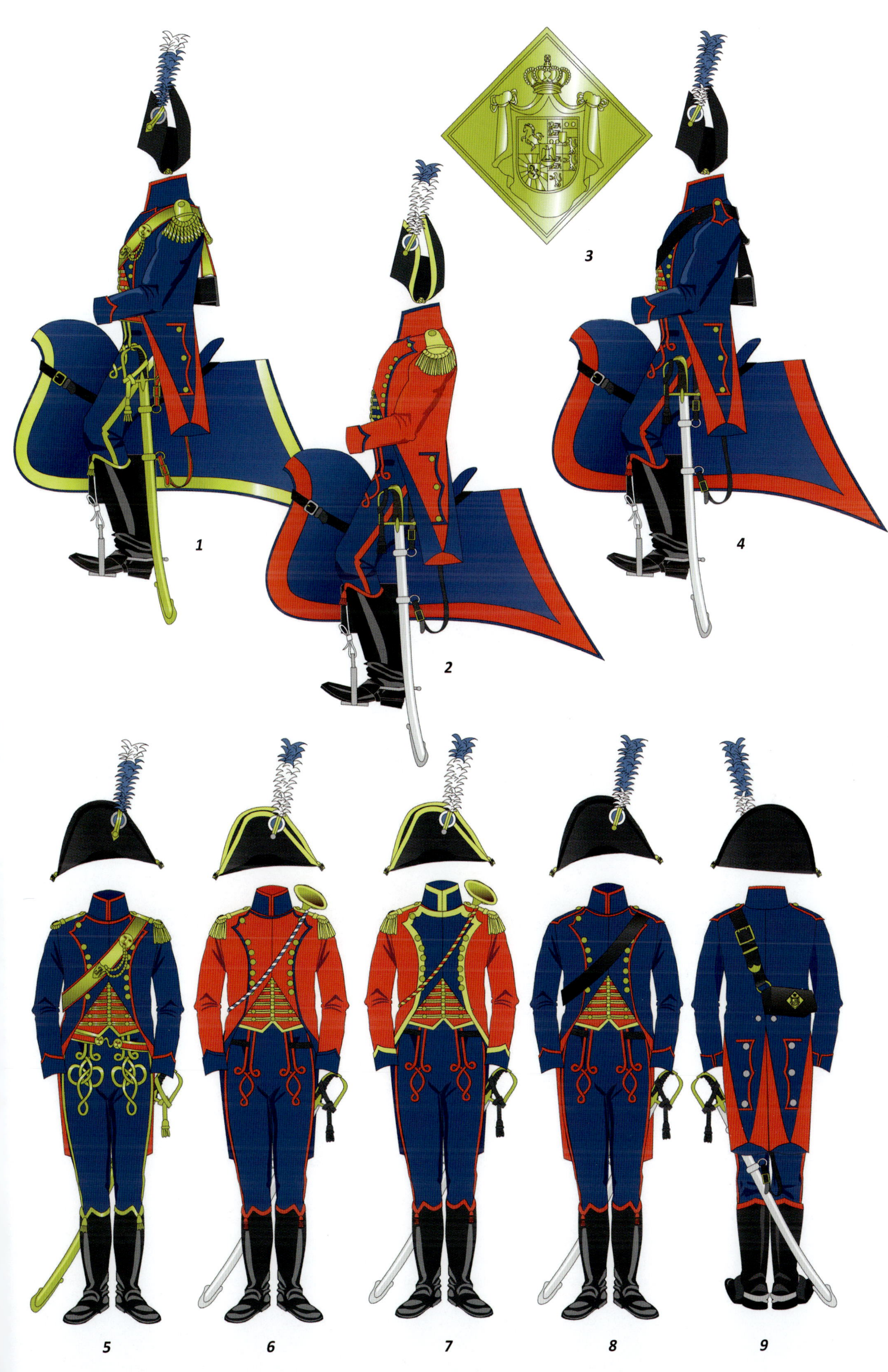

1
2
3
4
5
6
7
8
9

Captain, mounted company of the National Guard, 1812
Pinhas, Salomon: *Recueil de planches représentant les troupes des différentes armes et grades de l'armée Westphalienne, 1811–1813,* LWL-Preussenmuseum, Minden.

HONOR GUARDS *(EHRENGARDEN)*

Honor guards were formed in some cities in the Kingdom of Westphalia for whenever the King made an official visit to a city. This was in imitation of the French custom of greeting Emperor Napoleon with an honor guard in the towns and cities.

The honor guard members were assembled from well-to-do burghers who dressed in splendid uniforms for the appropriate occasions.

The Information about the attire is spotty and only sparsely documented.

Kassel

Entry of the royal couple in Kassel and the Wilhelmshöhe Palace on 7 and 8 December 1807.

Uniform: Tall bicorn with gilt edging. Red coat with black lapels, collar, cuffs. All the parts were edged with wide gold lace. White vest and pants with boots. As armament a saber.

A variation given by Wilhelm Hewig showed the honor guard's coat as follows: red coat with closed lapels and long coattails. The facings were made of black velour. Each lapel was decorated with 9 gilt lace pairs. There were also two laces on the collar and each cuff plus the waist pockets had two vertical laces each. The turnbacks were black, but did not reach to the middle of the tails. Epaulets were gilt and edged in red on both sides.

Brunswick

Arrival of the King in the city on 17 May 1807. Reception by the garrison and a formation by the mounted honor guard.

Uniform: Three-cornered hat with silver trim as headgear. Blue coat with white lapels and cuffs. The aiguillettes were silver; the vest and pants were white.
Saddlecloth was red shabraque with silvered trim.

Halberstadt

Coming from Brunswick, King Jérôme reached the city on 18 May 1807.

Uniform: Bicorn, coat dark blue with gilt collar trim. Saddlecloth: dark blue shabraque with silver trim.

Magdeburg

Stop by the King on 22 May 1807. A mounted company of 150 men was constituted.

Uniform: Three-cornered hat with white rooster feathers. White braiding on the edges.

Green coat with two rows of white buttons. Cuffs and collar in white. Large epaulets in silver. Short single-breasted white vest. Long pants with lace trim also in green. Hungarian boots with silver trimming and tassels. Sword silvered. waist belt of black lacquered leather. Gauntlets.
Shabraque white with dark blue trim.

Göttingen

Visit by the King in 1807.

Uniform: Three-cornered hat with white and blue plume. Coat dark blue with white closed collar, cuffs and gilt buttons. The vest was white with one row of buttons. Blue pants with half-boots.
As armament, a sword and carabine.

Osnabrück

On 13 September 1807 the King visited the capital of the Department of the Weser and was greeted by a mounted company. When he made a tour of the city he was accompanied by a formation on foot.

Uniform: Mounted: White coat with light blue facings. On foot: Black coat with red facings.

Minden

Visit to the city on 14 September 1807 with a reception by a mounted formation of 20 men.

Uniform: Bicorn with gilt loop and tassels on the sides, plus a white plume. Single-breasted blue coat with gilt buttons. Collar and cuffs in red. Gilt epaulet on the left shoulder, a trefoil epaulet on the right. Saber with gilt sword-strap. White vest and pants with half-boots which were decorated with white tassels.

Saddlecloth in white with a red border.

Marburg

Uniform: Mounted: bicorn with gilt edging, white and blue plume. Coat dark blue. Collar, cuffs and piping white. Two laces on the collar. On the right shoulder a gilt epaulette; on the left a contre-epaulette (i.e., without a fringe).

In 1811 the lands of the former Kingdom of Hanover were incorporated into Westphalia. Honor guards were also created in the more important cities there.

Hanover

Uniform: Bicorn with gilt trim. Dark green coat with gilt piping. White vest and pants. Boots with gilt edging and tassels.

Harburg

Uniform: Mounted: Three-cornered hat, coat dark green, saber. Dismounted: The shako for headgear, blue coat with red cuffs. Vest and pants white with gaiters.

Nienburg

Uniform: Mounted: Hat with a blue plume. Blue coat with white collar and cuffs and gilt epaulets. The vest and pants were white. The hussar boots had gilt trim and a tassel.

Verden

Uniform 1811: Mounted: bicorn with long silvered loop. White plume with red base. Blue coat with red distinctions on the collar, lapels and pointed cuffs. On the right shoulder was silver fringed epaulet, and on the left was a trefoil epaulet with aiguillettes. The vest and pants were white. The honor guard members had a red leather waist belt with a saber and silver sword-strap.

Honor guards were also formed in the cities of Salzgitter, Celle or Paderborn (mounted unit for 1808), but no information is available on the strengths or uniforms.

Honor Guards, 1807-1811

1: Verden Mounted Honor Guard, 1811; **2:** Kassel Honor Guard, 1807; **3:** Kassel Honor Guard, 1807, variation.

Sources: 1 – from a contemporary miniature picture in the collection of C. Vetterling, Kaltenkirchen; 2 – from a portrait by H. Knötel, in the estate in WGM; 3 – from a 1931 sketch from the Stadttheater Kassel, W. Hewig, pencil sketches in WGM.

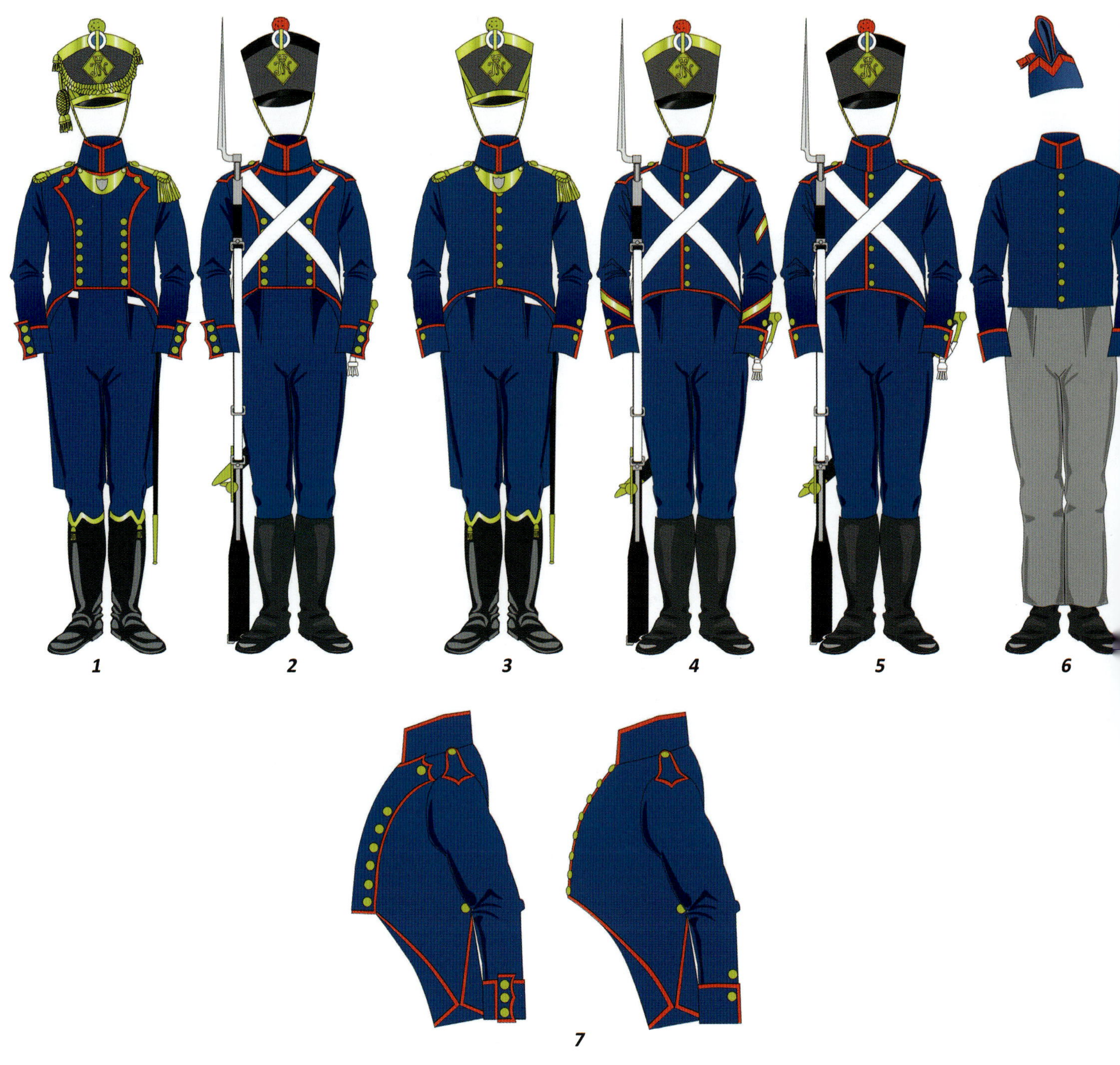

Veterans Companies, 1808–1813

1: Officer in dress uniform, 1808–1810; **2:** veteran in dress uniform, 1808–1810; **3:** officer in dress uniform, 1810–1813; **4:** NCO sergeant in duty uniform starting 1810; **5:** veteran, 1810–1813; **6:** veteran in fatigue uniform and inside service, 1808–1813; **7:** coat dress uniform, 1808–1810 and for 1810–1813.

Sources: 2, 4, 5, 7 – per the Decree of 1808 and H. Knötel, details in the estate in WGM; 1, 3, 6 – reconstructions.

VETERANS COMPANIES

ESTABLISHMENT

A veterans company was established in each of the eight Departments of the kingdom with the Decree of 9 February 1808. Soldiers who were no longer able to serve in the field were to be assigned to them. In the event of an enemy invasion, they were to be used as reinforcements for defending the country. Service was set at six years and linked to a subsequent lifetime pension.

ORGANIZATION

1 Captain (*Hauptmann/Kapitän*), 1 Lieutenant, 1 *Feldwebel*, 1 corporal quartermaster, 2 sergeants, 4 corporals, 2 drummers and 80 soldiers.

In 1808, the companies had a total strength of 648 men (of 720 authorized). The companies mostly were understrength; only after 1810 did they reach their full strength with the departure of the long serving soldiers.

UNIFORMS, 1808–1810

PRIVATES

Headgear: Shako with brass "JN" plate under a crown. Red pompom in spherical or carrot shape.
Field cap was made of blue cloth with red trim.
Coat: Completely dark blue coat with lapels and short coattails. Collar, shoulder-straps, cuffs, turnbacks were piped red. Flaps on the cuffs.
A coat without lapels and cuff flaps served as the undress uniform. A blue waistcoat with the collar and cuffs piped in red was worn for inside duty.
Trousers: Blue pants with black gaiters. For the undress uniform or for inside duty grey trousers were also worn.
Equipment and armament: White leather bandoliers. Former Kurhessian items like cartridge boxes and sabers were still used. In the beginning, the armament also came from Hessian M 1790 muskets that were later replaced by French and their own models.

NCOs

Like that for the privates but with NCO's rank insignia. Sergeants and *Feldwebels* had golden lace trim on the upper shako band.

DRUMMERS

There are no known details about the drummer's uniform.

OFFICERS

Uniform coats were like the privates but with long coattails. To that were added corresponding rank insignia. The pants were worn tucked into the boots. As armament a sword.

UNIFORMS, 1810–1813

In 1810 the coat with lapels was abolished for all ranks. The former undress uniform with the single-breasted coat became the new dress uniform. Everything else remained unchanged.

Departmental Companies, 1808

1: Officer of the Veterans; **2:** NCO in duty uniform starting 1809; **3:** drummer starting 1808; **4:** soldier 1808; **5:** soldier starting 1809.

Sources: 1 – per the *Decree of 1808* and H. Knötel; 2, 4, 5 – per the decree of February 1808; 3 – reconstruction.

DEPARTMENTAL COMPANIES *(DEPARTEMENTAL-KOMPANIEN)* (PREFECTURE GUARDS - *PRÄFEKTURGARDEN*)

ESTABLISHMENT

With the Decree of 9 February1808, Departmental companies were created in each of the Kingdom of Westphalia's eight departments to support the gendarmerie. Their mission was to guard public buildings, warehouses and prisons. The companies were paid, clothed and maintained by the Departments. The period of service was six years. The officers and NCOs were experienced veterans and were selected for the command by the Ministry of War.

STRUCTURE

1 Captain, 1 lieutenant, 1 sergeant major (*Feldwebel*), 2 sergeants, 1 *fourrier*, 4 corporals, 1 drummer and 39 soldiers.
Total strength: 50 men.

There were a total of eight companies. In 1809 the companies of the Departments of the Fulda and the Werra were each increased to 100 men.

UNIFORMS

According to the Decree of 9 February 1808.

PRIVATES

Headgear: Black bicorn with a flat blue pompom with the company number in white in the center; the cockade on a white loop.
Coat: Bluish grey; single-breasted uniform coat closed with eight buttons, in the pattern of the infantry undress coat. Collar, breast seam and cuffs were edged with red piping. The shoulder straps were in the same color as the coat and without piping. The buttons were white metal with the "JN" emblem.
Trousers: Bluish grey pants with long black gaiters. Starting in 1809 long trousers for daily duty.
Greatcoat: Made of grey cloth, closed in front with one row of buttons.
Armament and equipment: Musket boxes and cartridge boxes from old Prussian, Hanoverian or Kurhessian stocks. The bayonet was always carried fixed to the musket. White leather bandoliers. Cartridge box without a plate.

NCOs

Uniform was like for the privates but with white/silver rank insignia on the sleeves.

TAMBOUR

Details about the uniform are not known. There were probably no special distinctions.

OFFICERS

Headgear: Black bicorn with a flat blue pompom with white company number in the center; cockade on a silver loop.
Coat: Blue, single-breasted frock coat with red turnbacks. The horizontal coattail pockets were piped red; silver epaulets.
Trousers: Blue pants were worn tucked in boots.

DISCIPLINARY UNITS

DEPOT FOR DEFAULTING CONSCRIPTS
(DEPOTS RÉFRACTAIRES/DEPOT FÜR REFRACTÄRE)

Refractäre (from the French "*réfractaires*") were conscripts who did not appear for induction and attempted to go into hiding. They were sought out by the Gendarmerie who received a bonus for each apprehended *Refractäre*.

A depot for apprehended *Refractäre* was established by a decree of 27 October 1808, where they were each sentenced to two years of public work. For good behavior a *Refractär* could be transferred to the Army.
The location was initially Paderborn. In March 1809 the depot was moved to Braunschweig.

STRUCTURE

The *Refractäre* were combined into companies:

1 Captain *(Hauptmann)*
1 Lieutenant
1 Sub-lieutenant *(sous-lieutenant)*
1 Sergeant major
1 *Fourier*
5 Sergeants
10 Corporals
100 *Refractäre* (defaulting conscripts)

It is not known how many companies were formed. However a second planned depot was not set up.

UNIFORM

The uniform was like for the Line infantry but without distinction colors. It was simply the infantry undress coat. Brown forage caps as headgear.
The officers and NCOs probably already wore the uniform that was established for the cadre of the Public Workers Corps (*Korps der öffentlichen Arbeiter*) formed in 1813.

Depot for Defaulting Conscripts
(Réfractaires), **1808–1812**

Réfractaire in work uniform.

PUBLIC WORKERS CORPS

(KORPS DER ÖFFENTLICHEN ARBEITER)

At the beginning of 1813 the opposition of the population of the kingdom to conscription and military service appears to have increased significantly. The news about the enormous losses in Russia and the large requirements for personnel for re-establishing the units could have been the reasons for this. In any case, the Public Workers Corps (*Korps der öffentlichen Arbeiter*) was created in June of 1813. It was a unit of convicts who had been sentenced to forced labor. Four groups based on sentences were established

1. Those who refused to obey orders (*Befehlsverweigerer*) (*"indisziplinierte und nicht mehr zu bessernde Soldaten"* – "soldiers who were undisciplined and who could not be bettered")
2. Conscripts who had injured themselves to avoid duty
3. Pardoned deserters
4. Military personnel who were sentenced to public work.

The convicts in groups 1 to 3 were considered Class 1 workers, those in the fourth group as Class 2 workers. The corps was stationed in Braunschweig and probably merged into the *Refractäre* Depot located there.

In 1813 family members and village communities that aided desertions were also given severe punishments.

STRUCTURE

The corps consisted of several battalions. The number of personnel depended on the number of personnel being punished. Each battalion in turn was made up of six companies with 134 workers each.

Staff:

1 Commandant (staff officer)
1 Adjutant-major (captain)
1 Quartermaster
1 Surgeon *(chirurgien-aide-major)*
1 Drummer corporal *(Korporal-Tambour)*
2 Artisans *(Handwerker)*

Company:

1 Captain
1 Lieutenant
1 Sergeant major
3 Sergeants
1 *Fourier*
6 Corporals
2 Drummers
134 Workers *(Arbeiter)*

Total: 149 men

The officers and NCOs from Army were reassigned to the Corps. Service there was not respected and considered a punishment. An assignment to the Corps via a *"Tagesbefehl"* (King's order) had to be considered a as an "award." NCOs and corporals could also be named from the workers among the 1st class.

The corps was subordinate to the General Director of the Artillery and Engineer System.

UNIFORMS

PRIVATES

Headgear: grey forage caps of both the old and new pattern (*bonnet de police* and *pokalem*). Also a round, felt hat turned up in front was in use.
Coat: **grey** waistcoat closed with a single or two rows of buttons; the buttons were covered with cloth.
For the 1st Class Worker (*Arbeiter 1. Klasse*) a light blue collar on the jacket.
Pants: Grey pants with grey cloth gaiters.
Greatcoat: For inclement weather, a grey greatcoat closed with one row of buttons.

NCOs

Headgear: Shako with white metal plate and chin-scales and a red pompom.
Coat: Single-breasted, blue uniform coat. Only the collar was red with blue piping. White metal buttons.
Pants: Dark blue pants in black gaiters or blue trousers.
Rank insignia: Rank braids on the sleeves. For the sergeant major silver and red interwoven fringed epaulets.
Armament: Short saber without sword-strap.

DRUMMERS

Unknown.

OFFICERS

Headgear: Shako with silvered emblems and decorations.
Coat: Dark blue surtout with silvered buttons with the artillery emblem on them. The collar was red with dark blue piping.
Trousers: Dark blue pants with low boots.
Armament: Sword with silvered *portepée*, worn on waist belt made of white leather.

Public Workers Corps,
Worker 2nd class in greatcoat and work dress
Watercolor by H. Boisselier after W. Hewig and H. Knötel.

Public Workers Corps, 1813

1: officer; **2:** NCO – sergeant major; **3:** worker 1st class; **4:** worker 2nd class, **5:** worker 2nd class, variation.

Source: 1 – reconstruction, 2-6 – from information from W. Hewig and H. Knötel, WGM.

Westfalen
Knötel d. J.

MILITARY ADMINISTRATION AND SCHOOLS

Field hospital at Borodino, 7 September 1812: "… but I am certain that the countless cripples of the great Napoleonic Army, along the tremendously long monastery wall on a little befouled straw, … bivouacked using their shakos for bedpans and their helmets for cooking pots. The naked corpses of the departed laying stacked in piles at the entries to the monastery …"

From: Wachsmuth; *Leutnant 5. Infanterie-Regiment – Geschichte meiner Kriegsgefangenschaft in Rußland in den Jahren 1812-1813*, Magdeburg 1910.

Surgeon
Watercolor by Herbert Knötel, Serie *Westfälische Studien*; WGM, Rastatt.

***Inspecteur aux revues en Chef*, 1811**
Pinhas, Salomon: *Recueil de planches représentant les troupes des différentes armes et grades de l'armée Westphalienne.*

MUSTERING INSPECTION AND MILITARY OFFICIALS *(MUSTERUNGS-INSPEKTOREN AND MILITÄRBEAMTE)*

ESTABLISHMENT

The Ministry of War oversaw and steered all the affairs and tasks of the Army and established the regulations and the military administration.

The kingdom was initially divided into three and in 1810 into four military administrative entities, so-called Military Divisions (*Militärdivisionen*).

Each Division was commanded by a more senior officer who functioned as the *Gouverneur*. The weapons commandants (*Waffenkommandanten*) and site commandants (*Platzkommandanten*), the war commissars (*Kriegskommissare*) and numerous military officials (*Militärbeamten*) were under his command.

The most senior oversight authority was a Commission (*Kommission*) with the following composition:

Chief Review Inspector (*Generalmusterungsinspekteur/Inspecteur aux revues en chef*) in Kassel	1
Review Inspectors (*Musterungsinspekteur, Revue-Inspekteur/Inspecteurs aux revues*)	4
Junior Inspector 1st and 2nd Class (*Unter-Inspekteur 1. und 2. Klasse*)	8
Adjutants (*Adjutanten/adjoints aux inspecteurs aux revues*)	8

With the Decree of 1 January 1812 there were only the ranks of *Inspekteurs aux revues* and its subordinate grades.

These "authorities" ("*Behörde*") oversaw the call-up of recruits and they were in continuous contact with the respective regiments, who had to do checks at regular intervals on the strength and financial accounting. The Military Administration was completely set up in its division of duties and its organization on the French model, which based on its complicated construction was able to perform thorough and extensive administrative functions

The Review Inspectors (*Musterungsinspektoren / Revue-Inspektor*) maintained direct contact with the individual units. These inspectors were to monitor and control the administration, the budgeting system, as well as the discipline.

A *Waffenkommandant* or *Platzkommandant*, who was responsible for all military matters, was stationed in each of the larger towns and cities of a Department.

The War Commissars (*Kriegskommissare*) were responsible for the requisitioning and delivery of various necessary equipment and usually had the functions of the *Musterungsinspektoren* at the same time.

The troop units were inspected and had their readiness and equipment checked with regular parades and reviews (*Revuen* or *Musterungen*). The prescribed implementation of the training regulations also fell into the Commission's area of responsibility.

In wartime a Field War Commissariat (*Feldkriegskommissariat*) was created that had the difficult task of supplying the units in the field. It was often poorly organized and also over-tasked, plus in many cases officials misused their office for personal financial gains.

ORGANIZATION (OF THE WAR COMMISSARIAT *[KRIEGSKOMMISSARIAT]* IN 1812)

Commissariat (*Indendant*)	1
Mustering and/or Review Inspectors (*Musterungsinspektoren/Revueinspektoren*)	2
Inspectors' Assistants (*Adjonts der Inspektoren*)	4
War Commissars (*Kriegskommisare*)	8
Bakers (*Bäcker*)	41
Butchers (*Metzger*)	40

Plus a wagon park with additionally assigned Train soldiers (*Trainsoldaten*, i.e., drivers).

UNIFORMS

Dress/Gala Uniforms

Headgear: Tall bicorn with silvered hat tassels and loop. For the Chief Inspector (*Inspecteur en Chef*) with black plumage-feather trim on the hat.
Coat: Medium blue single-breasted frock coat cut in the pattern like for generals, here with silvered embroidery in the shape of oak leaves on the collar, on the breast seam, cuffs as well as on the coattails. The rank was indicated by the number and placement of the embroidery.
Chief Inspector of Reviews *(Inspecteur aux Revues en Chef):* Two rows of embroidery on the collar and cuffs. One wide set of embroidery on the chest, as well as on the coattail turnbacks and pockets.
On duty he wore a silver waist sash worked through with light blue; the fringes on the ends were silvered.
Inspector of Reviews *(Inspecteur aux Revues)*: A row of embroidery, a narrow pattern of embroidery on the chest.
Deputy Inspector of Reviews 1st and 2nd Class *(Sous-Inspecteur aux Revues 1er and 2em Classe)*: Only one row of embroidery on the collar and cuffs.
The "2nd Class" ("*2. Klasse*"/"2em Classe) rank only had collar embroidery.
Adjoints **(Adjunkt - Adjutanten)**: Only one silver lace on the collar.
Trousers: Tight fitting white pants with tall black straight-legged boots.
Armament: The sword, with silver *portepée,* was worn on the waist belt.

Undress Uniform

The coat for the informal uniform corresponded to the ones above, like before, but had red turned back coattails on which a silver eagle was situated.
The embroidery and the rank insignia also corresponded to the dress uniform.
The pants were dark blue worn with short Hungarian or Hessian boots.
Greatcoat: Blue, closed in front with two rows of buttons. The embroidery on the collar and cuffs was according to the rank.
Saddlecloth: Rectangular medium blue cloth shabraque and holsters with silver bordering.

Mustering Inspectors, 1811–1813

1: *Generalmusterungsinspektor* dress and undress uniform 1808–1812; **2:** *Revue-Musterungsinspektor* dress and undress uniform, 1812; **3:** *Generalmusterungsinspektor* in dress uniform 1811; **4:** *Revue-Musterungsinspektor* in undress uniform, 1812; **5:** *Revue-Musterungsinspektor* in the greatcoat (redingote), 1812–1813; **6:** *Unter-Inspekteur* in dress uniform; **7:** adjutant *(adjoint)* in undress uniform 1812; **8:** schema: *Unter-Inspekteur* dress uniform, *Unter-Inspekteur* 2nd class dress uniform, *adjoint* dress uniform.

Sources: 1, 2, 4 to 8 – from the 1812 decree and H. Knötel's schemata in his estate in WGM; 2 – from S. Pinhas 1811.

1
2
3
4
5
6
7
8

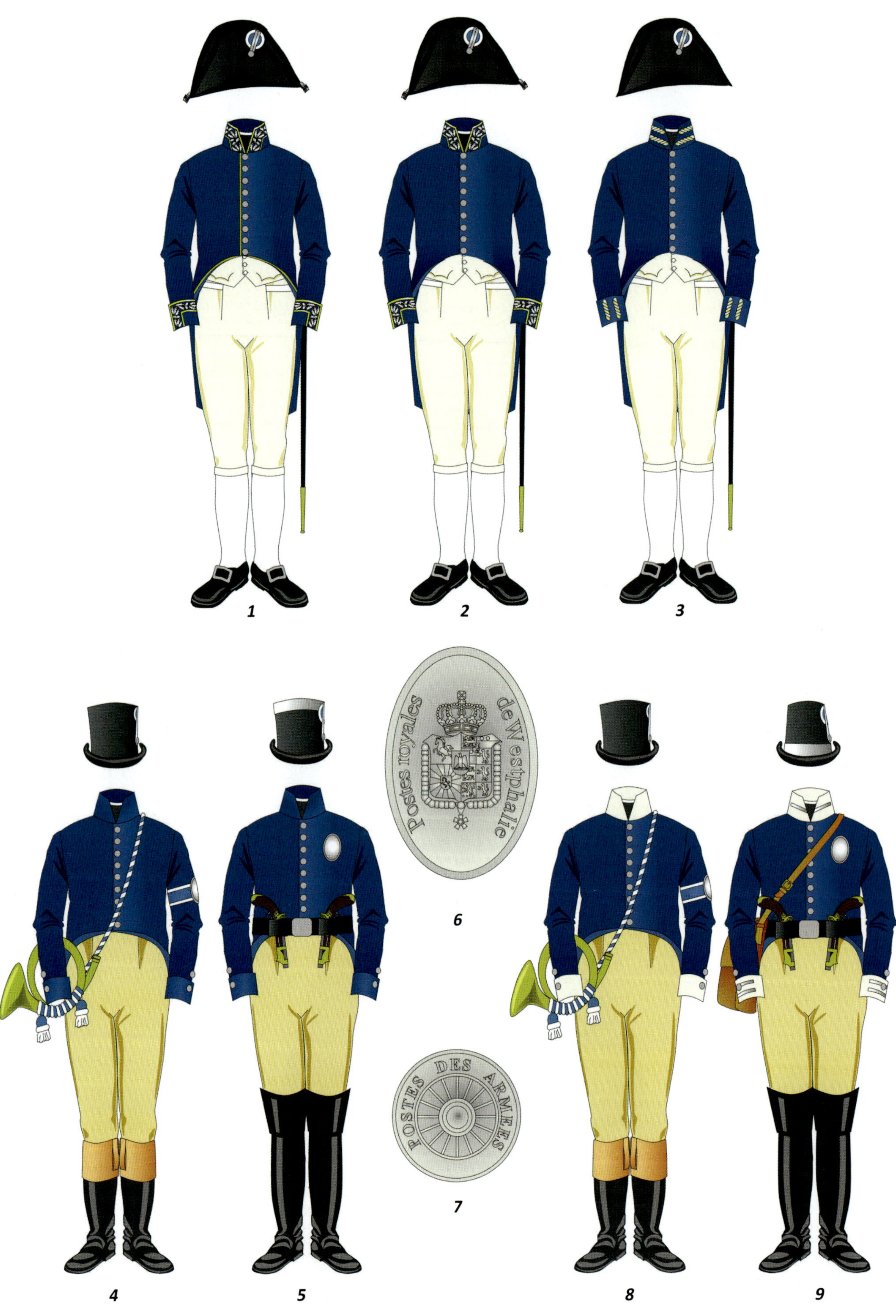
1
2
3
Postes royales de Westphalie
6
POSTES DES ARMEES
7
4
5
8
9

FIELD POSTAL SERVICE *(FELDPOST)*

The post office (*Post*) was a part of the Kingdom's civil administration. If the Westphalian Army went to war, a Field Postal Service was established. To do that, officials from the civil *Post* were assigned to the Field Postal Service (*Feldpost*). The field post office had the mission of delivering letters, dispatches and packages not only to the General Staff but also to members of the army and their families. Items mailed were delivered to the closest office of the particular Department in the Kingdom. Members of the *Post* were already operating in Spain from 1809 to 1811. Reports and dispatches were as a rule transported quickly to the capital, Kassel. In 1812 a field post office was organized for the campaign against Russia. The *Feldpost's* leaders were located in the headquarters of the Westphalian divisions.

The following structure was specified for 1812:

- 1 Senior inspector (*Oberinspektor*)
- 2 Postal directors (*Postdirektoren*)
- 1 Controller (*Kontrolleur*)
- 1 Cashier (*Kassierer*)
- 1 Accountant (R*echnungsführer*)
- 6 Field postmasters (*Feldpostmeister*)
- 8 Couriers (*Kuriere*)
- 16 Mailmen (*Postillione*)

Total: 36 men and 52 horses.

The mounted couriers (*Kuriere*) delivered the letters while the mailmen (*Postillione*) transported the packages with wagons. The sides of the wagons were marked with the initials "JN" with a crown above them and the designation *"Postes militaires"* (military mail). The size of the wagon park is not known.

UNIFORMS

All the Post's members wore a uniform (per the Decrees of 1808 and 1810). It was allowed to carry a sidearm (a sword for the officials; a short saber for the *Postillione* and *Kuriere*) when in uniform.

Inspectors, Directors, Controllers, Cashiers, Postmasters

Headgear: Bicorn with cockade and loop.
Coat: Blue coat with long coattails. Silver buttons with the royal coat of arms and the inscription *"Postes royales de Westphalie"* (Royal Post of Westphalia).
White vests and pants, shoes with buckles.

The officials; ranks were differentiated by varied embroidery on the coats:
Inspector: Silver oakleaf embroidery between lengthwise golden braids on the collar, cuffs and the flaps of the coattail pockets. Gold piping along the button seam and the turnbacks
Director, Controller, Cashier: like for the Inspector but without gold piping on the button seam and turnbacks.
Postmaster: the only embroidery was two woven, gold-silver mixed staffs on the sides of the collar and the cuffs

Field Postal Service, 1808–1813

1: Inspector; **2:** director, controller, cashier; **3:** postmaster; **4:** mailman, 1808; **5:** courier, 1808; **6:** courier's badge, 1808–1812; **7:** uniform button; **8:** mailman *(Postillion)*, 1810; **9:** courier, 1810.

Sources: 1–8 – from *Decree of 11 February 1808* and of *30 September 1810*, information from Dr. Klietmann; 9 – from W. Hewig.

Couriers *(Kurier)*, Postmen *(Postillion)*

Headgear: Round hat made of felt with the Westphalian cockade and loop on the left. The bell of the hat was decorated with a ca. 2cm/¾ inch broad white or silver band. It is uncertain whether this band ran around the bottom or the top of the hat.

Coat: Completely dark blue coat with short coattails. In the front was a row of nine white metal buttons. The buttons bore the inscription "POSTES DES ARMÉES." White vests.

In 1810 the collar and cuffs were changed to white. The couriers received narrow silver braids on the collar and cuffs. White stars on the turnbacks.

The Postman (*Postillion*) wore an armband with an oval metal badge with the royal coat of arms on his left arm. The armband was made of blue cloth with white border. The courier wore the same kind of badge on his right breast.

Trousers: Pants made of light leather. In addition, tall boots with cuffs or boots with brown turned down cuffs.

Equipment: The *Postillion*'s equipment included a *Posthorn* with light blue and white cording.

The sources show as armament two small pistols that were carried in holsters on a black waist belt.

Saddlecloth: White sheepskin shabraque probably with white wolves teeth.

Postal Service, 1812
Sketch by Wilhelm Hewig, Knötel estate, WGM, Rastatt.

MEDICAL SYSTEM *(SANITÄTSWESEN)*

A branch for medical units was not yet normal at the beginning of the 19th century. The medical officers and doctors were subordinate to the Military Administration. The level of medical care for sick and wounded soldiers was exceptionally poor at that time. This was due to the poor level of medical knowledge at that time and on the other hand on the medical personnel's lack of training. Only the actual doctors (*Ärzte/médecin*), the regimental doctors (*Regimentsärzte*), surgeons (*Wundärzte, Chirurgen/Chirurgiens de 1ère classe/chirurgien-mayor*) and the Senior Pharmacists (*Oberapotheker/pharmacien de 1ère classe*) had studied for their professions. The lower ranks usually learned through hands-on experience.

The general practitioners (*Allgemein-Ärzte/médecin*) at that time were considered responsible for "internal" conditions. There were only two ranks for them. They were, like the pharmacists, employed in the hospitals and in field hospitals. The surgeons or *Wundärzte* (*Chirurgien*) treated external conditions (accidents, injuries, wounds) and took over the care of the ill before they were sent to the hospitals. The surgeons served directly with the troops in the regiments. A 1st Class Surgeon (*Chirurgien-mayor/Chirurgien de 1ère classe*) and several senior surgeon's assistants (*Chirurgiens-aide-mayor*) and junior surgeon's assistants (*sous-aide-mayor/chirurgiens de 2me* and *de 3me classe*) served in each regiment's staff.
For the *Wundärzte* and the pharmacists (*Apotheker/pharmaciens*) there were four ranks for each.

The medical system was divided in three levels in the Westphalian Army:

1st - HOSPITALS *(Hospitäler)*
Hospitals existed in various cities as lasting institutions for the treatment and care of the ill and wounded. They were divided into three classes:

1st Class Hospitals (Hospitäler 1. Klasse):
In Kassel and Magdeburg with a capacity of 300 to 700 patients.
2nd Class Hospitals (Hospitäler 2. Klasse):
In Braunschweig and Hanover with a capacity up to 300 patients.
3rd Class Hospitals (*Hospitäler 3. Klasse*):
In Hameln, Halberstadt, Halle and Celle with a capacity up to 150 patients.

2nd - FIELD HOSPITALS *(Feldlazartte)*
Field hospitals were attached to the Army divisions when they deployed. The hospitals were set up a little distance from the battlefield. The wounded received initial treatment there before being transported to collection hospitals or hospitals.
The staffing of medical officers of a field hospital for a division in 1812 was:

Doctor (*Médecin/Stabsarzt*)	1
Surgeon 1st Class/Staff Surgeon (*chirurgien de 1ère classe/chirurgien-mayor/Stabschirurg*)	2
Surgeons 2nd Class (*chirurgien de 2me classe/ chirurgien-aide-mayor/Chirurg 2. Klasse*)	4
Surgeons 3rd Class (*chirurgien de 3me classe/ chirurgien-sous-aide-mayor/Chirurg 3. Klasse*)	8
Pharmacists 1st Class (*Pharmacien de 1ère classe/ Oberapotheker*)	1
Pharmacists 2nd Class (*Pharmacien de 2me classe /Feldapotheker*)	2
Pharmacists 3rd Class (*Pharmacien de 3me classe /Unterapotheker*)	4

The field hospital *(Feldlazarett)* was led by an administrative official, not by a doctor:

Inspecteur aux revues/Oberinspektor	1

3rd - REGIMENTAL SURGEONS *(Regimentsärzte)*
The regimental surgeons (*Chirurgien*) belonged to the staff of each regiment and accompanied the unit to the field.
The exact designation of the various doctors' and pharmacists' ranks cannot be determined with certainty. Especially the German translations that are used in the sources (e.g., in Lünsmann) change frequently and are not clearly defined.

Officer, medical system
Pinhas, Salomon: *Recueil de planches représentant les troupes des différentes armes et grades de l'armée Westphalienne*, 1811–1813, privately owned.

Doctors *(Ärzte/Mediziner/Medecins)*, 1812

1: *Médecin en Chef*, dress uniform; **2:** doctor, dress uniform; **3:** doctor, undress uniform; **4:** Hospital Administration Inspector; **5:** Hospital Administration employee; **6:** *Médecin en Chef* – **a:** dress uniform, **b:** undress uniform; **7:** *Médecin/Arzt* – **a:** dress uniform, **b:** undress uniform; **8:** Hospital Administration – **a:** inspector, **b:** director, **c:** employee.

Sources: 1-8 – Reglement Kapitel 28, *Von der Uniform der Gesundheitsbeamten der Militärhospitäler und der Corps* and H. Knötel, *Schemata der Gesundheitsbeamten 1811/1812,* estate in WGM.

UNIFORMS

Headgear: Bicorn with gilt loop and cockade.
Additionally a cornflower blue forage cap with red piping.
Coat: Cornflower blue uniform coat with long coattails, closed in the front with nine gilt buttons. On the buttons was the rod of Asclepius inside a wreath of oak and laurel leaves. Horizontal coattail pockets with three buttons. Golden eagle emblems on the turnbacks. Collar and cuffs were violet for the doctors *(Ärzte),* red for the surgeons (*Chirurgen* or *Wundärzte*) and green for the pharmacists (*Apotheker*). The surgeons' and the pharmacists' vests were also red and green respectively. The doctors wore blue or in the summer also white vests under the coat.
The medical officers' ranks were indicated by varying golden laces on the uniform coat.
The undress uniform coat had a folded down collar and somewhat reduced lace trim.

Trousers: Blue, in the summer also white pants. Boots with light brown cuffs or Hungarian boots.
Armament: Sword with a gilt *portepée* was worn on the waist belt made of white leather for the dress uniform and made of black leather for the undress uniform.
Greatcoat: Cornflower blue *Überrock* (redingote) with turned down collar and cuffs in red and green respectively.
Cornflower blue greatcoat; the cape collar was trimmed with a 4 cm/1½ inches wide golden braid. The collar was violet, red or green.
Saddlecloth: Rectangular, cornflower blue cloth shabraque with holsters. Golden edging with the outside edge piped in red, violet or green. The width of the braid depended on the rank.

Hospital and Field Hospital *(Lazarett)* Administration

Headgear: Bicorn gilt clasp/loop (*Agraffe*) and a cockade.
Coat: Dark blue coat cut like that of the medical officers with blue collar and cuffs. The buttons were gold-colored with the inscription *"Militär-Hospitäler"* surrounded my an oakleaf wreath. Vest in the same color as the coat, and in summer also in white.
Wide gilt braids were sewn on the collar and cuffs for the inspectors.
The *Direktor* wore only one braid on the collar.

For the employees or *"Angestellten"* had only a narrow gold braid on the collar.
Trousers: Blue pants with low boots. In the summer pants also in white or in calico.
Employees (*Angestellte*) wore black knee-high stockings with high shoes instead of the boots.

Surgeons *(Chirurgen/chirurgiens),* 1812

Dress uniform 1: *Médecin en Chef*; **2:** surgeon 1st class; **3:** surgeon 2nd class; **4:** surgeon 3rd class; **5:** surgeon's aid *(aide-chirurgien)*; **Undress uniform 6:** surgeon 1st class; **7:** surgeon 3rd class; **8:** surgeon 2nd class in the *Überrock* (redingote); **9:** surgeon 1st class in the greatcoat; **10:** surgeon 2nd class.

Sources: 1-10 – *Reglement Kapitel 28, Von der Uniform der Gesundheitsbeamten der Militärhospitäler and der Corps* and H. Knötel, *Schemata der Gesundheitsbeamten 1811/1812*, estate in WGM.

1
2
3
4
5
6
7
8
9
10

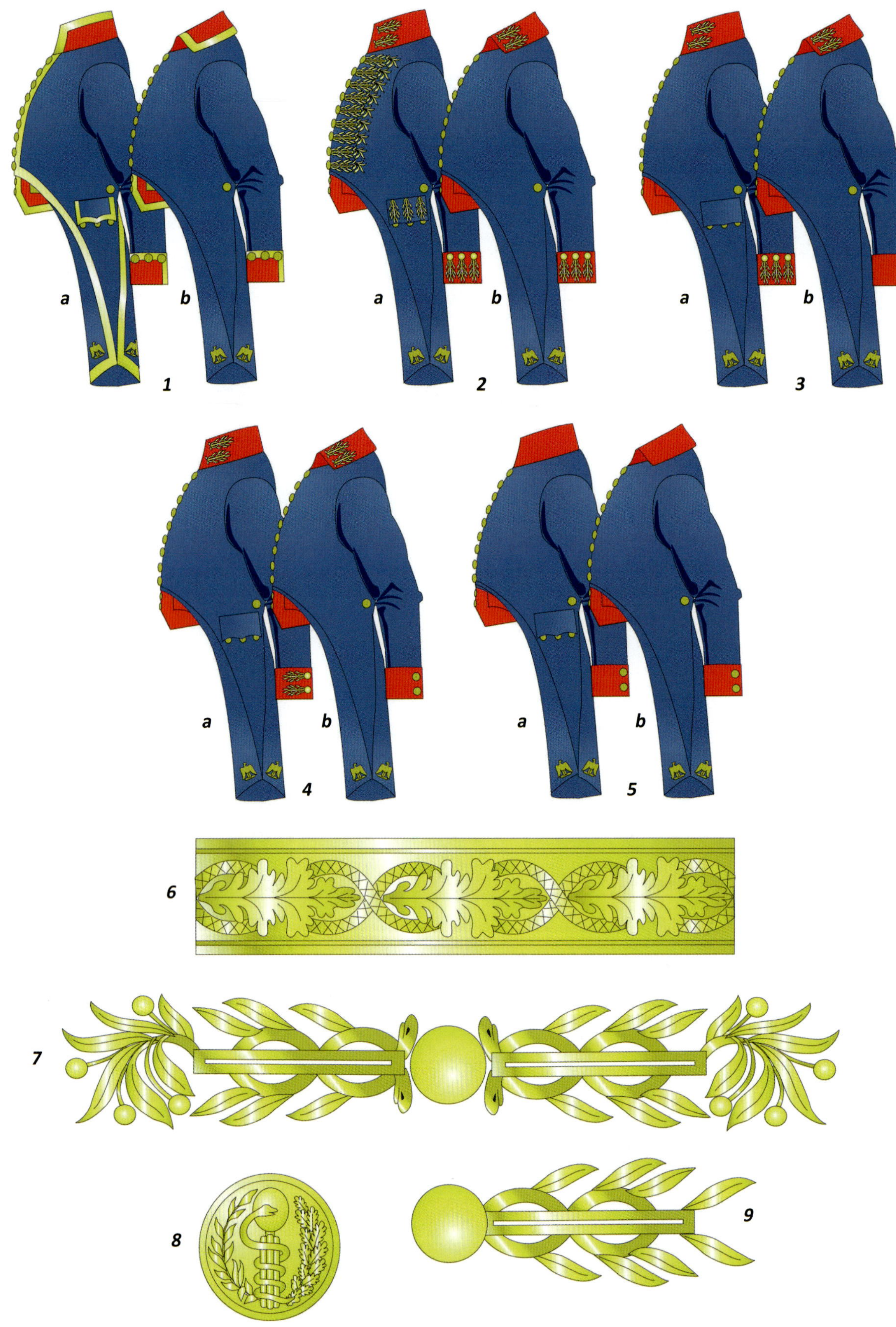

Surgeons' Coat Patterns 1812 and Health Officials' and Medical Officers' Braid Trim

1: *Chirurgien en chef* a – dress b – undress uniform; **2:** surgeon 1st class a – dress b – undress uniform; **3:** surgein 2nd class a – dress b – undress uniform; **4:** surgeon 3rd clase a – dress b- undress uniform; **5:** surgeon's aid; **6:** braid trim for chief medical officers; **7:** breast embroidery for medical officer 1st clase; **8:** button for medical officers and Medical Administration; **9:** collar and cuff embroidery for medical officers.

Sources: 1–5 – Reglement Kapitel 28, *Von der Uniform der Gesundheitsbeamten der Militärhospitäler und der Corps* and H. Knötel, *Schemata der Gesundheitsbeamten 1811/1812*, estate in WGM; 6–9 reconstruction and schema on buttons by W. Hewig.

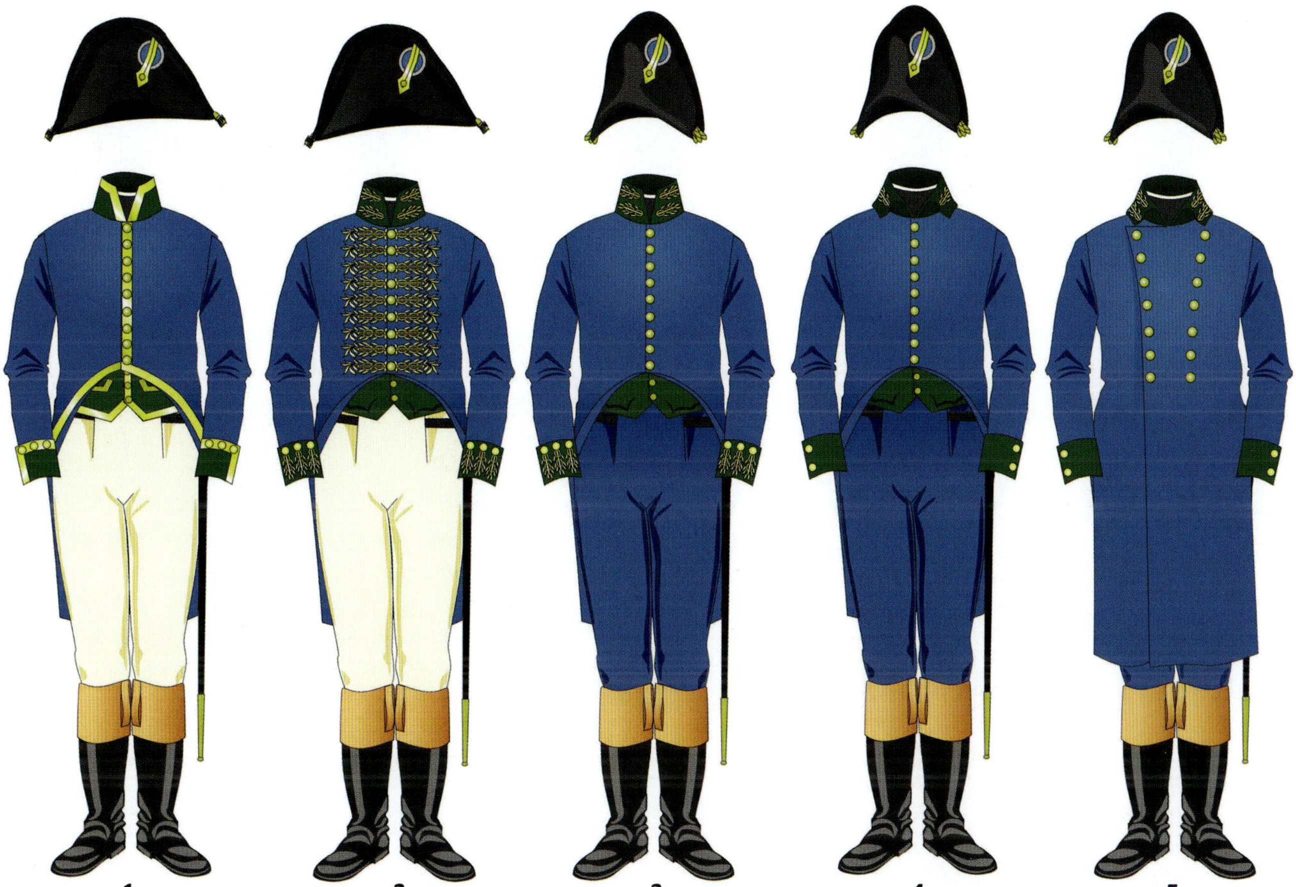

Pharmacists, 1812

1: Staff pharmacist, dress uniform;
2: pharmacist 1st class, dress uniform;
3: pharmacist 2nd class, dress uniform;
4: pharmacist 3rd class, undress uniform;
5: pharmacist 2nd class in redingote, undress uniform.

Coat patterns
6: Staff pharmacist
a – dress uniform, b – undress uniform;
7: pharmacist 1st class
a – dress uniform, b – undress uniform;
8: pharmacist 2nd class
a – dress uniform, b – undress uniform;
9: pharmacist 3rd class
a – dress uniform, b – undress uniform.

Sources: 1–9 – *Reglement Kapitel 28, Von der Uniform der Gesundheitsbeamten der Militärhospitäler und der Corps* and H. Knötel, *Schemata der Gesundheitsbeamten 1811/1812*, estate in WGM; 6–9 reconstructions and button patterns by W. Hewig.

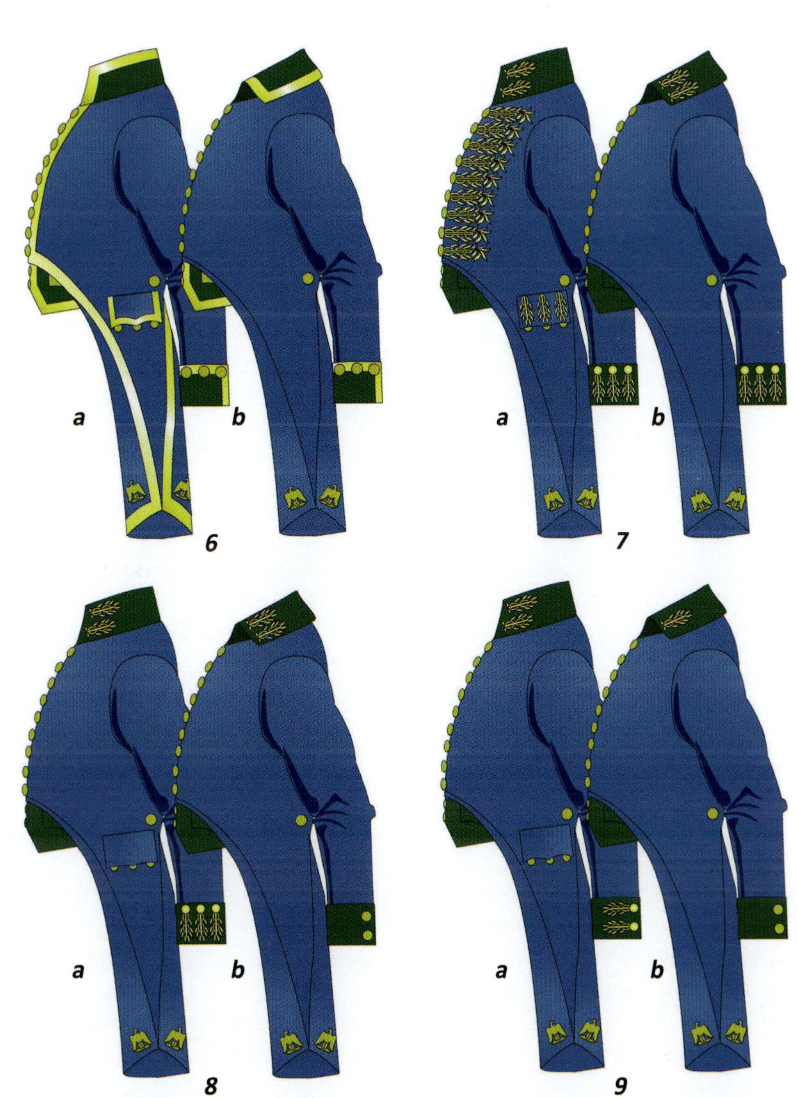

ROYAL MILITARY ACADEMIES *(KÖNIGLICHE MILITÄRSCHULEN)*

MILITARY ACADEMY *(KRIEGSSCHULE/ECOLE MILITAIRE)*

Cadet, Braunschweig Military School, 1812
Color drawing by Neumann,
collection of Paul Meganck, Brussels.

ESTABLISHMENT

Per a Royal Decree of 4 March 1808, a Military Academy (*École militaire* or *Kriegsschule*) was erected in Kassel to further educate the young and the successors of trained officers. The institution was moved to Braunschweig in October 1808. The school was directly subordinate to the Ministry of War.

The cadets had to be from 14 to 17 years old upon entry, have a good educational foundation and come from financially sound homes. There were stipendiums for selected, competent NCOs.

The general courses of instruction were writing, French, religion, history geography and mathematics. The military subjects were fortification science, mapmaking fencing, military administration, and drill. The training lasted from two to three years. Then the students were assigned to the Army as officers in the rank of a second lieutenant (*sous-lieutenant*).

The theoretical number of students was supposed to be 50 students. There were 49 students in 1809 and in the following year 47 students. By 1812 the number increased to 76 students. In mid-1813 there were 71. The first 16 students left the school in 1812.

STRUCTURE

1 Governor/*Gouverneur* (General von Heldring)
1 Director/*Direktor* (Major von Sommer)
1 *Adjudant-major*
1 War Commissar/*Kriegskommissar*
1 Quartermaster-Paymaster/*Schatzmeister* (*Quartier- und Zahlmeister*)
8 Professors

In 1812, the structure was increased with:
4 Professors
1 Deputy *Adjudant Major*/*Unter-Adjudant-major*
1 Doctor/*Arzt*
2 Senior Administrative Officials/*Oberbeamte* (*Verwaltungsbeamte*)
2 Drummers

UNIFORMS

Headgear: Shako with brass rhombus-shaped plate and chin-scales. The plate had the royal monogram with a crown above it; the spherical pompom was red. In 1812 red shako cording was introduced.

Coat: Dark blue with short coattails and pointed lapels, a red collar. The pointed cuffs, the shoulder-straps and the turnbacks were dark blue with red piping. On each turnback was a yellow cloth "JN" with a crown as an emblem. A variation had a yellow grenade as the insignia. Yellow buttons. A white, red or dark blue vest was worn and visible under the coat. In 1812 the vest was changed to red with yellow Hungarian knotting.

Trousers: Blue pants with white (summer) or black (winter) gaiters.

Armament: A short saber without a *portepée*, worn on a shoulder bandolier made of white leather.

ARTILLERY ACADEMY *(ARTILLERIESCHULE)*

ESTABLISHMENT

This institution was established in Kassel by orders of 29 October 1810 in order to bring this branch's education to a higher level (it opened on 1 January 1811). The educational focuses were mathematics and teaching about artillery. The training in various subjects lasted two years. The entry age was from 16 to 22 years old. In 1811 the first 16 students were being instructed. After passing the training the students went to the artillery as second lieutenants (*sous-lieutenant*). The first 20 students left the institution in 1813.

The school was subordinate to the commander of the Artillery Regiment, Major General Allix and it was led by Major von Heinemann.

UNIFORMS

The students wore the uniform of a foot artillery *sous-lieutenant*, however, without a gorget.

Braunschweig Military Academy *(Kriegsschule)*
1: Student 1808–1811; **2:** student, 1812–1813; **3:** coat pattern;

Kassel Artillery School
4: Student, 1810; **5:** coat pattern.

Sources: 1-5 – from information by W. Hewig, description by v. Poten, sketch by H. Knötel, WGM.

RETIRED OFFICERS *(PENSIONIERTE OFFIZIERE)*

The officers also continued to wear their uniforms after they were retired. In 1809 they were standardized and were kept simple and plain.

Headgear: Bicorn with Westphalian cockade.
Coat: Completely dark blue surtout; epaulets of the last rank attained, and gilt buttons. White vest.
Trousers: Blue breeches with boots or buckled shoes.
Armament: Sword worn on the waist belt.

Retired Officer (Captain)
Source: H. Boisselier, Darbou.

KARLSHAFEN INVALIDS' HOUSE *(INVALIDENHAUS KARLSHAFEN)*

In February 1813, the so-called *Invalidenhaus*, a house for veteran invalids was established in the northern Hessian town of Karlshafen. Wounded veterans were supposed to be able to spend their final years there.
Since the beginning of the 18th century a public institution having the same name already existed in Karlshafen that served as a rest home for the elderly former officers and soldiers from the Hessian Army. It was originally established by Landgrave Carl. The "*Invalidenhaus*" building which was built from 1704 to 1710 served this function until 1918 and still exists today in Bad Karlshafen.

UNIFORMS

Little is known about the uniform. H. Boisselier shows a variant with W. Hewig as the source.
Headgear: Bicorn or dark blue cloth *bonnet de police* with red piping and white braid on the turned-up part. Silver braid for the officers.
Coat: Dark blue single-breasted surtout. Red cuffs with two buttons. White fringed epaulets. The NCOs had rank insignia on the sleeves. The officers wore their respective epaulets in silver.
The undress uniform had a blue waistcoat with red cuffs for officers and NCOs, blue cuffs for privates.
Trousers: Dark blue breeches in short black gaiters or white trousers.
The officers wore boots or buckled shoes.
Greatcoat: Grey greatcoat with two rows of buttons. For officers also in blue.

Karlshafen Invalids, 1813

1. Officer in dress uniform; **2:** officer in undress uniform; **3:** NCO (corporal) in dress uniform; **4:** invalid (private/*Gemeiner*) in undress uniform.

Source: 1–4 – from H. Boisselier and information from W. Hewig and H. Knötel, WGM.

RANK INSIGNIA

Grenadier officer, 1813
This officer displays all the rank insignia elements: Lace trim on the shako, epaulets and gorget.
Pinhas, Salomon: *Recueil de planches représentant les troupes des différentes armes et grades de l´armée Westphalienne*, 1811–1813.

Essentially the Westphalian Army's rank insignia were patterned after those of Napoleon's army.

OFFICERS

The most obvious of the officers' rank distinctions were the epaulets. The staff (senior) officers wore them with bouillon, i.e., they were thick fringes made from a wire meshwork. The company-grade officers' epaulets had thin fringes. The color of the epaulets was gold or silver, according to the color of the metal buttons in the respective regiment. For majors, the epaulets' fields were always in the alternate color. In the Napoleonic army, the major was the colonel's deputy. The lieutenant colonel rank did not exist in this period. In the Westphalian Army the lieutenant colonel was the lowest staff/senior officer grade. That is confirmed by the existing memoirs of Westphalian officers. The The lieutenant colonel was designated as a "Bataillonschef" (battalion commander) and an "Eskadronschef" (squadron commander) for infantry and cavalry respectively.
The form of the *portepée*, sword-strap or sword-knot, also depended on the rank. The *portepée*' tassels were made with bullion for staff officers, and those for the company-grade officers had fringes.

On the officer's shako the upper band and possibly also the lower band were trimmed with a lace in the button color. A unique feature of the Westphalian officers' shakos was the angular lace trim on the sides: probably one chevron for the *second* lieutenant, two chevrons for the *premier-leutnant*, three chevrons for the captain, 4 chevrons for the *chef de bataillon* and *d'escadron* (battalion/squadron commander), 5 chevrons (mixed gold and silver) for the major, and 5 chevrons for the colonel. When on duty, the infantry and artillery officers put on a gorget as a rank insignia.
The light cavalry officers (hussars, chevaulegers) and the mounted artillery especially wore angular braid trim on their uniforms. These are described in more detail in the section on hussars.

Major of the Guard Jaegers (left) with shako
Detail from the painting *"Serment au drapeau Westphalien*, 1810" (Oath to the Westphalian Flag) by Louis Dupré (see also illustration on p. 17).

Officers' Epaulets (gold metal buttons)

1: Colonel; **2:** major; **3:**lieutenant colonel (*chef de bataillon or chef d´escadron/chef de bataillons/Eskadronschef*); **4:** captain (*Hauptmann/Capitaine*); **5:** first lieutenant (*Leutnant/Premier-lieutenant*); **6:** second lieutenant *(Unterleutnant/Sous-lieutenant)*.

1
2
3
4
5
6

NCOs

The NCOs' ranks were indicated by stripes on the sleeves. With straight cuffs they were placed diagonally, while with pointed cuffs they were in the form of chevrons.
The corporals wore two wool braids on each sleeve. The color corresponded to either the unit's distinction or button color. The sources show a number of variations. They also seldom show only a single braid on each side.
The *fourier* was not a rank per se, but a select duty position for a soldier in the grade of corporal or brigadier. He was responsible for staff and supply tasks within the company. The *fourier* wore, along with the corporal's stripes, an additional NCO's braid on his upper arm.
Sergeants and *Feldwebel*s wore lace rank insignia in the color of their regiment's metal buttons. Usually the laces were sewn on a cloth backing that was in a contrasting color. The upper shako band was also trimmed with lace. The lace trim was singular for the sergeants and double for the *Feldwebels*. The shako cording could have gold or silver thread mixed in. For the units that wore epaulets, the *Feldwebels*' epaulets could be decorated with silver or gold fringes and trimming.

The shako cording could have gold or silver threads mixed in. For the units that wore epaulets, the *Feldwebel*'s cording could be decorated with silver or gold fringes and trim.
The *Adjutant* was the most senior NCO rank; it was a kind of battalion or squadron sergeant major. As a rank insignia, he wore epaulets that were the reverse of those of a junior lieutenant, i.e., red with stripes in the button color. For the hussars, who did not wear epaulets, the adjutant was identified by three rank chevrons on the forearm.
There were also distinctions (insignia) given for years of service. These were braid chevrons (for privates and corporals) or lace chevrons (for NCOs) that were worn on the left upper arm. Pinhas shows them on the right, while Richard Knötel shows them on both sides.

1 Chevron - 8 years of service
2 Chevrons - 16 years of service
3 Chevrons - 24 years of service

Because Pinhas' graphic, which was done in 1811, shows a *Feldwebel* with three service chevrons, one can assume that years of service performed before joining the Westphalian Army were also taken into consideration.

Line infantry sergeant major of the grenadiers
Pinhas, Salomon: *Recueil de planches représentant les troupes des différentes armes et grades de l'armée Westphalienne,* 1811–1813.

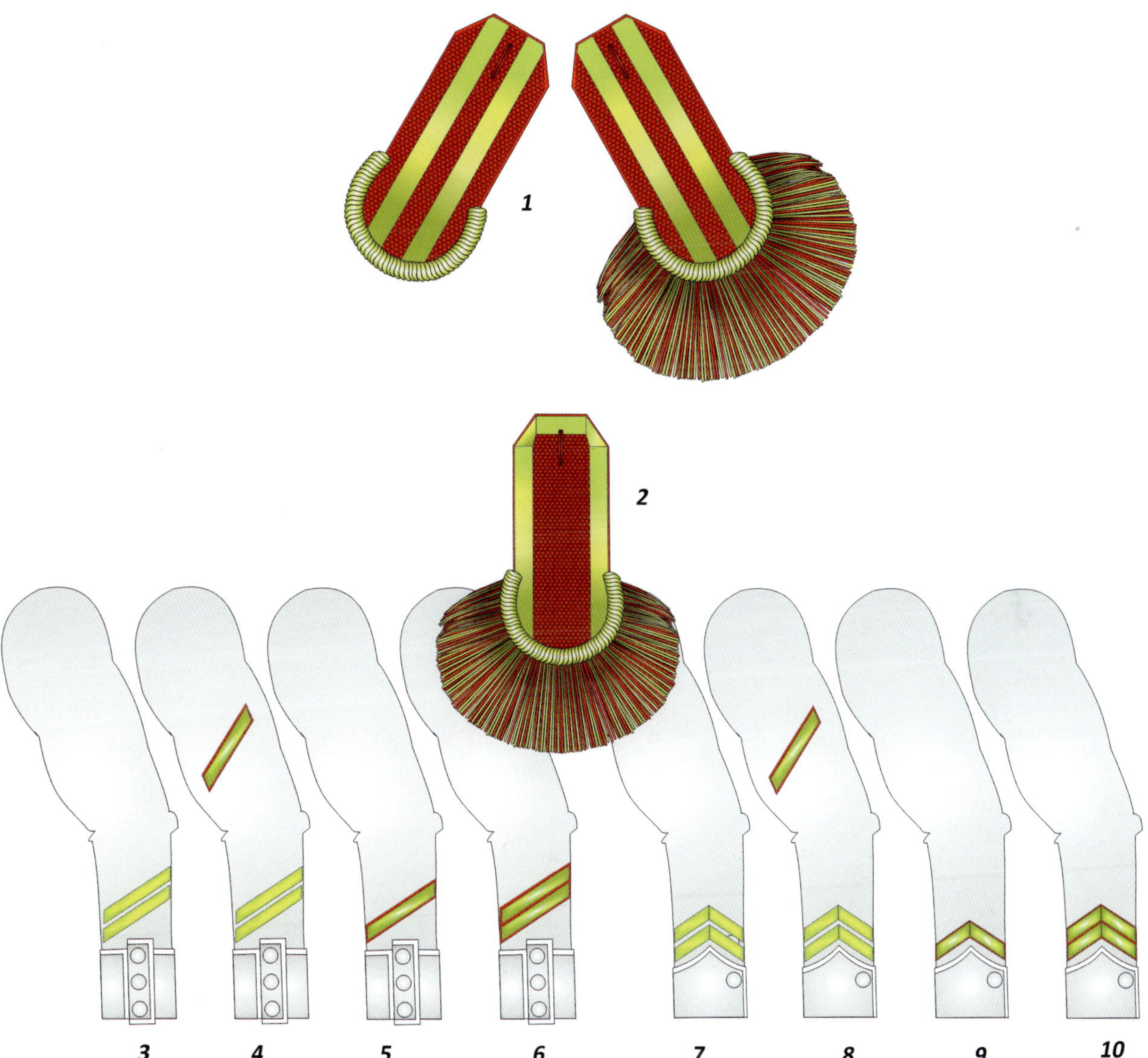

NCOs' Distinctions (gold metal buttons)

1: Adjutant's epaulets; **2:** *Feldwebel*/sergeant major's epaulets (uniform with red epaulets); **3:** corporal (sleeve with straight cuffs); **4:** *Furier/fourier* (sleeve with straight cuffs); **5:** sergeant/*Sergent/maréchal des logis* (sleeve with straight cuffs); **6:** *Feldwebel/sergeant major/maréchal des logis chef* (sleeve with straight cuffs); **7:** corporal/*Korporal* (sleeve with pointed cuffs); **8:** *Furier/fourier* (sleeve with pointed cuffs); **9:** Sergeant/*maréchal des logis* (sleeve with pointed cuffs); **10:** *Feldwebel/sergent-major/maréchal des logis chef* (sleeve with pointed cuffs).

RANK DESIGNATIONS

French	Westphalian (German)	English
Général de division	*Divisionsgeneral*	Major General
Général de brigade	*Brigadegeneral*	Brigadier General
	Officers	
Colonel	*Oberst*	Colonel
Major	*Major*	Major
Chef de bataillon (inf.)	*Bataillonschef*	Battalion Commander
Chef d´escadron (cav.)	*Eskadronschef*	Squadron Commander
Capitaine	*Kapitän*	Captain
Premier-Lieutenant	*Leutnant*	First Lieutenant
Seconde-Lieutenant	*Unterleutnant*	Second Lieutenant
	NCOs	
Adjudant-sous-officier	*Adjutant*	See NCOs above
	Infanterie	
Sergent-major	*Sergeantmajor/Feldwebel*	Sergeant Major
Sergent	*Sergeant*	Sergeant
Caporal-fourrier	*Fourier*	*Fourier* (see NCOs above)
Caporal	*Korporal*	Corporal
	Cavalry	
maréchal des logis chef	*Oberwachtmeister*	Sergeant Major
maréchal des logis	*Wachtmeister*	Sergeant
Brigadier-fourrier	*Fourier*	*Fourier* (see NCOs above)
Brigadier	*Korporal*	Corporal

Information above is based on Lünsmann (pp. 43-47) and Amsel and numerous memoirs.

Supposedly in practice, due to the close interweaving of the Westphalians with the French, the French as well as the Westphalian (German) rank designations were used. The French rank designations predominated when dealing with the French Army, but the German ranks were used internally in the Westphalian Army. In contrast to Lünsmann's work, the officers' memoirs overwhelmingly used the Westphalian and not the French designations for officers' ranks. It is unclear whether that also applied to the NCO ranks. Plus there is uncertainty about the German equivalents of the French designations for the more senior NCO ranks.

Voltigeur corporal
Pinhas, Salomon: *Recueil de planches représentant les troupes des différentes armes et grades de l´armée Westphalienne,* 1811–1813.

Voltigeur sergeant
Pinhas, Salomon: *Recueil de planches représentant les troupes des différentes armes et grades de l´armée Westphalienne,* 1811–1813.

ORDERS AND MEDALS

Decorative wooden freeze with the Westphalian state coat-of-arms
Museum Schloß Friedrichstein (Bad Wildungen), photo: Markus Gaertner.

ORDER OF THE CROWN OF WESTPHALIA

(ORDEN DER KRONE WESTPHALENS)

This award was supposed to be a decoration comparable to the French Legion of Honor (*Ordre national de la Légion d'honneur*) conferred when King Jérôme desired. The purpose was to tie as many people as possible who distinguished themselves through service or had made outstanding contributions in the military sphere, to the King and his system of rule. This addressed primarily officers and soldiers as well as officials performing military and civil functions.

On 25 December 1809 the King, in Paris, created the Order and at the same time named himself the Grand Master of this institution, which also received financial endowments from various domains.

The Order got the following organizational structure in February 1810: 10 Grand Commanders, 30 Commandants and 300 Knights. The awarding of the order was accompanied by a generous bonus. In August 1812 a 2nd Class award was created and with it another 500 Knights were taken into the Order.

In March 1810 the first awards were given, e.g., 117 officers and officials were awarded the Order.

Starting in April 1810, the medal was decorated with a crowned eagle. Under it was a ribbon with the inscription *"Je les uni."* Under that on the left side was a stylized lion. On the right side was a horse (for Hanover-Brunswick). Both were depicted rearing up and coming down toward the middle. In the center were the Westphalian eagle and again a lion, with each halved. Below them the award ended with the royal crown.

They were crafted in gold for the Knights of the 1st Class and in silver for those of the 2nd Class.

The Orden was officially worn on a gold necklace, however it was usually worn on a light blue ribbon worn on the chest. The necklace consisted of alternating sections with stylized, alternating sections with an eagle and with a horse within a green laurel wreath.

Plus, for the Grand Commanders there was a silver breast star with a gold center piece that was circled in light blue. The emblem in the center matched that of the Order.

MEDAL OF MERIT FOR BRAVERY AND GOOD CONDUCT

(VERDIENSTMEDAILLE FÜR TAPFERKEIT UND GUTES BETRAGEN)

On 17 June 1809, a medal for bravery was created for meritorious NCOs and soldiers who distinguished themselves by commendable service or in war had performed a distinguished act. There were silver and gold versions of the medal. The silver version was received by persons who had at least ten years of military service, the gold or thirty years. As a rule, the medal was awarded for bravery in the face of the enemy.

The medal was initially round in shape. On the front side, inside a zig-zag ornament on the wide rim, was a laurel wreath formed from two branches crossed at the bottom. Inside the wreath were two crossed swords with their points toward the top.

On the rear inside a linear decoration was the inscription in four lines:

- FÜR TAPFERKEIT UND GUTES BETRAGEN -

(For bravery and good conduct)

Below it were two crossed laurel branches. The gold version had the same pattern as described above.

By the beginning of 1810 it was modified and a second version, now oval, was introduced.

On the front side inside a broad oak branch (left) and a laurel branch (right) was the stylized "HN" monogram (for Hieronymus Napoleon) in Latin letters; above it the king's crown. Below the monogram was the year 1809.

Rear side: In the center was a stylized cuirass, above it was a caterpillar helmet on a staff. On the sides, it was surrounded by a musket and bayonet, two flags, two cannon barrels and a lance with a pennant. A pile of cannonballs formed the base. Around the edge was the inscription:

- FÜR TAPFERKEIT UND GUTES BETRAGEN -

At the very bottom was a five-leafed rosette.

The medal was worn on a light blue ribbon edged with two white stripes, pinned on the left breast. The gold version had the same pattern as the one described above.

Wearing the Order and the medal were forbidden in Kurhessen after the dissolution of the kingdom in December 1813.

Chest Star for Grand Commanders
Watercolor, Herbert Knötel's estate in WGM.

Medal of Merit in the 1st Version in Silver
Watercolor, Herbert Knötel estate, WGM.

Chain for the Order 1st Class in Gold
Watercolor, Herbert Knötel's estate in WGM.

Medal of Merit *(Verdienstmedaille)* 2nd Class in Silver,
Watercolor, Herbert Knötel estate, WGM.

Illustration at left:
Order of the Crown of Westphalia in Gold for the Knight 1st class
Original in Schloss Friedrichstein (Bad Wildungen). Museumslandschaft Kassel.

Medal of Merit in the Version in Gold,
Original in Schloss Friedrichstein (Bad Wildungen). Museumslandschaft Kassel.

LE ROI
DE WESTPHALIE
AU REGIMENT
DE HUSSARDS
DE LA
GARDE ROYALE
BOISSELIER

FLAGS AND STANDARDS

March 1, 1812: „... on the day established for the conferring of the new flags to the Guard, his Majesty went to the Orangeriepark, where were also the Guard Corps, the 2nd and 6th Line Regiments, the 1st Light Infantry Battalion, the 1st and 2nd Cuirassier Regiments, a squadron of the Royal Gendarmerie, a detachment from the 1st Chevauleger Lancer Regiment and the Artillery Regiment - a total of ten thousand men - marched out..."

From: *Westphälischer Moniteur vom 2. März 1812.*

Standard bearer of the Guard Hussars with Model 1813 flag
Watercolor by Henri Boisselier, collection of Paul Meganck, Brussels.

State coat of arms of the Kingdom of Westphalia
Central emblem of the "dedication flag" of the Salt Workers Brotherhood (Salzwirker Bruderschaft), Salinenmuseum Halle.

The infantry units and the cavalry regiments of the Guard and the Line carried flags. For the infantry each battalion had a flag while for the cavalry only one standard was issued per regiment. There are very few original sources about Westphalian flags. The best known is certainly a drawing in the work by Christian Suhr. The original Garde du Corps' Model 1812 standard still exists. The other flags and standards were lost or were destroyed. Also the flags of the 1st, 2nd, 3rd, 4th and 6th Infantry Regiments that were displayed in Saint Petersburg in the Kazan Cathedral with the trophies from 1812 no longer exist. Additionally there are very few orders or receipts for deliveries of flags.

Wilhelm Hewig, Roger Forthoffer and Pierre Charrié attempted research in order to reconstruct the development of the flags. After analyzing the many, frequently contradictory publications on Westphalian flags, we present our version of their evolution here. Unfortunately, much of the information on the flags' appearance remains speculative.

The Artillery Regiment and the Gendarmerie Legion also received a flag.

The National Guard units were supposed to have received flags, but there is no further information about them.

Garde du Corps standard, Model 1812, front with inscription
Former collection of the Prince of Monaco.

Garde du Corps standard, Model 1812, rear side with coat of arms
Former collection of the Prince of Monaco.

INFANTRY FLAGS

Between 1808 and 1813 various models were issued. All were square with a length of 33 inches (ca. 85 cm) on the sides.

The flags were carried by a junior lieutenant or a long-serving NCO (*sergent-major* or *Feldwebel*). In addition two sergeants, four *fouriers* and two corporals were assigned as a color guard.

GUARD FLAGS

Model 1808 Guard Flag

In 1808 the Guard Grenadier and Guard Jaeger Battalions each received a flag. They were made in Paris in the French 1804 Picot pattern. The silk base cloth was medium blue with a white rhombus in the center. A gold laurel wreath, possibly with the royal initials "JHN" inside, was located in each corner. Also the rhombus itself was surrounded with a gold laurel garland. Inside, the inscription in gold read:

Front (avers):
LE ROI / DE WESTPHALIE / AU BATAILLON DE / GRENADIERS / DE LA GARDE

Or correspondingly:
LE ROI / DE WESTPHALIE / AU BATAILLON DE / CHASSEURS / DE LA GARDE

Rear (revers):
VALEUR / ET DISCIPLINE

The flags were painted. The staff was 170 cm/67 inches long and painted white. The finial was spear-shaped and made of polished steel or brass with the initials "JN". Both flags were burned during the fire in the palace at Kassel in November 1811.

Model 1812 Guard Flag

After the fire at the King's palace, the Guard received new flags. The Jaeger-Carabiniers was also granted a Guard model flag at this time.
The cloth field of blue silk had a white Cross of Saint Andrew (*Andreaskreuz*). The triangular blue side fields displayed the initials "HN" (for Hieronymus Napoleon).

Golden inscription on the obverse side:
Der König / von Westphalien / dem Bataillon / Grenadier-Garde / Jäger-Garde / Jäger-Carabiniers

In the center of the rear side was the kingdom's coat of arms.
The staff was painted in blue and white spirals. The pierced finial had the cypher under a crown.

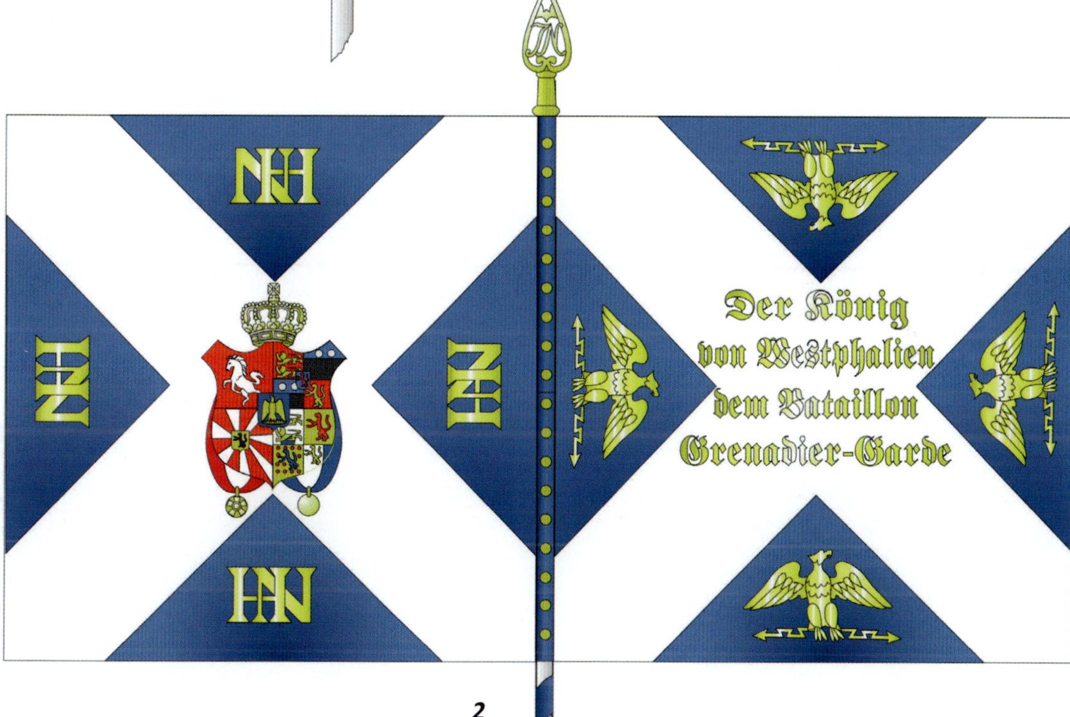

Guard Infantry Flags

1: Model 1808; 2: Model 1812.

LINE FLAGS

Model 1808

The flags corresponded to the Guard's Model 1808. An eagle and the "JN" royal monogram were painted alternatingly within the laurel wreaths in the corner fields.

The obverse side displayed the following inscription:
LE ROI / DE WESTPHALIE / AU ... REGIMENT / D'INFANTERIE / DE LIGNE

On the reverse side:
VALEUR / ET / DISCIPLINE / ... BATAILLON

The inscription for 1st Light Battalion was correspondingly:
LE ROI / DE WESTPHALIE /
AU 1er BATAILLON / D'INFANTERIE / LEGERE

Reverse side:
VALEUR / ET DISCIPLINE

The flags were painted. The staff was 170 cm/67 inches long and painted blue. The finial was in the shape of a spear and made of polished steel or brass.

Model 1810

Starting in 1810 the newly raised units were issued a modified flag model. This version largely resembled the 1808 model but the inscriptions were in the German language and a star replaced the initials in the corner medallions.

Front (avers) side:
DER KÖNIG / VON WESTPHALIEN /
DEM ... LINIEN / INFANTERIE / REGIMENT

On the reverse side:
TAPFERKEIT / UND / GUTES BETRAGEN / ... BATAILLON

Model 1813

After the campaign against Russia, in which the majority of the flags were lost, a new model flag was issued again in 1813. It was a simplified version of the 1810 model but without the laurel leaf surrounding the central rhombus. The regiment's or battalion's respective unit number replaced the corresponding eagle in the corner medallions.

Line Infantry Flags

1: Model 1808; **2:** Model 1810; **3:** Model 1813.

CAVARY STANDARDS

GUARD CAVALRY STANDARDS

Model 1808

In July 1808 the Garde du Corps and the Chevauleger Guards were each issued a standard. It was in the same form as the flag of the Grenadier Guards and measured 60 x 60 cm or 23.5 x 23.5 inches. On the reverse side in the center was the Westphalian coat of arms. The royal monogram in the form of "JHN" was inside the laurel leaf wreath in each of the flag's corners. Gold fringe edging. The staff was painted white.

Obverse side:
LE ROI / DE WESTPHALIE /
AU COMPAGNIE DE / GARDE DU CORPS

Or correspondingly:
LE ROI / DE WESTPHALIE / AU RÉGIMENT DES /
CHEVAULEGERS / DE LA GARDE

Model 1812

After being destroyed in the 1811 palace fire, new standards were issued. Again, they were the same as the Guard infantry model with a white St. Andrew's cross on a blue field. Gold fringed edging. On the obverse side were golden eagles in the blue side fields.

The inscription on the obverse side read:
Der König / von Westphalien / an seine Leibgarde

Or correspondingly:
Der König / von Westphalien / an seine /
Chevaulegers / der Garde

On the reverse side the Westphalian coat of arms in the middle and the initials "HN" in the fields on the sides. The staff was painted blue and white and the finial was pierced with the royal cypher "JN" under a crown.

Model 1813

The Guard Hussar Regiment possibly received another model standard in 1813. It was supposed to be divided vertically in the center – staff-side blue, flag side white – with golden inscriptions. There is no evidence for this.

Guard Cavalry Standards

1: Model 1808; **2:** Model 1812.

LINE CAVALRY STANDARDS

Modell 1808

The standards corresponded to the infantry flags but measured 60 cm or 23½ inches on each side. The inscriptions were in French. In the blue corner fields were alternatingly an eagle and the "JN" royal monogram. The flag staffs were blue.

The standards were produced in France like the 1808 flags.

Modell 1810

The new model was again a smaller version of the infantry flags with a side length of about 60cm or 24 inches. It had the following changes from its predecessor.:

A German inscription replaced that in French in the center and a star replaced the royal monogram "JN" in the laurel wreath.
The 2nd Cuirassier Regiment and both hussar regiments received this version of the standard in 1811.

Standard bearer – NCO, 6th Line Regiment until 1812
Watercolor by Herbert Knötel,
collection John, R. Elting Collection, USA.

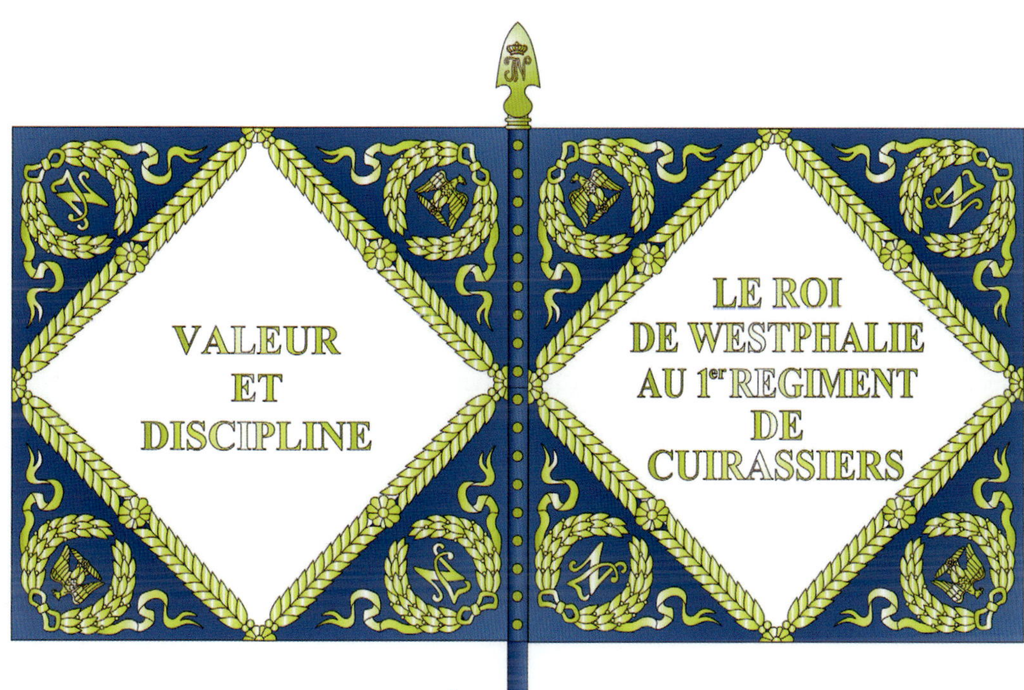

1

2

Line Cavalry Standards

1: Model 1808; **2:** Model 1810.

LIST OF THE CONFERRED FLAGS AND STANDARDS

GUARD

Grenadier Guards:
M 1808: one flag conferred on 1 July 1808, this was burned on 25-26 Nov 1811
M 1812: one flag conferred on 1 Mar 1812; remained unburned.

Jaeger Guards:
M 1808: one flag conferred on 1 July 1808, this was burned on 25-26 Nov. 1811
M 1812: one flag conferred on 1 Mar 1812; remained unburned.

Jaeger Carabiniers:
M 1810 Line Model: one flag conferred on 19 May 1811; this was burned on 25-26 Nov. 1811
M 1812: one flag conferred on 1 Mar. 1812; remained unburned.

Fusilier Guards:
M 1810: two flags conferred on 22 Nov. 1812
Remained unburned.

Garde du Corps:
M 1808: one flag conferred on 1 July 1808, this was burned on 25-26 Nov. 1811
M 1812: one flag conferred on 1 Mar. 1812
In November 1813 the King took it with him; today privately owned.

Guard Chevauleger Regiment:
M 1808: one flag conferred on 1 July 1808, this was burned on 25-26 Nov. 1811
M 1812: one flag conferred on 1 Mar. 1812
In October 1813 brought back from the campaign and saved during the withdrawal from Kassel; afterwards the status unknown.

Guard Hussar Regiment:
M 1813: one flag probably conferred in the autumn of 1813
According to W. Hewig, it was handed in at the end of October 1813, and later lost by the French side?

LINE

INFANTRY

1st Regiment:
M 1808: two flags conferred on 1 July 1808
M 1810: one flag conferred in the middle of 1810 on the 3rd Battalion
In December 1813 two flags lost to the Russian Army in Danzig.

2nd Regiment:
M 1808: two flags conferred on 1 July 1808
M 1810: one flag conferred in April 1811 on the 3rd Battalion
3 flags burned at the palace on 25-26 Nov. 1811
M 1810: three new flags conferred on 1 Mar. 1812
1813 three handed in and two new M 1813 conferred in early summer
In November 1813 both flags lost in Dresden.

3rd Regiment:
M 1808: one flag conferred on 1 July 1808; later another flag was issued.
In November 1812 one flag lost to the Russian Army in Kovno
M 1813: two flags conferred in the spring of 1813
In November 1813 both flags lost in Dresden.

4th Regiment:
M 1808: two flags conferred
1812: one flag lost to the Russian Army on the retreat
1814: one flag lost in the Küstrin Fortress

5th Regiment:
M 1808: two flags conferred in the spring of 1809
On 29 July 1809, two flags lost in the fighting around Halberstadt
M 1810: two flags conferred on 6 Jan. 1810
1814: two flags lost in the Küstrin Fortress.

6th Regiment:
M 1808: two flags conferred on 20 June 1809 in Sonderhausen
On 6 Oct. 1812 one flag lost in the Russian campaign to the Russian Army at Vereya
1813: one flag handed in in Westphalia.

7th Regiment:
M 1810: two flags conferred on 15 Aug. 1810 in Hanover and in April 1811
M 1810: one flag additional issued to the 3rd Battalion
March 1813 three flags handed in in Westphalia, in exchange in September
M 1813: one flag issued again, this handed back again on 7 Oct. 1813.

8th Regiment:
M 1810: three conferred on 28 Oct. 1810, April 1811 one handed in
In March 1813 two handed in, in exchange,
M 1813: two flags new ones received; these lost in October 1813.

9th Regiment:
M 1813: two flags conferred
In autumn of 1813 two destroyed by the French in Magdeburg.

1st Light Battalion:
M 1808: one flag conferred
March 1813 handed in, and in exchanges a new
M 1813: one flag conferred, lost in November 1813 in Dresden

2nd Light Battalion:
M 1810: one conferred at the end of 1810 or beginning of 1811
March 1813 handed in, in exchange new
M 1813: one flag issued; lost in the autumn of 1813.

3rd Light Battalion:
M 1810: one conferred at the end of 1810 or the beginning of 1811
March 1813 handed in, in exchange a new
M 1813: one flag was newly issued, in the autumn of 1813 lost after the Battle of Leipzig.

4th Light Battalion:
M 1813: one conferred in the summer 1813
In October 1813 lost.

CAVALRY / ARTILLERY / GENDARMERIE

1st Cuirassier Regiment:
M 1808: one flag conferred on 20 June 1809 in Sonderhausen
1813 one flag M 1810; in October 1813 lost.

2nd Cuirassier Regiment:
M 1810: one flag conferred in 1811
March 1813, this was handed in and in exchange received one new flag in the summer 1813; lost.

1st Chevauleger Regiment:
M1808: one conferred on 1 July 1808
Lost in December 1813.

2nd Chevauleger Regiment:
No standards were conferred.

1st Hussar Regiment:
M 1810: one conferred the end of 1810 or beginning of 1811
March 1813 returned; in the summer of 1813 one flag issued again
On 31 Aug. 1813 publicly burned in Ziegenhain

2nd Hussar Regiment:
M 1810: one conferred on 28 Oct. 1810
March 1813 returned, in the summer of 1813 one flag issued again
On 31 Aug. 1813 publicly burned in Ziegenhain

Additionally the Artillery Regiment and the Gendarmerie-Legion each received a flag in the pattern used by the Line units:

Artillery Regiment:
M 1808: one conferred 1808, this was burned on 25-26 Nov. 1811
M 1810: one flag conferred 1812

Gendarmerie-Legion:
M 1808: one flag conferred on 1 July 1808, this was burned on 25-26 Nov. 1811
M 1810: one flag conferred on 1 Mar. 1812
In October 1813 handed in; whereabouts unknown.

FIREARMS AND EDGED WEAPONS

Staff officer's *Pallasch*, 1st Cuirassier Regiment 1813
The royal coat of arms was removed after 1813 and the saber was used further in the Kurhessian era.
Museum Schloß Friedrichstein (Bad Wildungen), photo: Markus Gaertner.

ARMAMENT

During the organizing of the units, the stores of muskets from the Kassel and Braunschweig arsenals were used initially, also models of Prussian origin, in order to equip the formed regiments (Hessian Legion and later Regiments Nos. 1 through 4). The examples of firearms and edged weapons that still exist today show a wide selection of various models.

At the same time additional armaments and equipment were obtained from France, for example, and up to 1811 also from the factory in Mutzig. At first the production of firearms in Westphalia advanced haltingly; for example reverse engineered and modified models were developed and produced in its own workshops in Herzfeld and Schmalkalden (Pistor).

The main firearms of the foot troops were the French model muskets – 1777 – Model AN IX modified to XIII. The voltigeurs used the light infantry model that had a shorter barrel.

The musket had a smooth bore and no sight. It was 15.5 mm caliber and was 147 cm or 59 inches long without the bayonet.

The effective range was about 300 to 400 meters or 330 to 435 yards even though the musket ball could have a range of up to 1,200 meters or 1,300 yards.

The Model AN IX bayonet was three-sided and ground hollow; it had a length of about; 46 cm or 18 inches.

Furthermore the elite companies and NCOs of the various branches carried the short saber. Initially, Prussian models were used. Starting in 1809 the French model (briquet M 1803) was used more and more. It had a length of 75 cm or 29.5 inches. The saber had a rippled grip and basket made of brass and a curved blade.

The Jaeger Carabiniers as elite sharpshooters were equipped with rifles, but which exact models are not known. It can be assumed that various versions were used along side one another. The accuracy at up to 220 meters/240 yards was clearly better than for the standard model smooth bore muskets.

The officers used thrusting swords of different origins and manufacture because they were often acquired privately. The hilt usually was like the general shape of the Prussian or Hessian pattern with a wire-covered grip and

Rifle, Jaeger-Carabiniers, detail
Schloß Friedrichstein (Bad Wildungen),
Museumslandschaft Hessen-Kassel.

Left
Model 1777 musket
Schloß Friedrichstein (Bad Wildungen).
Museumslandschaft Kassel.

Right
Jaeger's rifle, Jaeger Carabiniers
Schloß Friedrichstein (Bad Wildungen).
Museumslandschaft Kassel.

an oval handguard with a basket, all of brass. The swords were from 75 to 80 cm or 29½ to 31½ inches long and had a straight blade.

The grenadier companies' officers carried a saber with a shortened curved blade in many cases.

Furthermore in the Spanish campaign, officers armed themselves, especially with additional pistols. Various models (e.g. Model 1777, Model 1786 or Model An IX – 1800–1801) were in use at the same time there. Also models from the former Hessian Army were in use.

For the cavalry, different models were used at the outset of the kingdom. Also Kurhessian models, from old stores, were modified, for example the dragoon saber, whose hilt was decorated with a basket/knuckle-guard with the king's monogram under a crown.

For the Guard Chevaulegers, a unique shape following the French light cavalry model was introduced. It also had an oval basket with a monogram; surrounded by an oakleaf wreath. Additionally it had two bars on the side. The blade was slightly curved. The edged weapons were probably produced, also for the Garde du Corps, in the well-known Klingenthal factory.

The Garde du Corps received a special model saber that was recognizable by its more expensive construction. The hilt had a shape similar to that for the chevaulegers. The end of the grip, pommel, had a stylized helmet with a visor, curved handguard and in the center also an oval shield with oakleaves and the monogram.

For the heavy cavalry – cuirassiers – a *Pallasch* with a straight blade was in use. It could have been like the French model (AN IX to AN XI – 1802). That was 116.6 cm or 46 inches long, and the scabbard was made of iron. The hilt consisted of a main quillon and three loop guards (*Seitenbügeln*).

Pistol, Model 1812, Pistor Schmalkalden
LWL-Preussenmuseum, Minden.

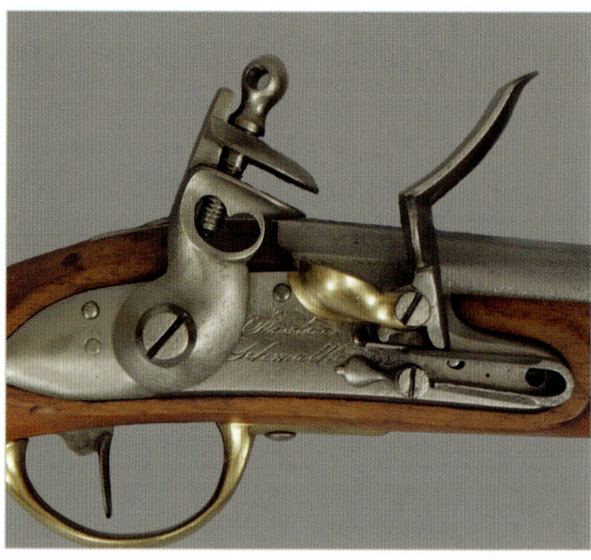

Musket lock – detail of a Model 1777 musket
Schloß Friedrichstein (Bad Wildungen), Museumslandschaft Hessen-Kassel.

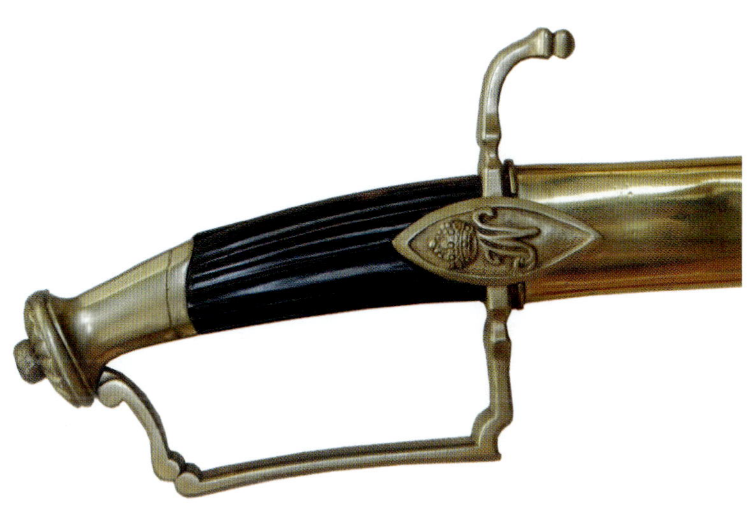

Saber – hilt, model for officers of the grenadiers
Schloß Friedrichstein (Bad Wildungen),
Museumslandschaft Hessen-Kassel.

Sword – hilt, model for officers
Schloß Friedrichstein (Bad Wildungen),
Museumslandschaft Hessen-Kassel.

Short saber – *sabre briquet* – for infantrymen and foot troops
Schloß Friedrichstein (Bad Wildungen),
Museumslandschaft Hessen-Kassel.

The light cavalry saber as well as mounted artillery (Model AN XI) saber had a slightly curved blade with a length of 107.6 cm/42.3 inches. The hilt was could be equipped with or without a handguard. The hilt was brass and the grip (tang) was wrapped with wire.

Further firearms armament for the cavalry usually included two cavalry pistols (AN IX to AN XIII), but they had only a limited range. In addition, there was a carbine.

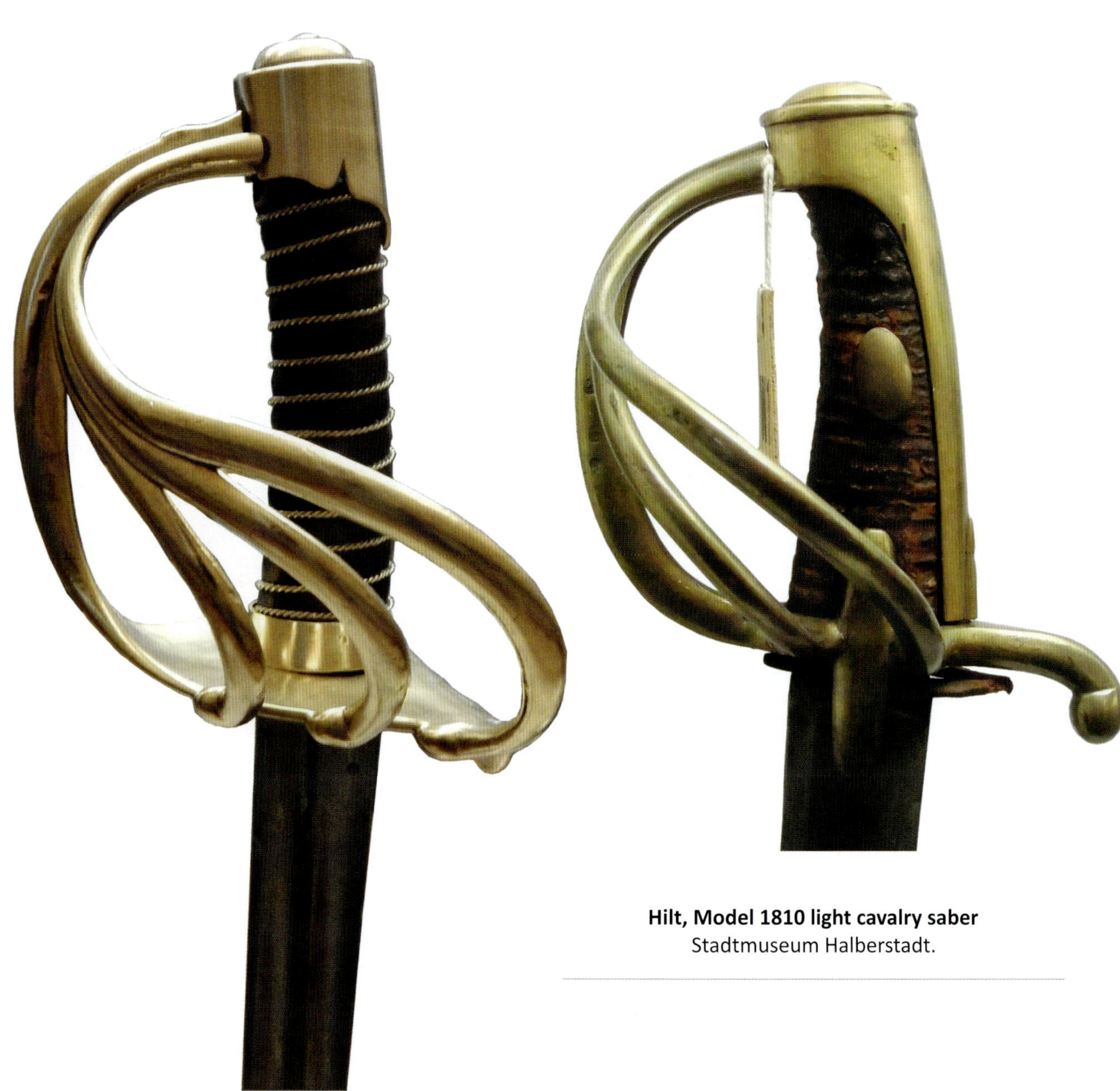

Hilt, Model 1810 light cavalry saber
Stadtmuseum Halberstadt.

***Pallasch* hilt, cuirassiers' model**
Schloß Friedrichstein (Bad Wildungen).
Museumslandschaft Kassel.

Pallasch **for cuirassiers with scabbard**
Schloß Friedrichstein (Bad Wildungen). Museumslandschaft Kassel.

PART III

THOMAS HEMMANN

THE ARMY IN ACTION – THE 1808–1813 CAMPAIGNS

"If we had only attacked then, the Russians would have been destroyed, and everyone, officers and soldiers, waited with feverous excitement for the order to advance. Our desire to fight was palpable, individual battalions shouted they wanted to be led forward, but Junot did not move and threatened with curses to have anyone shot who said another word. It was desperate ... and Junot, this incapable and hardheaded general did not seize the opportunity."

"Wenn wir jetzt angriffen, mussten die Russen vernichtet werden, und alles, Offiziere und Soldaten, warteteten mit fieberhafter Spannung auf den Befehl zum Vorgehen. Unsere Kampfeslust machte sich laut Luft, einzelne Bataillone riefen, sie wollten vorgeführt werden; aber Junot rührte sich nicht und drohte fluchend jeden erschießen zu lassen, der noch ein Wort sagte Es war zum Verzweifeln ... und Junot, dieser unfähige und dabei eigensinnige General, benutzte sie (die Gelegenheit) nicht."

On the employment of the Army Corps at Valutina-Gora on 19 August 1812
From: Conrady, L. W.v., *Aus stürmischer Zeit. Ein Soldatenleben vor hundert Jahren*, Berlin 1907

Vincenzo (Vincent) Poiret: "Entry of Jérôme Bonaparte in Breslau on 7 January 1807"
(Jérôme Bonaparte, Brother of Napoleon, as the Commandant of a Bavarian-Wurttemberg Army Corps, Accepts The Capitulation of the City and Fortress).
Oil on canvas, 189 x 295 cm. Inv. No. N 3101, Fontainebleau, Musée national du Château. akg-images.

THE CAMPAIGN IN SPAIN 1808–1813

THE CHEVAULEGER REGIMENT IN SPAIN 1808–1813

After the creation of the Kingdom of Westphalia, following the Peace of Tilsit in July 1807, the buildup of the Westphalian Army was started the beginning of 1808.[45] Initially, except for the Royal Guard (*königlichen Garde*) - four infantry of the line regiments, one light infantry battalion, one cuirassier regiment, one Chevauleger regiment and four artillery companies were raised. Originally, in 1808, Napoleon wanted to send a Westphalian division to Spain. Actually only after 10 March 1808, the Chevauleger Regiment, made up of former Hessian and Prussian cavalrymen, was mission capable. At the end of August 1808, as its organization was completed, this regiment was sent off to Spain to at least respond to the French Emperor's urgent demands.[46]

The Chevauleger Regiment had just barely 600 men and was commanded by Colonel Hans Baron von Hammerstein-Equord. It marched from Osnabrück via Wesel, Lüttich, Luxemburg, Metz, Orléans, Bordeaux, Bayonne, Irun, Vittoria, and Burgos to Madrid. It arrived there on 12 December with 390 cavalrymen. Napoleon, who had stopped in Madrid at the time, wanted to send back the numerically weakened regiment immediately. However, the ambitious Hammerstein succeeded in preventing this. The regiment was initially employed in the pursuit of the English army under General Moore that was retreating toward La Coruña. On 30 December, it arrived at Benavente, one day after the French advance guard's fight there. The Chevauleger Regiment participated in the further pursuit of the English to La Bañeza. It turned around there and marched in the vicinity of Zamora. On the 13th of January 1809 it took part in the Battle of Uclés. In the following months, it conducted reconnaissance on the Portuguese border and fought in the area of the Spanish Ciudad Rodrigo border fortress. The fate of the regiment proved to be unsettled. For a time, it formed a brigade with the 5th French Dragoon Regiment and operated with the Division Lapisse of II Corps (Marshal Soult).[47] A part of the regiment (1st Company and a part of the 3rd) under *Rittmeister* (cavalry captain) von Göcking was at this time indeed detached and participated, inter alia, in the Battle of Meza de Ibor (March 17, 1809). At the end of April, the regiment performed rear area service and security duties on the road between Mérida and Trujillo. On the 27 and 28 July, it took part in the Battle of Talavera, now as a unit in the Merlin Light Cavalry Division (VI Corps under General of the Division Sebastiani). The former regimental commander, Colonel von Hammerstein, who had been promoted to Brigadier General in the meantime, was replaced by Major von Hessberg on September 14, 1809 in Alcabón. The regiment was mentioned with praise many times in the French commander's correspondence and in the Westphalian newspapers. Starting July 16, 1810,[48] Colonel Stein commanded the Chevaulegers. At the end of November 1810, a small detachment left the regiment and returned to Westphalia, and there were supposedly also desertions.[49] At the Battle of Siguenza on February 7,1812, the regiment distinguished itself again; Chevauleger Mühe of the 2nd Company captured an enemy flag.[50] Additionally, the regiment was to have fought at Las Rozas on August 11, 1812, and at Villafranca on September 13, 1813.[51] In early 1813, the regiment, except for a squadron under Lieutenant Colonel von Plessen, was called back to Westphalia to fill out the newly organizing Westphalian cavalry for the Russia campaign. On December 23, 1813, after word was received in Spain about the dissolution of Kingdom of Westphalia, the Chevauleger-Squadron that remained there was disarmed and taken as prisoners of war by the French.

45 Additionally a *"Westphalen Regiment"* was established in French service, cf. Worringer.

46 For further information, cf. the sources: Bussche, Friedrich, Gaertner & Wagner, Hartmann, Kleinschmidt, Lünsmann and Staff.

47 Bussche, p. 93 and 96.

48 According to Friedrich, page 49, starting November 1811. The information in the - limited – literature is partially contradictory.

49 Kleinschmidt, p. 394.

50 *„Magdeburgische Zeitung"* from 21 April 1812, see Friedrich, p. 50.

51 Smith, pp. 385 and 454.

THE SIEGE OF GERONA 1809

Stand-Up of the Westphalian Corps

The beginning of February 1809, a division was formed from the existing units.[52] At the end of February this division departed in the direction of France and marching by way of Metz, Strasbourg, Chalon-sur-Saône and Perpignan, reached Spanish border on May 2, 1809.[53]

Spanish Theater of War in 1809.

52 See the Orders of Battle Appendix.

53 This section is based on a lecture by M. Gaertner at a workshop titled *"Die WestfälischeArmee 1807–1813,"* in Bornheim, 28/29 September 2002. Additionally the following sources were used: Bauer, Boedicker Bucher, Bussche, Gouvion-Saint-Cyr, Lünsmann, Morgenstern, Hohenhausen and Staff.

The Situation in the Spanish Theater of War

After the French forces had occupied the province of Catalonia, an insurgency broke out, as it did in almost all the other Spanish provinces. To stabilize the situation, three divisions with a strength of 16,000 men, forming VII Army Corps under the command of the General

AD. LUDW. v. OCHS

KURHESS. GENERAL-MAJOR.

General von Ochs

Gouvion Saint Cyr, was sent to the affected regions (also to Aragon and Valencia). After a short time, the Catalonian forces dispersed and the activities turned to more intense guerilla warfare against the occupiers. Until April, only the Gerona fortress, under the command of General Alvarez, put up any considerable resistance.

At the beginning of April 1809, a weak French corps under the command of Major General Reille advanced on Gerona and began the encirclement of the city. Until the beginning of May, a French brigade under General of Division Verdier was located in the region. In addition, a German brigade with forces from the Duchy of Berg, and two infantry battalions of Würzburgers as well as various contingents of the smaller German duchies were located in front of the fortress. Additionally, the French command had another two Italian divisions available. An additional Italian division occupied the line of communication to France. On 6 May, the 2nd Westphalian Brigade also reached Gerona, where it immediately got engaged in combat. The Westphalian division was supposed to occupy the right bank of the River Ter.

The City and Fortress Gerona

Gerona lies on the right bank of the River Ter in a strategically favorable position on the important main road to Barcelona. The eastern portion of the city extended along the steep slope of the tributary Ogna River, while the smaller part ran along the plain of Villarcir. Eight forts surrounded the city for protection. Of them, the heavily built up Fort Montjuic was the strongest. The Spanish garrison of Gerona consisted of ca. 12,000 men, of which barely half were regular military. The French initially could only employ 56 cannon and mortars against the 180 cannon along the fortress' walls. The craggy ground also impeded the besiegers' construction of bastions, batteries and parallel earthworks.

General Verdier, who relieved General Reille on 13 May, intended to attack the city from the east, to take Fort Montjuic and thus gain the key to capturing the city.

The Siege

Our description follows the chronology of the battle that was, for that time, the costliest siege and the hardest fought military employment of the Westphalian regiments involved.

6 May:

The Light Battalion had hardly gone into position on the left bank of the river when it had to repel a heavy attack by the Spaniards. With the help of the 1st Battalion of the 3rd Infantry Regiment, the Spaniards had to retreat to avoid being cut off.

8 May:

The 1st Westphalian Brigade fought a fierce battle in the north of the city and was able to capture a defensive tower named "Montagut."

The 2nd Westphalian Brigade under von Ochs along with the Light Battalion captured the village of Saria on the banks of the Ter and drove the Spanish line back to the walls of the city. In this engagement that lasted until the evening, the Light Battalion suffered losses of 40 men dead and wounded, and one officer was killed. The troops from Berg and Würzburg also crossed the Ter and advanced from the eastern side toward the fortress. The siege around Gerona was now being tightened.

Until the end of May:

The Westphalian and the French-German Division, together ca. 16,000 men under Division General Verdier, set up camp in the fortress. The Westphalians took part in forays in the vicinity, as well as to the coast of the Mediterranean, especially to gather provisions.

Gerona, Fort Montjuic.

30 May:

Approximately 600 Spanish peasants attacked the "Montagut" tower and drove off the 30 Westphalian occupiers. However, shortly thereafter, the 1st Battalion of the 4th Westphalian Infantry Regiment retook the tower and drove off the Spaniards.

1 June through 21 June:

After the bombardment that started on 13 June, French troops succeeded in taking some outlying defensive works and forts like St. Daniel, St. Louis and St. Narcisse. Thus the way was clear to storm the primary fort, Montjuic.

The end of June through 4 July:

General Gouvion Saint-Cyr arrived from Barcelona with the remainder of his Army Corps and covered the siege from any outside attack. On 4 July, a breach was shot in the main fort and 8 July was chosen for the assault.

1809 Gerona, Attack on Fort Montjuic.

8 July:

Fort Montjuic was situated close the city's north side and was only separated by an adjacent ravine. Montjuic consisted of a fortified rectangle with a star-shaped series of trenches cut into the cliffs. Three thousand men were designated for the assault, made up of the 12 Westphalian grenadier companies, the Elite of the Neapolitan 1st Infantry Regiment, twelve Berg and Würzburg companies and an additional ten elite companies from the French regiments.

Before the attack could begin that afternoon, the Westphalian 3rd Infantry Regiment, which was standing guard, was surprised by 800 Spanish infantrymen and 200 hussars under Colonel Claros and driven from their camp. Five companies from the Westphalian 1st Battalion of the 4th Westphalian Infantry Regiments were able to drive back the Spaniards. The Light Battalion took up the pursuit.

During this defensive action, the assault on Montjuic's works began. The attackers had to accept heavy casualties even before they reached the moats at the walls because the moats were not, as expected, filled with the rubble from the breaches shot into them, so crossing the moats was significantly more difficult. Franz von Morgenstern (Junior Lieutenant in the 2nd Westphalian Infantry Regiment), who was in the assault column during the attack, reported: "We had reached the top of the glacis, but in order to climb up from the deep ditch there was only a narrow '*appareille*' [aperture] in the otherwise undamaged contreescarpe [outer wall of a fortress] in which two men could barely pass through side-by-side. Because of this, a stoppage developed so that a growing cluster of men spread out on the upper edge of the glacis which presented an inordinately favorable target for enemy fire." Howitzer fire, grapeshot and hurled grenades in the breach tore new huge gaps into the attackers. Morgenstern described the situation in the breach: "... as we descended, we made the bleak discovery that at the wall under the breach there were only widely dispersed ladders and that the ladders were too short by about the height of a man. At the feet of the ladders, we were met with all conceivable manner of means of destruction: hand grenades, burning pitch and oil, boulders rolling down at us and exploding sacks of gunpowder." Each renewed advance was thrown back with heavy losses. The defender's resistance was tenacious; priests supported the fighters, even a battalion of women provided ammunition. The attack ended in a hopeless struggle; the losses for the units involved were monstrous. Thus, of the 3,000 men who entered the action, at the end 1,170 men were dead and wounded, of them 219 Westphalians. A total of 21 officers were lost! Johann Philip von Bauer (4th Regiment) reported the situation after the assault: *"All those remaining wounded in the moat after the assault were shot dead by the Spaniards, and because many of the officers were also sick, many companies had to be led by sergeants."*

8 July to the end of August:

Useless attacks and counterattacks were the order of the day. A sortie by the occupiers of Montjuic on 15 August was repulsed with heavy losses. Then the Spaniards evacuated Montjuic.

This period also brought changes for the Westphalian forces: General Morio became ill with a fever and had to be transported back to Perpignan in France. Westphalian Brigadier General von Hadeln, his successor, was killed just a few days after taking command; also his successor Brigadier General Jouba fell as well (on 6 September 1809). Finally, on September 7, General von Ochs took over command of the division, but shortly thereafter had to be taken back to Perpignan due to serious illness. By the same token, the situation of the troops and the relationship to the French allies did not develop for the best. Their handling by the French led to numerous complaints. The sick and wounded, whose care was neglected, were especially impacted and which led to further losses. Von Bauer wrote in a letter on 21 August 1809: *"...the French and Italians are put into the rooms and our poor fellows are given with a little straw on the floors or in the courtyard, it is horrid to thus treat the troops who suffered the most at Gerona."* The continuous work on the redoubts and the guard duty also weakened the troops. The Westphalian Division alone had to permanently provide 900 workers. On 5 August, a battalion of Westphalians occupying Fort San Juan was attacked, but was able to repel the attackers after a short fight.

On August 10, the Spaniards made two sorties: one against the monastery of Sant Daniel, that was fiercely held by the Würzburgers; in another sortie on the trenches in the vicinity Westphalian forces were violently attacked. Portions of the trenches were abandoned; the Spaniards were able to spike cannon and set a portion of the defenses in fire. Only after the approach of reserve units and subsequent close combat with bayonets could the old situation be restored. The Westphalians lost eleven dead and 48 wounded in the action.

31 August:

The Spanish General Blake had already carried out a surprise attack on 20 August with his corps against the somewhat more distant forces of General Saint Cyr. On the assumption that it was a relief maneuver, General Verdier received orders to engage with part of his corps as reinforcements. Following those orders, the besieging corps, i.e., the remaining German forces – except for the Westphalian Division - and an Italian division, moved out. General Verdier, as expected, arrived at the main army on 31 August 1809. General Blake however, did not plan to fight the reinforced French units, instead, after a few diversionary skirmishes, he marched quickly with about 8,000 men toward Gerona. On 1 September, advancing along both banks of the Ter, he attacked the camp of the weak Westphalian guard force, destroyed the headquarters, and allowed all the wounded to be killed. Furthermore, he succeeded in delivering the urgently needed food and ammunition on 800 pack mules to the occupants of Gerona. This was a serious setback for the besiegers. General Verdier immediately directed his forces back in the direction of the city, but when the French arrived, Blake had long since disappeared.

Fort Montjuic today.

19 September:

After many weeks without decisive success for either side, an attack from the north of the city was ordered. Four columns were to capture varies locations. The assault by the Würzburgers and Westphalians was directed against the "French Gate" as the primary objective. After renewed heavy losses of over 600 men dead and wounded, the assaults had to be broken off without results. The Westphalians lost about 100 men in the action. After these repeated failures, the weakened besiegers limited their actions to cutting off and blockading the city. Additionally, lack of provisions and increasing illnesses further weakened not only the besieged, but also the exhausted besiegers.

October:

In the middle of the month, Marshal Augereau received command of VII Army Corps. To defend against further sorties, two redoubts were constructed. The Westphalians provided the work force. The positions were strengthened with numerous cannon.

November - December:

Major General Amey took over command from General Verdier. The encirclement of the city was strengthened in order to bring the occupants to surrender, however numerous demands remained without results. Little by little, the forward defenses were taken, and on December 7, Fort Calvaire and portions of the city's outskirts were captured. On December 10, the bombardment of all the batteries of the remaining outposts and of the city was intensified. That same evening, the city capitulated.

12 December:

The Gerona Fortress surrendered after more than seven months. The siege had cost the French and German contingents almost 20,000 men. The Westphalian losses were very considerable, with 47 officers and almost 6.000 men dead and wounded. On 12 December the Westphalians also moved into the city to take up better quarters. Even though over the previous months reinforcements had arrived many times, the entire Westphalian Division had only 1,500 men remaining. With that ended the first bloody chapter in the Spanish theater of war.

THE WESTPHALIAN CONTINGENT IN CATALONIA 1810–1813

In March1810, an approximately 650-man relief force with four cannons arrived in Gerona from Westphalia. The Westphalians did not take part in the further conquest of Catalonia by forces under Marshal Augereau except for a light battalion deployed forward to Riudellots de la Creu.[54]

In May of this year, the cadre of each of the 2nd battalions of the Infantry, about 200 men, were sent back to Westphalia. About 1,000 men under the command of Colonel Zink remained in Spain. In May, the remainder of the Westphalian Division under Colonel Bosse carried out a punitive expedition against the rebellious Catalonians. During a further undertaking on June 10, the 4th Infantry Regiment was attacked by the Spaniards near the Mortera monastery and suffered considerable losses. On June 14, a company from the same regiment under Lieutenant Pflüger was taken captive. On 1 April, the remnants of 1st Battalion under Colonel von Bosse were set in march toward Westphalia. Only 500 able-bodied men remained in Spain and comprised the so-called *"Westphalen"* Battalion along with a small artillery detachment, all under Lieutenant Colonel von Winkel. The battalion took part in the 1811 siege of Figueras, where it was involved in fighting during a sortie by the Spanish garrison on 24 May 1811.[55] Starting 3 September 1811, the *"Westphalen"* Battalion was commanded by Vigelius. In April 1813 the remainder of the Westphalian detachments, with about 300 men, headed back to Westphalia and were used for the new raising of the 3rd Light Battalion or were incorporated into the Artillery Regiment.

54 For more on the fates of the Westphalian detachments in Catalonia see Friedrich, Kleinschmidt and Lünsmann.

55 Friedrich, p. 56f.

King Jérôme with his Staff at a Parade in Leipzig during the 1809 Campaign Drawing by Gottfried Geissler from the series on wartime scenes (*Kriegsszenen*) 1809.

THE 1809 CAMPAIGN IN GERMANY

Internal Unrest in the Kingdom

The situation in Westphalia was relatively unstable starting with the establishment of the kingdom in 1807.[56] Unrest erupted many times because the military conscriptions and the heavy tax burdens put constant pressure on the entire population, while at the same time only a few people profited from the wasteful excesses of the court. Even the letters of Jérôme and the French Emissary in Kassel, Reinhard, from the beginning of 1809 highlight the popular dissatisfaction.[57] The resentment was increased even more by the dispatching of the 2nd Westphalian Division to Spain planned for February 1809, where the Westphalians would be offered up for the sake of foreign interests.

The former Prussian Senior Lieutenant von Katte delivered the first blow. After he had made secret contacts, on 2 April 1809 von Katte appeared with about 60 men on the left side of the Elbe in Stendal, called for an uprising, and confiscated weapons and horses from the Westphalian gendarmes, as well as the royal and Imperial treasuries. Then he turned toward Magdeburg. The governor of Magdeburg, General Michaud, sent some troops against von Katte, defeating von Katte's forces at Wolmirstedt and taking eleven of the rebels captive. The remainder fled over the Elbe to Prussia. A simultaneous attempt by cavalry captain (*Rittmeister*) von Thilo and a Lieutenant von Wedell among others, to raid the fortress itself failed due to the vigilance of the fortress occupants. On the 5 April, the newly raised 5th Westphalian Infantry Regiment, with 1,900 men, reentered Magdeburg; on the 8th, so did the 6th Regiment, with 1,300 to 1,400 men, which was also part of the organization. In the vicinity of Magdeburg, the Westphalian government carried out numerous arrests in order to pacify the situation.

At the same time, attempts to rebel were sprouting in old Hessen. Their leader was, of all people, a Westphalian officer and favorite of Jérôme, Colonel Wilhelm von Dörnberg.[58] Additionally, many of the resistance's strings were being pulled in a woman's monastery in Homberg an der Efze, where a sister of the well-known Freiherrn von Stein was the dean. In the countryside, connections were made everywhere to mobilize the peasants, by the Justice of the Peace Martin among others.

Originally, February 15, 1809 was set for the date for the start of the revolt. At the last moment, the leaders of the revolt gave a counter command, because two different events upset the plans. The first was that Dörnberg's Jaeger-Carabinier Battalion was selected to deploy to Spain. Simultaneously, i.e., during the march through Mainz, Dörnberg received orders reassigning him to the Battalion *Jaeger-Garde*; also the Jaeger-Carabinier Battalion was called back again. The other hindering circumstance was the transit of two French divisions coming from Mainz through Westphalia.

In mid- April, after the outbreak of war between Austria and France (see below) a favorable instant for the revolt seemed to have arrived again. Orders had already been given for the Westphalian troops to depart on 25 April for the lower Elbe. A council of war by the rebels, meeting in Kassel from 16 to 18 April, therefore decided to strike the blow in the night of 22-23 April. Dörnberg thought he could count on his Garde-Jaeger Battalion as well as on the Jaeger-Carabinier Battalion that had recently arrived in Kassel. During the parade on 22 April, a Saturday, a coconspirator brought Dörnberg news that the alarm bells had already sounded in the countryside, i.e., that the uprising had prematurely begun. Naturally this disrupted the plans in the residence in Kassel. The plan to overpower and capture the king could no longer be accomplished; on the contrary, Jérôme immediately ordered two Chevauleger squadrons and a few Guard companies to occupy the palace. Shortly thereafter, Dörnberg received the news from a confidant that his name had been betrayed and he should expect to be arrested soon. Dörnberg decided to flee from Kassel and to go to join the rebels in Homberg, where he arrived about 17:00. On the way from Wilhelmshöhe to Kassel, Dörnberg attempted in vain to convince the Jaeger-Carabinier Battalion to go over to the rebels. However, after some of the Jaegers pointed their weapons at him, he gave up and rode on further to Homberg. In the meantime, both of the squadrons of the 1st Westphalian Cuirassier Regiment located there, led by Captain von Weissen[59] and Premier Lieutenant von Girsewald[60] had almost completely gone over to the side of the rebels. Dörnberg and his coconspirators attempted to inject some order into the mass of peasants and prepare them to march on Kassel. Detachments of the cuirassiers were sent out to make contact with other reb-

56 We are basing this on the descriptions in Kircheisen Kleinschmidt, Lynker, Heitzer, Baumann, Bodenhausen, Dörnberg, Meibom and Gill.

57 See Kleinschmidt, p. 225.

58 Wilhelm von Dörnberg, born 1768, at the age of 14, joined 1st Hesse-Kasselsche Garde Battalion, in 1788 became an officer, 1792-95 campaigns against France, 1796 service in Prussian, 1807 left service, 1808 Battalion Commander in the Westphalian Grenadier Guards, in the same year became a Senior Major in the 3rd Line Infantry Regiment and Colonel with the Chasseur-Carabiniers. This battalion, which consisted in for the most part of former Hessian foresters' sons and forestry employees, was loyal to Dörnberg, some of the officers were witting of the plans for the uprising.

59 In Lünsmann, p. 233, named by Weissem.

60 Both of the squadron commanders authorized for the unit were absent.

els in Wolfhagen, Ziegenhain and Felsberg. Among them was Colonel of the 1st Cuirassier Regiment, von Marshal, with the remaining squadrons from Melsungen. He indignantly took Dörnberg to task. Dörnberg responded that the rebellion had generally broken out in northern Germany and persuaded Marschall to turn back toward Melsungen and to remain neutral until the next day. The rebel's main column, several thousand men, now departed and marched to Kassel. At 3:00 in the morning on 23 April, General Rewbell, left Kassel to engage them. He commanded two companies of the Garde-Jaeger, one detachment of the *Garde-Chevaulegers* and two cannons. The first contact occurred at the *"Knallhütte"* inn in the Frankfurter Straße. The well-trained professional soldiers easily repulsed the rebels. The Westphalian troops advanced further and after about a one-half hour march met the rebels from Felsberg, who were also immediately scattered. Afterwards, the soldiers encountered the main force of the rebels in a copse on the Bertingshäuser Höhe (Heights). The latter were showered with grapeshot, Dörnberg attempted in vain to hold them together and to convince them to attack. Also his attempts to persuade the Garde-Jaegers to quit their king remained unsuccessful. Thus, the rebellion collapsed, and they all tried to save themselves by fleeing.

Jérôme searched for Dörnberg using wanted posters: *"Description of Colonel von Doernberg of the Jaegers of the Guard of the King of Westphalia – approximately forty years old, five foot eight inches tall, lean and rather well built, black but slightly greying hair and eyebrows, bald-headed, high forehead, black eyes, large, long nose, average mouth which when he speaks is large and pulls a little to the left, brown complexion, long rounded and a little slender face, an erect gait, bearing, and a pleasant look. He normally wears a black à la Titus wig, speaks French well and stammers a little when speaking. When he fled, he was wearing the uniform der Guard Jaegers, a green coat with yellow collar and cuffs trimmed with silver braid."*[61] Nonetheless, Dörnberg succeeded in escaping to the Duke of Brunswick (see below).

Jérôme appointed a court martial under General Rewbell that handed down relatively mild sentences. Only two of the soldiers who participated in the plot were sentenced to death: Cuirassier Lieutenant von Hasserodt and Cuirassier *Wachtmeister* (Sergeant) Hohnemann. A few others were sentenced to prison or fines. Cuirassier-Colonel von Marschall was punished by assigning him as the commandant of Homberg, and Squadron Commander von Schenck was reassigned as Commandant at Wolfenbüttel. The officers of the 1st Cuirassier Regiment who remained loyal to the king were promoted as a reward and Major von Würthen became the new regimental commander.

61 Dörnberg, p. 55.

The Campaign in Germany up until the Ceasefire with Austria

At the end of 1808, the indications increased that Austria planned to renew hostilities against Napoleon. Based on this intelligence, Napoleon returned from Spain to Paris in January 1809 and began preparations for the coming war with Austria. Austria initiated hostilities on April 9, 1809. The primary theater of operations was initially Bavaria. On April 18, Napoleon named Jérôme commander of X Corps.[62] The X Corps had the task of protecting the North Sea coast from a British landing and to form a reserve for the French main army (against Austria). The Corps was supposed to be deployed from Bremen to Stralsund, with its headquarters in Hamburg.[63]

The Battle at Dodendorf

After putting down the Westphalian peasants' uprising (see previous section), the Westphalian Army's first combat was on 4 May at the Battle of Dodendorf (south of Magdeburg) against Prussian Major von Schill's Corps.[64] Schill, along with the 2nd Brandenburg Hussar Regiment had departed Berlin on 28 April and entered Westphalia north of Bernburg via Wittenberg, Dessau and Köthen. On 4 May, French General Michaud, Governor of the Magdeburg Fortress, sent six companies of infantry (four from the 1st Westphalian and 2 from the 22nd French Infantry Regiment) as well as two 6-pounders under the command of Westphalian General von Uslar to oppose Schill. Von Uslar had barely arrived in Dodendorf (about 15km south of Magdeburg) when he had to hand over command to French Colonel Vauthier (Commander of the 1st Westphalian Infantry Regiment). Von Uslar had fallen into disfavor with Jérôme because of the slow organization of the Westphalian 5th and 6th Infantry Regiments. Because of being in the immediate vicinity of Schill's forces, von Uslar remained as a volunteer with the Westphalian troops.

As Schill advanced with about 400 hussars, 60 mounted Jaegers and 40-50 infantrymen, Vauthier only left behind a company of grenadiers under Captain Legat in Dodendorf as a reserve. Vauthier vacated the other five companies from his favorable position behind the Sulzebach creek near Dodendorf, formed three squares for the attack and engaged Schill. The latter succeeded in breaking the squares with simultane-

62 Lünsmann, p. 287; according to *Memoiren et Correspondance du Roi Jérôme*, Vol. III, p. 405.

63 For further sources, see the following sources: Kleinschmidt, Baumann, Borcke, Kircheisen, Meibom, Petersdorff, Wesemann, for the opposite: Ernstberger, Dörnberg, Hessen, Dehnel, Oppen and Wachholtz.

64 In the description of the battle, we used Lünsmann, p. 288f, Bock, pp. 145-151 and Conrady, pp. 174-177. The details, e.g., participation of the two French companies, number of cannon, etc. in the individual descriptions differ slightly from one another.

Westphalian and Allied Forces' Engagements Against the Brunswick Corps in the 1809 Campaign.
Map by Bernhard Glaenzer.

ous frontal attacks and bypassing and forcing back the squares and taking about 200 prisoners (including the badly wounded Vauthier).[65] The remnants of the French and Westphalian infantry fled in the direction of Magdeburg; many Westphalians deserted and went back to their homeland. Also General von Uslar escaped being captured by a hair. After this partial success, General von Uslar took his forces westward around the Magdeburg Fortress and marched further north in the direction of the Baltic coast, pursued by portions of the Westphalian Garde under General Bongars. Schill crossed the Elbe[66] near the small Mecklenburg fortress at Dömitz. The Dutch Division Gratien took over the pursuit; the Westphalians remained on the Elbe.

Fighting in Saxony and Franconia

While since April, heavy fighting was occurring in Bavaria, Austria, Italy and Illyria between the Austrians on one side and the French and their allies on the other side, initially the theater of war in central Germany remained relatively peaceful. Austrian forces under General Am Ende first took Dresden on June 11, 1809. Under his command was also Duke Friedrich Wilhelm of Braunschweig-Oels[67] with his Freikorps and the Hessian Legion, which the former Electoral Prince (*Kurfürst*) of Hessen had raised. Prior to this, the Duke of Brunswick had withstood battles in and near Zittau against Saxon forces under Colonel Thielmann with mixed success.[68]

The threat to Saxony had prompted the King of Saxony to leave his capital and flee to Frankfurt am Main in several moves. Because the mass of the Saxon forces under Marshal Bernadotte were in Napoleon's *Grand Armée*, i.e., located in the vicinity of Vienna, and the few remaining in the country under Thielmann (ca. 2,000 men) could not hold off the Austrians, the Saxon King Friedrich August turned to Jérôme and requested him to go on the offensive. Jérôme dispatched a part of the Guard and the Berg regiment (see the Orders of Battle Appendix, Composition of X Corps, April 1809) to Eisenach where, at the time, Friedrich August had set up his court camp. On 21 June, Jérôme already had 12,900 men available after the D´Albignac and Gratien Divisions had arrived. With these forces he could risk facing Am Ende, particularly since Am Ende tended to act hesitantly. Thielmann's Saxons linked up with D'Albignac on 22 June, and on 24 June these forces began their advance from Sondershausen to Querfurt. On 25 June, Jérôme was in Merseburg; on 26 June he entered Leipzig, after it was cleared of the Austrian's allied forces. In Leipzig, Jérôme issued a braggartly proclamation in Leipzig.

Meanwhile, a change of command occurred for the Austrians. The energetic General Kienmayer took the high command. He sought to shift the theater of war from Saxony to Franconia, supposedly to go against the advancing French General Junot and also to be better able to act against the French lines of communication.

Jérôme departed Leipzig on 28 June, after Gratien Division had already left the city the day before. D´Albignac, who had marched off earlier, already had an engagement with the Duke of Brunswick on the 28th. However, Jérôme had not noticed that the main force of Austria's allies had moved into Franconia via Chemnitz. Jérôme followed the wrong track: that of a few Austrian *Landwehr* battalions, that had withdrawn to Dresden. On 1 July, Jérôme celebrated being the liberator of Dresden, but the enemy had disappeared. General Bongars, who was moving in the direction of Halle to engage the Brunswickers, also found no one there. Jérôme remained in Dresden until July 4 and then turned toward Chemnitz. He intended to march to Hof, to join with Junot there but Kienmayer frustrated this intension. Kienmayer escaped this dangerous situation, namely coming between Junot's and Jérôme's fires, in that he immediately began operations against Junot (in the direction of Hof). On July 8, Kienmayer soundly defeated Junot at Berneck and Gefrees and forced him to retreat toward Amberg. After this liberating blow, Kienmayer again turned toward the north against Jérôme. In the meantime, he was located with X Corps at Plauen, utterly defeated Junot at Berneck and Gefrees and forced him to retreat to Amberg. On 11 July, the vanguards of both armies were facing one another. Jérôme, although numerically clearly superior, pulled back in the direction of Schleiz where his forces had a small melee with Kienmayer's on the 13th. Jérôme evaded him once again and marched to Neustadt an der Orla where there was renewed fighting. Jérôme withdrew again toward Erfurt where he arrived on July 17.

In the meantime, Jérôme received two messages. The more important one stated that France and Austria had agreed to a ceasefire. Additionally, there was a - false - report that the British had landed in northern Germany.[69] This gave Jérôme, after his very inglorious retreat, the excuse to immediately return to Kassel with the Guards, the Cuirassier Regiment, the 1st and 6th Westphalian Regiments as well as the Berg Line Infantry Regiment. The Guards remained in Kassel starting on 19 July, while the other regiments, under General Rewbell, continued moving toward Hanover. In the end, on 27 July, Jérôme received a letter from Napoleon that severely admonished the Westphalian military leadership, although less so chastising the king, who was placing the blame on the division commanders.

65 Vauthier later died of his wounds.

66 Schill left behind a 400-man force to occupy and defend the small fortress.

67 The Duke was, as a result of a convention with Austria, declared an independent war power allied with Austria.

68 . Sources: Kleinschmidt, Smith, Baumann, Borcke, Kircheisen, Meibom, Petersdorff, Wesemann; Opposing side: Ernstberger, Kortzfleisch, Dörnberg; Hessen, Dehnel, Oppen and Wachholtz.

69 However, the English had landed on the Dutch island of Walcheren.

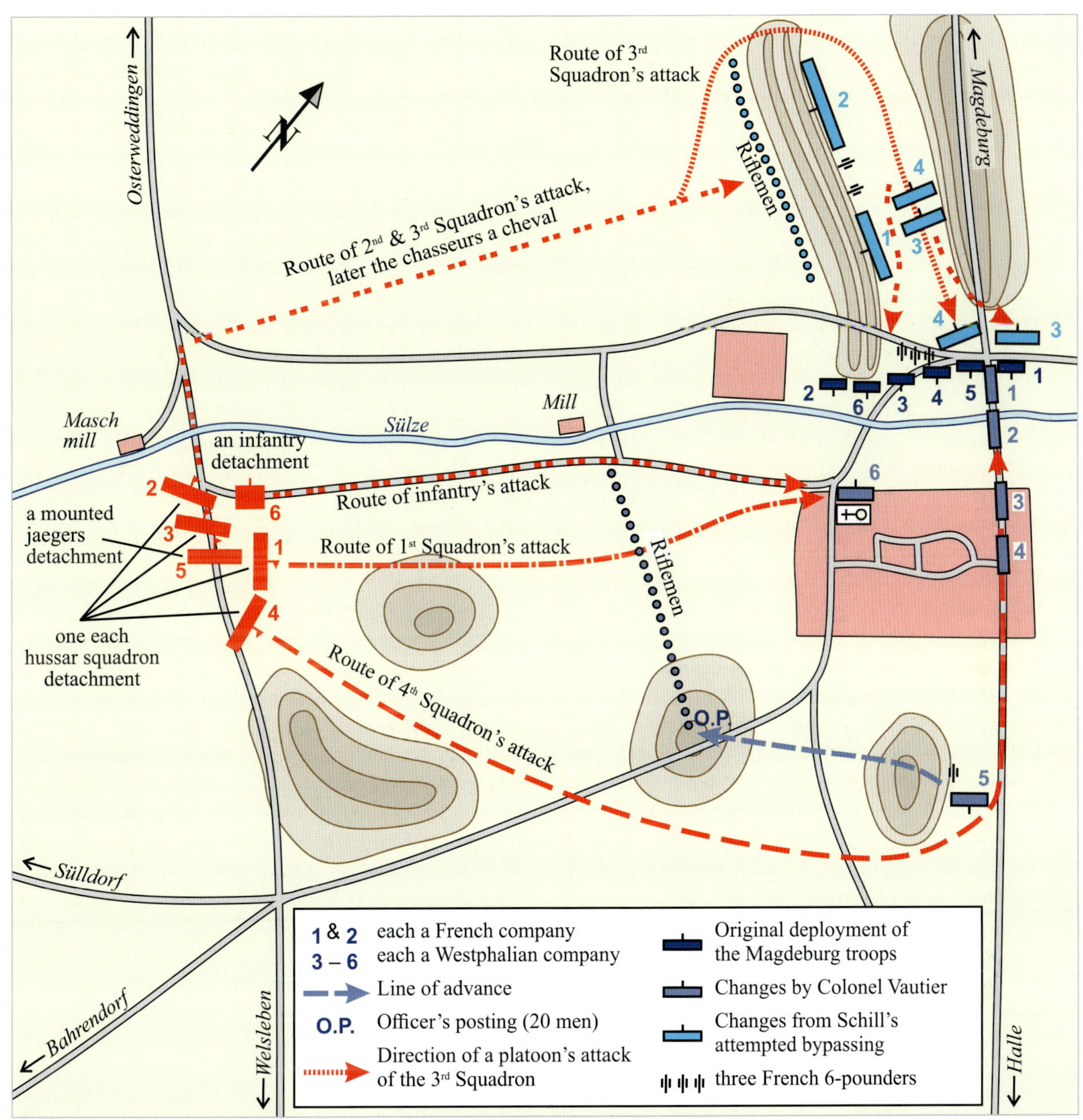

The Battle of Dodendorf, 4 May 1809
Copyright Dr. Frank Bauer,
Map revised by Bernhard Glaenzer.

After the Ceasefire: Against the Duke of Brunswick

Between 17 and 24 July, the Duke of Brunswick decided to not join into the ceasefire, but to push through to the Baltic Sea coast to the English.[70] Naturally, he kept his plan secret so as not to alert the Westphalian king through whose lands the forces would have to pass to reach the Baltic Sea. In Zwickau the Duke made his final preparations for this bold undertaking by bringing his forces up to strength, rapidly finishing up uniforms and organizing the supplying of ammunition. On 24 July near Zwickau, Duke Friedrich Wilhelm informed his officers and let them choose to accompany him or depart service. Thereupon, about thirty officers chose to take their leave, which he granted them on the spot. The duke proceeded similarly with the troops whom he first informed in Gössnitz during the following movement. Of the latter, about 200 men left the Duke's flag. After those resignations, the Brunswick forces had about 2,100 men and 100 officers remaining. See the Orders of Battle Appendix.

After the reorganization, the Duke immediately left the Zwickau area and marched via Borna to Leipzig where he arrived on 26 July. From there he turned toward Halle and took the route along the northeastern edge of the Harz Mountains on the evening of the 27th, where he spread false rumors in order to mislead the Saxon and Westphalian forces as to his actual direction of march. The Black Corps' route actually was via Hettstedt and Quedlinburg to Halberstadt, where they arrived on 29 July.

The Battle at Halberstadt

About the same time, on 28 July, the 5th Westphalian Infantry Regiment under Colonel Meyronnet (Count Wellingerode) left Magdeburg heading west to meet up with Westphalian General Rewbell's forces. They reached Halberstadt about midday on the 29th. The regiment, just recently organized, had 59 officers and 1,921 men. It consisted of two field battalions, each battalion with six companies (a voltigeur company, a grenadier company and four fusilier companies each). The Westphalian and Brunswick forces had observed one another throughout 29 July, so both sides were forewarned. Admittedly, Colonel Count Wellingerode did not think he was at risk of being attacked immediately, but instead planned to avoid the danger by a night march. The Westphalian infantry regiment was at that moment, unarmed, standing formation in the Halberstadt's Cathedral Square (Domplatz) when a Westphalian Gendarme brought a report that the Brunswick vanguard was already located at Harsleben, just four kilometers from Halberstadt. The forces available to the Westphalian side are given in orders of battle.

Colonel Count Wellingerode and the Westphalian Commandant of the Saale-Department, Major Stockmayer, who was present in Halberstadt, consulted immediately. Two voltigeur companies from the 5th Infantry Regiment were sent southeast in front of the city. Both grenadier companies, together with the soldiers from the Department and the veterans, received orders to barricade all the city gates. Subsequently, wagons were brought to block the streets, with the exception of the Kühlinger Tor (Kühling Gate) through which the deployed voltigeur companies would need to reenter the city. The old city walls were similarly occupied (see the attached city map of Halberstadt). A strong reserve was left at the Cathedral Square.

In the meantime, the Duke of Brunswick had assembled all the available forces for the battle. Through the interaction of his infantry, cavalry and artillery (a cannon and a howitzer under Ensign Dehnel) the Westphalian voltigeur companies were quickly forced to withdraw and flooded back into the city. Duke Friedrich Wilhelm ordered an immediate attack on the city.[71] Thus the west (the Breites Tor - Wide Gate) and south side (Kühlinger, Harslebener and Johannis Gates) were chosen for the direction of the main attack. The first attack, around 19:00 hours, against the well defended Kühlinger Gate came to a standstill. The attacking jaeger company, but also the artillerymen, suffered serious losses. Even senior Brunswick officers had to personally assist with the cannon in order to keep up the fires. After repeated attempts, they succeeded in taking the Kühlinger Gate. The courageous Duke immediately pushed through the gate at the head of his infantry and engaged in hand-to-hand fighting. A pitched battle with man against man developed in the adjacent streets. Irresistibly, the Brunswickers forced their way to the Fish Market (Fischmarkt), i.e., toward the city center. The Harslebener Tor (Gate) in the south was initially the objective of just a diversionary attack by the Brunswickers under Lieutenant von Hertell and set ablaze. On the other hand, the more westerly Johannis-Tor (Gate) that was stormed by a detachment under Captain von Rabiel was more heavily contested. After a cannon was brought up, whose crew was shown by a Halberstädter locksmith master exactly where the lock was located, they succeeded in bursting the gate. At the same time, a side gate was smashed in with axes and troops climbed over the wall. After the attack at this location succeeded, the barricades located behind were cleared. Rabiel's assault column also pushed toward the city center.

70 Sources: Kleinschmidt, Baumann, Conrady, Borcke, Kircheisen, Meibom, Rogge-Ludwig, Wesemann; for the opposing side: Ernstberger, Kortzfleisch, Reher, Dörnberg, Franckenberg-Ludwigsdorff, Hessen, Dehnel, Oppen and Wachholtz.

71 The Duke, whose father's Prussian regiment had been stationed in Halberstad, was obviously familiar with the city. Similarly familiar"were some of his officers (cf. Voss, von Radonitz), who had been stationed there.

By 21:00 hour, three gates had been taken by the Brunswickers and with that they were prepared to successfully storm the city, even though success was not completely certain. For the Duke, it was now a matter of dislodging the Westphalian reserves at the Domplatz (Cathedral Square) in the heart of the city and defeating the remaining resistance. In bitter street fighting, all the Brunswick branches, i.e., infantry, cavalry and artillery, worked together and provided mutual support. About an hour after the capture of the Kühlinger Tor, Premier-Lieutenant Genderer had gathered all the Brunswick cannon at the Holzmarkt. The von Girsewald officers, who were brothers, took Colonel Count Wellingerode captive in the midst of the rest of his troops.[72] The severely wounded Commandant, Major Stockmayer, was also captured by the Brunswickers. Senior Major Grissot (Westphalian Regimental Deputy Commander), who was wounded, was also taken captive at the Domplatz. Several hundred Westphalians surrendered by and by. Only the Westphalian Gendarmes were given no pardon. About 100 Westphalian soldiers succeeded in escaping over the northern city wall. Only the Breite Tor and the Breite Weg (Broad Street) in the east of the city remained in Westphalian hands. Two Elite Companies (the grenadier-companies) of the 5th Infantry Regiment were fighting there. They did not surrender until about 5:30 in the morning on 30 July, after the Brunswick howitzers were brought into position and an assault column had arrived. The 5th Westphalian Infantry Regiment had ceased to exist. Circa 50 Westphalian officers and about 1,500 NCOs and soldiers had been captured, the remainder killed, wounded or missing. Around 300 Westphalians, among them at least three NCOs (however no officers), accepted service with Brunswick.[73] The remaining prisoners were released to go home after a few days. The Brunswick losses were also considerable. To be added is that the 5th Westphalian Infantry Regiment was recreated immediately after these events; as early as 10 August 1809, the "*Westphalian Moniteur*" called for the remnants of the devastated troops to gather in Magdeburg.

The Battle of Oelper

On the afternoon of July 30, the Duke left Halberstadt and marched in the direction of his native city of Braunschweig. Major von Oppen, who had been dispatched to the North Sea coast a few days earlier was waiting for the Duke in Wolfenbüttel, and delivered the important news that the corps could be rescued by English ships at the mouth of the Weser River. The volunteer corps arrived in Braunschweig on July 31. The Duke's situation was critical. From the south, Dutch General Gratien with his division was pursuing him. From the northwest, Westphalian General Rewbell was approaching. Each of these corps by itself was already stronger than the Brunswickers, together they could effortlessly defeat the Duke. Duke Friedrich Wilhelm therefore had only two options: either to avoid a fight and sneak between his opponents, or attempt to defeat Rewbell (who blocked the route to the North Sea) and thus clear the way. From the Duke's perspective, a breakthrough through Rewbell's forces also had the advantage that a defeated Rewbell could not energetically take part in a pursuit.

Rewbell, coming from Hoya, arrived in Celle the evening of 31 July. Getting the news of the approach of the Duke, he ordered his troops on the morning of 1 August to continue moving to Braunschweig. This was haphazardly implemented, parts of the infantry remained behind due to exhaustion or lock of motivation. Rewbell's vanguard was sighted by the Duke's pickets near Ohof, about 20 km northwest of Braunschweig. Duchy of Brunswick Major Korfes recommended the Duke to engage the Westphalians at the village of Oelper located outside Braunschweig's gates. Additionally, all the bridges on the Oker River from that at Oelper and back as far as Wolfenbüttel were destroyed, so that the right flank was protected by the Oker River.

The Duke dispersed his forces as follows: the 1st Infantry Battalion on the right flank on the Oelper Berg (hill south of Oelper) with 2 cannon; 2 companies under Captain von Rabiel in Oelper; the Riflemen (*Schützen*) along the Schmölke-Graben (moat) toward the southeast to the Schäferbrücke (Shepherds' Bridge); two cannon on the Schäferbrücke, the Uhlan Squadron and the Hussars Regiment (left flank) and further to the rear, the 2nd Infantry Battalion. A hussar squadron was moved up to Lehndorf on the road to Hannover as an observation force, and a small Sharpshooter picket force was placed at the Pawel´sche Holz (woods) west of Oelper (*Oberjäger* Ulrich with 15 men). The actual reserve force (detachments of the Independent Jaeger Battalion and the Uhlans) was located at the Petritor (Petri Gate) in Braunschweig.

Rewbell's division attacked with the Westphalian Cuirassiers on the left wing, i.e., opposite the Brunswick cavalry. Then the 6th Infantry Regiment was next to it, and then the 1st Infantry Regiment on the east wing. The Berg Infantry Regiment formed the reserve, approximately behind the gap between the 6th and 1st Regi-

72 The Duke of Brunswick took Count Wellingerode with him as a prisoner to England and in February 1810 exchanged him for the English Major Lestrange who was a captive in Spain; see Kleinschmidt, p. 352.

73 This probably dealt for the most part with former members of the1st Line Battalion of English King's German Legion, who were stranded with their ship on the Dutch in1807 and forced to join the Westphalian Army, cf. Kortzfleisch; p. 34.

The Storming of Halberstadt on 29 July 1809
Copyright Dr. Frank Bauer,
Map revised by Bernhard Glaenzer.

The Duke of Brunswick at the Battle of Halberstadt on 28 June 1809
On the right in the picture are Westphalian prisoners (in white uniforms)
Watercolor by Richard Knötel, in the collection of Thomas Hemmann.

ments. The Westphalian cannon were placed west of Oelper, approximately across from the front of the 6th Regiment. However, the placement was made from a poorly led assault column, and as a result the battle line developed rather chaotically.

Shortly after 15:00, the cuirassiers, which formed Rewbell's advance guard, received fire from *Oberjäger* Ulrich's sharpshooters who were deployed in the Pawel´schen Holz. As the Westphalian infantry arrived in wagons (requisitioned in Ohof), Ulrich and his sharpshooters had to withdraw. The 1st Westphalian Infantry Regiment advanced toward Oelper. Because the village could not be defended due to its unfavorable location, and both companies under Captain von Rabiel were in danger of being cut off, the Duke withdrew them again and pulled them back to the Oelper Berg (hill). Rewbell had the 1st Regiment occupy the southern edge of the village and prepare to attack the Duke's main position. This attack began about 20:00 but was immediately repulsed with grapeshot from the two Brunswick cannon on the Oelper Berg. After that, the Duke ordered a counterattack on the village. But this also failed due confusion because he had his horse shot out from under him and Captain von Rabiel was killed. The fighting also was going back and forth on the west wing. The 6th Westphalian Regiment advancing there suffered costly casualties from a crossfire from Oelper and the riflemen's line along the Schmölke-Graben (moat). At the same time, the Brunswick hussars succeeded in forcing back the Westphalian cuirassiers, so that the cuirassiers disrupted their own infantry's line. The Westphalian batteries (seven cannon) were in danger of being captured by the Brunswickers, after they had already destroyed one of two Brunswick cannons. The leader of the Westphalian battery, Captain Guériot, had been mortally wounded. Brunswick Major von Reichmeister, who was commanding the wing, missed a good opportunity to roll up the Westphalian flank due to his hesitation, so that Rewbell's reserve (the Berg Infantry Regiment) was able to restore the situation. Now the Brunswickers pulled back on this side. Because the position on the Oelper Berg could not be held, the Duke also had to give orders to the right wing to withdraw toward Braunschweig. The Westphalians pursued only hesitatingly; the Duke left an infantry detachment under Captain von Pröstler in place to hold them off.

From a tactical perspective, the Battle of Oelper was initially a defeat for the Duke of Brunswick. There was in fact the danger that he would be encircled and defeated the next day between Rewbell and Gratien who was pursuing from the southeast. The Duke was pressed by his own officers to leave the corps and force

The 5th Infantry Regiment in the Battle of Halberstadt 1809
Plate by Richard Knötel, in ***Uniformkunde*** Vol. IV.

his way through to the coast. He refused this request. The sixteen officers who did not want to fight any longer were immediately dismissed. Under pressure from the Westphalian Prefect Henneberg who was threatening to storm Braunschweig, the Duke decided on the morning of 2 August about 8:00 o'clock, to leave Braunschweig with his troops.

Up until then, Duke Friedrich Wilhelm was completely unaware that around 22:00 that night Rewbell had already ordered his forces to withdraw, an activity which very rapidly resulted in confusion in the darkness. The reasons for the withdrawal remain unclear to this day. Possibly Rewbell's concern was that his right flank might be enveloped, due to a nighttime skirmish between the Westphalian right wing battalion and the Brunswick von Pröstler Detachment. Also, Rewbell completely misjudged the relative strength of the forces, misled by the participation of Braunschweig citizens (mostly in dark civilian clothing) and the arrival of Westphalian prisoners or defectors from the 5th Westphalian Regiment,[74] whom Rewbell thought were Austrians or members of the Hessian Legion.

The Pursuit of the Duke von Brunswick to the North Sea

Actually, General Rewbell did not pursue immediately, but crossed over the Oker River at Gross Schwülper heading east, sought to join with General Gratien who was coming from Wolfenbüttel, and arrived in Braunschweig the evening of 2 August. Although the commander of the Westphalian-Dutch troops had promised them they could plunder the city of Braunschweig, this was prevented at the last minute by the Westphalian Prefect Henneberg!

The Duke departed Braunschweig on 2 August[75] and marched as far as Burgdorf, north of Hannover that day.[76] On 3 August the Brunswickers initially occupied Hannover - where the Duke spread the rumor he wanted to head to Kassel - and he then turned northwest again toward Neustadt am Rübenberge. From there, he marched further via Nienburg to Hoya an der Weser (47 km) on 4 August. Thus they reached the west bank of the Weser River before his Westphalian pursuers. General Rewbell reached Hoya with his advance guard the morning of 5 August and first of all had to re-erect the bridge over the Weser that had been destroyed by the Duchy's troops. Then Rewbell continued his pursuit of the Duke, but alone, because General Gratien

74 From the Battle of Halberstadt, see above.

75 Major von Oppen had just received news that the way to the Duchy of Oldenburg was open and there were enough ships there to take on the Duke's forces.

76 This was the first one-day march of about 50 km and more would follow. This amazing movement accomplishment was only possible because the infantry, wounded etc. were driven in wagons, of which the Black Corps had about 400.

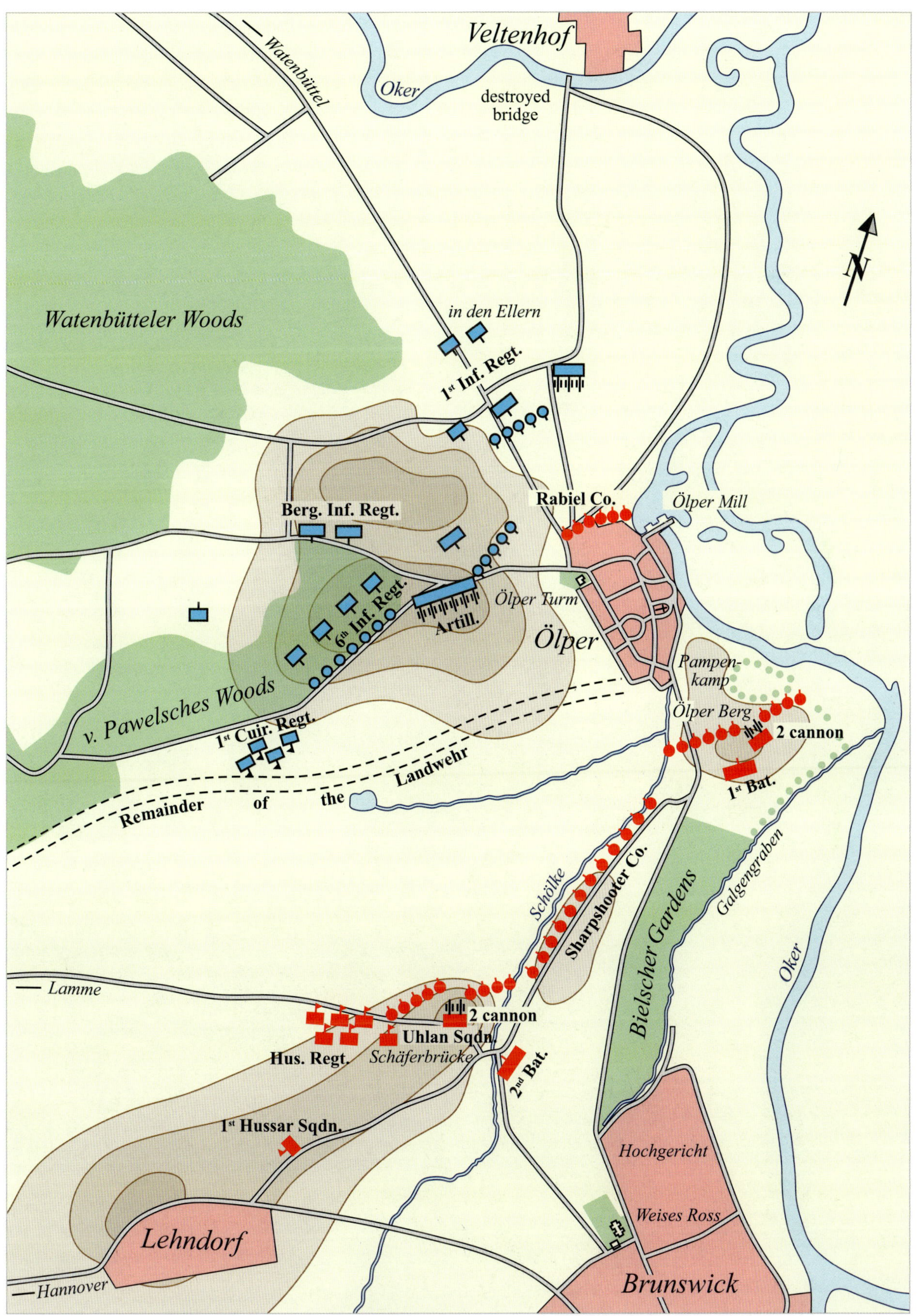

The Battle of Oelper, 1 August 1809
Copyright Dr. Frank Bauer,
Map revised by Bernhard Glaenzer.

The Duke of Brunswick in the Battle of Oelper, 1 August 1809
Watercolor by Richard Knötel, in the collection of Thomas Hemmann.

had received orders from Jérôme to march to Holland in order to engage the English who had landed on Walcheren Island.[77] In order to deceive the Westphalians, the Duke sent a detachment from multiple branches (60 Jaegers, 60 hussars and two cannon) under Major von Korfes to Bremen, while he himself turned with the bulk of his forces toward Delmen which he reached late the evening of 5 August (over 50 km in one day!). About 1:30 AM on 6 August, the Brunswick troops were again alerted and advanced via Huntebrück to Elsfleth, skirting around the Oldenburg territory.[78] In Huntebrück a company under Captain von Wachholtz stayed behind to guard the crossing against the Westphalian pursuers.

General Rewbell reached Delmenhorst that day about 14:00 and decided, on 7 August, to march to Bremen where the Duke was suspected to be located. Thus the Duke's ruse, namely the deception of Major Korfes' movement as being that of the whole Corps was a success. Korfes remained in Bremen until midday on 7 August (two of the city gates remained in Brunswick's possession until the evening of 7 August) and the tried to join up with the Duke. In doing so, his force ran into Rewbell's lead elements that were marching from Delmenhorst to Bremen, at Langenwisch. A small battle ensued in which Korfes – with the right perception of the situation – tried to draw the Westphalians after him in a northwesterly direction. At Rabelingshausen an der Weser, Korfes embarked on a large Weser boat[79] with his 60 to 70 remaining men and a howitzer and sailed down the Weser River. At the same time, during 6 and 7 August, the mass of the Brunswick forces at Elsfleth and Brake completed embarking. About 14 ships sailed down the Weser toward the English. Furthermore, hussars, uhlans and the company under Captain von Wachholtz mentioned above, got onto seven ships in the lake at Brake. On the evening of 8 August, the Brunswickers met up with the English ships under Lord Stewart sent for them - the Black Corps was saved.

In the meantime, General Rewbell entered Bremen the evening of 7 August where he obviously recognized his error. On the 8th, Rewbell marched back to Delmenhorst, from where he wanted to follow the Duke to Varel. During that day, Rewbell learned from a Danish hussar patrol about the successful debarkation of the Duke, whereupon he had his Chief of Staff, Colonel von Borstell, occupy Brake and Elsfleth with ca. 900 Westphalians. On 9 August, Rewbell received the news that he had been relieved of command;[80] General Bongars took over then as the commander.

77 The third set of opponents, the Danes under General Ewald, were still located at Cuxhaven on 5 August.

78 The Duke von Oldenburg avoided an engagement by his forces with the Brunswickers, in that he allowed the Oldenburg infantry regiment in the west of the country to depart.

79 On a so-called *"Weserbock."*

80 He left the kingdom and went to America with his wife, see Kleinschmidt, p. 305.

THE 1812 CAMPAIGN AGAINST RUSSIA

To the Russian Border

In the years 1809 through 1811 the relations between France and Russia became increasingly strained. During 1811, the French emperor came to the decision to subjugate Russia. On 27 January 1812, Napoleon ordered Jérôme to mobilize the Confederation of the Rhine's (*Rheinbund*) Westphalian contingent by 15 February,[81] since France was forced to defend itself against an increasingly hostile Russia. On 25 February, Jérôme reported that the Westphalian forces were ready for the campaign and that the army was in excellent spirits. On 1 March, before the deployment, a splendid revue of the Westphalian Army took place in Kassel to which the diplomatic corps was invited.[82] At this revue, the troops learned of the impending deployment.

On 9 March, Jérôme traveled with a few confidants to Paris to negotiate with Napoleon about the employment of the army and the filling of senior positions in the Westphalian officer corps. Despite the Emperor's original intention to occupy all the division and brigade commanders' positions with French officers, Jérôme was able to grant command of a division to General von Ochs and numerous brigade command positions to other Westphalians. On the other hand, Jérôme's request to have an independent overall command was initially rejected by Napoleon. The proven French Major General Vandamme was named as the commander of the Westphalian forces that were to form VIII Corps of the *Grand Armée*. On 23 March, he took over command in Dessau. On 25 March, Jérôme returned to Kassel. The third battalion of each infantry regiment (except for the 2nd and 7th Regiments), the seventh company of the Light Battalions and the ninth companies of the cavalry regiments remained behind as depot units.

Both Westphalian divisions[83] crossed the Elbe on 24 and 25 March and marched via Luckau and Glogau in short daily movements to Kalisch (on the border between Prussia and the Grand Duchy of Warsaw). After crossing the Elbe, the Westphalians, on Vandamme's orders, had to march as if at war and post guards in their military quarters, in order to get used to field duty.[84] On 13 April, Jérôme arrived in Kalisch and had the troops pass in review. The Adjutant von Borcke reported about the following weeks:

"With the entry into Poland, any excess in supplies ended and even the well laid tables of the generals disappeared. Shortages had already set in because stores of goods were nowhere to be found. Confusion and dwindling discipline began to show in the troops who were used to strict discipline, who before and after being quartered among their poor Polish peasant hosts who were unable to give them anything. No man was able to remedy the many incoming complaints and a dangerous requisitioning system at large began in which the order of the day authorized the troops to supply their needs for food and cattle for the continued march. One can only look with dismal glances to a future under such conditions. The war had not yet been declared and one already faced the danger of starving."[85]

The beginning of May, the Westphalian forces marched further to Warsaw, where von Ochs' Division took up quarters, while on 15 May the Tharreau Division crossed the Weichsel River above Warsaw, near Gora and then went into an encampment. Also, on 15 May, von Ochs and Tharreau exchanged division commands, so that Tharreau henceforth led the 1st Division (23rd of the *Grand Armée*) and von Ochs the 2nd Westphalian Division (24th of the *Grand Armée*).

Jérôme also traveled to Warsaw and took command of the *Grand Armée's* Westphalian VIII Corps, the Polish Corps (led by the Polish Major General Prince Poniatowski), the Saxon VII Corps (under the French Major General Reynier) and the combined VI Cavalry Corps (French commander: Major General Latour-Maubourg). Napoleon decided the named corps were to form the right (southern) wing of the *Grand Armée*. The Westphalian forces spent a month engaged in musters, target practice, exercises and other preparations.[86]

On 15 June, VIII and V Army Corps began moving eastward in the direction of the Russian border. The forces (the Polish Corps always a day's march in advance) marched via Pultusk, Ostrolenka and Szczuczyn[87] to Grodno (on the Neman river, the Polish-Russian border river) where the advance guard arrived on 28 June, the bulk arriving on 2 July.

81 Kleinschmidt, p. 480.

82 Kleinschmidt, p. 482.

83 We are basing this description of the 1812 campaign primarily on the following sources: Nafziger, Esposito, Elting, Gerdes, Kleinschmidt and the available memoirs of Westphalian officers and soldiers. For the opposing forces, see Bernhardi, Wolzogen, and Clausewitz, among others.

84 Hohenhausen, p. 219.

85 Borcke, p. 166f.

86 Borcke, p. 167ff.

87 The spelling of the Polish and Russian place names differ significantly in the various sources.

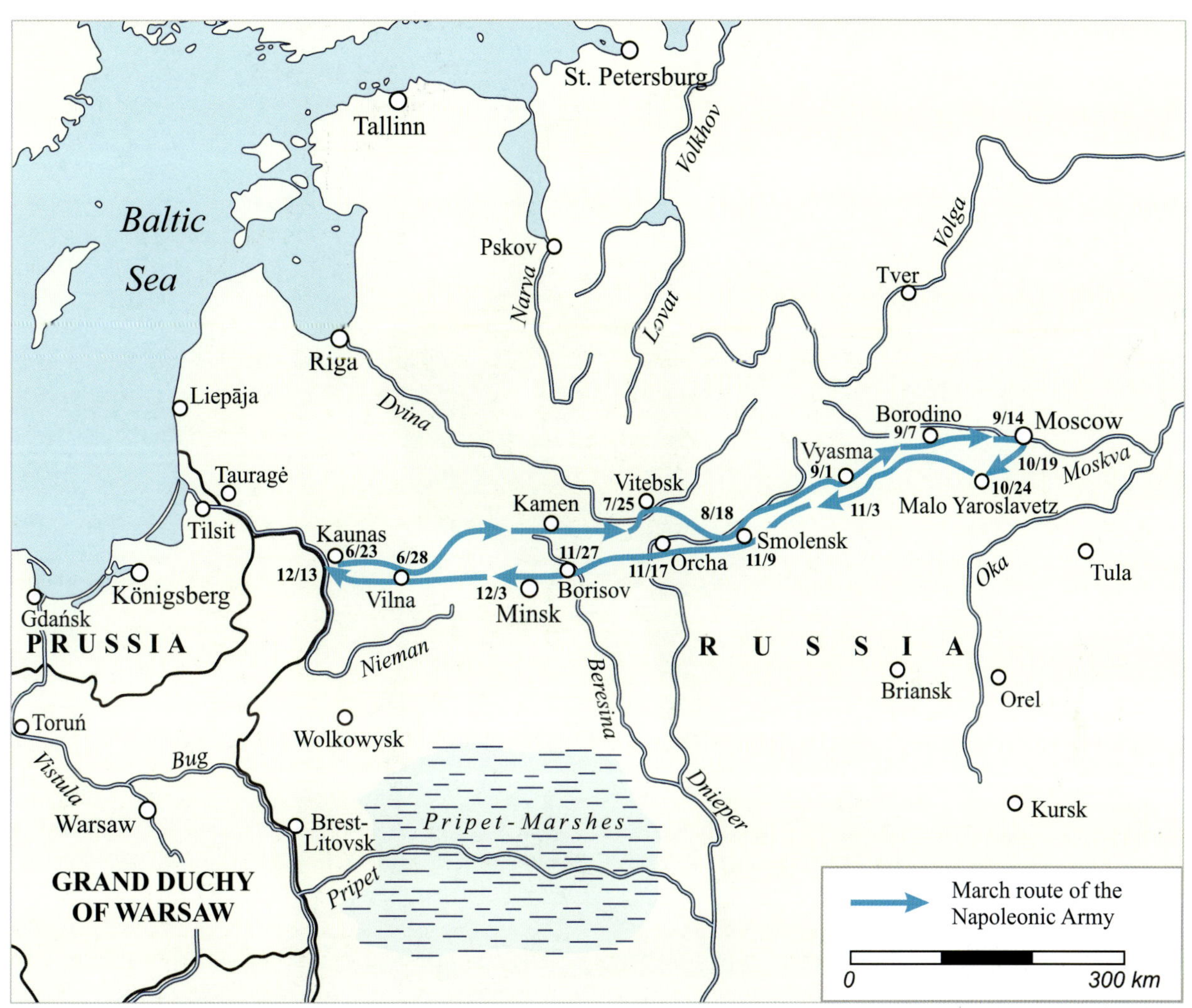

The Main Movements of the Grand Armée in the 1812 Campaign Against Russia.
Map revised by Bernhard Glaenzer.

Major General Vandamme
Commander of the VIII Corps until july 1812.
Anne S.K. Brown Military Collection,
Brown University Library.

The Beginning of the War and Advance Toward Moscow

The Emperor's proclamation on the outbreak of war, which had already been proclaimed on 22 June, was announced to the troops. Hostilities began with crossing of the Neman - the Westphalian cavalry was successful in a minor skirmish against Russian Cossacks and took about 100 prisoners. Starting at the beginning of the march to Grodno, the Westphalians and Poles suffered through sandy roads, rain, heat and poor rations. Jérôme gave the troops two days of rest before resuming the pursuit of the retreating Russians.

The strategic situation at the beginning of July 1812 was that Jérôme was located where the Russian 1st (General Barclay de Tolly) and 2nd (General Bagration) Western Armies abutted one another. Napoleon's objective was to isolate both armies from one another and then to defeat them separately as quickly as possible. In any case, smoldering differences of opinion by Jérôme and General Vandamme had already broken out in Grodno. Jérôme relieved Vandamme of Command of VIII Corps and temporarily turned it over to General Tharreau. Both Jérôme and Vandamme wrote to the Emperor to justify their own position. Napoleon decided in favor of Jérôme and sent Vandamme home, although Vandamme remained with the army as far as Bielica. Thus the Westphalian Corps lost an able, if also a blunt commander, who was concerned for his soldiers' wellbeing. Vandamme's departure evoked complaints from many Westphalians.

Napoleon pushed Jérôme to stay in close pursuit of Bagration. Because Bagration already had a few days' march head start, Jérôme sent the entire available Westphalian and Polish light cavalry after him in order to delay him wherever possible. The Poles, who formed the advance guard, were defeated three times by the Russian rear guard under Platov – at Korelic on 9 July, at

Mir on 10 July and at Romanow on 14 July. Thus Bagration was able to cross the Berezina at Bobruisk unopposed, and to turn northeast via Mohilev to attempt to unite with Barclay. Jérôme called off the pursuit on 13 July in Neswisch after he became convinced it would be impossible to catch up with Barclay and allowed his troops a few days' rest. Napoleon was highly enraged that Jérôme had let Bagration escape and issued an (initially secret) order putting Jérôme under Marshal Davout's command. In the meantime, the marshal had reached Minsk with I Corps, but could no longer prevent Bagration's retreat due to his long dalliance in that city. Davout notified Jérôme with a copy of the in an imperial note on 14 July with the information of change of command. Jérôme, indignant about his opinion and undeserved affront, immediately resigned his command and on 16 July departed for home. He took his Garde du Corps company and the Westphalian Guard Infantry Battalions with him.[88] However, Napoleon saw to it that after a few days march from Korelic, the Guard Infantry under Brigadier General Wolff had to turn around.

VIII Corps, under the command of Tharreaus, marched to Borissov,[89] where they crossed the Berezina, and then turned toward Orcha on the Dniepr, which they reached on 27 July. The exhausted troops made camp there and remained there for almost two weeks and were able to recuperate and get their military equipment back into condition.[90] Some of the battalions were melded together,[91] because many soldiers were no longer able to keep up with the corps due to the great tribulations. About 2.000 men were dead, wounded or sick. The Westphalian Borstel Brigade, which was detached to Alexandria (about 14 km south of Orcha), sent four companies of the 3rd Infantry Regiment under Lieutenant Colonel Lossberg across the Dniepr to occupy the city and Fort Kopys, which led to a small battle a flanking corps under Bagration.[92]

On 30 July French General Junot, Duke of Abrantes, sent by Napoleon, arrived at VIII Corps and took over command. On 4 August he held a review of the Corps and found the troops' condition and maneuver capabilities above his expectations.[93] The Guard Infantry, about 3,000 men, joined up with the Corps on 1 August after forced marches. During both weeks in camp at Orsrscha the Westphalians only had minor skirmishes with the Russians. Cossacks crossed the Dniepr (which could be forded at Orcha), but were regularly driven off by the Westphalian Hussar Brigade.

On 12 August, the VIII Corps had to leave Orcha in order to advance to the right of the important military road and on the same plain as I Corps (Davout) to Smolensk. VIII Corps marched in one single column in the following march sequence: General Hammerstein with three light infantry battalions, nine squadrons of light cavalry and a mounted battery, as the advance guard. Following them were both infantry divisions, between which were two cavalry squadrons, the remaining artillery as well as the Reserve Artillery Park and the baggage train. An infantry battalion and a squadron of hussars formed the rear guard. Due to the poor roads, the inadequate construction of many bridges, and the orders to keep troops close together on the march, there were many back-ups. On 13 and 14 August the Westphalian march column crossed paths with a Polish one that led to further delays. The troops were only able to make camp during the night and could not cook meals. On 14 August they crossed the old Russian border at Buyevo.[94]

On 15 August, Junot lost his way, the Westphalians had to march back and forth for great distances before they were able to finally make a bivouac at midnight, having only gained 15 kilometers. Entire brigades remained in place and soldiers bivouacked individually in the woods. Only during the 16th were the troops able to join up and continue movement toward Smolensk. Due to the delays of the previous day they only got as far as Tolstikyt[95] - VIII Corps, was about one day behind the other corps advancing on Smolensk.

The Battle of Smolensk took place on 17 August. In the battle, the primary units engaged were I, III and V Corps (Davout, Ney and Poniatowski, respectively); the Guard and parts of the Reserve Cavalry under Murat were in reserve. VIII Corps marched toward the cannon fire; Napoleon had an officer order Junot to speed up his advance if possible. Junot allowed a several hour pause at midday in order to have lunch in a palace. While there, he received the Emperor's order, whereupon he had his forces depart for the 20-kilometer distant Smolensk, with cavalry and light infantry at a run. Nevertheless, the Westphalian advance guard only reached the battlefield in the evening after everything was over and the Russians had evacuated the burning district on the south bank of the Dniepr.[96] VIII Corps bivouacked in the vicinity of the French Imperial Guard. The French and

88 The King returned to Kassel on 12 August, see Kaisenberg, p. 239; with him, among others, were Minister-State Secretary Le Camus (Graf v. Fürstenstein), General Prinz von Hesse-Philippsthal und Colonel zu Salm-Salm. The Garde du Corps reached Kassel at the end of that month, per Lünsmann, p. 301.

89 A few kilometers south of Studyanka, where Napoleon completed his famous Berezina crossing at the end of November 1812.

90 Napoleon had ordered a general halt of operations and a rest period because he could no longer prevent the link-up of both Russian armies and the *Grand Armée* desperately needed a rest.

91 Borcke, p. 174.

92 Hohenhausen, p. 228 and Lossberg, p. 62ff. Marshal Davout ordered the advance on Kopys, as his I Corps passed Alexandria.

93 Hohenhausen, p. 230.

94 From there on it was difficult to find guides who knew the area because no Jews were allowed to live in Old Russia and the Russian civilians fled into the forests from the French and their allies.

95 Located a good 35 kilometers from Smolensk. For this and the following, see Hohenhausen, p. 231ff.

96 The left bank, because the Dniepr flows from east to west at Smolensk.

Major General Jean Andoche Junot
Duke of Abrantes, Commander of VIII Corps 1812
Contemporary engraving, collection: Markus Gaertner.

their allies used 18 August to occupy the southern part of Smolensk, to put out the fires, and to throw several temporary bridges across the Dniepr after the Russians had burned the permanent Dniepr bridges during their withdrawal. The temporary bridges were needed to allow the pursuit of the retreating Russians on the main military road to Moscow north of the Dniepr.

Napoleon planned an envelopment operation for 19 August that had the objective to at least cut off the Russian rearguard. To do this, I Corps (Davout) and III Corps (Ney) and portions of the reserve cavalry in Smolensk crossed over to the north bank of the Dniepr and took up the tracks of the retreating Russians. Initially, they had to clarify whether the main retreat was via the Petersburg Road to the north or via the Moscow Road to the east. Actually the Russians had retreated northward during the night of 18-19 August on the main road from Smolensk, but then turned right outside the city, to go by a semicircle through the forests to get back to the Moscow. This march in a circle during the night, almost unavoidably – led the Russian forces to delays and confusion, so that the Russian rearguard were only about two kilometers from Smolensk on the morning of 19 August. III Corps forces that arrived just then on the Moscow Road attacked the Russians there.

On the same day, about 13:00 - 14:00, VIII Corps crossed the Dniepr a few kilometers further southeast at Prudisczy on two just erected pontoon bridges and thus were in the position to advance on the Moscow military road in short order and to attack the Russians from the rear. After about an hour-and-a-half, the Westphalians had reached the village of Szenkovo, from which one could see to the right the Russian rearguard in combat with the retreating I Corps and III Corps. The situation for Junot was especially favorable; he needed to only advance a little bit and the 10,000 men of the Russian rearguard would unquestionably be lost. Many Westphalian generals advised Junot to advance immediately. The latter however called a halt and the Westphalian advance guard was actually ordered back again. Junot told the generals, that he had advanced too quickly in contradiction to the orders he had received. The Russians, who immediately recognized the danger of their situation, formed a front against the Westphalians and immediately deployed some cavalry regiments. At the same time, some Russian infantry divisions that had already marched further along the Moscow Road were called back again to re-form the Russian rearguard. The favorable moment for the Westphalians was lost. Meanwhile, the commander of the French Reserve Cavalry, King Joachim of Naples (Marshal Murat) hurried to Junot at the center of the battlefield to order him to advance immediately. Junot would not let himself be hurried; only the Westphalian cavalry had to mount up again and the 2nd Light Infantry Battalion (under Lieutenant Colonel Boedicker) and the voltigeur company (Captain Wurmb) of the I (1st) Light Infantry Battalion were sent to skirmish against the Russian cavalry. Thereupon Russian Cossacks attacked the light infantry line. The 2nd Battalion succeeded in withdrawing into a nearby thicket, while the Voltigeur company of the 1st, which had formed a square and fired a volley, were all killed by the Cossacks after a brave defense. The 2nd Battalion suffered only one dead and 11 wounded.[97] The *Garde-Chevauleger* Regiment was also attacked by the Cossacks, suffered some losses and had to be helped to break out by the two Westphalian hussar regiments.

After 16:00 the King von Naples rode to Junot a second time, admonished him sharply because of his inactivity said that the Westphalian Corps' cavalry (the *Garde-Chevauleger* Regiment and both hussar regiments) under General von Hammerstein could attack.[98] Initially the Westphalian riders were able to repulse the opposing Cossacks, however afterward the Westphalians were forced to retreat in the face of numerically superior Russian cavalry of the line and Russian jaegers.[99] Junot rejected Hammerstein's request for support from the Westphalian infantry divisions, and only a battery was sent to Hammerstein. The line infantry, which had been withheld, had to form squares due to Junot's excessive need for safety and they just observed the events without taking any action.[100] After repeated requests from General von Ochs, he received permission at least to have two light battalions and the Jaeger-Carabiniers chase the Russians out of a forest that they were using to protect the right flank of the Russian cavalry line. During this action the commander of the Jaeger-Carabiniers Battalion, Lieutenant Colonel von Hessberg was fatally shot. General Legras then, with the *Jaeger-Garde Battalion*, supported by a few cannon, captured a thicket located further forward that formed the seam between two Russian corps. Thanks to this partial success it was possible for the Westphalians to make contact with III Corps (Ney). Von Ochs who was informed about this success, was allowed by Junot to have four Voltigeur companies from the 2nd and 6th Infantry Regiments advance, who were to skirmish against the Russian sharpshooters. General Allix, the commander of the Westphalian artillery, brought up several more batteries that began firing. The Westphalian cavalry also had to advance again. About 20:00 the Russians were forced to retreat on the Moscow Road. Thus the Battle of Valutina-Gora was over for the Westphalians. Only the light troops (corps cavalry, parts of the light infantry and some Voltigeur companies of the heavy infantry) and the artillery had come under fire; in total the losses came to 16 officers and 450 men.[101] Napoleon, in his initial anger about Junot's passivity, wanted to relieve him as the Corps Commander. The advocates for the Duke, among them Adjutant General Rapp, figured out how to help Junot retain his position.[102] Junot's behavior that day can only be explained with the beginning of mental illness from which he died in July the following year.

Napoleon, dissatisfied with VIII Corps' actions, ordered the Westphalians to leave the Valutina-Gora battlefield. This took several days while the army corps that had been planned for the advance on Moscow marched across the battlefield. The cavalry reserve under Murat was in the lead, then I Corps on the major military road, followed by III and the Guards; to the left of the military road IV Corps and to the right the Army Corps. VIII Corps departed on 24 August and followed the *Grand Armée*. The difficulties of supplying the forces increased considerably because the entire area around the military road had already been stripped and all the inhabitants had fled to the surrounding forests with all their belongings and livestock. The Westphalians were therefore forced

97 Linsingen, p. 278.

98 Before the beginning of the fight, Hammerstein engaged in a man-to-man fight with a Russian hussar officer whom he pushed from his horse, cf. Rüppell, p. 88.

99 The to and fro of the fighting was vividly described by Rüppell, then a lieutenant in the 2nd Westphalian Hussar Regiment. Rüppell was captured in a counterattack by the Russians and taken to the interior of the country, Rüppell, p. 81ff.

100 Lieutenant Colonel Conrady of the 6th Infantry Regiment, mentioned about this day: *"We stood as idle spectators gnashing our teeth, where honor and fame waved to us. Never before is the opportunity to gain a glowing success been squandered in such an unprincipled, cowardly way! I saw many officers and men with tears of anger and shame running down their cheeks."* Conrady, p. 255.

101 Lünsmann, p. 303, according to an official report in the *"Westphälischen Moniteur"* of 26 September 1812.

102 Junot had once gained favor with Napoleon at the siege of Toulon. The Emperor was grateful to him for the rest of his life. In 1813 he finally went insane (probably due to a head wound suffered in Spain) and died.

to conduct distant patrols to the left and right of the road in order to find any food. Due to the constant detaching of personnel there was increasing disorder in the units. Often it was especially difficult for the detachments to find their troops after several days' absence. Additionally, there were problems in this relatively arid part of Russia finding usable drinking water. It was unbearable for the marching troops, especially with the prevailing heat, and the thick dust kicked up by the endless columns. In contrast, the nights were already severely cold. Hundreds of stragglers were left behind daily due to exhaustion or illness. Dead horses lined the sides of the roads and gave off a pestilent stench. The resting places, which could only be occupied at night, frequently were already contaminated by the Russians, French and other allies who had preceded them. Along the road were pillars of smoke from the plundered villages or the burnt remains. Also the larger cities on the road to Moscow, like Dorogobusch, Vyasma and Gschatsk,[103] had been consumed by flames, after they had been thoroughly plundered. So it is not surprising that the Westphalian Corps lost many personnel to illness and exhaustion, as well as many soldiers who had gone foraging and killed by the peasants or Cossacks.[104] Many a soldier eagerly saw the old capital of Russia, which they were nearing closer and closer every day. One hoped to find a place to rest and of peace there. Even a battle that the Russians could offer at the gates of Moscow would be welcomed because it would bring the decision about the campaign sooner. On 2 September, it was learned that that General Kutuzov had taken over as Commander in Chief of the Russian armies. The news brought hope for a decisive battle. The French headquarters requested reports on troop strength, ordered detachments be pulled in - everything pointed to the approach of a major battle.

103 The VIII Corps reached Dorogobusch on 26 and Vyasma on 30 August, Gschatsk on 4 September.

104 Hohenhausen, p. 246f.

Borodino - The Westphalian Army's Greatest Battle

After the Westphalian Corps had taken a day of rest on 5 September at Gschatsk, on 6 September, it had to join the lines of the *Grand Armée* in front of the redoubts of Borodino. That same day the French captured the advanced defenses at Schevardino. VIII Corps still had 15 battalions,[105] 3 cavalry regiments and all its artillery. Its strength was just under 10,000 men.[106]

Early in the morning of 7 September, troops donned their parade uniforms[107] and a German translation of Napoleon's proclamation was read to the troops in each company. The troops received it with a joyous *"Vive l'Empereur!"* (Long live the Emperor" – in case of a victory – because they were promised wealth, good winter quarters and a quick return home. That day the Emperor intentionally put VIII Corps under Marshal Ney's command; the Westphalian division commanders received their orders directly from him, so that Junot would be left out in the cold that day.

About 5:00 in the morning, VIII Corps moved into its position behind III Corps;[108] both Westphalian infantry divisions deployed in two long lines like on a drill field. The Westphalians were located somewhat to the right of the center of the French position, initially as the reserve of III Corps and their own corps. The battle began around 6:00 o'clock, initially at the village of Borodino and in the Utiza Forest.[109] While III Corps attacked several of the redoubts located to their front at Semenovskoye, the Westphalians pulled to the right[110] of III Corps and filled the gap which had existed up to then between III and I Corps (Davout) and V Corps (Poniatowski), which were fighting further to the south. The 1st Brigade Damas (1st Westphalian Division) received orders to take a piece of woods from which the Russians were delivering harassing fire. The 1st Brigade drove off some Russian cuirassiers, who were charging, by fire from a quickly formed square, and afterwards took the woods and thus a link-up was established with V Corps. Now the 2nd Westphalian Division under General von Ochs that

105 The 2nd Battalion of the 5th Infantry Regiments was in Dorogobusch, the I. Battalion of the same regiment and 200 Westphalian Hussars were in Vyasma and the III. Battalion of the 2nd Infantry Regiment in Gschatsk were left behind in order to secure the rear areas.

106 Other information in Giesse, p. 123: 9,870 infantry, 1,530 cavalry, 474 foot artillery personnel, 229 Train soldiers, 56 mounted artillery personnel plus 41 Train soldiers; totaling around 12,200 men. However, on the day of the Battle of Borodino, Giesse was located far to the rear at Dorogobusch.

107 Wearing the dress uniform was a standard practice in the French and their allies' armies before a battle.

108 We essentially rely on Hohenhausen, p. 251ff. for the description of the battle.

109 Morgenstern, p. 68ff.

110 This departure to the right in front of the Russian's front resulted in many personnel receiving wounds on their left side, cf. Giesse, p. 124.

had been located in reserve also advanced to the plain at the front. The 1st Light Battalion under Lieutenant Colonel Rauschenplatt that belonged to the Division was also attacked by Russian cavalry and fended off the attack with the battalion's fires. After Ney's III Corps' partial successes at Semenovskoye, the Westphalians received the order to break through the Russian lines. The Russians, sensing the danger, also called reserves into their front line. A murderous artillery barrage ensued. At Ney's expressed orders, the Westphalian Jaeger-Carabinier Battalion had to deploy in dispersed formation in front of the Russian artillery line in order to knock out the Russian cannoneers with rifle fire. Renewed Russian cavalry attacks were repulsed. The 2nd Brigade Borstel advanced in assault column formation toward the Russian infantry line and pushed it back a bit. However, they did not succeed in mastering the strong Russian artillery that was positioned on high ground in some woods. Westphalians, French, Württembergers and Poles suffered heavy losses in the attempt. Ney ordered von Ochs, who had taken over command of the 1st Division (all of its generals were dead or wounded in the meantime) and to force the Russians out of the woods, which succeeded despite fierce opposition. The Russians were forced to give up this position on the battlefield; their artillery had to leave the heights. This last, decisive attack took place about 17:00. The exhausted Westphalians collapsed on the spot.

At the same time, the Westphalian Light Cavalry under General von Hammerstein in the center withstood heavy fire and also attempted a few successful charges, although admittedly they were not that successful in dispersing the Russian squares. Both heavy cavalry brigades, both cuirassier regiments under General von Lepel, had also taken part in the storming of the Great Redoubt at the center of the battlefield.

The Westphalian losses at Borodino were enormous. About 500 men were killed, another 2,500 wounded[111] (which by the prevailing conditions were almost tantamount to death) and many were missing. Thus the total losses that day amounted to about one third![112] Light Battalion II, that entered the battle that morning with about 700 men, lost 10 officers and 341enlisted, so approximately one half its personnel.[113] For the Jaeger-Carabiniers Battalion that went into battle with around 550, only 30 men remained under arms by that evening! The three light cavalry regiments only formed three squadrons (less than 300 men), thus were reduced to about one-sixth of their authorized strength. Except for von Ochs, all the Westphalian generals were dead or fatally wounded (Generals Tharreau, Damas and von Lepel) or injured (Generals von Hammerstein and von Borstel among other). Among the staff officers, Lieutenant Colonels von Cölln and von Knorr had been killed, and later Colonels von Hesberg and von Gilsa and Lieutenant Colonels von Stockhausen and von Crammon died of their wounds. Colonels Müller, von Zandt, Humbert and von Füllgraf, Lieutenant Colonels von Reiche, von Czernitzky, von Schmidt, von Lossberg, von Lepel, von Conrady and Boedicker as well as Major Müldner, among others, were wounded.

After the battle, the Emperor and Marshal Ney expressed their satisfaction with the Westphalian forces. A few weeks after the battle, many officers received the Order of the Westphalian Crown (*Orden der westphälischen Krone*)[114] for their bravery. Non-commissioned officers and soldiers were awarded 14 gold and 56 silver Medals for Merit (*Verdienstmedaillen*) from the king.

Until the Retreat

As they had already done at Valutina-Gora, VIII Corps had to remain on the battlefield for a few days in order to care for the wounded and as best they could to clean up the area and pick up weapons. Afterwards, the corps received the task of securing the extended (Smolensk-) Moschaisk - Moscow line of communication. Only the Cuirassier Brigade and the mounted battery went with the IV Cavalry Corps to Moscow. The Westphalian headquarters remained in Moschaisk. A combined brigade (3rd Infantry Regiment, Light Battalions II and III, and 60 hussars) under the command of Colonel Bernard maintained communication between Moschaisk and Moscow. It accompanied the French treasury wagons carrying the Imperial strongboxes to Moscow and at the end of September brought a column of Russian prisoners of war and some booty back from there. Otherwise, they were left behind at numerous rear area points as security forces.[115]

The battalions stationed further to the rear (in Dorogobusch, Vyasma and Gschatsk) were relieved by units from other Army Corps and moved closer to Moschaisk.[116] One searched for the sick and wounded who could be transported back to Smolensk.

After General Tharreau's death, a single Westphalian division with three brigades (Danloup-Verdun,[117] Legras and Borstel) was formed from the remaining troops. All

111 According to Giesse, p. 123, about 3,500 wounded.

112 Borcke, p. 188, gives the number of present for duty on the evening of 6 September as only 1,500 men "in shattered condition" (*"in zerrüttetem Zustand"*). This can only be explained with a very high number of dispersed and missing.

113 Boedicker, p. 273 and Linsingen, p. 284

114 *"Westphälischer Moniteur"* of 7 and 10 October 1812.

115 In Szelkovka Captain Brethauer of Light Battalion II; in Kubinskoe Captain Wolf from Light Battalion IIIone with one detachment each; in Perchuszkovo Lieutenant Colonel Rauschenplatt with Light Battalion I; in Buzayeva Captain Bardeleben of the 3rd Infantry Regiment with one company and in Prokosewo (west of Moschaisk) two Companies of the 2nd Infantry Regiment, cf. Giesse, p. 124.

116 cf. Giesse, p. 126 and 129ff. Giesse also describes the transport of Russian prisoners of war of whom many who could not go any further were executed by the accompanying troops.

117 General Danloup-Verdun arrived at the corps the end of September, at the 8th Infantry Regiment in October Hohenhausen, p. 259.

Jaeger Carbiniers in the Battle of Borodino
Förster Fleck's Story of his Fate on Napoleon's Campaign to Russia *(Förster Flecks Erzählung von seinen Schicksalen auf dem Zuge Napoleons nach Rußland)*, Cologne 1912.

of General von Ochs' efforts went toward making the division combat ready again. Moschaisk was secured against the threat of fire, and the grain from the surrounding fields was harvested and milled. So during those six weeks, Moschaisk was at least secured against the most urgent shortages. Any surpluses were used for the wounded who lay by the thousands in the Kolotzkoi Monastery (near the Borodino battlefield), which had been converted, to a field hospital. Also some foraging parties were conducted a little further afield in the area. To do this, increasingly stronger detachments (up to entire battalions with cannon) were put together, because the Russian militia was active and smaller detachments were neutralized. Many useful measures that von Ochs planned remained unaccomplished, because the Corps Commander, Junot, refused approval unless he received justifications.

Because of increasing Russian attacks, Junot had detached the Jaeger Guard Battalion (under Major von Picot) to Ruza and the 1st battalion of the 6th Infantry Regiments (under Colonel Ruelle) with both regimental cannon to Vereya. Both battalions were located too far away for the main corps to support them in a timely manner in case of danger. Since this did not escape the Russians' notice, the 1st battalion of the 6th Infantry Regiments in Vereya was attacked by a detachment under General Dorochov during the night of 10/11 October, overpowered despite fierce resistance and taken into captivity.[118] A Westphalian relief column under Colonel Bernard came too late to prevent the disaster.

The Retreat from Russia

Napoleon, who remained in Moscow for almost six weeks based on Russian misleading peace proposals, decided on 18 October to withdraw from the city. On October 19, the French left Moscow and initially directed their march to the southwest. On 24 October, Kutuzov used the Russian Army to block the path of the French Army. In the bloody battle at Malo Yaroslavetz Napoleon was unable to force a breakthrough. On 26 October, the French Emperor decided to march further to the northwest and at Moschaisk to take the great Military Road to Smolensk. With this decision to take the army back on the old route into Russia and thus through completely exhausted regions, the fate of the *Grand Armée* was sealed.

On 28 October, Napoleon passed Moschaisk. The Westphalian Army Corps received orders to make room for the approaching corps and to march ahead as the advance guard of the *Grand Armée*.[119] At this time, VIII

118 Conrady, p. 291-307. Conrady, the battalion commander, remained a Russian prisoner until the beginning of 1814. On the King's orders, the 6th Regiment was not raised again after the Russian campaign.

119 For the following, cf. Hohenhausen, p. 263ff.

Westphalian Cuirassiers in the Battle of Borodino
Detail from the painting by Peter Hess, Artillery Museum, St. Petersburg.

Corps was only about 5,000 – 6,000 men strong. Some of the 19 infantry battalions only had 300 - 500 men; similarly the Light Cavalry Brigade was only reinforced to 600 men. The artillery moved all the cannon (except for those not lost at Vereya). Only the Westphalian Cuirassier Brigade, under Murat, that had been located on the Nara (south of Moscow), could be considered as destroyed.

The Westphalian Corps hurried in forced marches - i.e., so well as the already malnourished soldiers were able – in the direction of Vyasma. On 28 October they passed the gruesome Borodino battlefield and reached Vyasma in relatively good order on 31 October. Up to then, the food supplies brought from Moschaisk has sufficed. But despite all promises, there were no provisions on hand in the stores in Vyasma, so the troops had to suffer even more on the following march toward Smolensk. Every day sick and exhausted soldiers were left behind to starve. On 5 November the first snow fell (near Dorogobusch). With that the suffering became unfathomable. In the bivouacs on the snow, without food, blankets or tents, countless men died every night. Discipline began to dissolve, small groups departed at any time to search for food. Many of these foragers never returned because they were killed or captured by embittered peasants or patrolling Cossacks. The Train wagons and cannon could only be moved on the snow and ice with great exertion, since the horses were exhausted and not adequately shoed. Every night 50 to 100 men had to be detailed to guard Junot and his baggage, and dozens of them froze to death. This mistreatment only ended when General von Ochs complained about it to Marshal Berthier.

VIII Corps arrived at Smolensk on 9 November with barely 1,500 men. Around Smolensk, bit by bit, all the Westphalian cannon had to be spiked and left standing, and the ammunition wagons blown up[120] because they could not be transported over the icy heights. On 12 November, the Westphalians departed Smolensk for Orcha. Three battalions were formed from the remaining troops in order to have tactically functioning formations. At Krasnoi, Russian units threw themselves in front of the Westphalian advance guard on 15 November[121] and

120 See Wesemann, p. 52f.

121 According to Borcke, p. 202, on 16 November.

blocked the single road for the retreat. The Westphalians led by von Ochs were able to break through with a desperate attack. On 16 November, they reached the old Russian border at Liady again and for the first time for weeks the troops could be properly housed and fed. On 19 November another 400 or so Westphalians crossed the Dniepr at Orcha in formation.[122] Among them were about 100 horsemen of the Westphalian Light Cavalry, who General von Hammerstein had kept together and had led mostly on side roads where they could find meager food and places to spend the nights.

The already bitterly cold temperatures eased up somewhat at Orcha, so that all who had trudged there could take heart again. Also the other conditions got somewhat better, e.g., one could purchase food and converse with the Jewish inhabitants they met, who mostly spoke a kind of German dialect. At the same time, fresh troops of the corps had been coming to support those from Moscow arrived, so that the pressure from the pursuing Russians abated somewhat. On 22 November they reached Bobr and formed an approximately 300-man strong battalion under Lieutenant Colonel Rauschenplatt (previously the Battalion Commander of the Light Infantry Battalion I) using the remnants of the Westphalian infantry there. At Bobr, General von Ochs ordered that all Westphalian flags be removed from their flagstaffs and handed over to the battalions' commanders or their deputies.

The next objective was to reach Borissov on the Berezina. When Napoleon learned that a Russian Army coming from the south had taken Borissov and burned the bridges there, he decided to deceive the Russians and to cross the Berezina on two quickly erected trestle bridges at Studyanka, a few kilometers north of Borissov. The remainder of the Westphalians, who had arrived there, crossed the Berezina on 27 November in the midst of an indescribable chaos of fleeing people of all kinds. With this, any organization of the Westphalian forces ended; except for almost 100-man strong cavalry unit under Hammerstein, all the other soldiers were on their own, even though from 1,000 to 1,500 Westphalians had been able to save themselves on the west bank of the Berezina. On the 14-day march via Zembin (28 November) and Smorgoni (where Napoleon left the Army) to Vilnius (8/9 December) the rest of the Westphalian troops perished, above all because the cold had increased.[123] Shortly before Vilnius the 4th Westphalian Infantry Regiment, that had participated in conjunction with VI Corps (Bavarian), met with the ruins of the *Grand Armée*. It was still in relatively good condition but was pulled into the vortex of the defeat through the fighting at Vilnius. After a brief pause in Vilnius the last survivors attempted to reach the Russian border at Kaunas. Almost all the remaining wagons and sleds had to be abandoned shortly behind Vilnius at the narrow pass in the Ponary Mountains. Those who were able to save themselves crossing the Neman at Kaunas on 12-13 were lucky! Many also fell into the hands of the Cossacks even so far east as in Prussia and the Grand Duchy of Warsaw.[124] Indeed anyone who could reach Schirwind (present Kutuzovo, Kaliningrad, Russia) in East Prussia could take a sigh of relief because the Westphalians generally were treated well by the Prussian population. The remnants of VIII Corps were directed to Thorn (present Torun) thanks to posted directional signs. Up until 8 January 1813, 184 Westphalian officers and 683 enlisted troops arrived there.[125] Half of the enlisted belonged to the 4th Infantry Regiment mentioned above, of whom only part had participated in the Russian campaign and therefore had suffered less. Besides them, the 1st Infantry Regiment returned relatively intact. It had been located with X Corps (Prussians and Poles under Marshal Macdonald) during the entire campaign and returned with 46 officers and 888 enlisted personnel[126] to fortified Danzig. Danzig was soon surrounded by the Russians and besieged until the end of 1813.

122 A moving scene happened here: General von Ochs was taken to a seriously ill Westphalian officer, and recognized him as his own son. He was able to take his son with him and transport him back home. cf. Hohenhausen, p. 271f, and Borcke.

123 On 7 and 8 December temperatures far below minus 20 degrees Celsius prevailed, cf. Hohenhausen, p. 276. The soldiers could no longer touch their firearms without sticking to them. Other sources report that birds fell dead out of the sky from the extreme cold.

124 For example, Westphalian *Rittmeister* Baumann of the *Garde-Chevaulegers*, among others, see Baumann, p. 175ff.

125 Description in Giesse, p. 315.

126 Lünsmann, p. 313.

The Reorganization in Thorn, Beginning of 1813

In Thorn a column of 1,294 replacements under Colonel von Boecking ran into the ruins of the Westphalian Army Corps. It consisted of depot personnel from the 1st, 2nd, 3rd, 5th, 6th and 7th Infantry Regiments and three light battalions, the light cavalry regiments and the artillery.[127] General Hammerstein took command of the horsemen of the relief column and set off for Westphalia with them and about 90 cavalrymen whom he had brought back from Russia. On 15 January, two so-called "March Regiments" ("*Marsch Regimenter*") were formed from all the able-bodied Westphalian infantry in Thorn. Colonel von Goeben temporarily took command of the 1st March Regiment, Major von Winkel took the 2nd March Regiment. General von Füllgraf commanded the brigade that was formed from the two regiments. All the non-able-bodied and excess officers (108) and soldiers (402) were sent to the Kingdom of Westphalia. On 31 January (per the Order of 16 January), the two March Regiments received the designations as the 4th and 5th Line Infantry Regiments ("*4. and 5. Linien-Infanterie Regiment*"). Major von Winkel was relieved of command of the 4th Infantry Regiment by Count (*Graf*) Seyboldsdorf and also returned to Westphalia. On 12 February both regiments formed up to march to Küstrin (present Kostrzyn, Poland). On 18 February in Wrietzen (Neumark), Russian Lieutenant Colonel von Benkendorf with 500 Cossacks attacked Colonel von Seyboldsdorf with part of the troops and a large portion of the young, inexperienced men were taken prisoner. The rest of both regiments arrived as reinforcements for the French who occupied the (actually Prussian) Küstrin Fortress and were besieged there by Prussian forces until early 1814. On 20 March 1814, the fortress surrendered to the Prussians, about five months after the dissolution of the Kingdom of Westphalia.

Jaeger Carabiniers Being Taken Prisoner by Cossacks
Förster Fleck's Story of his Fate on Napoleon's Campaign to Russia *(Förster Flecks Erzählung von seinen Schicksalen auf dem Zuge Napoleons nach Rußland),* Cologne 1912.

127 Lünsmann, p. 308.

THE 1813 CAMPAIGN IN GERMANY

The Spring Campaign and the 1813 Ceasefire

From the beginning of the fateful year of 1813 the reorganization of the army was carried out under high pressure in the kingdom.[128] No state in the Confederation of the Rhine had more reason than Westphalia to do this, for the survival or extinction of the country and its ruling class depended on the coming campaign.[129] Through the exploitation of all available resources and the Military Administration's more intense activity, it was possible to begin reestablishing the Army. Each Military Division had a Division or Brigadier General as its commander to whom all troops located in the Division's area were subordinated. Furthermore, the Commander of the Military Division had a *Gendarmerie* squadron available. Each Division was divided into two Departments, which as a rule had a Brigadier General or Colonel commanding, although sometimes also the Division Commandant (compare with the Orders of Battle Appendix). A connection to the so-called "High Police" ("*Hohen Polizei*")[130] was made certain to guarantee the problem-free calling up of recruits and the ability to nip in the bud any possible unrest by the populace.

The depots (ca. 7,000 men) that remained behind during the 1812 Russian Campaign were available as the foundation for the new organization:

- 8 Battalions (each of four companies) from the Line Infantry
- 7 Depot companies from the Guard and from the Jaeger-Carabiniers Battalion
- 6 Cavalry squadron depots
- The Artillery Depot

In addition there were those troops conscripted in 1812 along with 6,000 recruits who were called into service per the decree of March 8, 1813. In the workshops, especially the foundry in Kassel, people worked nonstop to replace the military materiel lost in Russia.

Thanks to these exertions until May-June a considerable portion of the Westphalian Army could be mobilized and sent to Saxony to join the French *Grand Armée*. This included:

- The Queen's Regiment (*Regiment der Königin*) (Guard Fusiliers - *Füsiliergarde*)[131]
- 2nd, 3rd, 8th and 9th Infantry Regiments[132]
- Light Infantry Battalions I, II and IV
- Chevaulegers-Garde
- 1st and 2nd Hussar Regiments
- Three 6-pounder foot batteries, one 6-pounder horse battery, each with 6 cannon

According to authorized strengths, this came to 15,960 infantry, 1,350 cavalry, and 824 artillerymen, for a total of 18,134 men. Napoleon supposedly questioned the loyalty of the Westphalian troops and – as opposed to in the 1812 campaign – mixed the Westphalian regiments into various corps of the *Grand Armée*.

Besides the usual depots of the units that had deployed to the field, forces that remained in the Kingdom of Westphalia were the 7th Infantry Regiment, Light Infantry Battalion III, both cuirassier regiments, parts of the Artillery Regiment and the Guard Brigade. Per the Imperial Decree of 6 August 1813, Jérôme received a hussar regiment as a present from Napoleon.[133] Also there were Veterans- and Departmental Companies and the *Gendarmerie*. All the units were pulled together in Kassel, Braunschweig, Berka, Magdeburg, Melsungen and Ziegenhain; the rest of the country was stripped of forces.

No actual fighting by the Westphalian Army in a battle during the early 1813 campaign has been documented.[134] On 1 April 1813, a mobile corps under the command of Major General von Hammerstein set off to protect Westphalia's eastern border and the access to the kingdom via the Harz Mountains from the Allies' roving *Streifkorps* ("Patrolling or flying corps").[135] In this way, the Westphalian Army experienced a number of misfortunes.[136] On 16 April, a squadron of Chevaulegers

128 For a general description of the "Wars of Liberation" (*Befreiungskriege*) cf. Friederich 1913.

129 For the history of the Westphalian Army throughout 1813 cf. Specht. Additionally Kleinschmidt and Hohenhausen provide numerous details.

130 As in the political arm of the police (Secret Police - *Geheimpolizei*).

131 Newly raised by the Decree of 15 August 1812.

132 We remind the reader that the 1st, 4th and 5th Infantry Regiments were located in the Danzig and Küstrin Fortresses, cf. Bauer and Giesse. The 6th Infantry Regiment was not raised again.

133 However it arrived in Kassel mostly without mounts and had to be organized (as part of the Westphalian Guard) throughout August and September, see Stein.

134 Except for the Guard Light Horse *(Garde-Chevauleger)* Regiment. This unit took part in the Battle of Grossgoerschen and a few smaller skirmishes in Saxony, see Lehsten, p. 99ff.

135 Consisting of two battalions of the Guard Fusiliers, Light Battalions II and IV, two squadrons of the *Chevauleger-Garde*, two squadrons from each of the two hussar regiments and two artillery batteries, cf. Lünsmann, p. 315 and Borcke, p. 250.

136 See Kleinschmidt, p. 574ff among others.

under Lieutenant Colonel von Göcking was attacked and taken prisoner by the Russians at Bleicherode. On 18 April, Prussian Major von Hellwig surprised the village of Wanfried, where a company of Westphalian light Infantry and the 2nd Squadron of the 2nd Hussar Regiment were located. About 50 Westphalian infantrymen and 80 hussars, with 100 horses, surrendered without a fight.[137] On 19 April another three officers and 103 men of the *Garde-Chevaulegers* were taken prisoner by Russian patrols. Additionally, Russian Major von Löwenstern, commander of several Cossack regiments, was able to destroy a Westphalian weapons factory in Herzberg in the Harz and take a large quantity of edged weapons as booty.[138]

A few weeks later, on 30 May 1813, a Westphalian-French march column under the command of General von Ochs (Commander of the 3rd Military Division), that was escorting an artillery park, was surrounded by a Russian "*Streifkorps*" ("Patrolling" or "flying" corps) under General Chernyshyov at Halberstadt. Besides von Ochs, who was wounded, about 550 men were taken prisoner, and the Russians captured 14 cannons, some ammunition wagons and 800 horses.[139] However, with the entry into effect of the ceasefire of 4 June 1813, further attacks were initially averted.

At the beginning of May, von Hammerstein`s corps joined the *Grand Armée*. It was divided there with the infantry and artillery going to the *Grand Armée's* XI Corps as the Lageon Brigade (see the Orders of Battle Appendix). Von Hammerstein returned to Kassel – but not with a rank corresponding to his command. An additional Westphalian division under Major General Danloup-Verdun was dispatched to the field the end of June and also divided up in July. A part of these forces were posted in the Torgau Fortress; the rest marched to Dresden where the Westphalian Bernard Brigade was formed from the infantry and artillery. General Danloup-Verdun remained – now without a command – at the Imperial Headquarters in Dresden until the beginning of September.[140]

The Autumn Campaign in Silesia and Saxony up to the Battle of Nations at Leipzig

The ceasefire between France and the Allies expired on 17 August 1813. The first drumbeat for the Westphalian Army sounded the end of August. During the night of 22 to 23 August, two squadrons each of the 1st Hussar Regiment (2nd and 3rd squadrons) and the 2nd Hussar Regiment (1st and 3rd squadrons) at Reichenberg in Silesia under the leadership of their commanders Colonel William von Hammerstein and Major von Pentz went over to the enemy en masse. The remaining squadrons of the 1st (1st squadron) and 2nd (2nd squadron) Hussar Regiments allowed themselves - intentionally – to be taken captive by the Austrians at Freiberg on 18 September. Jérôme, who feared further treason, arrested many officers of both hussar regiments and their families[141] and had both hussar regiments' standards publicly burned in Ziegenhain. Another notable incident was the September 1813 defection of a battalion of the 3rd Infantry Regiment under Lieutenant Colonel Bretthauer.[142]

On the other hand, the Bernard Brigade in Dresden successfully participated in the defense of the city during the two-day Battle of Dresden on 26-27 August 1813. Special laurels went to the Westphalian artillery under Colonel Pfuhl, to whom Napoleon personally tipped his hat.[143] To boost the motivation of the Westphalians, the Emperor incorporated a battalion under Major Pasor (from the remnants of the Guard Fusiliers, four grenadier companies of the 2nd and 3rd Infantry Regiments) and the Normann Foot Battery into the French Guard.[144] The battalion ultimately fought in the Battle of Nations at Leipzig from 16 to 19 October.

In September the 2nd Infantry Regiment (originally part of the Bernard Brigade) accompanied a large artillery and ammunition park to Dresden, where it remained, was later disarmed, and on 11 November – after the handover of the fortress to the Allies – was disbanded.[145]

137 Fabricius, p. 57ff. It is indicative of the Westphalian soldier' lack of loyalty that many of the prisoners immediately joined the Prussian Army. Also the number of desertions in Westphalia increased significantly with the news of the Russians' and Prussians' advances as described in Borcke, p. 249 and Specht, p. 82ff.

138 Löwenstern, Vol. 2, p. 13.

139 For more details see Hohenhausen, p. 292ff.

140 According to Borcke, p. 264.

141 The most prominent prisoner was Major General Hans von Hammerstein, brother of Colonel William von Hammerstein. General von Hammerstein was initially taken to the French fortress in Metz, then in the Kastell of Ham, and was finally released just after the capture of Paris in 1814, cf. Hartmann, p. 50.

142 See Kleinschmidt, p. 601.

143 For details see Normann, p. 8ff. Colonel Pfuhl (also spelled Pfuel) and Lieutenant Normann were recommended to be awarded the Officer's Cross *(Offizierskreuz)* and Cross of the Legion of Honor (Kreuz der Ehrenlegion) respectively for their bravery.

144 cf. Specht, p. 71.

145 According to Morgenstern, p. 128f. The bitter separation of the German and French elements of the Westphalian Army after the handover of Dresden on 11 November 1813 is described movingly there. The French nationals became prisoners of war while as a rule the Germans returned to their respective homelands (Prussia, Kurhessen, Brunswick and Hannover, among others) and got positions there in newly created formations in order to fight against France in the 1814 campaign.

The Chevauleger-Garde as part of XII Corps (Oudinot) had a separate fate. It took part in the costly battles of Grossbeeren (however without actual combat there), Dennewitz and Leipzig. The rest of the regiment then marched to Kassel where the regiment was disbanded.

The fate of the Westphalian Lageon Brigade was similar. It fought as part of XI Corps (Macdonald) in Silesia and Saxony and was also disbanded after the Battle of Nations at Leipzig.

The history of Westphalian 1st, 4th, 5th and 9th Infantry Regiments that were trapped in the fortresses at Danzig, Küstrin and Magdeburg is described in the Orders of Battle Appendix.

The Events in the Kingdom until October 1813

The Prussian Attack on Braunschweig

On 22 September 1813, Prussian Lieutenant Colonel von d. Marwitz with the 3rd *Kurmärkischen*[146] Militia (*Landwehr*) Cavalry Regiment (about 400 men) crossed the Elbe below Magdeburg and marched toward Braunschweig, not without first having deceived the enemy about his true objective by detouring via Neuhaldensleben and vicinity of the Magdeburg Fortress.[147] On 25 September, Marwitz arrived in front of Braunschweig after a forced march via Borsfelde.

In Braunschweig, Brigadier General von Klösterlein, commanded the 2nd Military Division (see the Orders of Battle Appendix). He had the following forces available: a veterans company under Bn. Commander Duroi,[148] a Departmental company under Bn. Commander Stutzer (40 men), a detachment of Gendarmes (about 16 men), the depots of four Line infantry regiments (about 620 men), the depot of the Jaeger-Carabiniers under Captain Metzner (approximately 70 men) and a still unarmed detachment of a combined Lippe-Waldeck Regiment (circa 250-300 men). The City Commandant was Gendarmerie Brigadier, Lieutenant Colonel Hartert. The morale of the troops was rather poor (except for the longer serving NCOs and Gendarmes), so that their actual fighting capability was far below how their numerical strength of about 1,000 men might appear.

Major von Lossberg with the Depot of the 3rd Infantry Regiments stationed in Braunschweig told General Klösterlein about Braunschweig's vulnerable situation and the populace's hostile attitude[149] and suggested pulling back the available troops to more easily defended Wolfenbüttel.[150] Klösterlein, who underestimated the danger from the Allies' "flying corps" at first could only decide to evacuate the magazine and transport the officers' baggage wagons via Salzgitter to Kassel. However, shortly after their departure about 6 o'clock in the morning of 25 September, General Klösterlein changed his mind and departed with the troops toward Wolfenbüttel. Initially only a few sentries and the weak Jaeger-Carabiniers Company, under the command of the oldest staff officer, Colonel von Bork, stayed behind In Braunschweig.

Marwitz, who was waiting in front of the city to gather more intelligence, decided to attack Braunschweig after Klösterlein's departure. The few remaining

146 Specht on p. 97 mistakenly mentions the 3rd *neumärkische* Landwehr-Cavalry Regiment.

147 We use the description in Specht, p. 97ff, Lünsmann, p. 319, and Marwitz, Vol. 1, p. 562f.

148 Alternate spelling: Düroi.

149 In 1809, during a short stop by the Duke Wilhelm von Brunswick in of the city, the population had clearly expressed their dislike of the Westphalian government.

150 Wolfenbüttel had walls and moats, so it was better protected against attacks.

sentries threw away their muskets after a weak defense; only at the August Gate (Augusttor) where Colonel von Bork was commanding did the Jaeger-Carabiniers put up a longer defense until they were overpowered and captured. Prussian Lieutenant Count (*Graf*) von Finkenstein was thereupon ordered to take fifty horsemen and pursue the Westphalian column marching to Wolfenbüttel and disrupt them as much as possible. Klösterlein, who had already reached Wolfenbüttel, was informed about the events in Braunschweig by a Gendarme and decided to immediately march further toward Goslar, although a defense of partially fortified Wolfenbüttel - especially against cavalry – would have been a better decision. In the vicinity of the village of Halchter the Westphalian march column was attacked from the rear by Prussian militia cavalry (*Landwehrreitern*) under Count (*Graf*) von Finkenstein. Finkenstein's shouted "You certainly would not fire on your German brothers!" sufficed so that the Westphalian soldiers threw away their weapons, ignoring Klösterlein's and his officers' orders to open fire.[151] The mounted Westphalian officers, realizing that further resistance was futile, put spurs to their horses and fled. The Prussians with their already fatigued horses were not able to pursue, so the Westphalians were able to escape. They turned toward Bielefeld, where in the coming days they learned of King Jérôme's flight from Kassel. In Bielefeld, after the recapture of Kassel, they received General Allix's order to go to the capital. In Braunschweig and at Halchter the Prussians captured about 25 officers (including Colonel von Bork) and 350 NCOs and soldiers,[152] the rest had fled. Using volunteers among the prisoners and from the pupils of the Brunswick Military School, Lt. Col. von d. Marwitz raised a volunteer jaeger squadron for the 3rd Kurmark Landwehr Cavalry Regiment (*3. kurmärkische Landwehr-Kavallerieregiment*). In Braunschweig a large number of Westphalians, so-called "recalcitrant" (*widerspenstigen*) and conscripted soldiers and deserters were freed from the prison. Also, some Secret Police (*Geheimpolizisten*) were arrested and taken to Berlin; there were even violent actions by the angry population against captured Westphalian officers. Marwitz confiscated 20,000 Taler from the Westphalian coffers and military equipment left behind, and departed in the direction of the Elbe. The Westphalian rule in Braunschweig and Luneburg lands was virtually ended.

The Russian's Taking of Kassel

In the evening of 28 September, people in Kassel got word of Marwitz´s attack on Braunschweig. Together with the existing intelligence from the theater of war in Saxony[153] (the allies were gradually pulling the noose around Napoleon ever tighter after the victories at Grossbeeren, on the Katzbach, at Kulm and Dennewitz), Jérôme accepted the situation was a disaster. At the same time, the King received news that Russian forces had appeared in the Harz Mountains again and their patrols ("*Streifkommandos*") had advanced as far as Mühlhausen and Nordhausen. Jérôme decided to send his orderly officer, Colonel von Hessberg, to Generals von Bastineller[154] and von Zandt to let them know about the impending dangers and in case of a threat to Kassel, to order them to come there. Certainly no one in the capital figured that a large enemy *Streifkorps* of appreciable size could advance on Kassel unobserved and surprise the capital. The Westphalian forces available in Kassel the end of September are shown orders of Battle.

From the Allies' side, as already mentioned, several *Streifkorps* were active in the French Army's rear.[155] The corps under Russian General Chernyshyov, that operated in conjunction with the Northern Army under Crown Prince Karl Johann of Sweden, belonged to them.[156] General Chernyshyov had already made a name for himself as a *Streifkorps* commander in the 1812 Russian and the early 1813 campaigns.[157] Chernyshyov, located in Bernburg an der Saale (Bernburg on the Saale River), had – probably in mid- September – recommended to the Crown Prince to attack Kassel. The Crown Prince accepted this recommendation under the condition that Chernyshyov had to return within two weeks. Additionally, the Crown Prince assigned to the general some officers knowledgeable of the area to facilitate as much as possible the difficult mission. Among these officers was also a Major von Dörnberg, brother of the former Westphalian, Colonel Wilhelm von Dörnberg, mentioned earlier.[158] Chernyshyov had a detachment conduct a patrol in the direction of Nordhausen to divert Bastineller's attention there. Simultaneously he skirted to the south of the road from Heiligenstadt to Nordhausen and in the course of 26 September marched by way of Sondershausen to Mühlhausen. There he feigned being the advance guard of a strong corps force. Chernyshyov carefully had anyone passing through the area detained so news of his arrival would not spread. On the 27th,

151 *"Ihr werdet doch nicht auf eure deutsche Brüder feuern!"* Present, were Major von Lossberg, Major von Winkel (Winckel), Lieutenant Colonel Hartert, Squadron Commander von Schenk, Squadron Commander von Schmidt and Captain Grinzky, amongothers.

152 According to Marwitz, more than 600 prisoners.

153 The Westphalian government attempted in any case to suppress all news that was unfavorable to the French, while Napoleon's victory at Dresden was exaggerated. Most of the population was informed about the true situation only through rumors, cf. Specht, p. 136.

154 Bastineller was located at Heiligenstadt and observed the road toward Nordhausen.

155 The Thielemann, Mensdorff-Pouilly, Platow, Hellwig, Colomb, Marwitz, Tettenborn flying corps (*Streifkorps*) among others.

156 The former French Marshal Bernadotte.

157 We remind the reader that he among others took Westphalian General von Ochs prisoner at Halberstadt in early 1813, see above.

158 It was planned that Major von Dörnberg would form a battalion for the English King's German Legion from Westphalian line-crossers.

Chernyshyov made a further forced march of about seventy kilometers[159] via Wanfried, Eschwege and Waldkappel to Kassel. He arrived there – under cover of a thick fog – about 6:00 o'clock on the morning of 28 September. However, in the meantime, earlier that morning - about 4:00 o'clock, personnel in Kassel had been warned because the authorities In Mühlhausen had sent a courier there.[160]

Westphalian Major General von Bongars, who was also the Police Commander, received the Gendarme's news and immediately informed the King. Jérôme gave the alarm to the palace guards (sixty men of the Guard Grenadiers under Captain von Specht). Then he went into the city where he assembled the generals and some higher officials. Some hastily cobbled together units[161] were assigned under the command of Major Boedicker, later under Brigadier General Danloup-Verdun, to occupy the entrances to the city and to do reconnaissance.

The hussars sent out to reconnoiter very soon encountered a Cossack detachment of around 200 men and were thrown back to the Jaeger Guards. The 6th Company of the Jaeger Guards formed a *tirailleur* (skirmish) line with Soutiens[162] at the so-called "Forst" (woods south of the city), while the 2nd Company stood in close formation for their support, somewhat to the rear on the road leading to the woods. The four remaining companies and two cannons were in reserve (i.e., further to the rear) on the bridge over the Wahlebach. The Russians also brought up two cannons, fired grapeshot at the 6th Company and then attacked with their cavalry. Whereupon the mostly young Westphalian recruits ran in different directions and tried to escape. Some of them, including Captain von Hugo, were able to pull back to the village of Bettenhausen to rejoin the bulk of the battalion.

The Russians seized the six cannon that were located at the Forst but that no one among the Westphalians were thinking about. The fighting then came to a standstill at the Wahlebach stream, where Major Boedicker was in command, and there was a small pause in the fighting. About 9:00 o'clock, the Russians attacked again and bypassed the Westphalians. Major Boedicker, who had already feared a flanking maneuver and therefore already sent back four companies, started the withdrawal to the so-called *Siechenhof*, in front of the Leipziger Tor (Kassel's eastern city gate). Both Westphalian cannon fell into the hands of the advancing Russians because some of the gun crews were dead, and some were trying to pull the cannon back with ropes. The Russians also quickly overpowered the resistance at the Leipziger Gate (many Westphalians threw down their weapons and tried to flee),[163] so the bridge over the Wahlebach stream was captured on the first assault. The Russians captured entire companies.[164]

The fighting now shifted to Kassel's city walls, which were occupied by the remainder of the Westphalian infantry. At the same time, Major Boedicker and Lieutenant Colonel von Lepel had the Fulda Bridge blocked with manure wagons in order to erect a barricade, and have it manned by infantry and dismounted Jérôme-Napoleon Hussars. Around 10:00 o'clock the Russians succeeded in storming the Leipziger Gate and to shift the fighting into Kassel's Unterneustadt (Lower New City) district. Next they took the Kastell (castle) and fired on the barricade on the Fulda Bridge. A firefight now developed on the bridge, through which the citizenry of the Altneustadt (Old New City) district – that is on the Fulda's left bank still held by Westphalians - became restless and decided to disarm the Jérôme-Napoleon Hussars. Westphalian Captain von Berlepsch even needed to threaten some citizens at gunpoint in order to keep his back open. About 11:00 the Russians pulled back out of the Unterneustadt district leaving four dead in the square.[165]

While the fighting described above was playing out in Kassel's east side, Jérôme had any available forces[166] on the other side of the city assemble on the street leading to Frankfurt. A war council was held In the palace; finally the king decided to leave Kassel via the Frankfurt road and to take up a position behind Niederzwehren so as not to be captured in the city. Indeed, contributing to this decision were, above all, the lack of any urgently awaited news from General Bastineller as well as reports that Cossacks had already crossed the Fulda at many places and were patrolling in the direction of the Frankfurt road. Couriers were sent to Generals von Zandt and Bastineller in order to hasten their arrival at Kassel. Major General Allix, as governor of the city,

---

159 In total, Chernyshyov covered about 180 kilometers in three days – also a considerable achievement for cavalry, especially when one considers that they also took along cannon.

160 Chernyshyov had Cossacks pursue the courier and actually caught up with him just before Kassel. However, a Gendarme escorting the courier succeeded in escaping and brought the report to Kassel.

161 Among them were a platoon of the Jérôme-Napoleon-Hussars (30 men, commanded the King's Orderly, Lieutenant Colonel von Lepel), a detachment of Gendarmes and the 6th Company of the *Jaeger-Garde* under Captain von Hugo. The 2nd Company of the *Jaeger-Garde* (under Captain von Bardeleben) and finally the rest of the *Jaeger-Garde* Battalion eventually followed. Except for the officers and some older NCOs, these were almost exclusively young inexperienced troops.

162 Small, closed groups as reserves of the Tirailleurs (sharpshooters - *Schützen*).

163 The Westphalian senior leadership had failed to establish defenses for the Siechenhof, the gardens, the buildings, and even the city itself. This is at first incomprehensible because most of the Westphalian senior officers were experienced, battle-tested veterans, and it can only be explained as the result of the confusion from the surprise attack and the general mood.

164 Specht, p. 158.

165 Chernyshyov had received news that General Bastineller was on the way and had already occupied the village of Helsa.

166 The *Grenadier-Garde* Battalion, some companies of the Jaeger-Carabiniers, the Garde du Corps, the (mounted) remnants of the (Jérôme-Napoleon-) Guard Hussars and other parts of the garrison including eight cannons.

received the order to defend the city. As reports arrived essentially indicating that the Russians apparently had begun a wide flanking maneuver via the Nuremberg Road (Nürnberger Straße), it raised worries, so Jérôme gave an order to take up a new position further to the west. Thus the decision was made to retreat; Kassel was de facto given up by the King.[167] Jérôme, who was driven by impatience and worries finally road with his close associates (among them the French envoy) and the Garde du Corps in the lead, which evoked great dissatisfaction among the foot soldiers in his escort,[168] and the group hurried via Herborn, Wetzlar and Weilburg finally arriving at the secure Koblenz on the Rhine.

We return here in our story to General Bastineller's corps. On 26 September, the General, who was located with his forces at Heiligenstadt, received the news that Russian *Streifkorps* had been seen in the area. He dispatched patrols to Nordhausen and Mühlhausen and pulled his units closer together, in some cases in bivouacs in order to have the troops more readily available. The patrols that had been sent out could not clarify the actual situation, i.e., Chernyshyov's attack on Kassel, so that Bastineller was not immediately clear about the needed actions. In the course of 27 September, however, he decided to return to Kassel, the capital, because he correctly guessed that his presence there could be of great use in case the Russians had broken through. Now instead of taking the shortest route via Kaufungen, he let himself be scared by the possibly dangerous movement through the defiles there and decided to use a time-consuming and difficult indirect route via Lichtenau, Spangenberg and Morschen, to get to the Kassel-Frankfurt road. This march on byways resulted in the march column being stretched out and gave more and more soldiers the opportunity to desert. During 29 September, the march finally degenerated more and more into a stampede. In the end, from the two cuirassier regiments only forty men (mostly officers and NCOs) arrived in Friedberg, the infantry got to Wetzlar in similarly reduced numbers.[169] Thus General Bastineller's attempt at relief failed. A similar attempt by General von Zandt, who was at Göttingen, had the same outcome.[170]

On the other hand, Chernyshyov was also uncertain what to do after his first withdrawal from Kassel. He was aware that his rear area was threatened by General Bastineller's and General Zandt's corps that could cut off his communication to the east. Therefore, Chernyshyov cautiously withdrew toward Melsungen. When he learned from the Melsungen inhabitants and deserters from Bastineller´s corps who were now incorporated there about the corps' dissolution, he decided to halt at Melsungen and have a detachment of 100 Cossacks under Ensign Sebastyanoff follow the remnants of Bastineller´s corps. Among other things, Sebastyanoff succeeded in capturing twenty Westphalian cuirassiers at Rothenburg. Additionally he was able to recover both of the Bastineller corps' cannon from the Fulda River. Furthermore, during these days, Chernyshyov organized a 300-man infantry battalion from Westphalian line-crossers and volunteers that would be of use to him in a renewed assault on Kassel.

As of 29 September, there were still about 350 mounted soldiers and around 500 infantrymen, artillery and Gendarmes, in total 850 men, under General Allix's command in Kassel. Allix tried to weaken the adverse impact on his soldiers' morale from the Russian attacks and that day he inserted a proclamation in the *"Westphälischen Moniteur."* However, he did not direct any serious defensive measures, e.g., erecting barricades, presumably because he no longer considered the Westphalian troops to be reliable.

On 30 September, Chernyshyov deployed anew with his cavalry corps, reinforced with ten captured cannon and 300 Infantrymen to take the Westphalian capital. About 13:00, he reached Kassel, where rumors of his renewed approach were already circulating. The remnants of the Kassel garrison, under the command of General von Schlotheim, assisted by Lieutenant Colonel von Stockmayer of the General Staff, were ready for the defense. As already mentioned above, this was about 850 men, reinforced with four cannon in front of the Friedrichstor. After a brief rest, an artillery duel began in which the Russians with their thirteen cannon quickly gained the upper hand. Numerous Russian cannonballs crashed into the city and killed and wounded some Westphalian soldiers. This led the citizenry, who were already upset about the coming events, to be alarmed. Many burghers demanded that the Westphalian commanders surrender the city in order to spare lives and property; they even went so far as wanting to open the gates to the enemy. After the Russians sent forward

167 Specht, p. 170, comments: "This unhappy condition, in its results for the king, which with less fear of the Russians and more calm consideration would have certainly had no influence on him or his counselors... dissolved the Kingdom four weeks earlier than would otherwise have been the case. *("Diese in ihren Folgen für den König unglückliche Voraussetzung, die bei weniger Angst vor den Russen und mehr ruhiger Überlegung gewiss keinen Einfluss auf ihn und seine Umgebung erlangt haben würde, (...) löste das Königreich 4 Wochen früher auf als es sonst der Fall gewesen wäre.")*.

168 On the first day's march to Wabern, the Grenadier Guards already lost one third of its personnel through desertion. Only 180 Grenadiers arrived in Marburg, only 100 in Wetzlar. The situation was similar with the Garde du Corps

169 Bastineller's two cannon were sunk in the Fulda River at Melsungen.

170 As an example, the battalion of the 7th Infantry Regiment, located with von Zandt´s corps, lost over 600 of its 816 men through desertion.

their infantry with two cannons, a Westphalian company went over to them. The nervous Kassel residents disarmed the defenders at the Fulda Bridge and pushed away the remaining obstacles. With that, the attackers stood with this side of the city wide open. But first a resolute counterattack by the remainder of the 7th Infantry Regiment under Major von Meibom restored the situation. Meanwhile, Chernyshyov sent a negotiator to Allix to suggest an orderly handover of the city. Allix agreed to the suggestion after a few negotiations because he could no longer hold the city given the mood of the population, the condition of the Westphalian forces and the dwindling hope of relief by the king. The capitulation consisted essentially of the following points:

4. Departure of the French and Westphalian forces with purely military baggage, however without cannon on the evening of 30 September.
5. Kassel would be occupied by Russian troops on the same evening.
6. A Cossack regiment would escort the departing French and Westphalians two "*Meilen*"[171] outside of Kassel.

Allix signed the capitulation document at sunset and about 19:00 marched away with his few remaining troops on the road to Arolsen. Allix released the Westphalians who marched out with him to either accompany him to the Rhine or to go back to the capital; the majority preferred the latter. A portion of the Westphalian soldiers and officers had also remained Kassel because they had not learned of the concluded capitulation.

On 1 October, Chernyshyov formally entered Kassel. In the following days, he let Dörnberg form a volunteer battalion of 1,000 men for the (English) King's German Legion, from former Westphalian soldiers among others. A large portion of the Westphalian officers who stayed behind even gave the Russian city commandant a written oath of honor to no fight against the Allies.

Chernyshyov quickly came to the decision to pull back to the Northern Army because it was clear to him that Kassel, being very far forward, could not be held against a French attempt to recapture it.[172] He guessed correctly that the forces of Marshal Kellermann, who was in Mainz overseeing the establishment of the French Reserve Corps, were deploying. Therefore the last Russians (the City Commandant Raschanovitsch with some Cossacks) hurriedly left the city on 4 October.

General Allix had remained in Marburg at the beginning of October. The King appointed him as his deputy (*lieutenant*) there. Kellermann sent him some hastily pulled together French units[173] for assistance under the command of Westphalian General Danloup-Verdun. On 7 October, General Allix reentered Kassel with these forces and the remnants of the Westphalian forces (two squadrons of Jérôme-Napoleon Hussars and some Garde du Corps). He immediately published a proclamation, had some people arrested[174] and reestablished order. On 8 and 9 October, strict orders were issued to gather together the scattered troops and materiel. On 12 October, regulations in the Military Law Book (*Militärgesetzbuch*) were reissued regarding instigation, forming groups, spying, hoarding of military materiel etc. in the kingdom. On 14 October, Allix issued a far stricter decree that any disturbance would carry a death penalty. On 16 October, the king entered his capital for the last time in order to return to his throne. But this was to no avail – the Kingdom was already in its death throes. On 25 October, Jérôme received definitive news that the French had lost the decisive battle at Leipzig. That same day, the French Honor Guards marched away through the Frankfurter Gate. In the morning of the next day, Jérôme called for the officers of the Grenadier Guards to come to him and granted all of them who desired to leave the service.[175] Shortly thereafter, the King left his capital for the second time, and this time forever. With that, the Kingdom of Westphalia collapsed.

171 Two German miles *(Meilen)* correspond to about 15 kilometers, or 9 U.S./U.K. miles.

172 The decisive battle in the German theater of war was still to come and fought from 16 to 19 October at Leipzig. This "Battle of Nations" (German: *"Völkerschlacht"*) was the catalyst for the complete evacuation of the French from Germany.

173 Many squadrons of French honor guards, lancers, dragoons and *chasseurs*, in addition to some artillery train and infantry; in total about 2,000 men, cf. Specht, p. 261.

174 Among them high-ranking officers, e.g., Lieutenant Colonel Boedicker. The prisoners mostly went into the Kastell.

175 Only one officer, Captain Kleinschmidt, did not leave. He was thereupon immediately promoted to Lieutenant Colonel and named the Orderly Officer to the King.

EPILOGUE: THE DISBANDING OF THE WESTPHALIAN ARMY

At the same time as the news of the defeat at the battle at Leipzig arrived, the remnants of the Westphalian field forces returned to Kassel. They were a modest little group, visibly having suffered the hardships of the spring and autumn campaigns in Saxony and Prussia. Some units never returned at all because they were bottled up in Dresden with Marshal St.-Cyr's French corps.

The officers who were still fit for field duty looked for the most part to immediately find other military positions. During the last months, many of them who had once loyally served King Jérôme were deeply conflicted between their duty to serve and their budding national patriotism.[176] Most of them went back to their old employment, mostly in the military service of the Electorate of Hessen,[177] Brunswick,[178] Hanover[179] or Prussia.[180] Others joined foreign allied[181] armies. A few officers remained true to King Jérôme and accompanied him to France.[182]

176 These internal struggles are movingly described by Borcke.

177 Among others Boedicker, Bauer, Lossberg, Müldner, Normann, Weiss, Ochs (after a few years).

178 E.g., Morgenstern.

179 Doernberg, Wuendenberg.

180 Conrady, Borcke, Bussche, Wagner.

181 E.g., Rueppell, who first returned from captivity in 1814 and joined the Austrian Army.

182 Colonel von Zurwesten and Colonel von Berger.

Guard Chevaulegers Fighting with the Hellwegischen Freikorps in the Autumn Campaign of 1813
Watercolor by Herbert Knötel, collection: Markus Gaertner.

105
104

APPENDICES

The End fof the Garde du Corps: The Guards' Equipment was used in the Carnival Parade in Cologne after 1815
(Das Ende der Garde du Corps: Ausrüstung der Gardisten wird nach 1815 im Karnevalsumzug in Köln genutzt)
Contemporary engraving by an unknown artist in the, Stadtmuseum Köln, photo: Markus Gaertner.

ORDERS OF BATTLE

Composition of the Westphalian Division for Spain, February 1809

Commander: Major General Morio[183]
Chief of the General Staff: Senior Major (*Gross-Major)* von Hessberg (later Colonel von Borstel)

1st Brigade Brigadier General Börner (later von Hadel)
2nd Westphalian Infantry Regiment (2 Bns.):[184] Colonel Legras (later Colonel von Bosse)
4th Westphalian Infantry Regiment (2 Bns.): Colonel von Benneville (later von Lassberg)

2nd Brigade Colonel von Ochs[185]
3rd Westphalian Infantry Regiment (2 Bns.): Colonel Zink
1st Light Bn.:[186] Bn.Commander von Meyern
Artillery (2 companies of foot artillery):[187] Bn. Commander Heinemann
Division total in May 1809: ca. 7,000 men

Composition of X Corps, April 1809[188]

Commander: Jérôme Napoleon, King of Westphalia
General Staff Chief: Major General Rewbell

1st Westphalian Guard Division: Major General Count *(Graf)* Bernterode (Ducoudras)
Garde du Corps, 1st Sqdn. (140 men): Brigadier General von Bongars
Grenadier-Garde, 1 Bn. (840 men): Colonel Langenschwarz
Jaeger-Garde, 1 Bn. (600 men): Major Füllgraf
Jaeger-Carabiniers, 1 Bn. (360 men): Prinz von Hessen-Philippsthal
Chevauleger-Garde, 3 Sqdns. (550 men): Colonel Wolff
Guard Division total: 2,490 men

2nd Westphalian Division: Major General D´Albignac
1st Westphalian Infantry Regiment (1,680 men): Colonel Vauthier
5th Westphalian Infantry Regiment (1,800 men): Colonel Graf Wellingerode (Meyronnet)[189]
6th Westphalian Infantry Regiment (1,700 men): Major-Commandant von Bosse
1st Westphalian Cuirassier Regiment, (260 horses): Colonel von Wurthen
Division total: 5,440 men

3rd The Dutch Division: Major General Gratien
6th Dutch Infantry Regiment
7th Dutch Infantry Regiment
8th Dutch Infantry Regiment
9th Dutch Infantry Regiment
2nd Dutch Cuirassier Regiment
3 Companiesof artillery
Division total: 5,300 men

4th Various forces on the march from Mainz: Colonel Chabert
3rd Berg Infantry Regiment (1,000 men), at Kassel
Detachments from the 28th French Light, 27th, 30th, 65th, 33rd and 22nd Infantry Regiments; 6th, 7th and 8th Artillery Regiments, portions in Homburg, portions in Magdeburg (3,000 men)

5th The occupation forces in Pomerania and in the Oder River fortresses[190]
400 men in Stettin: Brigadier General Liebert
1,100 men in Stralsund: Brigadier General Candras
2,000 men in Küstrin (among the previously named forces were 800 Oldenburgers and 2,300 Mecklenburgers).

Composition of the Brunswick Corps at Zwickau, 24 July 1809, in the evening[191]

Commander: Duke Friedrich Wilhelm of Brunswick
Chief of Staff: Colonel von Doernberg (absent)
1st Light Bn. (500 men): Major von Fragstein
2nd Light Bn. (500 men): Major von Reichmeister
3rd or Independent Jaeger Battalion (150 men): Major von Herzberg
Sharpshooter *(Scharfschützen)* Co. (150 men): Major von Scriever
Hussar Regiment (550 men): Major von Schrader
Uhlan Squadron (80 men): *Rittmeister* Graf (Count) von Wedell
Horse Battery (80 men): 1st Lieutenant Genderer

183 Lünsmann, p. 281f, Morgenstern, p. 9, and Hohenhausen, p. 171f.

184 The authorized strength of a line infantry regiment with two field battalions was 1,722 men (plus a depot battalion of 560 Men). cf. Lünsmann, p. 186.

185 Originally the Jaeger-Carabiniers Battalion was assigned to the brigade. However, during the march in France, it had to turn back again.

186 The authorized strength of a light infantry battalion was 873 men (plus a depot company of 140 men), p. Lünsmann, p.187.

187 The authorized strength of a foot artillery company was 107 men (data for 1812), cf. Lünsmann, p. 253.

188 Lünsmann, p. 287f and Kleinschmidt, p. 232.

189 In Lünsmann this is erroneously designated as the 2nd Infantry Regiment. The 2nd Regiment was actually sent to Spain.

190 Only nominally subordinated to King Jerome, but actually under the command of the respective fortress commanders.

191 Kortzfleisch, p. 11.

Composition of the Westphalian-French Forces in Halberstadt, 29 July 1809[192]

5th Westphalian Infantry Regiment
(ca. 2,000 men): Colonel Meyronnet
Departmental Guard
Veterans
Gendarmes (20 men)
French *March* Detachment (35 men)

Compositionof the Westphalian-Berg Division at Oelper, August 1, 1809[193]

Commander: Major General Rewbell
Chief of Staff: Colonel von Borstell
1st Westphalian Infantry Regiment
6th Westphalian Infantry Regiment
3rd Berg Infantry Regiment
1st Westphalian Cuirassier Regiment
1 mounted battery, 1 foot battery (10 cannons)
Division total: at least 5,000 men

Order of Battle, VIII (Westphalian) Corps of the *Grand Armée*, March 1812[194]

Commander in Chief: King Jérôme (returned to Kassel in July)
Orderly officers: *Graf* (Count) von Oberg, Capt. von Bodenhausen *(Kammerherr)*, Baron von Slicher, Lt. von Lehsten-Dingelstädt (a page), (returned to Kasselwith the King in July)
Commanding General: Major General Graf (Count) Vandamme (later replaced by General Colonel Junot, Duke of Abrantes)
Adjutants: Lieutenant Colonel Zeron, Captain Mynheer, and Lt. Delude
Chief of Staff: Colonel Revest
Adjoints of the Staff: Lieutenant Colonel Stockmayer (also Headquarters Commandant), Lieutenant Colonel von Longe, Capt. von Lamberty, Capt. von Linden
Commander der Gendarmerie:
Lieutenant Colonel von Kalm
Ordonnateur: Obermusterungsinspekteur (Senior Mustering Inspector) Ducrot
Senior Inspector of the Field Post Office: Emmermann
Inspector of the Field Hospital and the Apothecary: Isoard
General Staff Doctor: Merrem
Chief Pharmacist: Boutry
Headquarters total: 254 men (incl. Field Bakery, Butcher etc.)
1st (23rd) Division, Lieutenant General von Ochs
Adjutants: Capt. von Saint Paul, Capt. von Borcke, Capt. von Baurmeister
Chief of Staff: Colonel Humbert
Adjoints of the Staff: Captains von Quernheimb, Backer von Loewen, von Bobers, and von Wolf
1st Brigade, Brigadier General Damas
Adjutants: Capt.Liebhaber, Lt. von Lochhausen
Light Bn. III, Lieutenant Colonel von Hesberg (Hessberg)
2nd Infantry Regiment, 3 Bns., Colonel Baron von Fuellgraf
6th Infantry Regiment, 2 Bns., Colonel Ruelle
2nd Brigade, Brigadier General Graf von Wickenberg alias Zurwesten (returned to Kasselwith the Kingin July, therefore starting 21 July commanded by Brigadier General von Borstel)
Adjutants: Capt. Hoelke, Lt. Cordemann
Light Bn. II, Lieutenant Colonel Boedicker
3rd Infantry Regiment, 2 Bns., Colonel Bernard
7th Infantry Regiment, 3 Bns., Colonel Lageon
2nd (24th) Division, Major General Tharreau
Adjutants: Squadron Chief Liebhaber
Chief of Staff: Colonel Baron von Borstel (later Brigadier General, see above.)
Adjoints of the Staff: Captains Puttrich, von Diepenbroick, von Lindern, and Laumann
1st Brigade, Brigadier General Graf Wellingerode
Adjutants: Lieutenant Colonel Smallian, Capt. Vainclair
Grenadier-Garde, 1 Bn., Colonel Legras
Jaeger-Garde, 1 Bn., Maj. Picot
Jaeger-Carabiniers, 1 Bn., Maj. Müldner
Light Bn. I, Lieutenant Colonel von Rauschenplatt
5th Infantry Regiment, 2 Bns., Colonel Gissot
2nd Brigade, Brigadier General Danloup-Verdun (initially remained behind with the 8th Inf. Regt.)
Adjutants: Capt. von Alles, Lt.?
1st Infantry Regiment, 2 Bns., Colonel von Plessmann (located in Danzig, transferred to X Corps)
4th Infantry Regiment, 2 Bns., Colonel von Rossi (initially with XI Corps Augereau, then transferred to VI Corps St. Cyr; on 9. December arrived at the remainder of the *Grand Armée* at Vilnius)
8th Infantry Regiment, 2 Bns., Colonel Bergeron (on 29 October joined VIII Corps at Gschatsk)
Total infantry: 22,315 men
Cavalry Division, Major General Chabert (returned to Kassel with the King in July)
Adjutants: Capt. von St. Paul, Lt. Noel
Chief of Staff: ?
Adjoints of theStaff: Lieutenant Colonel von Reiche (from the Light Cavalry Brigade), Capt. von Hoyer (from the Heavy Cavalry Brigade)
Light Cavalry Brigade, Brigadier General Baron von Hammerstein
Adjutants: Capt. von St. Cernin, Capt. von Bothmer
Chevauleger-Garde, Colonel Müller (later set up an individual Guard Brigade under Maj. Gen. Wolff)
1st Hussar Regiment, Colonel von Zandt

---

192 Kortzfleisch, p. 26.

193 Borcke, p. 138 and Kortzfleisch, p. 44.

194 See Giesse, p. 14ff, Morgenstern, p. 121f, Kleinschmidt, p. 487, and Nafziger, p. 478f.

2nd Hussar Regiment, Colonel von Hesberg (Hessberg)
Heavy Cavalry Brigade, Brigadier General von Lepel
Adjutants: Capt. Barth, Lt. von Bourbon
Garde du Corps, 1 Escadron, Lieutenant Colonel Lallemand (the Garde du Corps went back to Kassel with the King in July)
1st Cuirassier Regiment, Colonel von Gilsa
2nd Cuirassier Regiment, Colonel Bastineller
(1st and 2nd Cuirassier Regts. under Brigadier General von Lepel transferred to IV Cavalry Corps)
Cavalry total: 3,374 men, 3,659 horses

Artillery and Engineers *(Genie)*, Major General Allix
Adjutants: Capt. Lachapelle, Lt. Spangenberg
Artillery Regt., 1 Mounted Battery of the Guard, 1 mounted battery of the line (transferred to the IV Cavalry Corps), 2 foot batteries of the line, and to each infantry regiment 2 regimental cannon (totaling 40 cannon and 8 howitzers), Colonel von Pfuhl
Engineer *(Genie)* Corps, Colonel Ulliac
One sapper company
Four train companies (of them, one to IV Cavalry Corps)
Handwerker (Artisans) Detachment
Reserve Park, Lieutenant Colonel Schulz
Total Artillery and Genie: 977 men (incl. regimental artillery), 558 men Train, 1,196 horses, Baggage Train: 324 men, 1,206 horses
Grand total: 27,802 men, 6,061 horses

Comments:
VIII Corps consisted almost exclusively of Westphalian units, therefore, the nationality is omitted in the Order of Battle. During the course of the campaign, there were numerous newly appointed and reassigned commanders. General Count Vandamme resigned his corps command directly after the beginning of the war and was temporarily replaced by General Tharreau, and then finally by General Junot, the Duke of Abrantes. King Jérôme left the army in mid-July and took the Garde du Corps with him back to Kassel. The 1st and 8th Infantry Regiments were located in Danzig, the 4th in Swedish Pomerania. The 1st Westphalian Infantry Regiment was later assigned to X Corps under Macdonald. The 8th Infantry Regiment went to VIII Corps at Gschatsk on 29 October only after their retreat of the *Grand Armée*; the 4th Infantry Regiment belonged to XI Corps Augereau, was then transferred to Division Wrede of VI Corps St. Cyr and arrived at Vilnius on 9 December. Both Westphalian cuirassier regiments were incorporated into IV Cavalry Corps Latour-Maubourg during the advance on the Vistula.
In the sources, German and French rank designations were used next to one another, e.g., *"Général de Brigade/Major General"* or *"Capitaine/Hauptmann."*

Administrative Composition of the Kingdom of Westphalia in Military Divisions, in Early 1813[195]
1st Division (Kassel), Major General Graf (Count) von Heldring
Department of the Fulda, Brigadier General von Schlotheim, Commandant of Kassel
Department oft he Werra, Colonel von Dalwigk
Gendarmerie: Squadron Chief von Grosskreutz
2nd Division (Braunschweig), Brigadier General von Klösterlein
Department oft he Oker, Brigadier General von Klösterlein
Department of the Harz, Colonel von Mauvillon (later dismissed)
Gendarmerie: Squadron Chief Hartert
3rd Division (Magdeburg), Major General von Ochs (captured by the Russians on 30 May 1813)
Department of the Elbe, Major General von Ochs
Department of the Saale, Colonel Melzheimer
Gendarmerie: Squadron Chief von Kalm
4th Division (Hanover), Brigadier General von Diemar
Departmentof the Leine, Brigadier General von Diemar
Departmentof the Aller, Colonel von Würthen
Gendarmerie: Squadron Chief von der Gree

Operational Composition of the Westphalian Army in 1813[196]
Guard Brigade, Major General Chabert (Generalkapitän der Garde)
Adjutant: Capt. Noel
Chief of the General Staff: Colonel von Humbert-Verneuil
Colonel Adjoint: Gauthier
Capitains Adjoints: von Putrich O`Lusma, Szimanieski (Orderlies to the King)
Infantry
Grenadier-Garde (1,000 men), Maj. Ries
Jaeger-Garde (840 men), Maj. Boedicker
Jaeger-Carabiniers (370 men), Colonel von Hesberg
Total infantry: 2,210 men
Cavalry
Garde du Corps, one squadron (286 men), Colonel Wolff
Chevauleger-Garde, two squadrons (290 men), Squadron Chief Bolte
Hussar Regiment Jérôme Napoleon (600 men), Colonel Brincard
Total Cavalry: 1,176 men
Artillery
Foot Battery, Captain Heinemann (later Captain Wille)
Total Artillery: 209 men

---

195 According to Specht, p. 64ff. The Military divisions were named after rivers in the kingdom and were geographic structures.

196 According to Specht, p. 67ff and Kleinschmidt, p. 570f.

Grand total Guard: 3,595 men

The Guard Brigade remained stationed in the kingdom. It was disbanded when the kingdom was dissolved. Some of the Garde du Corps accompanied the king onward to Cologne and were dismissed there on 3 November 1813.[197]

Chevauleger-Garde Regiment, Colonel Berger

The regiment wasunder the command of Westphalian General Wolff in a mixed brigade in XII Corps (Oudinot).[198] After participating in the Battle of Nations at Leipzig, the survivors went back to Kassel and were bid farewell on 26 October 1813.[199]

Westphalian Brigade, Brigadier General Lageon

Guard Fusiliers, Colonel von Benning
8th Infantry Regiment, Colonel von Bergeron
Light Battalion II, Lieutenant Colonel von Lepel
Light Battalion IV, Lieutenant Colonel von Gauthier
Foot Battery, Captain Schultheis
Foot Battery, Captain Wille (later Captain Schleenstein)

This brigade along with the Italian Brigade Pino formed the 31st Division (General Ledru) in X Corps (Macdonald) of the *Grand Armée*, which operated in Silesia and Saxony. It was disbanded after the Battle of Nations at Leipzig. The depots remained in Kassel.

Westphalian Brigade, Brigadier General Bernard

2nd Infantry Regiment, Colonel von Picot
3rd Infantry Regiment, Colonel von Hille
Light Infantry Battalion I, Major Bechtold
Foot battery, Lieutenant Orges
(late Lieutenant Normen)
Mounted battery, Lieutenant Wissel

The brigade was stationed in Dresden and Torgau[200] and was disbanded after Dresden's capitulation on 11 November 1813. The depots were located in Kassel (2nd Infantry Regiment and Light Battalion I) and in Braunschweig (3rd Infantry Regiment).

1st Infantry Regiment, Colonel von Plessmann

Part of the occupation force of Danzig until the end of 1813.[201] The depot remained in Braunschweig.

Westphalian Brigade, Brigadier General von Fuellgraf

4th Infantry Regiment, Colonel von Seibelsdorf (later Colonel Wetzel)
5th Infantry Regiment, Colonel von d. Groeben (later Lieutenant Colonel von Laborde)

Part of the occupation force of Küstrin, until March 1814.[202] The depots remained in Kassel (5th Infantry Regiment) and in Braunschweig (4th Infantry Regiment).

6th Infantry Regiment, vacant

Raising of the regiment ceased in 1813.

7th Infantry Regiment (840 men), Colonel von Meibom

Was raised again in September 1813 in Kassel. The 1st Battalion was ready to deploy the end of September and took part in the fighting around Kassel (against Chernyshyov), after which it was disbanded. The core of the 2nd Battalion remained in Kassel.

9th Infantry Regiment, Colonel von Lindern

Part of the occupation force of Magdeburg (until December 1813), then disarmed and dismissed from the fortress.[203] The depot remained in Braunschweig.

Light Infantry Battalion III (1,000 men), Lieutenant Colonel Vigelius

The battalion was newly created from the core of the Westphalian battalion that returned from Spain and remained stationed in country until the dissolution of the kingdom (initially in Kassel). In September 1813 it was located in Heiligenstadt (together with both cuirassier regiments) to protect the capital city.[204]

Westphalian Cuirassier Brigade, Brigadier General von Bastineller

1st Cuirassier Regiment (4 squadrons), Colonel von Lallemand[205]
2nd Cuirassier Regiment (4 squadrons), Colonel von Scheffer

Cuirassier Brigade total: 1,200 men

The Cuirassier Brigade initially remained in Ziegenhain, later in Berka. It dissolved as a result of desertions at the end of September (during Chernyshyov'sassault).

1st Chevauleger Regiment, Colonel von Stein

One squadron, Squadron Chief von Plessen
Regimental depot (90 men), *Rittmeister* Merkel

The single field squadron located in Spain was disarmed by the French and declared prisoners of war on 23 December 1813 (two months after the dissolution of the Kingdom of Westphalia). The depot was in Melsungen.

197 The flight to Cologne and the dismissal are described by Kaisenberg, p. 295ff and Gebauer, p. 17ff

198 Compare Lehsten, p. 91ff.

199 Described similarly in Lehsten, p. 149f and Kleinschmidt, p. 650f according to the diary of Lieutenant von Ochs of the *Garde-Chevauleger* Regiment.

200 The 2nd Infantry Regiment was originally intended to be the occupation force in Torgau, see Morgenstern, p. 127.

201 A detailed description of the victories is provided by Bauer.

202 See Giesse, p. 335ff.

203 According to Borcke, p. 267.

204 Also according to Borcke, p. 267.

205 Alsacian, other spellings: L`Allemand or Lallement.

Westphalian Hussar Brigade,
Brigadier General von Zandt
1st Hussar Regiment (3 squadrons),
Colonel von Hammerstein
2nd Hussar Regiment (3 squadrons), Major von Pentz
Hussar Brigade total: 580 men

Was assigned as the Corps Cavalry for the II Corps (Victor), which was deployed on the Bohemian border. Two squadrons of each of the two hussar regiments defected to the Allies at Reichenberg in Silesia on 22-23 August 1813; both the remaining squadrons let themselves be taken prisoner on 18 September at Freiberg in Saxony. The regiments were disbanded, the standards burned in the Ziegenhain depot, and the officers and depot troops who had remained in the kingdom were assigned to other regiments.

Westphalian Artillery, Major General Allix (General Director of the Artillery and of the Engineers (Genie), later Lieutenant du Roi)
Artillery Regiment[206] (104 of the men in depot), Colonel von Pfuel[207]
Ouvrier (Workers) company (103 men)

The Artillery Regiment mobilized multiple batteries (see above), while the rest including depots remained in Westphalia until the kingdom was dissolved.

Gendarmerie (Military Police)
One detachment each was in Kassel and Braunschweig; there were possibly also detachments in Hannover and Magdeburg (compare "Composition of the Military Divisions").

Departmental Companies
One company each in Kassel and Braunschweig.

Veterans
One company each in Kassel and Braunschweig.

Grand total in the army: ca. 30,000 men[208] and 5,078 horses

206 The *"Ordrebuch des Artillerieregiments"* (The Books of Orders of the Artillery Regiment) from 22 February to 19 September 1813 was published in extract form by Gerland.

207 Other spelling: Pfuhl.

208 According to calculations by Specht, p. 77: 29,046 men (including Gendarmerie, excluding the Veterans).

Composition of the Westphalian Forces Around Kassel, at the End of September 1813[209]

Governor Brigadier General *Graf* (Count) von Wickenberg (alias von Zurwesten), simultaneously Commander of the 1st Military Division
Adjutant: Capt. Biskamp
Chief of the General Staff: Major von Stockmayer[210]
Adjoints: Capt. von Lamberti, Capt. Bauermeister
Commandant of the Gendarmerie of the 1st Military Division: Squadron Chief von Grosskreutz
Weapons Commandant *(Waffen-Kommandant)*: Brigadier General von Schlotheim, simultaneously Commandant of the Departmentof the Fulda
Adjutants of the Place *"vom Platz"*: Capt. Feetz, Capt. Arnemann, and Lieutenant Stübing
Commandant of the Kastell:[211] Capt. Kaufmann

Infantry
Grenadier-Garde, 1 Bn. (1,000 men)
Jaeger-Garde, 1 Bn. (840 men)
Jaeger-Carabiniers (160 men)
Depot of the Guard Fusiliers (160 men)
Depot of the 2nd Infantry Regiments (150 men)
Depot of the 5th Infantry Regiments (150 men)
Core of the organization of II Bn./7th Infantry Regiment (150 men)
Depot of the 8th Infantry Regiments (150 men)
Depots of the four light infantry battalions (300 men)
Total infantry: 3,060 men

Cavalry
Garde du Corps, 1 squadron (286 men)
Depot of the *Chevauleger-Garde*, (140 men)
Hussar Regiment Jérôme Napoleon (450 men, of them about 300 men mounted)
Gendarmerie (30 men)
Total Cavalry: 906 men

Artillery
Foot Battery of the Guard, six 6-pounders[212] (209 men)
Remainder of the depots of the field artillery (24 men)
Ouvriers[213] company (103 men)
Total Artillery: 336 men
Grand total: 4,302 men,[214] 756 horses, 34 cannon

209 According to Specht, p. 137ff.

210 Other spelling: Stockmeier.

211 Also commandant of the Kassel prison.

212 In Kassel there were an additional 28 cannon on hand. Of them, a battery was located in the "Forest" *("Forst")* (i.e., outside the city) with four cannon and two howitzers for training purposes.

213 Military workers.

214 An additional 600 sick personnel were in the Kassel dispensaries.

Composition of the Russian Chernyshyov *"Streifkorps"* ("patrolling or flying corps"), at the End of September 1813[215]

Commander: Major General Count Chernyshyov

Attached officers: Colonels von Barnikow, von Podewils, von Arnim, Rothe,[216] Major von Doernberg
Combined[217] Hussar Regiment, 3 squadrons (301 men)
Isumski Hussar Regiment,
3 squadrons (398 men), Colonel Baedriaga
Finnlandski Dragoon Regiment, 2 squadrons (207 men)
Cossack Regiment Lieutenant Colonel Zizocv (355 men)
Cossack Regiment Colonel Girov (298 men)
Cossack Regiment Colonel Grekov (334 men)
Cossack Regiment Colonel Vlasov (319 men)
Cossack Regiment Colonel Balabin (280 men)
½ battery of mounted artillery, four 6-pounders and two "Unicorns" (100 men)
Grand total: 2,592 men,[218] 6 cannons

215 According to Specht, p. 137ff.

216 In Specht spelled as: Podewilz, Roteh.

217 The composition of this combined hussar regiment is unclear. According to the official Prussian General Staff document about the Wars of Liberation *(Befreiungskriege)* Friederich 1904, Vol. 1, p. 588, Chernyshyov commanded in mid- August 1813 except for the named cavalry regiments of the line, also the Riga Dragoon Regiment. Possibly Specht meant this.

218 Status: 10 August, possibly only about 2,300 more men (all mounted).

SHORT BIOGRAPHIES

OF KING JÉRÔME NAPOLEON AND GENERALS OF THE WESTPHALIAN ARMY[219]

Jérôme Napoleon, King von Westphalia
Detail from a painting by Kinson.

Jerôme Napoleon, King of Westphalia
Born 15 Nov. 1784, in Ajaccio, Corsica, as Napoleon Bonaparte's youngest brother. In 1793 he fled with their mother to Marseille, in 1800 joined the Consular-Guides Regiment. Shortly thereafter he entered the Navy and undertook many voyages to America (where he married Elisabeth Patterson without permission) and in the Mediterranean. In 1806 he became a brigadier general, in 1807 a major general, commander in Silesia and King of Westphalia; on 12 Aug. 1807 married Princess Katharina of Württemberg; took part in the 1809 campaign in Saxony; in 1812 named commander of the right wing of the *Grand Armée* during the campaign in Russia. In July he left the Armée due to quarrels with Marshal Davout and Napoleon; in October 1813 he fled from his kingdom, afterwards in exile in France and in Trieste. In 1815 at Waterloo was a French division commander, subsequently remained in Wurttemberg and Austria. In the aftermath of the July Revolution he returned to France, after Katharina's death in 1835 he went back to Italy and married the Marquise Bartolini-Badelli there. In 1847 he again returned to France, after the coup by his nephew (the later Emperor Napoleon III) he was temporarily the President of the Senate. Died on 24 June 1860 in Villegenis near Paris.[220]

D´Albignac, Philippe François Maurice de Rivet, Count of Ried
Born 15 Feb. 1775 in Milhaud, page to Louis XVI, then in the French Emigrants Corps; 1807 Aide de Camp to Jerôme; 21 Jan. 1808 in the State Council; 28 July 1808 brigadier general; 29 Jan. 1810 provisional Minister of War; 3 May 1810 Count of Ried; 24 Sep. 1810 dismissed and returned to France; 1812 under Gouvion St.-Cyr Chief of Staff of the VI Corps (Bavarian) of the *Grand Armée*; after the Restoration became Governor of the St. Cyr Military Academy; died 31 Jan. 1824 in Paris.[221]

Allix de Vaux, Jacques Alexandre Francois
Born 21 Dec. 1768 in Percy (Manche), left French service; 1808 as brigadier general in Westphalian service; 1810 General Director of the Artillery and Engineer Corps; April 1812 major general; October 1813 *Lieutenant du Roi* (King's Deputy); at the end of 1813 back in French service as a brigadier general; in 1814 defended Sens against the Württembergers; 1815 Division Commander with I Corps of the Army of the North; exiled in the Restoration; lived in Waldeck, then returned to France; in 1827 published a work about his field artillery system (*"System der Feldartillerie")*[222] died 26 Jan. 1836 in Courcelles.[223]

219 This section includes biographic information from Lünsmann, Kleinschmidt, Kircheisen and – special for the French generals - from Six, and further from the Online-Enzyklopädie www.Wikipedia.de. There were also generals who were not (no longer) carried in the official roster of positions (Rangliste), e.g., Brigadier Generals Girard, von Wurmb, von Hessberg, Legras and Zinck. No information about them is provided here. Beyond that, some French generals temporarily held command positions in the Westphalian Army, among others, Major Generals Eblé, Delaunay, Léfèbvre-Desnoettes, Rivaud de la Raffiniere and Tharreau. They are also not addressed here; for their biographies see Six.

220 See Kircheisen and Six, Vol. 1, p. 119f.

221 See Six, Vol. 1, p. 8, and Sauzey.

222 See Allix.

223 See Six, Vol. 1, p. 10f.

Bastineller, Karl Gottlob Baron v.
Born 1767 in Wittstock / Dosse, left Hessian service; 1808 as senior lieutenant of the Garde du Corps in Westphalian service; 1810 in the *Garde-Chevaulegers* Regiment; 20 Apr. 1811 colonel of the 2nd Cuirassier Regiment; 1812 in Russia; 20 Feb. 1813 brigadier general; 1813 commanded the Westphalian Cuirassier Brigade; after that did not serve any further, died 1839 at his estate Steckenthin in der Priegnitz.

Bernard, Jacques- Bernard
Born 22 Oct. 1774 in Draguignan (Var); left French service on 1 Nov. 1809 to be battalion commander and orderly to the King of in Westphalian service; 8 Jan. 1810 major in the 6th Infantry Regiment; 3 Nov. 1810 major of the Guard Jaeger Battalion; 14 Sep. 1811 Colonel of the 3rd Infantry Regiments; 1812 in Russia; 5 Mar. 1813 brigadier general; 1813 captured in Dresden; 1814 returned to French service as a colonel; 1831 departed as brigadier general; died 12 Jan. 1852.[224]

Börner, v.
Born 13 Sep. 1762 in Ravensburg (Swabia). Soldier in the (Irish) Walsh Infantry Regiment, later French 92nd Line Regiment. 1792 junior lieutenant, 1793 captain, 1796 battalion commander, various assignments in French staffs. On 30 Dec. 1807 Westphalian Brigadier general; 1808 Commandant of the Werra Department; 1809 Commander of the 1st Brigade in Spain (returned due to illness in June); 5 Oct. 1809 departed. 1814 recognized as *maréchal de camp* (brigadier general). 1817 naturalized French citizen; died 4 May 1829 in Nordheim, Lower Rhine.

Bongars, Jean Francois Marie Baron v.
Born 11 Mar. 1758 in Rieux (*Seine Inferieure*), page at the French court; emigrated in October 1791, arrived in Holland in 1792, entering Dutch service; 1803 Grand Equerry (*Großstallmeister*) of the Prince of Hohenzollern-Hechingen; 1807 entered French service; in December 1807 as the *Fourier* of the Palace in Westphalian service; 12 Feb. 1808 Chief of the Gendarmerie and aide-de-camp to the King; on 12 Jan. 1808 colonel of the 1st Light Battalion; on 28 Apr. 1809 promoted to brigadier general; 1809 with the X Corps in Saxony; 20 Apr. 1811 General Inspector of the Gendarmerie and Chief of the High Police (*Hohe Polizei*); 4 Sep. 1811 Chamberlain (*Kammerherr*); December 1811 State Councilman (*Staatsrat*); on 9 Jan. 1813 promoted to major general; at the end of 1813 returned to French service as a brigadier general; 1815 released; died in Gournay-en-Bray *(Seine-Inferieure)* on 11 Mar. 1833.[225]

Borstell[226], Karl Heinrich Emil Albrecht Baron v.
Born 2 Feb. 1778 in Tangermünde, left Prussian service and entered Westphalian service in December 1807, on 1 Jan. 1808 *Eskadrons-Chef*; 3 July 1808 Major in the 1st Chevauleger Regiment; 18 July 1809 colonel, then chief of staff of the division in Spain; 28 Jan. 1811 chief of staff of the Guard; 1812 chief of staff in the *Grand Armée*; 24 June 1812 Commandant of Grodno; on 2 Aug. 1812 promoted to brigadier general; 1813 Honorary Equerry of the King (*Ehrenstallmeister des Königs*); in October 1813 returned to Prussian; 1845 retired; died 11 July 1856 in Stralsund.

Chabert, Pierre Baron
Born 30 Sep. 1770 in Joyeuse, son of a backer, fought in the Revolutionary Wars and rose through all the ranks to a colonel; in 1809 went as a colonel into Westphalian service; 1810 *aide de camp* to the King; 4 Sep. 1810 brigadier general; 10 Dec. 1811 Captain General of the Guard; 1812 Chief of staff of the Westphalian Corps; in August 1812 returned with Jerôme to Kassel; 1 Jan. 1813 major general; in 1814 returned to French service as a brigadier general; 1830 retired; died 1839 in Besançon.[227]

Du Coudras, Graf von Bernterode
01 Jan. 1809 left French service; 17 Jan. 1808 colonel and King's Aide de Camp; 13 June 1808 brigadier general; 1 Jan. 1809 Count of Bernterode; in 1809 command ed the Guard Division in Saxony, 1 Jan. 1810 major general and Colonel-General (*Generaloberst*) of the Guard, due to illness went to France; died 13 July 1810 in Epernay.

Damas, François Auguste
Born 2 Oct. 1775 in Paris, 1789 - 1792 in the Paris National Guard; in 1798 fought in Egypt, named by Napoleon to *Eskadronchef*; in 1800 promoted to colonel; in 1806 entered Dutch service; in October 1809 entered Westphalian service as a colonel; 7 Aug. 1810 promoted to brigadier general and Commandant of the 4th Military Division; 1812 brigade commander with the Westphalian Corps; then Chief of the Westphalian General Staff; killed at Borodino on 7 Sep. 1812. Had the nickname "the Westphalian Bayard" ("*der westphälische Bayard*").

224 See Morgenstern and Six, Vol. 1, p. 82f.

225 Another spelling: Bongard. See Six, Vol. 1, p. 121f (with minor differences from Lünsmann).

226 Another spelling: v. Borstel.

227 See Six, Vol. 1, p. 210f (with differences from Lünsmann).

Danloup-Verdun, Louis
Born 17 July 1769 in Paris; in 1789 entered the Paris National Guard as a volunteer and advanced to Major (1807); on 30 Mar. 1808 entered Westphalian service; 3 May 1808 colonel of the 2nd Infantry Regiment and 11 June became the King's Aide de Camp; 22 June Colonel of the 8th Infantry Regiment; 5 Apr. 1811 brigadier general; 1812 in Russia; 17 July 1813 major general; at the end of 1813 re-entered French service as a brigadier general; died 1847 in Versailles.[228]

Diemar, Justus Heinrich Friedrich Wilhelm v.
Born in Walldorf 1755; came from the Hessian service in 1807 entering Westphalian service as a brigadier general; on 1 Jan. 1808 named Commandant of the Weser Department; on 8 Oct. 1810 designated the Commandant of the 1st Military Division (but declined); in 1810 aide-de-camp to the King; in 1813 Commandant of the 4th Military Division; 1814 returned to Hessian service; 1821 retired; died in poverty on 1822 in Bad Hersfeld.

Dumas de Polart, Jean Baptiste Char-les René Joseph Baron
Born 29 Mar. 1775 in Paris; came from French service on 21 Oct. 1808 entering Westphalian service as a colonel; 25 Nov. 1809 aide-de-camp to the king; on 1 Jan. 1810 became a brigadier general; 12 Sep. 1810 "Captain" of the Garde du Corps; worked on the drill regulation (*Exerzierreglement*) of the Westphalian cavalry; in April 1812 departed Westphalian service; in 1814 re-entered French service as a brigadier general; in 1842 was mayor of La Ferté-Milon; died 1843 in Courtefontaine (Doubs).[229]

Füllgraf, Friedrich Wilhelm Baron v.
Came from Hessian service, in 1808 captain in the Guard Jaeger Battalion; in February 1809 became battalion commander of the Jaeger-Carabiniers; on 23 Apr. 1809 was the Major of the Guard Jaeger Battalion; on 3 Nov. 1810 became the colonel of the 1st Light Infantry Battalion; on 5 May 1811 colonel of the 2nd Infantry Regiment; on 4 Nov. 1811 promoted to Chamberlain *(Kammerherr)*; 1812 wounded at Borodino; 13 Nov. 1812 promoted to brigadier general; 1813 imprisoned in Küstrin. After the ceasefire he went to Trieste to ex-King Jerôme, where he shot himself (suicide) the same year.

Hadel[230], v.
Born in Brunswick; in 1808 was a Westphalian brigadier general; in March 1809 temporarily retired; in June 1809 succeeded Brigadier General v. Börner as the commander of the 1st Brigade in Spain; on 1 Sep. 1809 killed at the siege of Gerona.

228 See Six, Vol. 1, p. 285f and Borcke.

229 Another spelling: Mas de Polart. See Six, Vol. 2, p. 164.

230 Another spelling: v. Hadeln.

Hammerstein-Equord, Hans Georg Baron v.
Born 17 Sep. 1771; 20 Nov. 1807 squadron commander (*Eskadronchef*) and chamberlain (*Kammerherr*); on 29 Feb. 1808 *Eskadronchef* of the 1st Chevauleger Regiment; on 26 June 1808 was colonel of the 1st Chevauleger Regiment in Spain; on 2 Aug. 1808 promoted to brigadier general; Sept. 1811 Inspector of the Light Infantry; 1812 Commander of the Hussar Brigade; on 1 Jan. 1813 promoted to major general; on 28 Sep. 1813 dismissed (because of his brother's desertion); restricted to barracks in France until 1814; died 9 Dec. 1841 in Hildesheim.[231]

Heldring, Gerhard Heinrich v.
Born in Rinteln 14 Sep. 1751; in 1768 entered Dutch service; in 1776 entered English service; fought in the United States; in 1785 was again in Dutch service; 1794 colonel, then in Bavarian service; in 1807 entered in Westphalian service as a brigadier general; in 1808 Commander of the Military Academy (*Kriegsschule*); 18 Nov. 1808 Commander of the 2nd Military Division; on 1 Jan. 1809 promoted to major general; 23 Sep. 1810 became a State Councilman (*Staatsrat*); on 6 Nov. 1812 named Governor of Kassel; 1813 Commandant of the 1st Military Division, later removed from his post; in 1814 entered Dutch service as a lieutenant general; Governor of Breda; in 1835 retired; died 19 Sep. 1835 in Nijmegen.

Hessen-Philippsthal, Ernst Konstantin Prince of *(Prinz von)*
Born 1771; left Hessian service; 23 Apr. 1809 (after the Dörnberg Rebellion) colonel of the Jaeger-Carabiniers Battalion attached to the Guards; on 15 Aug. 1810 senior chamberlain (*Oberkammerherr*) and brigadier general; 1811 briefly Grand Marshal of the Palace (*Großmarschall des Palasts*). In April 1813 requested to be released from his military offices as aide-de-camp *(Flügeladjutant)* and general. Dismissed as Senior Chamberlain on 9 Oct. 1813 (arrested at the same time).

Klösterlein, Karl Friedrich Adolf v.
Born 1756 in Saxony; in 1773 entered Saxon service; 1799 in Brunswick's; 1807 in Westphalian service; March 1808 became colonel of the 1st Cuirassier Regiment; 28 July 1808 brigadier general; 25 Sep. 1810 Commandant of the 2nd Military Division; after the Wars of Liberation did no further military service; died 3 Jan. 1819 in Strahlwalde (Saxony).

231 See Hartmann.

Lageon
Frenchman; in 1807 was a battalion commander in Westphalian service; on 10 Mar. 1809 promoted to major; 15 July 1810 colonel of the 7th Infantry Regiment; 24 June 1812 Chief of Staff of the 24th (2nd Westphalian) Division; 1813 promoted to brigadier general, Commander of the Westphalian Brigade in the 31st Division (XI Army Corps of the *Grand Armée*); on 8 Jan. 1814 returned to French service.

Langenblack, Georg Julius Baron v.
Born in Nentershausen (Hesse) 21 June 1766; came from Hessian service; on 5 Mar. 1808 entered Westphalian service as the battalion commander of the Grenadier Guards; on 3 July 1808 promoted to major; 25 Apr. 1809 became colonel of the Grenadier Guards; 20 Apr. in 1811 was a brigadier general and chamberlain (*Kammerherr*); in 1814 went back to Kurhessian service; 1846 retired; died on 29 Dec. 1852 in Kassel.

Lehsten-Dingelstädt, Ludwig August Detlef Baron v.
Born Lunow (Silesia) 24 Aug. 1743; came from Hessian service; on 3 Jan. 1808 entered Westphalian service as a brigadier general; 1810 Commandant of the Leine Department and major general; August 1810 retired; died 1819 in Lessendorf (Silesia). Father of Karl August Unico v. Lehsten-Dingelstädt.[232]

Lepel I, Christoph Gottlieb Gustav Baron v.
Born on 1 Mar. 1746 in Grabzow bei Wolgast; 1760 served as a page in Kassel; 11 Dec. 1807 became a Westphalian brigadier general; on 5 Apr. 1808 Commander of the 2nd Military Division; on 27 June 1808 promoted to major general; 29 Nov. 1808 Commander of the 1st Military Division; on 1 Apr. 1809 became President of the State Council (*Präsident Staatsrat*); 15 Oct. 1809 provisional Governor of Kassel; died on 22 Aug. 1813 in Kassel.

Lepel v. Grambow II, Hellmuth August Alexander Freiherr (*Graf*/Count)
Born in Hessen; in 1807 was Württemberg lieutenant colonel, then Jerôme's aide de camp; came with the queen to Kassel; in December 1807 entered Westphalian service as a major and honorary instructor *(Ehrenbereiter)*; in January 1808 colonel of the Chevauleger Regiment; on 19 Jan. 1810 became a count; on 2 June 1810 became aide de camp to the King; on 24 Nov. 1811 promoted to brigadier general; on 7 Sep. 1812 severely wounded at Borodino; died in Russia on 21 Oct. 1812 from his wounds.

Pierre Simon Meyronnet de Saint-Marc
Oil painting by an unknown artist,
photo: by Yves Martin

Meyronnet de Saint-Marc, Pierre Simon Count of Wellingerode
Born in Martiques on 3 Oct. 1772; left French service, joined the French Navy and in 1803 was a Lieutenant on the brig *"l'Épevier"* (the Sparrow Hawk) commanded by Jerôme; in 1807 joined Westphalian service and in December 1807 Grand Marshal of the Palace; 26 Feb. 1808 State Counsel; 12 June 1808 named a count; April 1809 colonel of the 5th Infantry Regiment; captured when the Duke of Brunswick's corps attacked Halberstadt and later exchanged for the English Major Lestrange; on 15 Mar. 1810 named Colonel General of the Chasseurs de la Garde; 25 Sep. 1810 Colonel General of the Garde du Corps; 13 July 1810 brigadier general; on 12 Sep. 1810 became Captain of the Garde du Corps; in 1812 commanded a brigade of the Westphalian Corps; but due to illness returned from Kalisch to Kassel; went from there to Paris, where he died on 10 Sep. 1812.

232 See Lehsten-Dingelstädt.

Joseph-Antoine-Morio-de-Marienborn,
Oil painting by an unknown artist, photo Wikipedia

Morio, Joseph Antoine Graf von Marienborn
Born 16 Jan. 1771 in Chantelle Chateau; French Navy cadet, then in the French Engineer Corps; 1806-07 Aide de Camp to Jerôme in Silesia; 11 Aug. 1807 as brigadier general in Westphalian service; 2 Feb. until August 1808 Westphalian Minister of War; 28 July 1808 major general, commander of the Westphalian Division in Spain; became ill in December 1809 and returned to Kassel; December 1810 named Grand Equerry *(Großstallmeister)*; murdered on 24 Dec. 1811 in Kassel.[233]

Motz, Carl Reinhard v.
Came from Hessian service; 1 Jan. 1808 as brigadier general in Westphalian service and Commandant of the Saale Department; 24 Aug. 1810 retired; died 1823 on his Bodenhausen estate.

Ochs, Adam Ludwig v.
Born 24 May 1759 in Rosenthal (Hesse); 1777 entered Hessian service; fought America; 1806 Kurhessian lieutenant colonel; in 1807 entered Westphalian service (Ministry of War); 31 Aug. 1808 promoted to colonel; 17 Feb. 1809 Commandant of the Harz-Department; 9 Mar. 1809 colonel in the General Staff of the Westphalian Division in Spain; 15 June 1809 brigadier general and Commander of the Westphalian Division; in 1810 led the cadre back from Spain; July - September 1810 Commander of the Westphalian Brigade on the Baltic Sea coast; 14 Nov. 1810 major general; 1 Nov. 1811 Captain General of the Guards (*Generalkapitän der Garden*); 1812 Commander of the 23rd then the 24th Division in Russia; 27 Mar. 1813 Commander the 3rd Military Division; 30 May 1813 taken prisoner in Halberstadt; at the beginning of 1814 returns from Dorpat to Kassel; enters Hessian service as colonel; died 21 Oct. 1823.[234]

Reubell, Jean Jacques
Born 12 Aug. 1777 in Colmar, son of a former member of the French Directorate; Jerôme's adjutant; on 8 Dec. 1807 became a Westphalian brigadier general, Governor of Kassel; 25 Dec. 1807 promoted to Westphalian major general, Commandant of the 1st Military Division; in April 1809 put down Dörnberg´s rebellion; afterward Chief of the General Staff of the X Army Corps; pulled back his forces after the unsuccessful battle at Oelper on 1 Aug. 1809, was dismissed and went to America. In 1817 he went back into French service. Died in 1847.[235]

de Salha, Valentin Graf v. Hoene
Born 13 Jan. 1758[236] in Bardos (Basses Pyrénées), from an old noble family; entered the French Navy and in 1805 was a lieutenant on the warship *"Le Vétéran"* commanded by Jerôme; in Sept. 1806 became aide-de-camp to the prince; in December 1807 entered Westphalian Service as a colonel; Commandant of the House of Pages; on 20 Apr. 1808 became the colonel of the Guard Jaeger Battalion; on 26 Dec. 1808 promoted to brigadier general; on 1 Sep. 1809 named a state councilman (*Staatsrat*); on 25 Sep. 1810 named Count of Hoene; on 29 Sep. 1810 became Minister of War (*Kriegsminister*) and a major general; in 1813 reorganized the Westphalian Army; on 21 Feb. 1814 went back into French service as a colonel; died 1841 in St. Palais.

233 See Kircheisen.

234 See Ochs.

235 Another spelling: Rewbell. See Six, Vol. 2, p. 358f.

236 See Communay.

Salm-Salm, Wilhelm Florentin Ludwig Karl, Prince zu *(Fürst zu)*
Born 1786 in Sens (France), 4th Prince zu Salm-Salm. King Jerôme's adjutant (in 1810 was included in the list of the General Staff Officers of the Guard as a colonel). August 1812 colonel of the newly created Queen's Regiment (*Regiment der Königin* or *Füsilier-Garde*). On 21 February 1813 he gave up command of the regiment and became the King's adjutant again. On 24 October 1813 he was named a Westphalian brigadier general. Ultimately entered Dutch service. Died in 1846 at the Anholt Palace *(Schloss)* at Isselburg.

Schlotheim, Ernst Wilhelm v.
Ca. 1808 Westphalian brigadier general, King's Honorary Equerry (*Ehrenstallmeister*), for some time the Commandant of Kassel; in September 1813 organized the defense of the city against Tschernyscheff; died 4 Nov. 1845 at Wietersheim.

Uslar, Leopold Wilhelm Freiherr v.
13 Apr. 1808 Westphalian brigadier general, Jerôme's Adjutant; organized the 5th and 6th Infantry Regiments in Magdeburg; fought at Dodendorf 5 May 1809 against Schill; 29 May 1809 left the service; died 30 Sep. 1830 in Hanenburg.

Webern, Johann Heinrich Karl v.
Born in Gerthausen (Franconia) 24 June 1745; left Hessian service, December 1807 entering Westphalian service; 1 Jan. 1808 brigadier general and Commandant of the Harz Department; 23 Feb. 1808 Commander of the 2nd Westphalian Brigade in Spain; called back because of his age; 1810 in the Harz Department again; 22 July 1810 dismissed from service. Died as a retired Prussian major general on 3 Feb. 1829 in Heiligenstadt.

Wolff, Marc-Francois Jerôme Baron v.
Born 4 Mar. 1776 in Strasbourg; left French service in December 1807 and entered Westphalian service as a major; organized the Westphalian cavalry; 10 Aug. 1808 Colonel of the *Garde-Chevaulegers*; 6 Apr. 1812 promoted to brigadier general; in August 1812 accompanied the King back to Kassel; on 1 Jan. 1813 became Jerôme's aide de camp; reorganized the Chevaulegers Regiment; fought at Grossbeeren, Dennewitz, Wartenburg and Leipzig; followed Jerôme to France and entered France's service as a brigadier general; on 31 Dec. 1835 promoted to lieutenant general; died 1848.[237]

Zandt, Ferdinand Baron v.
1806 Bavarian *Rittmeister* (cavalry captain); then in Westphalian service; 24 Feb. 1809 squadron commander in the *Garde-Chevaulegers* Regiment; in the beginning of 1810 Major of the 1st Hussar Regiment; 1812 in Russia; 28 Feb. 1813 Honorary Equerry (*Ehrenstallmeister*); 5 Mar. 1813 promoted to brigadier general; followed the King to Aachen; in 1827 was living as Prussian pensioner in the Rhine Province.

Zurwesten, Johann Baptist Hyron*imus Graf von* (Count of) Wickenberg
1805 entered Bavarian service; January 1807 Jerôme's aide de camp; in July 1807 entered Westphalian service; 3 July 1808 colonel and senior adjutant of the royal palace; 23 July 1810 colonel of the Jaeger-Carabiniers; 28 Aug. named Count of Wickenberg; 9 Feb. 1812 promoted to brigadier general; 1812 initially with the *Grand Armée*; 26 Aug. 1813 Commandant of the 1st Military Division and Governor of Kassel; on 24 Oct. 1813 as a major general accompanied Jerôme to France and was still in his service in 1815, then entered Kurhessian service; died before 1839 in Hanau.

237 See Lehsten-Dingelstädt and Six, Vol. 2, p. 574f (some differences from Lünsmann).

SOURCES AND LITERATURE

GRAPHIC SERIES – PRIMARY SOURCES

Anonymous: *"Dresdner Soldatenblätter,"* ca. 1813, 129 sheets of which two are on Westphalia, available in the Militärhistorisches Museum der Bundeswehr, Dresden.

Anonymous: *Collages anoymes*, ca 1820, series of pictures by an unknown artist, Westphalia sheet, Anne S. K. Brown (ASKB) Military Collection, Hay Library, Providence, Rhode Island.

Anonymous: *Almanach Royal de Westphalie pour l'an 1810* (Cassel: 1810).

Anonymous: *Verordnungsmäßige Instruktion ... Zur Bekleidung, der Remonte* etc., Cassel 1811.

Hahlo, Samuel: *Manuscrit du Canonier Hahlo, 1807–1808*, 30 watercolors. Small illustrations of which 13 are of Westphalian troops. Original in Universitätsbibliothek Kassel. Worked by Roger Forthoffer, Lyon 1973.
Copy by Wilhelm Hewig, without year, privaty owned.

Hemmann; Thomas: Samuel Hahlo's illustrated manuscript from 1807–1808, Norderstedt: Books on Demand, 2010.

Pinhas, Salomon: *Recueil de planches représentant les troupes des différentes armes et grades de l'armée Westphalienne*, 34 pages, 1811–1813, Cassel.

Sauerweid, Alexander Iwanowitsch: *Uniformen der Königlich westphälischen Armee*, 19 colorized engravings, ca. 1810, Dresden, Lipperheidesche Kostümbibliothek, Berlin.

Suhr, Christoph: *Album du Bourgeois de Hambourg, 1806 - 1815*, 158 lithographic watercolors in **Lipperheidische Kostümbibliothek**, Berlin. For Westphalian units: 7 sheets, 1809–1812.

Weiland, Carl Ferdinand: *Représentation des uniformes de l' armée imperiale royale française et des alliés*, 148 colorized engravings, Weimar, 1807 and 1812; of them, 10 pages on Westphalian units. Available at: Musee Marmotan, Paris; Lipperheidesche Kostümbibliothek, Berlin, Nationalbibliothek Paris, and Anne S. K. Brown (ASKB) Military Collection, Brown University Library, Providence USA.

Winkler, Karl-Alexander: *Freiberger Bilderhandschrift*, 1813, 156 watercolors of which 6 are on Westphalia. Originals in various collections; worked by Alfred Umhey, *Napoleons Last Grande Armee*; Berkeley: Military History Press, 2005.

GRAPHIC SERIES – SECONDARY SOURCES

Boisselier, Henri and Darbou, René, *L'armée du royaume de Westphalie 1807–1813*, 250 black and white plates with textual descriptions, 1950, facsimile by Henri Achard, Saumur: undated.

Forthoffer, Roger, *Fiches Documentaires*, plates Nos. 61-80, 152-156, 172-176, 246-247. Lyon, undated.

Hewig, Wilhelm and Dr. Klietmann, Kurt-Gerhard, *Heer und Tradition* -– "Brauer-Bogen" Nos. 181-188, 193 196, LXVI and LXVII, (Berlin: Die Ordenssammlung 1970).

Kieffer, Fritz und Carl, Theophile, *Collections alsaciennes* - Strasbourg paper soldiers, diverse series int the Musee historique Strasbourg.

Knötel, Richard: *Mittheilungen zur Geschichte der militärischen Tracht, bildliche Darstellungen* in the *"Großen Uniformenkunde,"* see its contents *(Inhaltverzeichnis)* (Rathenow: Verlag Babezien, 1890–1914).

Lienhart, Constant, Dr. and Humbert, René, *Les Uniformes de l'Armee Francaise depuis 1690 jusqu'a nos Jours*, Vol. V. (Leipzig: Ruhl, 1895 – 1906).

Neumann, Friedrich, *L'armée du Royaume de Westphalie*, undated, diverse series in the Lipperheidesche Kostümbibliothek, Berlin; Royal Library Brussels; Vinkhuijzen Collection - Digital Gallery and Library. New York; Collection Ridder, and National Library of France, Paris.

Norie, Orlando, *Skizzen – Armee des Königreichs Westphalen*, 12 sheets, worked on by Wilhelm Hewig, 1955, in Wehrgeschichtliches Museum (WGM) Rastatt.

Olmes, Jürgen (ed.), *Heere der Vergangenheit*. Plates 21-23 Königreich Westphalen 1808–1813 worked on by W. Hewig, Krefeld, undated.

Scharf, Ludwig, "*Frankfurter Tagebuch*" - Frankfurt Collection (manuscript), ca. 220 sketches, 1808–1811, of them 30 depictions are of Westphalian forces. In a private collection.

DEPICTIONS OF AND TREATISES ABOUT UNIFORMS AND ORGANIZATION

Carnet de la Sabretache, "Les decorations du Royame de Westphalie 1809–1813," in *Carnet de la Sabretache* (magazine), 1900, Paris.

--------, *Décret Royal portant Organisation de la Garde Royale vom 1. Januar 1811,* Hannover: Niedersächsische Landesbibliothek

Charrié, Pierre, *Drapeaux et Etendards de la Revolution et de l'Empire* (Paris: Copernic, 1982).

Dawson, Anthony L., Dawson Paul L., Summerfield Stephen, *Napoleonic Artillery* (Ramsburry: Crowood, 2007).

Dempsey, Guy C.: *Napoleon's Mercenaries 1799–1814* (London: Greenhill, 2002).

Elting, John R., *Napoleonic Uniforms, Volume III* (Rosemont: Emperors Press, 2000).

Forthoffer, Roger, *Troupes du Roi Jerôme Napoleon de Westfalie*, unpublished manuscript, undated.

Gaertner, Markus, "Die Armee des Königreichs Westphalen. Quellenspiegel für die Darstellung des königlich westphälischen Heeres 1807–1813," in *Zeitschrift für Heereskunde* (*ZfH*), Beckum, 1989.

--------, "La legion franco-hessoise 1806–1807," in *Tradition*, No. 248, Paris, 2010.

-------- and Wagner Edmund, "Westphälisches Militär," in *Deutsche Gesellschaft für Heereskunde*, Beckum, 1990.

Gerland, Otto, "Auszug aus dem letzten Ordrebuch des westphälischen Artillerieregiments von 1813," in *Zeitschrift des Vereins für Hessische Geschichte*, 1865.

Große-Löscher, Gerhard, "*Westphälische Blankwaffen*," in *Zeitschrift für Heereskunde*, 1989, p. 346.

-------- "Kurhessische Kavallerie Helme 1813–1866," ZfH. 1989, pp. 344-345.

Hellrung, Carl Ludwig, "Die Organisation der westphälischen Armee" in *Minerva-Ein Journal Historischen und Politischen Inhalts* (magazine), Jena, 1840.

Hewig, Wilhelm, "Die Armee des Königreichs Westphalen 1808 - 1813," in *ZfH*, 1955, pp. 49 and 78; 1956, p. 23.

Hewig, Wilhelm, "Uniformen der Zimmerleute, Trommler, Pfeiffer, Hornisten, Trompeter und Musiker der Armee des Königreichs Westphalen 1808–1813," in *ZfH*. 1958, p. 27.

Hewig, Wilhelm, "Fahnen und Standarten des Königreichs Westphalen 1807–1813," in *ZfH*, 1937, p. 7.

Klietmann, Dr. Kurt-Gerhard, "Zur Geschichte der Armee des Königreichs Westphalen," in *Die Zinnfigur* Nr. 3, 1984, Kassel: Thiele und Schwarz

-------- "Kurzer Abriß der Geschichte des 1. und 2. Kürassier-Regiments des Kgr. Westphalen 1808 - 1813," in *Die Zinnfigur Nr. 6, 1989*, Kassel: Thiele und Schwarz.

-------- "Die Nationalgarde des Königreichs Westphalen 1808–1813," in *Depesche* (magazine) No. 17, 5th year.

-------- "Die Post und Feldpost des Königreichs Westphalen 1808–1813," in *Depesche* No. 12, 3rd year.

-------- "Die Artillerie des Königreichs Westphalen von 1807 bis 1813," in *Die Zinnfigur*, No.4 and No. 5, Kassel: Thiele und Schwarz, 1973.

Klöffler, Martin, Die Artillerie des Königreichs Westphalen 1807 bis 1813, lecture at the convention "Armeen des Rheinbunds – Königreichs Westfalen, published in the e-journal www.napoleon.online.de, 2008.

Knötel, Herbert, "Die Armee des Königreiches Westphalen 1808 - 1813," lecture in 1929, appeared in *ZfH* 1929, p. 29.

-------- *Westphälische Studie*, unpublished manuscript, WGM Rastatt, undated.

-------- "Uniformierung der Spielleute der Kgl. westphälischen Linien-Infanterie," in *ZfH*, 1963, pp. 25-26.

-------- und Weyr, S. Kaskett – *Handdruck zur Geschichte der militärischen Tracht*, Berlin and Vienna: 1924.

Knötel, Herbert estate - sketches, notes and correspondence, Wehrgeschichtliches Museum Rastatt.

Knötel, Richard, *Handbuch der Uniformkunde*, Leipzig 1896 (Hamburg: Schulz 1937, Knötel-Sieg).

Köhler, Herbert, "Ueberblick des Kriegswesens im gewesenen Königreiche Westphalen und gedrängte Uebersicht der Geschichte der Westpählischen Truppen," in *Braunschweigisches Magazin*, July 1845.

Dr. Link, Eva, Museumführer Schloß Friedrichstein (Fridingen: Klenau, 1982).

Löbell, Oberst z. D. "Die Armee des Königreichs Westfalen in den Jahren 1808–1813," in *Beiheft zum Militär-Wochenblatt*, 6th issue, Berlin 1887.

Lünsmann, Fritz, *Die Armee des Königreichs Westfalen 1807 - 1813* (Berlin: Leddihn, 1935).

Martinien, Aristide, *Tableaux par Corps et par Batailles des Officiers tues et blesses (1805 - 1815)* (Paris: Editions Militares, undated, reprint).

Morin C. J., "A propos de l'ordre de la couronne de Westphalie 1807–1813," in *Le Bivouac*, Marseille, 1991.

Nafziger, George, The Armies of Westphalia and Cleve-Berg 1806-1815, privately published 1991.

Oppermann, P., "Die Artillerie- und Genieschule im Königreich Westfalen," in: *Zeitschrift des Vereins für hessische Geschichte*, vol. 29, Kassel, 1905.

Pavkovic, Michael, "'The Palladium of Westphalian Freedom' - Conscription and Recruitment in the Westphalian Army" lecture at the "Workshop zur Armee des Königreichs Westphalen" in Bornheim, Germany, September 2002, see www.napoleon-online.de.

Petard, Michel, *Equipements Militaires de 1600 - 1870*, Vol. IV. 1st and 2nd parts (Olonne sur Mer: Stiol-Guibert, 1987 and 1988).

Pigeard, Alain, "Les Grenadiers à pied de la Garde Royale 1808-1813," *Tradition* magazine No. 191.

Pivka, Otto von, *Napoleon's Allies (1) Westphalia and Kleve-Berg* (London: Osprey, 1975).

Poten, Bernhard. v., "Das Königreich Westfalen." in *Geschichte des Militär-Erziehungs- und Bildungswesens in den Landen deutscher Zunge*, 5. Band (Vol. 5): "Sachsen - Schaumburg-Lippe - Schleswig-Holstein - Schweiz - Königreich Westfalen - Württemberg" (Berlin: A. Hofmann & Comp, 1897).

Pouvesle, Frédéric, *Uniformes de l'Armée de Westphalie* (no location, 2000).

Reglement Kapitel 28, Von der Uniform der Gesundheitsbeamten der Militärhospitäler and der Corps, *Cassel 1812*

Rigondaud, Albert und Charrié; Pierre, Le Plumet, Série D, Drapeaux du royaume de Westphalie 1808-1813, D22, D26, D 30 and D 34. Louannec, undated.

Rocheron, Christian, "Les gardes d'honneur de Westphalie," in *Le Briquet* 1/1991.

Ruttorf, Michael, *Übersicht über die Fahnen und Standarten der Westfälischen Armee unter König Jerôme Bonaparte 1808-1813* (Meckenheim: Eigenverlag, 1993).

Six, Georges, *Dictionnaire biographique des generaux et admiraux francais de la Revolution et de l'empire* (Paris: Saffroy 1934).

Street, George, *The Army of the Kingdom of Westphalia 1807-1813* (Nottingham: Paritzan, 2011).

Summerfield, Stephen, *Westphalian Guard* (Godmanchester: Ken Trotman Publication, 2016).

Tenge, Torsten, "Das Bataillon der westphälischen Grenadier-Garde," in *Depesche* No. 26.

-------- "Das Regiment der Husaren der Garde des Königreichs Westphalen," in *Depesche* No. 27.

Titze, Jörg, *Die Stamm- und Rangliste der königlich Westfälischen Armee auf die Jahre 1812 und 1813* (Sprotta: Independant publishing, 2009).

Tohsche, Klaus, "Die leichte Infanterie des Kgr. Westphalen 1808 - 1813," in *Depesche* No. 11, 3. Jahrg. (3rd year).

Woringer, August, "Die königlich westfälische Post," in: *Zeitschrift des Vereins für hessische Geschichte und Landeskunde*. Kassel, 1916.

Woringer, August, "Das Regiment Westfalen," in: *Zeitschrift für Heereskunde*. Berlin 1932.

-------- *Die hessisch-französischen Regimenter 1806 bis 1808* in *Zeitschrift des Vereins für hessische Geschichte und Landeskunde* (ZVHessG) No.39 (Kassel, 1905), pp. 121-144.

HISTORIES OF THE KINGDOM AND THE ARMY'S CAMPAIGNS

Alcala, Cesar, *Los Sitios de Gerona1808-1809* (Madrid: Almena, 2009).

Bauer, Frank, *Der Zug des Schwarzen Herzogs 1809* (Potsdam: Edition König und Vaterland, 2012).

Bernhardi, Theodor v, *Denkwürdigkeiten des kaiserlich russischen Generals von der Infanterie Carl Friedrich Grafen von Toll*, 5 vols., (Leipzig: Verlag Otto Wigand, 1856).

Clausewitz, Carl von, *Der russische Feldzug von 1812. Feldzüge von 1813, 1814 und 1815* (Stuttgart, 1999, reprint).

Connelly, Owen, *Napoleon's Satellite Kingdoms*, (Toronto: The Free Press, 1965).

Dehnel, Heinrich, *Rückblicke auf meine Militair-Laufbahn in den Jahren 1805 bis 1849 im königlich-preußischen Heere, im Corps des Herzogs von Braunschweig-Oels, im königlich-großbrittanischen und im königlich-hannoverschen Dienst* (Hannover, 1859).

Ernstberger, Anton, *Die deutschen Freikorps 1809 in Böhmen* (Prague: Volk und Reich 1942).

Esposito, Vincent J.; Elting, John R., *A Military History and Atlas of the Napoleonic Wars* (London: AMS Press, 1999).

Fabricius, Hans, *Der Parteigänger Friedrich von Hellwig und seine Streifzüge im kriegsgeschichtlichen Zusammenhange betrachtet* (Berlin, 1896).

Franckenberg-Ludwigsdorff, F. W. H. v., *Schilderungen denkwürdiger deutscher Zustände vom Jahr 1806 bis zur Gegenwart* (Göttingen, 1863).

Friederich, Rudolf, *Die Befreiungskriege 1813–1815*. 4 vols. (Berlin: Mittler und Sohn, 1913).

Gerdes, Anton, *Westphälische und Großherzoglich bergische Truppen im russischen Feldzug*, (Langendreer, undated).

Gouvion-Saint-Cyr, Laurent, *Tagebuch der Operationen der Armee von Catalonien in den Jahren 1808 und 1809* (Mannheim, 1823).

Hessen, Rainer von, *Wir Wilhelm von Gottes Gnaden. Die Lebenserinnerungen Kurfürst Wilhelms I. von Hessen 1743–1821* (Frankfurt a. M.: Campus Verlag; New York, 1996).

Gill, John H., With Eagles to Glory, Napoleon and his German Allies in the 1809 Campaign (London: Greenhill, 1992).

Holzhausen, Paul, *Die Deutschen in Russland* (Berlin: Morawe und Scheffelt, 1912).

Kleinschmidt, Arthur, *Geschichte des Königreiches Westphalen* (Gotha: Hamecher, 1893).

Kortzfleisch, von, *Des Herzogs Friedrich Wilhelm vpn Braunschweig Zug durch Norddeutschland im Jahre 1809*, (Berlin, 1894; Krefeld: Heere der Vergangenheit, 1974).

Löwenstern, Woldemar von, *Denkwürdigkeiten eines Livländers*, 2 vols., (Leipzig & Heidelberg, 1858).

Marwitz, Friedrich August Ludwig v. d., *Ein märkischer Edelmann im Zeitalter der Befreiungskriege*, 3 vols. (Berlin: ed. F. Meusel, 1908).

Morillon, Marc, Troupes ayant assiégé Gerone en 1809 (Girona, 2008).

Nafziger, George F., Napoleon's Invasion of Russia. (Novato: Presidio, 1998).

Oppen, Friedrich Wilhelm von, *Bericht über den Feldzug des Herzogs Wilhelm von Braunschweig-Lüneburg. Im Jahr 1809.* (London, 1810).

Overkott, Franz, *In Rußland vermißte aus Rheinland und Westphalen 1812–1813* (Neustadt: Degener, 1963).

Petersdorff, Herman von, *General Johann Adolph Freiherr von Thielmann: ein Charakterbild aus napoleonischer Zeit* (Leipzig: Verlag S. Hirzel, 1894).

Pigeard, Alain, *L'Allemagne de Napoléon, La Confederation du Rhin 1806-1813* (Paris: Bisquine, 2013).

Reher, Eik F. F., *Elsfleth und der Schwarze Herzog* (Oldenburg: Isensee Verlag, 1999).

Sauzey, Camille, *De Munich à Vilna: A l'état-major du Corps Bavarois de la Grande Armée en 1812 d'après les "Papiers du général d'Albignac"* (Paris: Chapelot, 1911).

Schwertfeger, Bernhard, *Geschichte der Königlich Deutschen Legion 1803–1816*, 2 vols. (Hannover, Leipzig: Hahn'sche, 1907).

Smith, Digby, *Napoleon's Division in Spain, Volume II* (Huntington: Ken Trotman, 2014).

Specht, Friedrich August Karl von, *Das Königreich Westphalen und seine Armee im Jahr 1813* (Kassel: Luckhardt, 1848).

Staff, Hermann v., *Der Befreiungskrieg der Katalonier, in den Jahren 1808 bis 1814.* 2 vols. (Breslau & Berlin, 1821-1827).

Stein, Markus, "Westphalen im Jahre 1809: Innere Unruhen," lecture at "Workshop zur Armee des Königreichs Westphalen" in Bornheim, September 2002, published under www.napoleon-online.de

Wachholtz, Friedrich Ludwig von, *Aus dem Tagebuche des Generals Fr. L. von Wachholtz* (Braunschweig, 1843).

Wolzogen, Ludwig Freiherr von, *Memoiren des königlich preußischen Generals der Infanterie Ludwig Freiherr v. Wolzogen* (Leipzig, 1851).

MEMOIRS, DIARIES AND LETTERS

Allix de Vaux, Lieut. Gen. Jacques Alexandre Francois, "Mes Souvenirs militaires et politiques" in *Journal des sciences militaires*, 1828–1832.

Bartheld, Carl.ilhelm Friedrich von, "*Memoiren des kurhessischen Majors Carl Wilh. Friedr. v. Bartheld aus Lispenhausen, Ritters des preußischen eisernen Kreuzes und des hessischen eisernen Helmes. Aus der Zeit der Fremdherrschaft von 1806-1814,*" in *Zeitschrift des Vereins für hessische Geschichte und Landeskunde*, N.F., 1936, pp. 165-215.

Bauer, Gen. z.D., "Aus dem Leben des Kurhessischen Generallieutenants Bauer," in *Beihefte zum Militair-Wochenblatt*, (Berlin: E. S. Mittler und Sohn, 1887), pp. 89-137.

Baumann, Fritz, Eram, *Skizzen aus den Jugendjahren eines Veteranen* (Berlin: Verlag von Ferdinand Reichardt & Co., 1910).

Bodenhausen, Carl Bodo Freiherr von, *Tagebuch eines Ordonnanzoffiziers von 1812–1813, und über seine späteren Staatsdienste bis 1848* (Braunschweig: George Westermann, 1912).

Boedicker, Ludwig, "Die militärische Laufbahn 1788–1815 des Generallieutenant Ludwig Boedicker, zuletzt Stadtkommandant von Kassel: Eine Selbstbiographie," in *Beihefte zum Militär-Wochenblatt*, 1880, pp. 243-330.

Borcke, Johann von, *Kriegerleben des Johann von Borcke, Weiland Kgl. Preuß. Oberstlieutenants, 1806–1815* (Berlin: Ernst Siegfried Mittler und Sohn, 1888).

Bucher, Adolf W., *Tagebuch der Belagerung von Gerona, im Jahre 1809: Als Erläuterung zum Plane dieser Festung von A. W. Bucher, Hauptmann in Königlich Westphälischen Diensten* (Hildesheim: 1812).

Bussche, Carl von dem, *Auf Pferdesrücken durch Europa*, (Mainz: v. Hase & Koehler Verlag, 1997).

Communay, Arnaud, "Valentin de Salha: capitaine de frégate, ministre de la Guerre du Roi Jérôme de Westphalie" in: *Revue de Gascogne, Bulletin Bimestrial de la Société Historique de Gascogne*, Vol. 32, 1891, pp. 533-547.

Conrady, Ludwig Wilhelm von, "Aus stürmischer Zeit. Ein Soldatenleben vor hundert Jahren. Nach den Tagebüchern und Aufzeichnungen des weiland kurhessischen Stabskapitäns" in *Leibdragoner-Regiment L. W. v. Conrady* (Berlin: Verlag von C. A. Schwetschke und Sohn, 1907).

Dörnberg-Hausen, Hugo von, *Wilhelm von Dörnberg: Ein Kämpfer für Deutschlands Freiheit* (Marburg: N. G. Elwertsche Verlagsbuchhandlung, 1936).

Fleck, *Förster Flecks Erzählung von seinen Schicksalen auf dem Zuge Napoleons nach Rußland und von seiner Gefangenschaft: 1812–1814* (Cologne/Köln: Hermann Schaffstein, 1912).

Gebauer, Johannes Heinrich, "Aufzeichnungen eines jungen Hildesheimers aus den letzten Tagen des Kgl. Westfälischen Heeres. (27. September - 5. November 1813.), (Justus Süstermann)" in *Zeitschrift des Vereins für Hessische Geschichte und Landeskunde*, 1917, pp. 1-22.

Gieße, Friedrich, Kassel - Moskau - Küstrin 1812–1813. Tagebuch während des russischen Feldzuges geführt (Leipzig: Verlag der Dykschen Buchhandlung, 1912).

Haars, Johann Gottlieb, *Ein Braunschweiger im Russischen Feldzug von 1812* (Braunschweig: Verlag von Wilhelm Scholz, 1897).

Hartmann, Wilhelm, *Der General Hans Georg Freiherr von Hammerstein-Equord 1771–1841* (Alt- Hildesheim, 1969), pp. 42-55.

Hohenhausen, Ludwig Freiherr von, *Biographie des Generals von Ochs. Ein politisch-militairischer Beitrag zur Geschichte des nordamerikanischen und des französischen Revolutionskrieges, so wie der Feldzüge in Spa-*

nien, Rußland und Deutschland. (Aus den Originalpapieren des Generals) (Kassel: Verlag der Luckhardt´schen Buchhandlung, 1827).
Hüne, Carl, (ed. Hüne Peter), *Erinnerungen des Sergeanten Carl Hüne, Ein Braunschweiger im Dienste Napoleons, Augenzeugenbericht aus den Jahren 1810–1814* (Braunschweig: Ramdohr 1909).
Kaisenberg, Moritz. von, *König Jerôme Napoleon: Ein Zeit- und Lebensbild nach Briefen 1) der Frau von Sothen in Kassel an meine Großmutter, 2) des Reichserzkanzlers von Dalberg an meinen Großvater, 3) und meines Vaters als Westfälischer Garde du Corps an seine Eltern, sowie anderen Familienaufzeichnungen* (Leipzig: Verlag von Heinrich Schmidt & Carl Günther, 1899).
Keysser, Adolf, *Oberst Weiß 1796–1875: Ein Lebensbild aus der kurhessischen Heeresgeschichte* (Kassel, 1910), p. 43.
Kircheisen, Friedrich Max, *König Lustig. Napoleons jüngster Bruder* (Berlin: August Scherl, 1928).
Klinkhardt, Friedrich, *Feldzugs-Erinnerungen des Königlich Westfälischen Musikmeisters Friedrich Klinkhardt aus den Jahren 1812-1815* (Braunschweig: Verlag von Wilhelm Scholz, 1908).
Krollmann, Franz, *Erlebnisse in dem Kriege gegen Rußland im Jahre 1812 vom Landbereuter Fr. Krollmann damaligen Musikus beim dritten Chasseur-Bataillon Westfalen* (Hannover: Verlagsbuchhandlung Ernst Geibel, 1912).
Lehsten-Dingelstädt, Karl August Unico von, *Am Hofe König Jérômes: Erinnerungen eines westfälischen Pagen und Offiziers,* ***Hrsg: Dr: von Boltenstern*** (Berlin: E. S. Mittler und Sohn, 1905).
Leifels, Heinrich, *Napoleons Zug nach Rußland: Die Flucht durch Rußlands Eis- und Schneefelder* (Bocholt: Selbstverlag, 1906).
Linsingen, von, "Auszug aus dem Tagebuch des Hauptmann v. Linsingen während des Feldzuges in Rußland im Jahre 1812," in *Beihefte zum Militair-Wochenblatt* (Berlin: Ernst Siegfried Mittler und Sohn,1894), pp. 268-297.
Lossberg, Friedrich Wilhelm von, *Briefe in die Heimat: Geschrieben während des Feldzuges 1812 in Rußland* (Leipzig: Verlag von Georg Wigand, ca. 1913).
Löbell, von, *Die Armee des Königreichs Westfalen in den Jahren 1808 bis 1813. Beihefte zum Militair-Wochenblatt*, E. S. Mittler und Sohn: Berlin 1887, S. 161-200.
Meibom, Heinrich Wilhelm. von, *Aus napoleonischer Zeit* (Leipzig: Koehler & Amelang, 1943).
Meyer, Jakob, *Erzählung der Schicksale und Kriegsabenteuer des ehemaligen Westphälischen Artillerie Wachtmeisters Jakob Meyer aus Dransfeld während der Feldzüge in Spanien und Rußland,* (Göttingen: Friedrich Ernst Huth, 1837).
Morgenstern, Franz, *Kriegserinnerungen des Obersten Franz Morgenstern aus westfälischer Zeit* (Wolfenbüttel: Julius Zwisser, 1912).
Normann, Christian, *Aus den Papieren eines alten Offiziers: Ein Lebensbild Christian Normann`s, Kurfürstl. Hessischen Obersten u. zeitweilig beauftragten Brigadekommandeurs, Kommandeur der Bundesartillerie (Sächsischen, Braunschweigschen, Nassauschen, Oldenburgschen usw.)* (Hannover und Leipzig: Hahn'sche, 1896).
Rogge-Ludwig, Wilhelm, *Karl Müldner von Mülnheim: General-Lieutenant und General-Adjutant des Kurfürsten Wilhelm II. von Hessen: Ein hessisches Zeit- und Lebensbild* (Kassel: Georg H. Wigand, 1885).
Ruthe, Johann Friedrich, *Auf der Flucht vor den Streckreitern im Königreich Westfalen 1809 bis 1811: aus dem Leben, Leiden und Widerwärtigkeiten eines Niedersachsen"* (Braunschweig: Verlag von Wilhelm Scholz, 1906).
Rüppell, Eduard., Kriegsgefangen im Herzen Rußlands 1812–1814: Erinnerungen des Königlich Westfälischen Husarenleutnants Eduard Rüppell (Berlin: Verlag von Gebrüder Paetel, 1912.
Trott, Gustav, *Das Kriegstagebuch des Premierleutnants Trott aus den Jahren 1800–1815* (Berlin: Hugo Bermühler Verlag, 1915).
Wachsmuth, J. J., *Geschichte meiner Kriegsgefangenschaft in Russland in den Jahren 1812-1813: In gedrängter Kürze dargestellt von J. J. Wachsmuth, Leutnant in der Königl. Westfälischen Armee* (Magdeburg: Creutz´sche Verlagsbuchhandlung, 1910).
Wagner, F. L., "Tagebuch des Königlich Westfälischen Leutnants F. L. Wagner aus den Jahren 1809 bis 1813," in H. Heimke, Ed., *Jahrbücher für die Deutsche Armee und Marine, 1899*, pp. 198-221.
Weiß, Theodor, Aus den Briefen eines Offiziers über Kurhessen in den Jahren 1829–1836, 1894.
Wesemann, Heinrich, *Kanonier des Kaisers. Kriegstagebuch des Heinrich Wesemann 1808*-1814 (Cologne/Köln: Verlag Wissenschaft und Politik, 1971).
Wündenberg, Heinrich, "*My Military Experiences 1806–1816,*" (Newcastle upon Tyne: Napoleonic Association, 1991), p. 27.

MUSEUMS

Anne S.K. Brown (ASKB) Military Collection, Brown University Library, Providence, Rhode Island, USA
Bomann Museum, Celle.
Deutsches Historisches Museum (DHM), Berlin
Forum 1813 – Museum zur Geschichte der Völkerschlacht, Leipzig
Hessisches Landesmuseum (Staatliche Kunstsammlung), Kassel.
Landesmuseum Braunschweig.
Musée de l'Armée (Army Museum), Paris.
Musée Royal de l'Armée et d'Histoire Militaire, Brussels.
Musée de l'Empéri (Collection Brunon), Salon-de-Provence, France.
LWL-Preussenmuseum, Minden (LWL = Landschaftsverband Westfalen-Lippe).
Preussen-Museum Nordrhein-Westfalen, Standort Wesel
Schloss Friedrichstein (Bad Wildungen); Museumslandschaft Hessen-Kassel.
Wehrgeschichtliches Museum (WGM), Rastatt

ABBREVIATIONS

ASKB – Anne S. K. Brown Military Collection, Hay Library, Providence, Rhode Island
Bde. – brigade
BH – *Bilderhandschrift* (hand-drawn pictures)
Bn/Bns – battalion/battalions
Capt – captain
cf. – compare
Co – company
DHM – Deutsches Historisches Museum, Berlin
ff – and following pages
Inf. – infantry
Lt – lieutenant
Maj – major
MHK – Museumslandschaft Hessen-Kassel
NCO – Non-commissioned officer
Regt/Regts – regiment/regiments
Sqdn/Sqdns – squadron/squadrons
WGM – Wehrgeschichtliches Museum, Rastatt
ZfH – *Zeitschrift für Heereskunde*
ZVHessG – *Zeitschrift des Vereins für hessische Geschichte und Landeskunde*